Renovating Russia

RENOVATING RUSSIA

*The Human Sciences and the
Fate of Liberal Modernity,
1880–1930*

DANIEL BEER

Cornell University Press

ITHACA AND LONDON

First published 2008 by Cornell University Press

Printed in the United States of America

Library of Congress Cataloging-in-Publication Data

Beer, Daniel.
  Renovating Russia : the human sciences and the fate of liberal modernity, 1880–1930 / Daniel Beer.
    p. cm.
  Includes bibliographical references and index.
  ISBN 978-0-8014-4627-6 (cloth : alk. paper)
  1. Social sciences—Russia—History. 2. Social sciences—Soviet Union—History. 3. Medical sciences—Russia—History. 4. Medical sciences—Soviet Union—History. 5. Social engineering—Russia—History. 6. Social engineering—Soviet Union—History. 7. Liberalism—Russia—History. 8. Russia—Intellectual life—1801–1917. 9. Soviet Union—Intellectual life—1917–1970. 10. Russia—Moral conditions. 11. Soviet Union—Moral conditions. I. Title.
  H53.R9B44 2008
  300.947'09041—dc22   2008002007

For Gusztáv

Contents

Acknowledgments

Research and writing were generously funded by the Arts and Humanities Research Council, and King's College, Cambridge, but above all by a three-year research fellowship from Downing College, Cambridge, which enabled me to undertake substantial new research. I am very grateful to the fellows of that enlightened institution.

Susan Morrissey, Alexandra Oberländer, David L. Hoffmann, and Steve Smith all read the entire manuscript in various incarnations and offered constructive but challenging criticisms and suggestions for improvement that I fear I have not always been able adequately to address. Catriona Kelly, Stephen Lovell, Orlando Figes, Peter Holquist, István Hont, John Dunn, Hubertus Jahn, and Ze'ev Emmerich each offered important insights and comments on my ideas and pointed out deficiencies, implications, and connections of which I had been embarrassingly unaware.

I thank the staff of the National Library of Russia and the Library of the Academy of Sciences in St. Petersburg, who assisted me immeasurably in locating material for the book. Marina Pavlovna Podvigina not only eased my access to the holdings of the BAN but also provided me with a home away from home in Russia.

The Department of History at Royal Holloway has provided an intellectually stimulating and congenial environment in which to finish the book.

Family and friends have both supported and tolerated me throughout the writing and researching of this book. Above all, the opinion of Nóra Milotay has been a litmus test of everything I have written. She read innumerable drafts of my chapters, told me when they were not good enough and then told me again when they were.

I dedicate this book to our son.

D.B.

Introduction

In their rejection of the inevitability and permanence of the status quo, revolutionaries seek to identify, understand, and overcome their own inheritance. The Bolshevik Revolution was no exception. The Bolsheviks were obsessed with the legacy of both the tsarist social order and the economic and cultural forces of capital that had been gestating in the womb of the ailing autocracy since the 1880s. Aron Aleksandrovich Sol'ts (1872–1945), chairman of the Central Control Commission responsible for the morality and conduct of the Party's members, noted ruefully in 1924, "The Communist Party did not fall from the sky with its thoughts and tasks. It lived and grew in the capitalist system, it acquired all the customs that are characteristic of that order."[1] A year later in the pages of *Pravda*, Party ideologue Emelian Mikhailovich Iaroslavskii (1878–1943) lamented how "our weakness, our damnation inherited from the past [*nashu slabost', prokliatie nashe, unasledovannoe ot proshlogo*] is exploited by criminal elements who lead us by the nose, and who rejoice in our crimes and who live on our mistakes."[2] This book examines the genesis of the Bolsheviks' understanding of their inheritance: of the intellectual categories, assumptions, and theories with which they sought to make sense of, and overcome, their own past. In so doing, it explores an important paradox. Although the Bolsheviks were determinedly seeking to conquer the influences of liberal capitalism in their society, they did so with the backing of theories of social transformation and individual deviance first elaborated by their liberal forebears in the *fin-de-siècle*.

Caught up in the maelstrom of 1914–21 were Russian liberals and progressives who themselves had been seeking to transform state and society,

---

1   Aron A. Sol'ts, *O partetikete* (Moscow: PKK, 1925), 3.
2   Emelian Iaroslavskii, "Preduprezhdat' simptomy bolezni," *Pravda*, December 8, 1925.

steering a course of reform between the reactionary autocracy on the one hand and the threat of violent social revolution on the other. Their political creed embraced a number of key ideas: the primary aim of the state is to institute a social order that promotes human freedom; the need for political representation; adherence to the rule of law; and respect for private property.[3] Their political affiliations throughout the years of Russia's constitutional experiment between 1905 and 1917 were primarily to the centrist and left-liberal parties, including the Octobrists and the Constitutional Democrats, who lost out to their radical rivals in the chaotic year of the revolution.[4] Yet this constituency was recognizable not principally in terms of membership in a particular political party nor subscription to particular practical policies. Rather, Russian liberalism was a worldview that earnestly sought a gradual and controlled reform of the social, political, and economic order in accordance with the secular prescriptions of empiricism and rationality.

Just as powerful as the liberalism of Russia's reforming elites was their rationalist faith in the power of science and reason to shape and administer the world, and large numbers of progressive intellectuals were employed in the rapidly expanding scientific, medical, and legal professions.[5] Practitioners of the intersecting disciplines of psychiatry, psychology, criminology, anthropology, jurisprudence, and sociology offered their contemporaries a lens through which to examine and respond to the threats posed by rapid social change, the perceived spread of crime and subversion in Russia, and the challenges of building a unified society. In so doing, these intellectuals sought to make a fundamental contribution to the construction in Russia of a liberal civic modernity characterized by an emancipated, enlightened, and

3 · The category "liberal" is clearly diverse and expansive, and I deal here only with one particular instance of liberalism in vogue with a nebulous social grouping of educated Russians in the *fin-de-siècle*. For the sake of brevity, I refer to them as liberals throughout this study. On the etymology of the term "liberal" in the Russian context, see Charles E. Timberlake, "The Concept of Liberalism in Russia," introduction to *Essays on Russian Liberalism*, ed. Charles E. Timberlake (Columbia: University of Missouri Press, 1972), 1–17. On nineteenth-century rationalism, see Leonard Schapiro, *Rationalism and Nationalism in Nineteenth-Century Russian Political Thought* (New Haven: Yale University Press, 1967). On the liberals' attachment to the rule of law, see Michael Karpovich, "Two Types of Russian Liberalism: Maklakov and Miliukov," in *Continuity and Change in Russian and Soviet Thought*, ed. Ernest J. Simmons (Cambridge, MA: Harvard University Press, 1955), 129–43.

4 William G. Rosenberg has noted the extraordinary number of academics in senior positions within the Kadets and cites Alexander Kerenskii that they were a "faculty of politicians." Rosenberg, *Liberals in the Russian Revolution: The Constitutional Democratic Party, 1917–1921* (Princeton: Princeton University Press, 1974), 20–21. See also idem, "The Kadets and the Politics of Ambivalence, 1905–1917," in *Essays on Russian Liberalism*, ed. Timberlake, 139–63; Geoffrey Hosking, *The Russian Constitutional Experiment: Government and Duma, 1907–1914* (Cambridge: Cambridge University Press, 1973).

5 Harley Balzer, "The Problem of Professions in Imperial Russia," in *Between Tsar and People: Educated Society and the Quest for Public Identity in Late Imperial Russia*, ed. Edith W. Clowes, Samuel D. Kassow, and James L. West (Princeton: Princeton University Press, 1991), 183–98.

civilized citizenry governed by the rule of law and representative political institutions.

Traditionally seen by historians as Macbeth's "poor player who frets and struts his hour upon the stage and then is heard no more," the Russian liberals failed on their own terms to achieve their goal of unifying and modernizing Russia in the turbulent years that spanned the turn of the twentieth century. Yet although they were driven from the political stage in 1917, their intellectual efforts to articulate a vision of a modernized, rationalized society survived the upheavals of 1917 and went on to shape the Soviet regime's program of social transformation.

I argue this case by analyzing developments within the Russian human sciences across roughly fifty years spanning the turn of the twentieth century. Before the 1917 Revolution, the existence of unenlightened and disruptive constituencies in Russian society represented for liberals a significant obstacle in the path of reform. In their exploration of deviance and its causes, liberal practitioners of the human sciences constructed a conceptual framework within which social and individual disorders appeared both mutually constitutive and mutually sustaining. If individual deviants were powerfully shaped by their environments, they in turn wielded powers of destabilization and destruction that were awesome in their reach and intensity. Accordingly, influential elites came to articulate strategies for the attainment of national emancipation and harmony predicated on the gradual transformation not simply of the empire's social, economic, and political structures but ultimately of its human population as well. This progressive vision of modernization and improvement provided the Bolshevik regime with an arsenal of ideas that its own medical and scientific elites extended and radicalized into a program of massive and limitless social reconstruction.

Society as Artifact

Michael Halberstam has argued that "liberal democracy and totalitarianism share the idea that society is an artifact and that politics is a species of making."[6] Generally speaking, both ideological orientations argue that society is a creation of men and women in order to advance a politics of emancipation that rejects the mystifications of religion and tradition.[7] What separates

6   Michael Halberstam, "Totalitarianism as a Problem for the Modern Conception of Politics," *Political Theory* 26, no. 4 (August 1998): 463. Indeed, it is an interesting paradox that precisely in their rejection of the idea that the inherited social order is a necessary order, the biomedical sciences in revolutionary Russia were obsessively focused on hereditary forces that threatened to overdetermine the course of societal development.

7   This is a tradition stretching back at least as far as Hobbes's *Leviathan* (1651). Michael Halberstam, *Totalitarianism and the Modern Conception of Politics* (New Haven: Yale University Press, 1999), 15–16.

liberalism from totalitarianism in this account is primarily the factor of extent. Totalitarian ideologies aspire to a complete and unprecedented reconstruction of society. As sociologist Sigmund Neuman noted in 1937, "It is one of the major tenets of totalitarianism that man is manageable and that the whole problem of modern society thus boils down to a question of techniques and strategies for maintaining the 'human material.' "[8] Although classical liberalism does contain a number of components that potentially could offer robust resistance to totalitarian projects—the insistence on individual autonomy and sovereignty, for example—these were significantly diluted in the rationalist waters of late nineteenth-century Russian thought. As a consequence, proponents of certain forms of political and social change, which have subsequently come to be designated as "totalitarian" or "radical" on the one hand or "liberal" and "reformist" on the other, in fact shared a number of important assumptions about the need to remake not only the social and economic foundations of the state but also its human population.

The human sciences in Russia played a crucial role in elaborating and furbishing a conception of society as an artifact and of politics as essentially the endeavor to sculpt it. A central component of this project concerned the study of social disorder. Clinical accounts of its etiology repeatedly generated an insistence on human agency as both responsible for the given order and capable of its transformation. In Claude Lefort's formulation,

> It is by detecting the new relationship that is established between the viewpoint of science and the viewpoint of the social order, that we can best arrive at an understanding of totalitarianism. [The Soviet] regime represents the culmination of an artificialist project which begins to take place in the nineteenth century: the project of creating a self-organizing society which allows the discourse of technical rationality to be imprinted on the very form of social relations, and which, ultimately, reveals "social raw material" or "human raw material" to be fully amenable to organization.[9]

Following Lefort's definition then, I employ the term "totalitarian" not as a description of an empirical reality that obtained in the Soviet Union but rather as a description of the almost limitless ambition of the Stalinist regime to remake the social world and the population of Soviet Russia. It is in this sense that the designs of the human sciences in the Soviet period were totalizing in a way that those of the late imperial period were not. In other words, my intention in using the term "totalitarian" is not to intervene in debates about the actual nature of the Stalinist regime but to shed light

8   Sigmund Neuman, *Permanent Revolution* (New York: Praeger, 1937), 13. See also Hans Buchheim, *Totalitäre Herrschaft—Wesen und Merkmale* (Munich: Kösel, 1962), 14.
9   Claude Lefort, *Democracy and Political Theory*, trans. David Macey (Minneapolis: University of Minnesota Press, 1988), 234.

on a radicalization in elite ideas about the administration of society that gathered momentum across the period from the 1880s to the end of the 1920s.[10] The chapters that follow trace the development of the conceptual tools that the Bolsheviks ultimately used to articulate their transformative project and the obstacles in its path. Modernity in the Russian Revolution found both liberal-rationalist and totalitarian incarnations; to a large extent, the former was implicated in the latter.

Like Laura Engelstein, I use the term "modernity" because it was a contemporary concept employed by historical actors as a measure of the desirability and success of social and political change at the perceived margins of Europe.[11] Understood in these terms, "modernity" was a fact (or figment) of the contemporary imagination, one with which Russian intellectuals were explicitly engaged as something to be celebrated, tamed, or rejected.[12] The binaries of backwardness and progress (*otstalost'* and *progress*) and the past and contemporary world (*proshlyi i sovremennyi mir*) informed the thinking of Russian intellectuals in the revolutionary period.

For the specific purposes of the present study, a minimal definition of modernity might embrace three core features. Modernity is characterized by what Edward Ross Dickinson has termed "a distinctive '*Machbarkeitswahn*' or belief that things were doable, that anything can be done—or even by an '*Allmachtswahn*' or illusion of omnipotence."[13] The conviction that society could be comprehensively remade, that nothing lay beyond the technological and imaginative capacities of human beings, was expressed in any number of social engineering projects, including urban planning, public health and social welfare, educational reform, and so forth.[14] The moderns were in this sense profoundly optimistic, believing they could remake their social world as they chose. In 1923, Lev Trotskii offered a hyperbolic expression of this belief in the possibility of a virtual transcendence of existing humanity:

10   David D. Roberts has recently emphasized the disillusionment of European intellectuals with the promise, stability, and social cohesiveness of both liberal democracy and capitalism in the *fin-de-siècle*. *The Totalitarian Experiment in Twentieth-Century Europe: Understanding the Poverty of Great Politics* (New York: Routledge, 2006), chaps. 1–3.

11   Laura Engelstein, *The Keys to Happiness: Sex and the Search for Modernity in Fin-de-Siècle Russia* (Ithaca: Cornell University Press, 1992), 9. Yanni Kotsonis has similarly observed that "rather than measure what was not achieved and conclude that Russia was less than modern, the important fact is that historical actors debated within the terms of modernity." "A Modern Paradox—Subject and Citizen in Nineteenth- and Twentieth-Century Russia," introduction to *Russian Modernity: Politics, Knowledge, Practices*, ed. David L. Hoffmann and Yanni Kotsonis (Basingstoke: Macmillan, 2000), 3.

12   For a thoughtful attempt to capture the elusive nature of modernity in the Russian context, see Mark D. Steinberg, *Proletarian Imagination: Self, Modernity, and the Sacred in Russia, 1910–1925* (Ithaca: Cornell University Press, 2002), 5–9.

13   Edward Ross Dickinson, "Biopolitics, Fascism, Democracy: Some Reflections on Our Discourse about 'Modernity,'" *Central European History* 37, no. 1 (2004): 2–3.

14   See David L. Hoffmann, "European Modernity and Soviet Socialism," in *Russian Modernity*, ed. Hoffmann and Kotsonis, 245–60.

Man will make it his goal to master his own emotions, to elevate his instincts to the heights of consciousness, to make them transparent, . . . to create a higher sociobiological type, a superman, if you will. . . . Man will become incomparably stronger, wiser, and subtler. His body will become more harmonious, his movements more rhythmic, his voice more melodious. The forms of life will acquire a dynamic theatricality. The average human type will rise to the heights of an Aristotle, a Goethe, and a Marx. And beyond this ridge, other peaks will emerge.[15]

The moderns, however, were also haunted by a sense of permanent crisis, constantly unsettled by the erosion and relativization of older (Judeo-Christian) values, the collapse of traditional social structures and patterns of social interaction, the emergence of apparently chaotic new social forms (the modern city, popular or "mass" culture, the proletarian milieu), and the massive new "social problems" of the emerging order (pollution, urban public health disasters, criminality, industrial conflict, etc.).[16] Cultural histories of the revolutionary period have explored different aspects of this mood of dislocation and anxiety that accompanied Russia's entry into the twentieth century.[17] After 1917, these anxieties acquired a coloration particular to the postrevolutionary conjuncture. The Soviet state's ambiguous compromise with the forces of small-scale capitalism provided fertile ground for literary and intellectual explorations of motifs of decay, corruption, and loss of innocence.[18]

The moderns oscillated, so to speak, between these two extremes: optimism and the belief in progress and pessimism characterized by a sense of profound threat, a fear of dissolution, collapse, chaos, and degeneration.[19] Significantly, for the purposes of this study, science played a key role in defining both the optimism and the pessimism of modernity. On the one hand, it was constantly "discovering"—naming, defining, measuring, quantifying, investigating—new problems and threats. On the other hand, and on the

15   Lev Trotskii, *Literatura i revoliutsia* (Moscow: Krasnaia Nov', 1923), 192–94.

16   Heidi Rimke and Alan Hunt, "From Sinners to Degenerates: The Medicalisation of Morality in the Nineteenth Century," *History of the Human Sciences* 15, no. 1 (2002): 59–88.

17   Engelstein, *The Keys to Happiness;* Irina Paperno, *Suicide as a Cultural Institution in Dostoevsky's Russia* (Ithaca: Cornell University Press, 1996); Rosamund Bartlett and Linda Edmondson, "Collapse and Creation: Issues of Identity and the Russian *Fin de Siècle,*" in *Constructing Russian Culture in the Age of Revolution: 1880–1940*, ed. Catriona Kelly and David Shepherd (Oxford: Oxford University Press, 1998), 165–224; Susan Morrissey, *Suicide and the Body Politic in Imperial Russia* (Cambridge: Cambridge University Press, 2006).

18   Eric Naiman, *Sex in Public: The Incarnation of Early Soviet Ideology* (Princeton: Princeton University Press, 1997); Anne E. Gorsuch, *Youth in Revolutionary Russia: Enthusiasts, Bohemians, Delinquents* (Bloomington: University of Indiana Press, 2000); Kenneth Pinnow, "Violence against the Collective Self and the Problem of Social Integration in Early Bolshevik Russia," *Kritika* 4, no. 3 (Summer 2003): 653–77.

19   For an investigation of this contradiction, see Kevin Repp, "'More Corporeal, More Concrete': Liberal Humanism, Eugenics, and German Progressives at the Last *Fin-de-Siècle,*" *Journal of Modern History* 72, no. 3 (September 2000): 683–730.

basis of the codification of each, science was also constantly "identifying" new solutions to those problems, new fields of inquiry and expertise and new technologies to contain and resolve them. The eminent criminologist Dmitrii Andreevich Dril' (1849–1910) embodied this amalgam of fear and hope. He saw Russian society besieged by forces of irrationality, disorder, and a biologically determined barbarism and believed that the iniquities of the tsarist social order and the depredations of capitalism were destroying the moral, mental, and physical health of the population. He remained optimistic, however, that science would be triumphant and that "the phenomena of the physical and moral-mental degeneration of man, if possible, will almost completely disappear from the face of the earth."[20]

Within the human sciences, what I have chosen to call (with unavoidable imprecision) the "biomedical sciences" constituted the language both of crisis and of design. Each implied the other. Biopsychological theories of human nature and social interaction stood at the very center of the moderns' own conflicted relationship with their social world because these theories encapsulated the meshing moods of boundless optimism and apocalyptic despair. They also contributed to what Ulrich Herbert has termed the "biologization of the social."[21] Contemporaries with opposing interests could all selectively appropriate biomedical theories of social decline and individual deviance to portray society as an organic body that had to be guided by biological and psychological laws. These theories gave scientific authority to social fears and moral panics, lent respectability to theories of social transformation, and provided legitimacy to penal measures dealing with offenders. Powered by the prestige of science, they allowed modernizing elites to represent their prescriptive claims about the social order as objective statements irrevocably grounded in the laws of nature. The narrative of progress articulated within the biomedical sciences contained an important tension. On the one hand, it offered a biologizing vision of society in which the rights of individuals were subordinated to the rights of an abstract (and often medically conceived) community.[22] On the other hand, these sciences were also genuinely emancipatory in their aspiration, espousing the Enlightenment values of humanism and individual autonomy.[23]

---

20   Dmitrii A. Dril', "Iavleniia vyrozhdeniia i usloviia obshchestvennoi sredi v sviazi s voprosami vospitaniia," *Vestnik psikhologii, kriminal'noi antropologii i gipnotizma,* no. 10 (1906): 294.

21   Ulrich Herbert, "Rassismus und rationales Kalkül," in *"Vernichtungspolitik": Eine Debatte über den Zusammenhang von Sozialpolitik und Genozid im nationalsozialistischen Deutschland,* ed. Wolfgang Schneider (Hamburg: Junius, 1991), 28.

22   Charles E. Rosenberg, "The Bitter Fruit: Heredity, Disease, and Social Thought," in idem, *No Other Gods: On Science and American Social Thought* (Baltimore: John Hopkins University Press, 1961), 25–53.

23   Repp has emphasized this tension in his study of German progressives and eugenics in turn-of-the-century Germany. Modernity was, he writes, "still up for grabs." " 'More Corporeal, More Concrete,' " 686.

Disciplinary boundaries were decidedly fluid within the human sciences throughout the revolutionary period. The clinicians and theorists who made a significant contribution to the understanding of degeneration and moral contagion were drawn from a broad range of fields. For this reason, tracing the evolution of biomedical theories of deviance and their various clinical applications necessarily overruns any particular institutional setting or history of discipline-building. These theories constituted a "modern" way of talking about social problems in biologizing terms. They expressed the ongoing concern of Russia's professional elites with the nature and management of social change, with the proliferation of social and moral disorder within Russian and Soviet society and, crucially, with the need not simply to shape the structures of the social, economic, and political order but also to fashion a particular kind of personhood or humanity within the confines of that order. Biopsychological theories of evolution and change naturalized both the moderns' belief in the possibility (or inevitability) of progress and their acute sense of existential threat. They enforced the need for what Peter Fritzsche has termed, in the context of the Weimar Republic, "renovation."[24]

The Russian term *ozdorovlenie* (literally "healthification"), echoed throughout the period and denoted the iron necessity of change if dissolution and extinction were to be avoided. John F. Hutchinson has shown the currency of the slogan and its use by progressive *zemstvo* physicians keen to press for greater autonomy. And yet the specific meanings of the term *ozdorovlenie* remained rather vague. They clearly implied a thoroughgoing reform of the social and political order, the development of political freedoms, an end to the exploitative and degrading practices of late imperial capitalism, and a need to introduce improved living conditions in Russia's cities. Yet although the medical standard of health and illness implied a host of disintegrative forces that threatened dire and irreversible consequences if left unaddressed, the texts with which I deal were often rather short on detailed suggestions for a reform agenda. The term *ozdorovlenie* gradually came to serve, nonetheless, as a synonym for democratic reforms, however imprecisely conceived.[25]

Codifying Threats

The biomedical sciences were uniquely central to the project of renovating the human world, of defining and investigating the problems and potentials

---

24   Peter Fritzsche, "Did Weimar Fail?" *Journal of Modern History* 68, no. 3 (September 1996): 649.
25   John F. Hutchinson, *Politics and Public Health in Revolutionary Russia, 1890–1918* (Baltimore: John Hopkins University Press, 1990), xix–xx.

of human beings and human populations. The entwined visions of threat and possibility were forcefully articulated in discussions of degeneration, crowd psychology, criminality, and subversion. Psychiatry, criminology, and the study of the (alleged) inheritance of physical, intellectual, and social characteristics in human populations occupied a key place in the emerging biomedical model. Students of Western European societies in the *fin-de-siècle* have convincingly shown how fears of degeneration, the communicable nature of mass hysteria, criminal impulses, and revolt neatly summed up the moderns' sense of crisis.[26] In the 1880s, biopsychological theories of deviance also rose to prominence in Russia. They identified a particular type of deviant whose corrupted mental and moral capacities set him or her apart from the normal and healthy majority of human beings and who posed an urgent threat to the health of society. The human sciences conjured their own dragons with which they could do battle.

Historians of Russian medicine have concentrated on the institutional aspects of discipline-building in the revolutionary period and the struggle of the biomedical sciences for autonomy, status, and funding.[27] Indeed, the practitioners of these disciplines were quick to articulate in empirical or theoretical terms the fears and aspirations of educated society. Degeneration theory conceptualized a mutually constitutive relationship between the individual and the social world and, as a consequence, theorizations of individual deviance were necessarily also meditations on the broader health of the body social and its prospects for improvement or deterioration. In the absence of any credible competitor in the eyes of contemporaries, these theorists were able to articulate a privileged understanding of Russia's social and moral development in the period following the emancipation of the serfs and so were able to establish their authority in the public sphere and demonstrate their utility to the state and society.

Yet the reasons degeneration theory came to exert such fascination over clinical minds in the last four decades of the autocracy cannot be reduced

---

26   Daniel Pick, *Faces of Degeneration: A European Disorder c. 1848—c. 1918* (Cambridge: Cambridge University Press, 1989); Robert A. Nye, *Crime, Madness, and Politics in Modern France: The Medical Concept of National Decline* (Princeton: Princeton University Press, 1984); Ruth Harris, *Murders and Madness: Medicine, Law, and Society in the Fin de Siècle* (Oxford: Oxford University Press, 1989).

27   Nancy Mandelker Frieden, *Russian Physicians in an Era of Reform and Revolution, 1856–1905* (Princeton: Princeton University Press, 1981); Mark B. Adams, "Eugenics as Social Medicine in Revolutionary Russia: Prophets, Patrons, and the Dialectics of Discipline-Building," in *Health and Society in Revolutionary Russia*, ed. Susan Gross Solomon and John F. Hutchinson (Bloomington: Indiana University Press, 1990), 200–23; Julie V. Brown, "Psychiatrists and the State in Tsarist Russia," in *Social Control and the State*, ed. A. Scull and S. Cohen (Oxford: Blackwell, 1985), 267–87; Susan Gross Solomon, "The Expert and the State in Russian Public Health: Continuities and Changes Across the Revolutionary Divide," in *The History of Public Health and the Modern State*, ed. Dorothy Porter (Amsterdam: Rodopi, 1994), 183–223; Elisa M. Becker, "Judicial Reform and the Role of Medical Expertise in Late Imperial Russian Courts," *Law and History Review* 17, no. 1 (Spring 1999): 1–26.

to the proposition that clinicians strove to demonstrate their usefulness and authority. The rise of degeneration theory within the biomedical professions was more than a mere instrument for the advancement of institutional interests. To view it as such would be to ignore much of the theoretical uncertainty and reflexive self-scrutiny that pervaded the writing on the subject. Studies by clinicians reverberated with a palpable sense of disquiet at the elusive nature of the syndrome, its destructive powers, and medicine's apparent powerlessness to track its development and combat its spread. Moreover, the endurance of biomedical theories of deviance across the revolutionary period means that they are interesting not simply as expressions of a "moral panic" at a given moment of crisis. Rather, they serve as a sensitive register of, and meditation on, the concerns of contemporaries confronted with the risks, uncertainties, and opportunities of modernization, revolution, and state-building and the forms of social and moral disorder they appeared to entail.

Neither did the biomedical sciences simply speak to existing anxieties. With their emphasis on the destructive power of pathological heredity and contagion, biomedical theories were instrumental in the development, legitimation, and consolidation of new objects of popular anxiety. In their application of degeneration theory to an understanding of the effects of industrialization and urbanization, theorists of deviance generated for their contemporaries a powerful critique of capitalism. Medicalized discourses gave a particular form to already well-established concerns, such as the perceived increase in crime, by insisting on the existence of a criminal class that was biologically and psychologically distinct from the rest of society. Degeneration theory invested the person of the deviant with a nature more threatening than that of criminals understood to be acting from self-interest. A biopsychological deformity, he or she would be impervious to the moral and rational appeals of her contemporaries. In view of the deviant's biopsychological predisposition to vice, crime, and sedition, theorists argued that deterrence would be an ineffectual strategy. What was required was his or her coercive treatment or indeed isolation by the state.

The power of degeneration to transfer pathologies from parents to their offspring found a corollary in the power of certain disorders to infect the wider society. Theories of moral and mental contagion forged an enduring understanding of the relationship of psychological instability and constant mutual peril that existed between individuals and their societies. Deviant individuals had the power to contaminate those around them with irrational, overwhelming, and destructive urges. Large agglomerations of human beings in urban centers thus represented powder kegs of unrest waiting to be ignited by madmen and demagogues. Conceptualized in clinical terms, moral and physical deformity, crime, suicide, and political extremism were all the symptoms of a diseased and dysfunctional social order. The accumulation of vice, criminality, and sedition in a particular section of the population threatened to disseminate itself and destroy the empire's moral fabric, social order, and political institutions. Such a view lent a particular urgency to the battle with crime. Society could not aspire simply to contain the disorder within its midst; it was obliged to strive for its elimination.

The Influence of the Human Sciences in Revolutionary Russia

Science enjoyed extraordinary popularity in post-Emancipation Russia.[28] Educated Russia flocked to public lectures given by university professors and independent scholars and to public meetings of scientific societies. The "thick journals" contained a hefty quotient of popular science and discussions of scientific conferences, material which constitutes one of the primary sources of this book. Even specialist journals often enjoyed a broad and interdisciplinary appeal, providing arenas in which academics and clinicians advanced their own theories and debated a broad range of social and moral issues of pressing public concern. Scientists and clinicians undertook this outreach to the wider public in a conscious and deliberate manner. In a review of recent research into psychiatry published in 1893 in the liberal journal *Russkaia mysl'*, physician Aleksandr Nikolaevich Alelekov (1856–?) explicitly acknowledged that "moving out from a narrow and confined circle of specialization utterly inaccessible to the public, psychiatry has been trying to meet the demands of society, and the quantity of popular journal articles, pamphlets, and books devoted to various specialist questions is increasing every year."[29] Although frustrated by the tsarist regime's failure to implement its proposed criminal codes and reforms of medical and psychiatric care, on the public stage practitioners of the human sciences were highly influential in articulating the terms in which educated contemporaries came to view their changing world.[30]

28   Elizabeth A. Hachten, "In Service to Science and Society: Scientists and the Public in Late Nineteenth-Century Russia," in *Science and Civil Society*, ed. Lynn K. Nyhart and Thomas H. Broman, in *Osiris* 17 (2002): 171–209; Alexander Vucinich, *Science in Russian Culture, 1861–1917* (Stanford: Stanford University Press, 1970); Joseph Bradley, "Subjects into Citizens: Societies, Civil Society, and Autocracy in Tsarist Russia," *American Historical Review* 107, no. 4 (October 2002): 1094–1123; Irina Sirotkina, *Diagnosing Literary Genius: A Cultural History of Psychiatry in Russia, 1880–1930* (Baltimore: John Hopkins University Press, 2002); Francine Hirsch, *Empire of Nations: Ethnographic Knowledge and the Making of the Soviet Union* (Ithaca: Cornell University Press, 2005), chap. 1.
29   Aleksandr N. Alelekov, "Iz oblasti psikhiatrii," *Russkaia mysl'* (August 1893): 105.
30   See, for example, the fate of the rejected 1903 criminal code in Engelstein, *The Keys to Happiness*, 17–55. On the influence of the Russian academic community, see David Wartenweiler, *Civil Society and Academic Debate in Russia, 1905–1914* (Oxford: Clarendon, 1999), and the collection of conference papers in *Vlast' i nauka, uchenye i vlast' 1880-e—nachalo 1920-kh godov* (St. Petersburg: Dmitrii Bulanin, 2003).

As the literary works of Lev Tolstoi, Fedor Dostoevskii, Anton Chekhov and others explored, the mood among educated Russian society in the *fin-de-siècle* was characterized by mounting disquiet over the human costs of industrialization and urbanization, disillusionment with the impotence of legal and educational reform, and the sense that Russian society had lost its moral compass.[31] In this intellectual climate, clinical discourses of degeneration and moral contagion echoed all the more powerfully against the firmly established metaphorical language of social pathology and infection that featured prominently in journalistic and political writings.[32] Journalists frequently referred to crime and sedition as a plague or disease infecting Russian society, never more insistently than in the wake of the regicide of March 1, 1881.[33] Vladimir Osipovich Mikhnevich's (1841–99), chronicle of contemporary life in the capital, *Plagues of Petersburg*, first serialized in the literary journal *Nabliudatel'* in 1882, was full of allusions to the moral and social diseases of contemporary Russian society.[34]

The metaphorics of pathology and contagion also characterized the writings of influential Russian statesmen across the political spectrum. In an article entitled "Diseases of Our Time" (*Bolezni nashego vremeni*) published in 1896, the procurator of the Holy Synod, Konstantin Petrovich Pobedonostsev (1827–1907) lamented the mounting influence of a subversive mood among the empire's youth:

What are generated for the most part are unconscious imaginings and impressions, imbibed, and plucked by chance, out of the air, in the same way that the atoms of corrupt matter catch on and are imbibed during the development of any epidemic [*kak podkhvatyvaiutsia i vsasyvaiutsia atomy isporchennoi materii pri razvitii vsiakoi epidemii*]. The air is now teeming with the atoms of intellectual and moral epidemics [*v vozdukhe kishat teper' atomy umstvennykh*

---

31   Bartlett and Edmondson, "Collapse and Creation," 178–79.

32   The notion of a decaying or aberrant social order also formed part of the political lexicon of Populist writer Petr Lavrov. A manifesto he published in the influential Populist journal *Nedelia* in 1868–69 declared: "The present social order is a pathological order (*stroi patologicheskii*). . . . It is a decomposing society (*obshchestvo razlagaiushcheesia*) in need of radical reform." Petr Lavrov, *Istoricheskie pis'ma* (St. Petersburg: A. Kotomin, 1870), 54–55. For further examples of this language, see Paperno, *Suicide as a Cultural Institution*, 81–83; Daniel Beer, " 'The Hygiene of Souls': Languages of Illness and Contagion in Late Imperial and Early Soviet Russia" (PhD diss., University of Cambridge, 2002), chap. 1.

33   *Peterburgskaia gazeta* likened the spread of nihilist ideas in Russia's seminaries to a terrifying epidemic. "Our monasteries have more than once been the wellsprings of murderous miasma [*ubiistvennye miazmy*], which have been conceived and spread within their walls. Then, strengthened and shaped in the form of the most infectious epidemic diseases [*zarazitel'neishie poval'nye bolezni*], they were born out by the . . . inhabitants into the sinful world, where a widespread ruin [*paguba*] then began." *Peterburgskaia gazeta*, March 4, 1881.

34   Vladimir O. Mikhnevich, *Iazvy Peterburga. Opyt istoriko-statisticheskogo issledovaniia nravstvennosti stolichnogo naseleniia* (St. Petersburg: Limbus, 2003), 412, 419. The work was first published in book form in 1886.

i nravstvennykh epidemii] of all kinds; they are legion, and it is difficult to think of any other term to describe them.[35]

Biomedical understandings of national decline and individual deviance had gained tremendous currency across the European continent in the last two decades of the nineteenth century and continued to fascinate the contemporary imagination well into the twentieth. Max Nordau's *Entartung* (1892) enjoyed the same celebrity in Russia as elsewhere in Europe and within three years had been published in no less than three different Russian translations.[36] Russian literature also showed clear evidence of the theories of psychopathology and moral contagion. In Anton Chekhov's 1892 short story *The Duel*, for example, the Social Darwinist von Koren expresses his disdain for the dissolute Laevskii in terms that clearly show the popular currency of degeneration theory:

His harmfulness consists above all in his success with women, and he thereby threatens to have offspring and present the world with a dozen Laevskiis, just as sickly and corrupted as he. . . . Primitive man was protected from men like Laevskii by the struggle for survival and natural selection. But nowadays, since civilization has significantly weakened this struggle and the process of natural selection too, the extermination of the weak and worthless has become our worry. Otherwise, if people like Laevskii were to multiply, civilization would perish and humanity would degenerate [*vyrodit'sia*] completely.[37]

Chekhov's writing was no exception. Tolstoi's *Resurrection* (1899) made repeated, if unsympathetic, references to the theories of the Italian criminologist Cesare Lombroso (1835–1909) and the French sociologist Gabriel Tarde (1843–1904).[38] Over the course of the first six months of 1897, the

35   Konstantin P. Pobedonostsev, "Bolezni nashego vremeni," in idem, *Moskovskii sbornik* (Moscow: Sinodal'naia tipografiia, 1896), 125.
36   Maks Nordau, *Vyrozhdenie*, trans. and ed. R. I. Sementkovskii (St. Petersburg: P. P. Soikin, 1894). By 1896, in addition to the St. Petersburg edition, *Vyrozhdenie* had been published in two editions in Moscow and Kiev and was widely discussed in the Russian press. See, e.g., *Russkie vedomosti*, May 13, 1893; *Novosti i birzhevaia gazeta*, July 13, 1893. For a discussion of Nordau's influence, see Aleksandr Krinitsyn, "Problema 'Vyrozhdeniia' u Chekhova i Maksa Nordau," in *Chekhov i Germaniia*, ed. V. B. Kataeva and R.-D. Kluge (Moscow: MGU, 1996), 167–86. On Nordau, see George L. Mosse, "Max Nordau, Liberalism, and the New Jew," *Journal of Contemporary History* 27, no. 4 (October 1992): 565–81; Steven E. Aschheim, "Max Nordau, Friedrich Nietzsche, and *Degeneration*," *Journal of Contemporary History* 28, no. 4 (October 1993): 643–57; Hans-Peter Söder, "Disease and Health as Contexts of Modernity: Max Nordau as a Critic of Fin-de-Siècle Modernism," *German Studies Review* 14, no. 3 (October 1991): 473–87.
37   Anton P. Chekhov, "Duel'," in idem, *Polnoe sobranie sochinenii i pisem*, 30 vols. (Moscow: Nauka, 1974–84), 7:373, 7:375–76.
38   Lev N. Tolstoi, "Vozrozhdenie," in idem, *Polnoe sobranie sochinenii*, 91 vols. (Moscow: Khudozhestvennaia literatura, 1929–64), 32:72, 32:313.

Moscow literary journal *Russkoe obozrenie* serialized a novel by Vera Petrovna Zhilekhovskaia (?–1896) entitled *Degeneration;* in 1915, the Razsokhin theater in St. Petersburg staged an eponymous play by Aleksei Platonovich Vershinin (1871–1933).[39] Accordingly, when in 1912 the jurist Pavel Isaevich Liublinskii (1882–1938) declared that "few readers can today be unaware of the popular theories of social degeneration, of the role of mental and physical insufficiency in the spread of crime and vice," he was not guilty of exaggeration.[40]

By the first decade of the twentieth century, therefore, biomedical theories of social change, national decline, and individual deviance were thriving in the public sphere. Scientific scholarship and practice was central to the rapid coalescing of Russian civil society (*obshchestvennost'*), with its self-appointed mission of social reform and national enlightenment.[41] Indeed, the sources that constitute the base for this book are, in an important sense, inseparable from the emergence and self-definition of civil society in the late imperial period.[42]

In the postrevolutionary years, the human sciences found a more generous, if ideologically more inflexible, patron in the Soviet regime. Francine Hirsch has argued that the alliance forged after 1917 between ethnographers, along with experts in proximate disciplines, and the Bolshevik leadership

---

39   *Vyrozhdenie* is a mediocre novel which idealizes the pre-Reform era and particularly the generation of the 1840s. Its publication in the conservative *Russkoe obozrenie* was entirely congruent with the work's themes of deep disquiet at the perceived moral corrosion of the generation of the 1860s and underlying message that by the end of the 1880s Russia had lost its spiritual compass. Yet if the novel was undistinguished in terms of either its literary merit or the novelty of its representation of Russia's recent historical development, it remained striking for its explicit invocation of the degenerative model to understand these developments and argue its case for the need to rework the educational principles upon which the younger generation was being raised. V. P. Zhilekhovskaia, "Vyrozhdenie," *Russkoe obozrenie* 43 (January 1897): 41–67; (February 1897): 47–79; 44 (March 1897): 171–91; (April 1897): 620–44; 45 (May 1897): 42–66; (June 1897): 685–719; 46 (July 1897): 93–130. Vershinin's play chronicles, in melodramatic terms, the fall of the Vysol'tsov family, the moral and sexual corruption of whose children has been predetermined by the moral dissolution and ill-health of their parents. A. P. Vershinin, *Vyrozhdenie (Itogi zhizni)* (Moscow: S. F. Razsokhin, 1915). Vershinin was the pseudonym of A. P. Almazov, who published dozens of plays in the period, ranging from tragedies to farces.

40   Pavel I. Liublinskii, "Novaia mera bor'by s vyrozhdeniem i prestupnost'iu," *Russkaia mysl'*, no. 3 (1912): 31. In 1915, the criminologist Susanna A. Ukshe also declared that the phenomenon of degeneration "has attracted the attention of the entire cultured and educated world and has generated such heated debate and the most diverse theories." Ukshe, "Vyrozhdenie, ego rol' v prestupnosti i mery bor'by s nim," *Vestnik obshchestvennoi gigieny, sudebnoi i prakticheskoi meditsiny*, no. 42 (June 1915): 800.

41   Hachten, "In Service to Science and Society," 186–87. On the meanings of *obshchestvennost'*, see Samuel D. Kassow, James L. West, and Edith W. Clowes, "The Problem of the Middle in Late Imperial Russian Society," introduction to *Between Tsar and People, edited by idem, 3–9.

42   Wartenweiler is emphatic about this point. See *Civil Society,* chap. 3. See also Bradley, "Subjects into Citizens."

shaped the very formation of the Soviet Union.[43] Kenneth Pinnow has similarly examined the unfolding cooperation between practitioners of forensic medicine, many of whom established their careers in the prerevolutionary period, and the Soviet state in the 1920s.[44]

Like their counterparts in ethnography and forensic medicine, many psychiatrists, criminologists, and psychologists—sympathetic to the new Soviet state's program of rationalization and modernization, if not to its ideological excesses—sought an alliance with the regime. They often found themselves working in offices under the auspices of the repressive organs and judiciary of the new state. In the 1920s, they even published their psychiatric studies of criminals in volumes edited by the People's Commissar of Internal Affairs that bore the imprimatur of state approval and endorsement.[45] They offered influential interventions into Party debates about the morality and behavior of Soviet youth, and their ideas were reflected in the Party press and in literature intended to shape the formation of Soviet selfhood.[46]

As before the revolution, images of social pathology and degeneration continued to echo throughout the popular public discourse. Eric Naiman's subtle study of discussions of sex during the New Economic Policy (NEP) has illuminated the ways in which fears of sexually communicable diseases were in part displaced expressions of anxiety over the corruption of the innocence and purity of the revolution.[47] The Party was obsessed with curing its "illnesses." To take one representative example, a 1924 report of the Moscow Control Commission denounced NEP's influence over one particular Party cell in terms of "the origin of the deformed deterioration in their psychology [*urodlivyi nadlom psikhologii*], which degenerates [*vyrozhdat'sia*] into petty-bourgeois ideology."[48]

Important as it is, the public influence of the human sciences in the revolutionary period is not, however, the primary concern of the present study. The examples above demonstrate the broader metaphorical resonance of a language that in its scientific incarnation was anything but metaphorical.[49]

43   Hirsch, *Empire of Nations*, 24, 23. On the evolution of anthropology in the 1920s and 1930s, see also Frédéric Bertrand, *L'anthropologie soviétique des années 20–30: Configuration d'une rupture* (Bordeaux: Presses Universitaires de Bordeaux, 2002).

44   Kenneth Pinnow, "Cutting and Counting: Forensic Medicine as a Science of Society in Bolshevik Russia, 1920–29," in *Russian Modernity*, ed. Hoffmann and Kotsonis, 115–37.

45   Vladimir N. Tolmachev, ed., *Khuliganstvo i khuligany. Sbornik* (Moscow: NKVD, 1929).

46   See, for example, Martyn N. Liadov, *Voprosy byta* (Moscow: Kommunisticheskii universitet im. Sverdlova, 1925), 22, 28–29.

47   Naiman, *Sex in Public*.

48   *O rabote Moskovskoi KK RKP po 15 aprelia 1924* (Moscow: RKKI, 1924), 43–44. For further examples of the Party's discourse of moral and ideological pathologies, see Beer, "'The Hygiene of Souls'", chap. 4.

49   Indeed, the complex interplay between metaphorical and explanatory languages in this period might well be the subject of a separate study. See, for example, Jan Goldstein, "The Uses of Male Hysteria: Medical and Literary Discourse in Nineteenth-Century France," *Representations* 34, no. 1 (Spring 1991): 134–65.

Rather, the extent to which the precepts of degeneration theory, moral contagion, and psychopathology reverberated throughout the public sphere is, for my purposes, a reason to take seriously the status of the influential and authoritative texts documenting the responses of educated Russians to the challenges and dilemmas they confronted in the revolutionary era.

The Dilemmas of Liberalism

In its investigation of the fate of liberal modernity in the Russian Revolution through the prism of the biomedical sciences, this study must necessarily engage with what has become one of the most influential accounts of the role of these disciplines across 1917. In a seminal essay published in 1993, Engelstein argued that Michel Foucault's account of the relationship between discipline and law in Western modernity was fundamentally, and revealingly, inapplicable to Russia.[50] Foucault had argued that liberalism in the West had replaced the intrinsically ideological legality of juridical monarchy with the normative power of a no-less-inequitable and repressive disciplinary regime. The law no longer operated as the organizing principle for the exercise of power in modern societies, notwithstanding its claims to do so.[51]

Engelstein's basic objection to any attempt to transplant this explanatory model into a Russian setting (and by implication, she also challenges its adequacy in Western Europe) is that Foucault neglects the *restraining* influence that constitutions and civil and penal codes have historically exerted over the disciplinary regimes articulated and practiced by the human sciences. The late imperial period provides an instructive case study. Although the disciplines of the human sciences emerged in the nineteenth century under tsarism, Russia did not witness the development of a *Rechtsstaat* that was their corollary in the West. The Soviet regime subsequently instrumentalized these disciplines to further the aims of a political system reminiscent

---

50   Laura Engelstein, "Combined Underdevelopment: Discipline and the Law in Imperial and Soviet Russia," *American Historical Review* 98, no. 2 (April 1993): 338–53.

51   In Foucault's opinion, the judicial system "is utterly incongruous with new methods of power whose operation is not ensured by right but by technique, not by law but by normalization, not by punishment but by control, methods that are employed on all levels and in forms that go beyond the state and its apparatus. We have been engaged for centuries in a type of society in which the juridical is increasingly incapable of coding power, of serving as a system of representation. Our historical gradient carries us further and further away from a reign of law that had already begun to recede into the past at a time when the French Revolution and the accompanying age of constitutions and codes seemed to destine it for a future that was at hand." Michel Foucault, *The History of Sexuality: An Introduction*, vol. 1, trans. Robert Hurley (New York: Pantheon Books, 1978), 89, cited in Engelstein, "Combined Underdevelopment," 340.

of a *Polizeistaat* in its enthusiasm for untrammeled intervention into the lives of its citizens. The absence of a liberal legal framework meant that there was no competing discourse of individual rights and freedoms and no impediment to the excesses of such a disciplinary regime. In Engelstein's formulation,

> In Russia . . . liberalism failed and the custodial state survived by enlisting and absorbing the agencies of social self-formation it inherited in embryonic form. In contrast to the imperfect world of capitalist liberalism, which both extends and violates the promise of rights, the Soviet regime long offered discipline without rights. This was not merely the old *Polizeistaat* under new ideological auspices—the return of Catherine the Terrible—but its refurbishment with new tactics, by which society was enlisted to do its own policing but in which the discursive authority of the professional disciplines, speaking in the name of "science," function only as a dependency of the state.[52]

Engelstein's argument amounts, as Rudy Koshar has noted, to a sophisticated rendition of a Russian *Sonderweg* thesis that explains the country's disastrous departure from the path of liberal, Western European, civic modernity.[53] In Engelstein's analysis, confronted with a bewildering array of social, economic, and political crises on both the domestic and international scenes, Russian liberalism failed to gain traction in the country's political culture. This failure then opened up the way for an institutionalization of the radicals' contempt for the law, which, perversely, mirrored the disdain for due process of the tsarist regime they had overthrown.[54]

In Engelstein's widely shared account, "liberalism" may have failed, but it remains as an essentially benign, if naïve, political force. Engelstein cites the eloquent Cassandra of Russian liberalism, the legal scholar Bogdan Aleksandrovich Kistiakovskii (1868–1920), who deplored the contempt of the Russian radicals for the law, which they cursorily dismissed as a tool of class domination.[55] Kistiakovskii insisted that the protection of individual liberty and integrity was central to a civic order based on the guarantes of the law and that individual freedom was itself the defining feature of the rule of law.[56] Yet Kistiakovskii's own statements go to the heart of the dilemma for Russia's liberals. He bemoaned the backwardness of Russian legal culture,

52   Engelstein, "Combined Underdevelopment," 353.
53   Rudy Koshar, "Foucault and Social History: Comments on 'Combined Underdevelopment,'" *American Historical Review* 98, no. 2 (April 1993): 359–60.
54   Engelstein, "Combined Underdevelopment," 344.
55   For Kistiakovskii's career and influence, see Susan Heuman, *Kistiakovsky: The Struggle for National and Constitutional Rights in the Last Years of Tsarism* (Cambridge, MA: Harvard Ukrainian Research Institute, 1998).
56   Engelstein, "Combined Underdevelopment," 346.

declaring that it had yet to be internalized by the population and continued therefore to be perceived as a system of purely external constraints: "We [Russians] need external discipline precisely because we lack internal discipline. In this regard, once again, we understand the law not as a matter of legal conviction [*pravovoe ubezhdenie*] but as a form of coercive regulation [*prinuditel'noe pravilo*]. And this conception once again testifies to the low level of our legal consciousness."[57]

Sentiments like those of Kistiakovskii were common. Yanni Kotsonis has noted that from the earliest discussions of income tax in the 1860s to its adoption in 1916, even its authors argued that the gravest challenge to its effective operation was the absence of the required level of "culture" and "civilization" in most of the population. Accordingly, critics warned that the income tax would encourage dishonesty, cheating, and low moral standards and would necessitate coercion rather than reflect a common purpose.[58]

Of course, Kistiakovskii wished it were otherwise, but in a sense his analysis simply raised the question of how to forge a civil society in which legal norms would indeed be internalized by the empire's subjects. In Kistiakovskii's view the law was principally a means to enhance social discipline, and a law-bound state was in essence a disciplined society. Individual freedom—external, relative and determined by the environment—depended upon the establishment of such an order. But more absolute, internal freedom could not develop without the provision of this external freedom.[59]

The key concerns of Russian liberals, who were active in the empire's rapidly growing professional elites, might broadly be summarized as, first, a commitment to the rule of law, that is, adherence to the restraints of legality by the state itself; second, respect for individual rights; third, a belief in the power of science and education to help bridge the gap between an untutored populace (*narod*) and the liberals' vision of Russia's future political order. They saw themselves as the nation's spiritual guide but also as its physician, responsible for the moral, mental, and physical improvement of the population.[60] Their endeavor was, as Reginald Zelnik has noted, a "tall order," caught as the liberal professions were between the obduracy of the tsarist

---

57   Bogdan Kistiakovskii, "V zashchitu prava (Intelligentsiia i pravosoznanie)," in *Vekhi: Sbornik statei o russkoi intelligentsii*, 2nd ed. (Moscow: V. M. Sablin, 1909), 148. For a survey of critical Russian attitudes toward law and legal culture, see Andrzej Walicki, *Legal Philosophies of Russian Liberalism* (Oxford: Clarendon Press, 1989), 9–104. Richard Wortman and Benjamin Nathans have both noted educated society's ambivalence toward the legal profession. See Richard Wortman, *The Development of a Russian Legal Consciousness* (Chicago: University of Chicago Press, 1976), 288; Ben Nathans, *Beyond the Pale: The Jewish Encounter with Late Imperial Russia* (Berkeley: University of California Press, 2002), 345–46.
58   Yanni Kotsonis, " 'No Place to Go': Taxation and State Transformation in Late Imperial and Early Soviet Russia," *Journal of Modern History* 76, no. 3 (September 2004): 551.
59   Wartenweiler, *Civil Society,* 106.
60   See the provocative essay by Theodore H. von Laue, "The Prospects of Liberal Democracy in Tsarist Russia," in *Essays on Russian Liberalism,* ed. Timberlake, 164–81.

state and their own acute ambivalence toward the "dark masses" in whose name they believed themselves to be acting.[61] The human sciences were perhaps uniquely placed (or placed themselves uniquely) to speak to this invidious dilemma. They generated a persuasive explanation of the obstacles confronting the liberal state-building project in the late imperial period and suggested methods to address them.

The liberal intelligentsia was driven by a combination of intellectual and ethical urges. They labored under an acute sense of responsibility for the downtrodden and downcast in their society. As the Populist philosopher and sociologist Nikolai Konstantinovich Mikhailovskii (1842–1904) observed, "We have come to realize that our awareness of the universal truth could only have been reached at the cost of the age-old suffering of the people. We are the people's debtors, and this debt weighs down heavily on our conscience."[62] The liberal intelligentsia fervently sought the construction of a viable and harmonious civil society and political community; and they experienced profound anxiety at the attendant forces of social disorder and subversion that had accompanied the empire's modernization in the second half of the nineteenth century.[63]

Biopsychological analyses of the Russian Empire's troublesome constituencies underscored the extent to which a legal framework—and the civic order that would flow from it—could not be based on the presumption of rational subjects amenable to the claims of order and reason. The gulf between the peasantry and educated society, what Alexander Ivanovich Herzen (1812–70) had in 1851 famously called "the two Russias," had long been an object of despairing discussion among Russian intellectuals.[64] The concepts of progress and modernization in Russia were, in part, understood in terms of the ability of educated Russia to disseminate its values and culture among the Russian peasantry. Overcoming the ignorance, brutality, and poverty of peasant Russia would bring about the fusion (*splochenie*) of the people (*narod*) and educated society (*obshchestvo*). Christine Worobec

---

61   Irina Paperno et al., "Symposium," *Slavic Review* 53, no. 1 (Spring 1994): 199.

62   Nikolai K. Mikhailovskii, *Sochineniia*, vol. 1 (Moscow, 1896), cited in Tibor Szamuely, *The Russian Tradition* (London: Secker and Warburg, 1974), 201.

63   Wartenweiler, *Civil Society*, 11–42; George Fischer, *Russian Liberalism: From Gentry to Intelligentsia* (Cambridge, MA: Harvard University Press, 1958); Dietrich Geyer, "Zwischen Bildungsbürgertum und Intelligentzija: Staatsdienst und akademische Professionalisierung im vorrevolutionären Rußland," in *Bildungsbürgertum im 19. Jahrhundert*, Werner Conze und Jürgen Kocka (Stuttgart: Klett-Cotta, 1985), 207–30. Eric Lohr and Jane Burbank have, from different perspectives, each drawn attention to the attempts made by liberal elites to articulate a language of universal citizenship in late Imperial Russia grounded in a system of equal rights. Eric Lohr, "The Ideal Citizen and Real Subject in Late Imperial Russia," *Kritika* 7, no. 2 (Spring 2006): 173–94; Jane Burbank, "An Imperial Rights Regime: Law and Citizenship in the Russian Empire," *Kritika* 7, no. 3 (Summer 2006): 397–431 (especially 421–27).

64   Aleksandr I. Gertsen, "Le peuple et le socialisme," in idem, *Polnoe sobranie sochinenii*, 30 vols. (Moscow: Akademiia Nauk SSSR, 1954–65), 7:271–306.

has observed that the medical and scientific establishment's drive to civilize the Russian peasants was just as much cultural as it was medical. Convinced that they were a force of progress, clinicians used binary categories of absolutes to distinguish the civilized from the primitive, the modern from the traditional, the superstitious and the religious from the scientific and the secular, and ultimately, the normal from the abnormal.[65] The role of the human sciences was, therefore, both forensic and tutelary.

The application of these binaries to the prospects for political and social freedom in Russia was the subject of the introduction of the first Russian translation of Nordau's *Entartung* in 1893. The publicist Rostislav Ivanovich Sementkovskii (1848–1918) traced the gradual decline of the optimistic "broad, general-European current which emerged together with the philosophy of the eighteenth century, which manifested itself in the great revolution at the end of that century." The French Revolution had heralded

> the overthrow of the old forms; in the social realm, the gradual inclusion of all the new classes into the national culture; in the private, the emancipation of the individual from different structures that repressed one individual at the caprice or in the interests of others. There was, however, a single source of all these different phenomena; they were all reducible to the single conviction that the possibility of progress, the achievement of the greatest prosperity for all people in general and for each one individually, depended principally on the establishment of freedom.[66]

This sanguine attitude toward human development had, however, increasingly given way to doubts about the capacities of democracy and freedom. "Voices were ringing out, claiming not only that all the political innovations had simply served the interests of bourgeois elements but that the new political forms, created by the great revolution at the end of the last century, actually represented an obstacle to the achievement of a normal development of state life." Sementkovskii noted that many of those sharing this analysis of the consequences of the French Revolution in fact prized freedom but perceived the granting of widespread political rights to the masses to be "dangerous for the provision of all forms of freedom valued by society's more enlightened strata: freedom of religion, expression, and conscience." In an argument that surely resonated with an educated Russian audience living in post-Emancipation Russia, which heard persistent calls from radicals for the political emancipation of the peasantry and their inclusion into the government of the country, Sementkovskii continued, "There exists a kind

65   Christine Worobec, *Possessed: Women, Witches, and Demons in Imperial Russia* (DeKalb: Northern Illinois University Press, 2001), 150–51.
66   Rostislav I. Sementkovskii, "Nazad ili vpered?" foreword to Russian edition of Maks Nordau, *Vyrozhdenie*, trans. and ed. Sementkovskii, iv–v.

of dark foreboding that having secured political freedom, the mass of the people, who have for so many centuries remained distant from cultural life, who still wallow in ignorance and in religious and economic prejudice, will treat all that which is dear to enlightened people with scorn."[67]

Sementkovskii argued that the aspirations of the progressive intelligentsia to direct the peasantry's rational and orderly integration into Russian civil society were misplaced: "neither political nor social reforms, even far-reaching ones, justify the kind of brilliant hopes that were pinned upon them."[68] Rather than being a source of spiritual renewal, as Slavophiles and Populists alike had supposed, the Russian peasantry threatened educated society with dark and destructive forces of irrationality.[69] The human sciences had revealed substantial differences in the *material* composition of individuals, comprising the "people" (*narod*) on the one hand and "educated society" (*obshchestvo*) on the other:

> If at the turn of the nineteenth century it became obvious that one can in no way rely on human reason as an immutable given, so in the second half of our century it has been similarly established that neither does the nature of man with its born instincts constitute an immutable given. If reason and nature in all people are the same, nonetheless in particular cases they present such differences that in a practical sense, at a given time and in a given place, they must be necessarily reflected in political and social conditions and systems.[70]

In other words, in Russia the peasantry was a significantly different social animal than the educated elites, and its "born instincts" demanded specific social and political forms. In order to understand better these forms, argued Sementkovskii, a closer and more thorough examination of the psychological profile of the individuals and groups comprising the empire was required. "The passion with which research into the fields of sociology, psychology, and specifically psychophysiology is now undertaken testifies to the degree to which humanity has understood that general welfare, provided by knowledge and freedom, is highly dependent on a correct estimation of the mental

---

67   Ibid., vi.
68   Ibid.
69   Andzrej Walicki, *A History of Russian Thought from the Enlightenment to Marxism* (Oxford: Oxford University Press, 1980), 92–115, 222–68; idem, *The Controversy over Capitalism: Studies in the Social Philosophy of the Russian Populists* (Oxford: Clarendon Press, 1969). Sementkovskii was writing in the midst of the cholera riots of 1892–93, which had confronted educated Russians with the violence and irrationality of their rural brothers. Nancy Frieden, "The Russian Cholera Epidemic, 1892–1893, and Medical Professionalization," *Journal of Social History* 10, no. 4 (Summer 1977): 538–59; Jeff Sahadeo, "Epidemic and Empire: Ethnicity, Class, and 'Civilization' in the 1892 Tashkent Cholera Riot," *Slavic Review* 64, no. 1 (Spring 2005): 117–39.
70   Sementkovskii, "Nazad ili vpered?" xi.

life of individuals and the masses and the natural laws which direct it."[71] Estimation was the first step in a tutelary project of national improvement, because almost no self-respecting *intelligent* held the biopsychological differences between the masses and educated society to be immutable and ineradicable. The human sciences would be deployed not simply in the service of a better understanding of those social constituencies—backward peasants and a whole range of social misfits, deviants, criminals, and the socially ill—but also in their improvement, their enlightenment, their *ozdorovlenie*.

Sementkovskii's view clearly conflicted with a liberal vision of the primacy of individual autonomy and sovereignty. The dilemma, in sum, was how to construct a liberal civic and political order in the absence of a liberal citizenry. Rather than, like Kistiakovskii, simply lamenting its intractability, many liberal Russian medical and legal theorists embraced this dilemma as something with which any project for the construction of a civil society and political community had to contend. The answer in many circles was indeed an invigorated emphasis on the necessity of social discipline, but one which should not be understood in terms of the exclusive preserve of a *Polizeistaat* in either its tsarist or Soviet incarnations.

Liberal critics of the tsarist order were inescapably implicated in their own critique of its biopsychologically damaging nature, which they charged with the proliferation of deviance in society. The strengthening of a *Rechtsstaat* would constitute neither an adequate nor a timely response to the physical, mental, and moral depredations of late tsarist capitalism. The establishment of social discipline came to be seen as a necessary precondition for the constitution of civil society in late Imperial Russia, a project that was unavoidably coercive. Russian liberal elites, moreover, had to contend with the intensely powerful capacities with which the human sciences invested the individual subject. Individuals could exert a frightening influence over the society around them: both in terms of their diseased heredity, which threatened to inseminate the social organism, and the irrational or subrational power they could wield over their contemporaries through the contagious properties of the emotions. Theories of degeneration, psychopathology, and moral contagion all concentrated the minds of Russia's biomedical tutors on the threats posed by highly noxious minorities within their society.

A liberal defense of personal inviolability and the rule of law repeatedly ran up against the problem not only of how to forge the unification of Russian society but also how to negotiate and manage the maelstrom of deviance unleashed by the country's headlong plunge into urban, industrial modernity. Recourse to a defense of the right of individuals to determine their own lives appeared, in the face of the accumulating social pathologies of the late imperial era, to amount to an abdication of social responsibility.

71   Ibid., xiv.

Accordingly, not just the radical but also the liberal project of renovation (*ozdorovlenie*) was by definition coercive. Of course, the forms of coercion endorsed by late imperial liberals and early Soviet radicals were not identical. Although many of their proposals were indeed draconian, ranging from preventive detention to "coercive healing in labor colonies," Russian liberals by and large balked at the widespread application of state-sponsored violence to deal with society's deviants. The Bolsheviks showed far less inhibition. As Nikolai Bukharin was to declare in 1923, "Proletarian compulsion in all its forms, beginning with execution by shooting and ending with the compulsory labor obligation, is—however paradoxical this might sound—*the means for producing a Communist humanity from the human material of the capitalist epoch.*"[72]

The rationalism of Russian liberals and their commitment to an orderly transformation of society were always pushing at the limits of a liberal observance of individual sovereignty.[73] Halberstam has suggested that, "According to liberalism, individuals substantially institute their own meanings. Shared meanings are considered to arise out of the interplay and plurality of individual institutions of meaning. This is the case precisely because liberalism has to emancipate the subject from meanings that are imposed from without if it wants to conceive of the individual as free and self-determining." And yet, he acknowledges, "the problem of shared understandings . . . can only be reduced to a matter of choice where shared understandings are already given." Thus liberalism typically "takes for granted" that individuals will institute *shared* meanings.[74] However, taking shared meanings for granted was a luxury that Russian liberals believed they could ill afford. Laid bare in the attempts of the practitioners of the human sciences to articulate a vision of a future civic and political order was an acute tension between the transformative program, to which they all in varying degrees subscribed,

---

72   Nikolai Bukharin, *Problemy teorii i praktiki sotsializma* (1920; Moscow, 1989), epigraph: 168, cited in Peter Holquist, "State Violence as Technique: The Logic of Violence in Soviet Totalitarianism," in *Landscaping the Human Garden: Twentieth-Century Population Management in a Comparative Framework*, ed. Amir Weiner (Stanford: Stanford University Press, 2003), 19.

73   Melissa K. Stockdale has noted that even the leader of the Constitutional Democrats, Pavel Miliukov, "respected classical liberalism's espousal of individual rights and political liberty, but found these liberal touchstones insufficient to the needs of twentieth-century society. The modern, interventionist, democratic state had necessary social and economic tasks to perform that laissez-faire doctrines and natural law theory could ill accommodate." *Paul Miliukov and the Quest for a Liberal Russia, 1880–1918* (Ithaca: Cornell University Press, 1996), xiii.

74   Halberstam, "Totalitarianism as a Problem," 475–76. Lohr has observed that "late imperial Russia's peculiarity lay perhaps in the absence of a faith among contemporaries that existing law, institutions, and traditions could provide the basis for an evolutionary move from powerless subject to rights-endowed citizen. Lacking a usable past, for better and for worse, many Russian liberals turned to categorical imperatives and universal, moral sources to define the ideal citizen." Lohr, "Ideal Citizen and Real Subject," 194.

and the defense of individual autonomy and sovereignty enshrined in classical liberalism.[75]

Neither was this dilemma unique to Russia. Daniel Pick, for example, has argued that Lombroso's "criminal man" is to be understood in the context of an ongoing attempt by educated North Italians to forge a coherent nation by identifying and exorcising those elements of backwardness and disorder understood to be endemic in the south of the country.[76] Throughout most of the nineteenth century, classical legal codes based on a liberal-inspired system of punishments and deterrents had postulated a sovereign and rational individual. Toward the end of the century, however, a new generation of positivist penal theorists was challenging both the sovereignty and rationality of the offender. They adopted a "custodial," or tutelary, view of the criminal or deviant as an object upon which the coercive apparatus of the state could and should operate, in ways determined by the biomedical sciences, in the service of the social good.[77]

Russian practitioners of these sciences were engaged in a sustained dialogue with their counterparts in other Western European countries, such as Germany, Italy, France, and England, whose penal institutions were moving in a decidedly illiberal direction.[78] Although not discounting the cautionary voices of those like Kistiakovskii, public discourse in the late imperial period saw a draining away of support for the liberal rights of the individual, articulated in terms of citizenship, in part because these "rights" threatened to enshrine the injustices of the *status quo* and keep the dark masses locked in stupidity, ignorance, and poverty—that is to say, in darkness. What emerged on a number of different levels was a profound distrust of spontaneous action, of irrationality, and ultimately of democracy; and a preference for the ordered dictates of reason, even when the order was dictated.

Kistiakovskii was certainly not alone in his disquiet, but no explicit binary existed between the champions of the *Rechtsstaat* and those of the *Polizeistaat*. The endorsement of the preventative (and even indefinite) detention of criminals on the basis of a scrutiny of their biopsychological constitution was arguably one of the most draconian departures from a classical liberal view of a law-bound state. Preventive detention was the cause of a

---

75   On the tension within Russian liberal jurisprudence between respect for the rule of law on the one hand and a desire to forge a modern, rights-endowed citizen whose development was perceived to be at odds with the existing legal order on the other, see Lohr, "The Ideal Citizen and Real Subject."

76   Pick, *Faces of Degeneration*, 115, 145–52.

77   Richard Wetzell, *Inventing the Criminal: a History of German Criminology, 1880–1945* (Chapel Hill: University of North Carolina Press, 2000), 73–105.

78   In France, for example, the *lois scélérates* specifically defined in common law anarchist activities as offenses against society (*délits sociaux*) punishable by death. They also held the anarchist press liable for the provocation of such acts. Nye, *Crime, Madness, and Politics*, 178; Barton L. Ingraham, *Political Crime in Europe: A Comparative Study of France, Germany, and England* (Berkeley: University of California Press, 1979), 180–81.

great deal of agonizing among liberal legal scholars such as Vladimir Dmitrievich Nabokov (1869–1922) and progressive psychiatrists like Vladimir Mikhailovich Bekhterev (1857–1927). Yet although they were, respectively, sensitive to the potential for the abuse of civil rights and the injustice of punishing criminals for a deeply inequitable and unhealthy social order that had driven them to crime in the first place, neither was prepared to reject the measure as unnecessary and unjustifiable. In other words, when confronted by a stark choice between the coercive healing or renovation of society and a diligent observance of liberal legal strictures, both opted for the former.[79]

Paradoxically, seeing the perpetrator as partly a victim of pathological circumstances made it possible to continue to believe in the feasibility of reforming those on the margins of society—even while this perspective reinforced incarcerating and punitive impulses in policymaking circles. Concern over the possible abuses of a disciplinary regime did not amount to a rejection of the role of the law beyond the maintenance of the social order, that is to say, of the *status quo*. The human sciences, in Russia as elsewhere in the Europe at the turn of the twentieth century, were making compelling claims to the function of the law as a central constituent part of the state's disciplinary arsenal, an agent not of order but of transformation.[80]

This conceptualization of the law became all the more urgent in the wake of the 1905 Revolution, which dealt a body blow to the liberals' belief in the power of education and emancipation to produce rational, law-abiding citizens.[81] Rationality itself, once the holy grail of the empire's liberal elites, began to appear bewilderingly illusory, a veil cast over the true psychological powers that lurked beneath the surface of society. The discourse of the human sciences after 1905 shifted from one of tutelage to one of containment and circumscription. Legal theorists came to see the law not simply as a constraint on the arbitrariness of the autocracy and the violence and barbarism that threatened the stability of the social order from below. Instead, the law was a central constituent feature of the reformers' disciplinary arsenal, capable of transforming, rather than simply marshalling, the behavior

79   Vladimir D. Nabokov, *Ob "opasnom sostoianii" prestupnika kak kriterii mer sotsial'noi zashchity* (St. Petersburg: Obshchestvennaia pol'za, 1910), 29–30, 36–37; Vladimir, M. Bekhterev, *Ob"ektivno-psikhologicheskii metod v primenenii k izucheniiu prestupnosti* (St. Petersburg: V. Anderson and G. Loitsiaskii, 1912), 64.

80   Kotsonis has observed that "a succession of reformers and revolutionaries used taxation to introduce techniques of government that would implicate the population in official practices. In the process, they treated the state as an actor and as a space where people act, as an instrument of transformation as well as a locus of integration." " 'No Place to Go,' " 536.

81   Roberta T. Manning, *The Crisis of the Old Order in Russia: Gentry and Government* (Princeton: Princeton University Press, 1982), 329. See also Christopher Read, *Religion, Revolution, and the Russian Intelligentsia, 1900–1912: The "Vekhi" Debate and Its Intellectual Background* (London: Macmillan, 1979); Aileen M. Kelly, "Which Signposts?" in idem, *Toward Another Shore: Russian Thinkers between Necessity and Chance* (New Haven: Yale University Press, 1998), 155–200; Engelstein, *The Keys to Happiness*, 215–53.

of citizens.[82] In other words, liberal elites understood that the obstacles impeding the emergence of a liberal order in Russia were found not simply in the reactionary tsarist state but also in the damaged and recalcitrant human material of the empire's population. The discourse of social *ozdorovlenie* championed by liberals and radicals alike in the revolutionary period was unavoidably and irreducibly disciplinary.[83]

Kotsonis has pointed to the shared context within which liberals and Marxists from the 1890s to the 1920s drew on science, rationality, and enlightenment as legitimizing frameworks for their transformative projects.[84] These continuities and commonalities thread their way throughout this book. Rather than a battleground between modern liberals and antiliberal authoritarians, the period from 1880 to 1930 is a fascinating foreground against which to trace the dark shadows of modernity.

82   On the sharpening debate between Russian liberals over the status of popular emancipation and the desirability of revolution, see Rosenberg, *Liberals in the Russian Revolution*, 34–35; Karpovich, "Two Types of Russian Liberalism."

83   In a recent review of research into late imperial liberal thinkers, Richard Wortman has commented on the continuities that link these thinkers with their radical contemporaries: "These analyses of liberal thinkers give us a greater understanding of the attraction of radical doctrines at this time. They suggest that radical politics had rational justification and were not motivated by misled or pathological urges to employ violent means." Richard Wortman, "Intellectual Constructs and Political Issues," *Kritika* 7, no. 2 (Spring 2006): 282.

84   Yanni Kotsonis, "A Modern Paradox—Subject and Citizen in Nineteenth- and Twentieth-Century Russia," introduction to *Russian Modernity*, ed. Hoffmann and Kotsonis, 4.

1   "Morel's Children"

In Search of the "Degenerate"

We see the birth of a multitude of Morel's children with defective and extremely weak constitutions, representatives with perverted gastric and sexual urges, a breed of people distinguished by their diseased cruelty, bloodthirstiness, and the absence of any trace of what is called moral feeling.
                                                                —Dmitrii A. Dril', 1906

It might seem paradoxical that the degenerative model came to exert such a fascination over educated Russians in late Imperial Russia in the midst of the astonishing technological and material achievements of the empire's industrialization drive.[1] It might seem all the more peculiar that science—usually understood to be a source of inspiration for Russia's progressive forces—should articulate an anxious or even pessimistic vision of the future. Science was both ideologically and practically central to the educated public's desire for strategic action to bring about the renewal and reform of society. Empiricism, rationalism, and scientific modes of expression all confirmed and strengthened confidence in the possibilities of national improvement, progress, and modernization.[2] Yet it was from within scientific discourse that theories of degeneration rose to public prominence. How might this apparent paradox be explained?

---

1   Hans Rogger, *Russia in the Age of Modernisation and Revolution, 1881–1917* (London: Longman, 1990).
2   Elizabeth A. Hachten, "In Service to Science and Society: Scientists and the Public in Late Nineteenth-Century Russia," in *Science and Civil Society*, ed. Lynn K. Nyhart and Thomas H. Broman. *Osiris* 17 (2002): 172, 185.

27

The post-Emancipation era in Russia certainly witnessed the evolution of a vision of a secularized utopia of individual and societal progress that derived its inspiration and persuasive power from the developments of the natural sciences.[3] Scientists themselves were caught up in the tremendous sense of public optimism in the power of science to revitalize the nation on the basis of empirically verifiable foundations of reason and evidence. Ivan Mikhailovich Sechenov's (1829–1905) research into the ability of centers in the brain to inhibit the functioning of peripheral reflexes appeared to demonstrate that higher mental activity had to suppress the lower functions of the organism so that moral, disciplined behavior—the acknowledged guarantee of the social order—could be possible. Sechenov was explicit that his research should serve to naturalize the concept of morality prise it away from the realm of religious metaphysics: "It will be my task to describe the outward activity of a man with an ideal strong will, who acts in accordance with high moral principles and is aware of every step he takes."[4] Ivan Petrovich Pavlov's (1849–1936) research into physiology and subsequently psychology was inspired by the earnest desire to establish an empirical science of human behavior and its rational evolution that would supplant traditional metaphysical understandings of the soul and religion.[5]

Alexander Herzen gave voice to the hopes of many liberal and proreform Russians when he observed that "without natural science there can be no salvation for modern man; without that healthy nourishment, that vigorous elevation of thought based on facts, and that proximity to the realities of life . . . our soul would continue to be a monastery cell, veiled in mysticism spreading darkness over our thoughts."[6] The radical journalist V. A. Zaitsev remarked in 1863, "If that social order in which we live is so bad for the majority . . . this is because the natural sciences do not lie at its foundations, because human life is constructed [instead] . . . upon the basis of abstract ideas."[7] German materialism and French positivism, which shared a pure belief in science as the motivating force of social and

---

3   Alexander Vucinich, *Science in Russian Culture, 1861–1917* (Stanford: Stanford University Press, 1970).

4   Ivan Sechenov, "Reflexes of the Brain" (1863), in idem, *Selected Works*, trans. A. A. Subkov (Amsterdam: E. J. Bonset, 1968), 290–91, cited in Roger Smith, *Inhibition: History and Meaning in the Sciences of Mind and Brain* (Berkeley: University of California Press, 1992), 108.

5   Torsten Rüting, *Pavlov und der Neue Mensch: Diskurse über Disziplinierung in Sowjetrussland* (Munich: Oldenbourg Verlag, 2002), 79–166.

6   Aleksandr I. Gertsen, *Polnoe sobranie sochinenii i pisem*, 25 vols. (1919–25), 12:106, cited in Alexander S. Vucinich, *Darwin in Russian Thought* (Berkeley: University of California Press, 1988), 8.

7   "Bibliograficheskii listok," *Russkoe slovo* 5 (1963): 72, cited in Daniel P. Todes, *Darwin without Malthus: The Struggle for Existence in Russian Evolutionary Thought* (Oxford: Oxford University Press, 1989), 29.

cultural progress, had an enormous intellectual impact on the Russian intelligentsia in the 1860s and 1870s.[8]

The study of the life sciences in particular lent a dual impetus to the discourse of social progress in this period. With their studies of the biological constitution of humans and animals and the organic processes that governed their functioning, scientists insisted on empirical evidence and deductive reasoning in place of metaphysics and religion. Building on the traditional associations between the body and society in Christianity, the life sciences were particularly well equipped to offer indirect commentaries on the nature of Russia's social relations and its evolution as a state.[9] The two paradigms—biological and social—merged, and the object of medical science and the object of social science were defined in the course of mutual projection. In addition, theories of evolutionary biology, notably Darwinism, were themselves predicated on the idea of change and progress and constituted a powerful arsenal of ideas and evidence that could be deployed against the servitors of the autocracy and the status quo.[10]

The rapid growth of research into evolutionary biology across Europe in the last three decades of the nineteenth century underpinned the study of pathological heredity in the field of psychiatry. The Kishinev psychiatrist Petr Petrovich Tutyshkin (1868–1937) celebrated the intellectual revolution in "all fields of biology (botany, zoology, anthropology, psychology etc.) [which] have assimilated the *laws of evolution.*"[11] At the First Congress of the Russian Union of Psychiatrists and Neuropathologists, held in Moscow in 1913, Tikhon Ivanovich Iudin (1879–1950) reflected on the recent interest in hereditary pathologies and explicitly linked the developments in psychiatry with those of biology. He cited German biologist Oskar

---

8   Rüting, *Pavlov und der Neue Mensch*, 60–61; Vucinich, *Darwin in Russian Thought*, 9; James H. Billington, "The Intelligentsia and the Religion of Humanity," *American Historical Review* 65, no. 4 (July 1960): 812–13.

9   For a comprehensive discussion, see Francis W. Coker, *Organismic Theories of the State: Nineteenth-Century Interpretations of the State as an Organism or as a Person* (New York: Columbia University Press, 1910); and Judith Schlanger, *Les métaphores de l'organisme* (Paris: J. Vrin, 1971). Such analogies have a venerable heritage in Western Europe. For citations from Aristotle, Cicero, Livy, Seneca, and St. Paul, see A. T. von Krieken, *Über die sogennante organische Staatstheorie* (Leipzig: Duncker and Humblot, 1873), 19–26; Ezra T. Towne, *Die Auffassung der Gesellschaft als Organismus, ihre Entwicklung und ihre Modifikation* (Halle: C. A. Kammerer, 1903), 15–24. For references to examples in early medieval comparisons, see Otto Gierke, *Political Theories of the Middle Age* (Cambridge: Cambridge University Press, 1987; reprint of 1900 ed.), 103–4, 112, 122–23, 130.

10   As early as 1866, at the very height of the Great Reforms, Vasilii M. Florinskii had observed that the laws of heredity implicitly issued a challenge to the social order: "Many talented members of the lower orders are prevented from exploring their real potential, constrained as they are by their circumstances. It is a matter of regret that so much talent remains untapped." *Usovershenstvovanie i vyrozhdenie chelovecheskogo roda* (St. Petersburg: Riumin, 1866), 72–73.

11   Petr P. Tutyshkin, *Rol' otritsatel'nogo otbora v protsesse semeinogo vyrozhdeniia (Darvinizm v patologii)* (Kharkov: M. Zilberberg, 1902), 42.

Hertwig's (1849–1922) recently translated *Development and Heredity* (1910), declaring "never has so much work been undertaken in biology on questions of development and heredity as in the last ten years." He then went on to mention inquiries into "the nature of matter transmitted as hereditary characteristics . . . investigations into the transfer of features acquired by the parents over the course of their individual lifetimes; research is being undertaken into Mendel's laws of cross-breeding; studies are being conducted into individual variations and the laws governing their appearance . . . ; and, finally, researchers are working to elucidate the effect of different external conditions on the development of the embryo."[12] Having enumerated these developments, Iudin was unequivocal about their impact on the study of psychiatric disorders: "This revival of interest in the study of heredity could not but influence psychiatry, which has always been deeply interested in questions of heredity, having long considered it to be the main factor in the etiology of psychoses."[13]

Degeneration theory combined the precepts of the life sciences—notably evolutionary biology, physiology, and the study of mental illness—and applied them to the study of psychology, criminology, and human conduct in general. It claimed to account for a departure from the normal psychophysical human type, a condition that would become progressively more acute from one generation to the next. This conceptualization of the relationship between the individual and the social world effectively ensured that discussions of individual deviance could not but simultaneously be meditations on the broader health of the body social. The environment's supposed power to inscribe itself into the psychophysical constitution of the individual defined the latter as a document of social forces that could be "read" by the trained observer as a map of the contemporary social order. Yet the picture was also one of dynamic change, for the central role accorded to heredity in discussions of degeneration lent a diachronic dimension to the examination of deviance. The recent past and the nature of Russia's historical development also found a distilled expression in the person of the individual degenerate.

---

12   Tikhon I. Iudin, "O kharaktere nasledstvennykh vzaimootnoshenii pri dushevnykh bolezniakh," *Trudy Pervogo s''ezda russkogo soiuza psikhiatrov i nevropatologov* (Moscow: Tipografiia Shtaba Moskovskogo Voennogo Okruga, 1914), 854. The coexistence of both Mendelian and neo-Lamarckian theories of inheritance was instructively typical. Vucinich has noted that the rediscovery in 1900 of Gregor Mendel's research led to an expansion in the study of genetics in Russia, as elsewhere in Europe. Yet genetics was still slow to inform debates over degenerative disorders. Moreover, the perceived conflict between neo-Lamarckian theories of acquired inheritance and Mendelian theories of genetically determined heredity remained latent rather than actual. An understanding of genetic inheritance did not, at this stage, seem to pose a necessary or intractable problem for the belief that an individual's genetic composition would alter as a result of environmental adaptation in his or her lifetime. Vucinich, *Science in Russian Culture*, 287–89.
13   Iudin, "O kharaktere," 854.

Practitioners of the human sciences enthusiastically deployed degeneration theory in the public sphere just as their disciplines were coming of age in the post-Emancipation era. The theory enabled clinicians to engage the interest and support of the Russian educated public by providing an explanation for the apparent proliferation of deviance in late imperial society.[14] Yet the propositions of the theory, and the objects of knowledge it claimed for itself, cannot be reduced to an expression of institutional or professional interest. The very concept of degeneration was infused with an acute sense of anxiety and crisis felt by contemporary Russians in the turbulent years of rapid industrialization, urbanization, the rise of mass politics, war, and revolution. Accordingly, the studies of degeneration upon which this chapter draws cannot be interpretatively flattened into strategic deployments for the pursuit of a self-interest conceived by the members of late Imperial Russia's scientific establishment. Rather, they are to be read textually as sensitive registers of the ways in which the practitioners of the human sciences both explored and gave shape to the anxiety that so pervaded educated society in the empire's *fin-de-siècle*. For optimism in scientifically ordered progress coexisted with dark undercurrents of pessimism, which continually pointed toward the contingency, frailty, and reversibility of change.

The exponents of a science of society found it impossible to discuss the progressive aspects of social evolution without considering the negative effects that accompanied it and threatened to stall or even reverse the "normal" condition of advance. The positivist philosopher Vladimir Viktorovich Lesevich (1837–1905) hailed evolution as "the most popular idea of our century" but cautioned that "alongside the process of development [*vyrabotka*], the idea of evolution posits the process of degeneration [*vyrozhdenie*] or decomposition."[15] Indeed, contemporaries found it impossible to discuss the manifest technological and material progress of the second half of the nineteenth century in Russia without returning repeatedly to disturbing visions of its human cost. Degeneration theory threw the notion of progress into critical relief by suggesting that there were in fact natural limits to the degree of wrenching change that the social organism could withstand. In his speech to the First Congress of National Psychiatrists in 1887, professor of psychiatry at the University of Kiev Ivan Alekseevich Sikorskii (1845–1918) highlighted what was a central paradox for contemporaries: it was in "the age of steam

---

14   For accounts which emphasize the disciplinary struggles of the medical profession for status, autonomy, and funding, see the introduction, footnote no. 25.

15   Vladimir V. Lesevich, "Ekskursii v oblast' psikhiatrii," *Russkaia mysl'* (February 1887): part 2, 2. Nye has noted in his study of *fin-de-siècle* France that "integrated into sociological theory, the idea of degeneration was able to resolve the apparent paradox of misery amidst growing plenty, of individual pathologies in a vigorous and highly integrated social organism." Nye, "Sociology and Degeneration: The Irony of Progress," in *Degeneration: The Dark Side of Progress*, ed. J. Edward Chamberlain and Sander L. Gilman (New York: Columbia University Press, 1985), 67.

and telegraphs" that "the process of physical, mental, and moral degeneration had revealed itself all over Europe, including in our fatherland." Degeneration theory accounted for the terrible human cost of modernization, as
expressed in the proliferation of "suicide, insanity, and nervous illnesses,"
which were all "indicators of the nervous-mental health of the population
and point to those places and periods in which the population begins to
manifest a tendency toward physical, mental, and moral degeneration."[16]

Sikorskii was of course right that the phenomenon of degeneration respected no borders on the European continent.[17] Its existence in Russia
seemed to bind the fate of the empire together with that of its neighbors in
a vision of future moral dissolution, physical corruption, and intellectual
paralysis. Accordingly, theorizations of the genesis and nature of degeneration stood at the intersection of pan-European concerns with urbanization,
the apparent increase in crime and sedition, and the rise of mass politics and
domestic Russian anxieties concerning the particular status of the Russian
Empire as a society that lagged both materially and culturally behind its
Western neighbors. As theorists and clinicians struggled to make sense of
the social and moral disorder that was accompanying Russia's modernization in the late nineteenth century, they repeatedly returned to certain core
questions: Was degeneration endemic to modern, urban, industrial societies? Was it a generic feature of a certain stage of industrial development? Or
did it indicate that something had gone wrong with Russia's own particular
development? Opinion within the human sciences was divided. In his 1887
review of recent psychiatric research, Lesevich cited the English psychiatrist Daniel Hack Tuke (1827–95) to the effect that although civilization
in the abstract could not be said to be harmful to the biological and psychological welfare of individuals, civilization in its contemporary incarnation, plagued by the "diseases of poverty and vice," certainly was.[18] Yet Pavel
Ivanovich Kovalevskii (1849–1923), professor of psychiatry at the University
of Kharkov, rejected such claims, insisting that "true civilization [*istinnaia
tsivilizatsiia*] of itself produces neither moral nor physical degeneration,"
and any civilization so doing would "not be a true civilization but a false one

16   Ivan A. Sikorskii, "Zadachi nervno-psikhicheskoi gigieny i profilaktiki," *Trudy
Pervogo s"ezda otechestvennykh psikhiatrov proiskhodivshego v Moskve s 5 po 11 ianvaria
1887 g.* (St. Petersburg: M. M. Stasiulevich, 1887), 1055. Sikorskii's own professional activities
illuminate the growing public profile of psychiatry during the period; he appeared as a prominent expert witness for the prosecution at the notorious trial of Mendel Beilis in 1913 and published a popular pamphlet justifying his conclusions, *Ekspertiza po delu ob ubiistve Andriushi
Iushchinskogo* (St. Petersburg: A. S. Suvorin, 1913). On his biography, see Marina Mogil'ner,
"'Entsiklopediia russkogo natsionalisticheskogo proekta': predislovie k publikatsii," *Ab Impe-
rio,* no. 3 (2003): 227.

17   For a comparative study of the discourse of degeneration in France, Italy, and England,
see Daniel Pick, *Faces of Degeneration: A European Disorder, c. 1848–c. 1918* (Cambridge:
Cambridge University Press, 1989).

18   Lesevich, "Ekskursii v oblast' psikhiatrii," 31.

[*lzhe-tsivilizatsiia*]."[19] These were disturbing claims. If the symptoms of degeneration were increasing in the wake of the Great Reforms, they suggested that something had gone profoundly wrong in Russia's historical development and that the country was now piling pathology upon pathology.

The unresolved tension between heredity and the environment in most accounts of the degenerative syndrome provided a rich and varied lens through which contemporaries could consider the promises and disappointments of the reform era and its aftermath. The reform era had articulated change not simply as something incremental, subject to the vagaries of economic and social forces, but as something intentional, rationally structured, and an explicit feature of the contemporary public discourse. The identification of the hereditary component in the degenerative syndrome offered a conception of society overdetermined by the pathologies of its own past. National reform, or *ozdorovlenie*, was burdened with the legacy of serfdom, economic backwardness, and the enormous gulf separating Russia's elites from the mass of the peasantry. By contrast, environmental factors in the etiology of degeneration served to explore and highlight the dangerous perils of Russia's industrial modernization and the expansion of social and moral disorder that it seemed to incur.

Inherent in the notion of progress as espoused by the apostles and practitioners of science was a nagging doubt that Russia might be forging ahead in the wrong direction, deviating ever further from a loosely defined, but keenly felt, norm of moral, mental, and physical health. In 1910, Isaak Grigor'evich Orshanskii (1851–1923), professor of psychiatry at the University of Kharkov, declared that "organs or their components that find themselves on the path of rapid growth and progress are unable to resist all kinds of harmful influences. Consequently they fall prey to pathological processes and easily enter a state of degeneration." Degeneration, in his view, could "have as its source a violation of the normal condition of individual development."[20] If theories of evolution chimed with the educated public's breathless admiration of the astonishing technological advances of the nineteenth century, degeneration theory offered a persuasive meditation on the mounting human misery and social disorder they seemed to entail.

For if progress was one of the great obsessions of the nineteenth century, so was normality, and the two were far from synonymous. Educated contemporaries in the late nineteenth century explored the binary of normality and abnormality through the lens of degeneration theory.[21] Numerically

19 Pavel I. Kovalevskii, *Obshchaia psikhopatologiia* (Kharkov: Kaplan and Biriukov, 1886), 180–81.
20 Isaak G. Orshanksii, *Atavizm i vyrozhdenie* (Moscow: I. N. Kushnerev, 1910), 26.
21 On the rise of the binary normal-pathological in the nineteenth century, see Georges Canguilhem, *Essai sur quelques problèmes concernant le normal et le pathologique* (Clermont Ferrand: "La Montagne," 1943)

small, politically powerless, and caught between an anachronistic auto-cratic state jealous of its own normative prerogatives and "the mass of the people, who . . . will treat all that which is dear to enlightened people with scorn," Russia's modernizing elites within the human sciences lacked the self-assurance of their bourgeois counterparts in the West.[22] Writing in the midst of 1905, the eminent psychiatrist Nikolai Nikolaevich Bazhenov (1856–1923) lamented that "in the conditions of Russian reality in the country, which we know is 'imperiled by attacks on two fronts—beneath there is the power of darkness and above there is the darkness of power,' the only reliable guarantee of a successful struggle with the latter and a resound-ing victory over it is to create a realm of light beneath it."[23]

This realm of light consisted, in part, in the assertion of normality through the illumination, identification, and exorcism of the aberrant and the threat-ening. Science may have conjured degenerates, but it did so in the earnest denial of their metaphorical power. Only by insisting on their concrete, tan-gible, and immediate presence could it discursively expel degenerates from the body social. Yet unlike their Italian, French, or English counterparts, Russian practitioners of the human sciences could never seek merely to con-solidate the notion of an existing normality and defend it from the besieging forces of disorder and deviance. Rather, the very articulation of normality comprised an intellectual assault on the vestiges of feudal privilege and the encroaching deformities of late tsarist capitalism. It was, in sum, a weapon in the struggle for national enlightenment.

And yet, and this is one of the primary arguments of this chapter, estab-lishing the contours of the normal and the abnormal was, within the intel-lectual structures of the theory, akin to chasing the end of the rainbow. All and any attempts to identify and explain the origins of the deviant within the degenerative schema necessarily cast the diagnostic net much wider, em-bracing and scrutinizing the entire social fabric. Reflecting contemporary fears about the trajectory of the empire's development, the theory came to suggest that degenerate forces would ultimately inseminate the whole of society rather than remain contained within its margins.

22 Rotislav I. Sementkovskii, "Nazad ili vpered?" foreword to Russian ed. of Maks Nordau, *Vyrozhdenie*, trans. under ed. R. I. Sementkovskii (St. Petersburg: P. P. Soikin, 1894), vi. Peter Cominos has argued that anxieties over degeneration reflected the quintessential Vic-torian "illness"; the intemperate and dissolute behavior of the degenerate could be unfavorably compared to the continent and self-regulated ideal of the respectable Victorian or bourgeois gentleman. See his "Late Victorian Sexual Respectability and the Social System," *International Review of Social History* 8 (1963): 18–48.

23 Nikolai N. Bazhenov, *Psikhologiia i politika* (Moscow: I. D. Sytin, 1906), 7. The quotation originally comes from Vladimir Alekseevich Giliarovskii's (1853–1935) impro-vised short verse of 1886 in connection with the premiere of Tolstoi's play *Vlast' t'my*. See N. D. Teleshov, *Zapiski pisatelia. Vospominaniia* (Moscow: Khudozhestvennaia literatura, 1943), 30.

The Origins of Degeneration Theory

No discussion of the concept of degeneration in Russia can ignore developments in Western Europe, notably in France—a testament to the pan-European influence of the theory. Russian clinicians and theorists universally acknowledged Bénédict A. Morel's *Traité des dégénérescences physiques, intellectuelles, et morales de l'espèce humaine* of 1857 to be the theory's founding text. In 1900, the psychiatrist Bronislav Ivanovich Vorotynskii (1869–1925), hailed Morel's formulation of a compelling theory which explained that "all deviations [from the norm] occurred in human beings under the influence of diseased heredity, under the influence of unfavorable external circumstances, and as a consequence they generate that abnormal type, that pathological condition, which bears the name 'degeneration.'"[24] Psychiatrist Vladimir Bekhterev even dedicated his public lecture to celebrate the opening of the Psychoneurological Institute in St. Petersburg on March 1, 1908, to the "memory of B. A. Morel, the famous psychiatrist and the celebrated founder of the theory of degeneration." Pointing out that it was almost 50 years exactly since the publication of Morel's celebrated *Traité*, Bekhterev argued that it belonged to those few works of the human intellect that "illuminate, as it were, the way forward, opening up to humanity wide horizons, and what previously appeared to be unclear, murky, and confused, seems in a new light to be completely natural, simple, full of harmony and strictly logical."[25] At the same occasion, Mikhail Nikolaevich Zhukovskii (1868–1916) also eulogized Morel's achievements, pointing to his enduring influence across a wide range of disciplines: jurisprudence, psychiatry, psychology, and sociology.[26]

Morel's *Traité* was an anthropological-psychiatric view of European civilization arguing that degeneration was a "morbid deviation from the primitive human type." Initially resulting from the pathogenic modern social environment and the unhealthy condition of agrarian life, it became truly threatening because heredity tended to transmit the acquired pathological characteristics from one generation to another. Morel based his views on his own observations of families from industrial urban areas and isolated rural areas such as the valleys of the Tyrol. He claimed to have found that families "tainted" through alcohol abuse or poor nutrition

24   Bronislav I. Vorotynskii, "Psikho-fizicheskie osobennosti prestupnika-degenerata," *Uchenye zapiski Kazanskogo Universiteta*, no. 3 (1900): 94.

25   Vladimir M. Bekhterev, "Voprosy vyrozhdeniia i bor'ba s nim," *Obozrenie psikhiatrii, nevrologii i eksperimental'noi psikhologii*, no. 9 (1908): 518. On Bekhterev's career and influence, see David Joravsky, *Russian Psychology: A Critical History* (Oxford: Blackwell, 1989), 83–91.

26   Mikhail N. Zhukovskii, "Morel' i sovremennoe uchenie o psikhicheskikh priznakakh degeneratsii," *Obozrenie psikhiatrii, nevrologii i eksperimental'noi psikhologii*, no. 10 (1908): 613.

became sterile and extinct after three generations of mental alienation, idiocy, and imbecility.[27] Although inherited disorders were already an established theory in contemporary French medicine, Morel's work represented a new and disconcerting departure.[28] The established emphasis had been on the reproduction over generations of a single hereditary constant, but in Morel's narrative, the degenerational syndrome, once set in motion, could gather momentum and the condition become more acute from one generation to the next.[29] What underpinned Morel's schema was the theory of acquired heredity inspired by Jean-Baptiste Lamarck's (1744–1829) research into embryology at the beginning of the nineteenth century.[30] Within the neo-Lamarckian framework, an organism adapting to a pathological environment concealed this pathology as an "aptitude" or "tendency," which would then embed itself in the psychophysical constitution of the organism and be transmitted as an inherited disorder to subsequent generations.[31] Whereas the origins of the

27   Bénédict A. Morel, *Traité des dégénérescences physiques, intellectuelles, et morales de l'espèce humaine* (Paris: G. Baillière, 1857), 5. My aim is not to reprise those sophisticated discussions of degeneration theory in France which a number of other scholars have presented, but rather to identify what was for all Russian theorists effectively a point of departure. Robert A. Nye, *Crime, Madness, and Politics in Modern France: The Medical Concept of National Decline* (Princeton: Princeton University Press, 1984), 97–131; Pick, *Faces of Degeneration,* 44–59; Ruth Harris, *Murders and Madness: Medicine, Law, and Society in the Fin de Siècle* (Oxford: Oxford University Press, 1989), 51–79. On the discourse of degeneration more widely in Europe, see Peter Becker, *Vererbnis und Entartung: Eine Geschichte der Kriminologie des 19. Jahrhunderts als Diskurs und Praxis* (Göttingen: Vandenhoeck & Ruprecht, 2002); Gunter *Mann,* "Dekadenz—Degeneration—Untergangsangst im Lichte der Biologie des 19. Jahrhunderts," *Medizinhistorische Journal* 20, nos. 1–2 (1985): 6–35; and Sander Gilman, "The Mad Man as Artist: Medicine, History, and Degenerate Art," *Journal of Contemporary History* 20, no. 4 (October 1985): 575–97.

28   Ian Dowbiggin has commented that "by 1886 it had been established in most minds that heredity was a viable enough concept to justify making it the foundation for an entire classification of mental disorders and diseases of the nervous system." "Degeneration and Hereditarianism in French Mental Medicine, 1840–1890: Psychiatric Theory as Ideological Adaptation," in *The Anatomy of Madness: Essays in the History of Psychiatry,* ed. W. F. Bynum, Roy Porter, and Michael Shepherd, 3 vols. (London: Tavistock, 1985–88), 1:196.

29   See, for example, the second volume of Prosper Lucas's 1850 *Philosophical and Physiological Treatise on Natural Heredity,* which had termed heredity "a law, a force, and a fact," cited in Pick, *Faces of Degeneration,* 48.

30   Neo-Lamarckianism as it developed in the mid-nineteenth century contended that each individual organism was engaged in a permanent struggle to adapt its own organic constitution to the demands of the environment in which it found itself. Central to this account of evolutionary change was the conception of the embryo's "organic economy," in which diverse internal elements of the organism exhibit a solidarity of associative bonds that serve the organism in the task of adaptation. In this view, the organism possesses some interior force helping it to determine the "conditions in which it accepts combat." The organism's accommodation to any environment is negotiated between these solidaristic components and the milieu. This internal "organic economy," with its efficient division of labor, then becomes an *a priori* condition of successful adaptation. For a discussion of Lamarck's life and work, see Ludmilla Jordanova, *Lamarck* (Oxford: Oxford University Press, 1984).

31   See, for example, Elizabeth Lomax, "Infantile Syphilis as an Example of the Nineteenth Century Belief in the Inheritance of Acquired Characteristics," *Journal of the History of Medicine* 34, no. 1 (1979): 23–39.

theory lay in Lamarck's study of embryology and were initially applied to biological changes in organisms, between 1850 and 1875 several thinkers elaborated a neo-Lamarckian theory of heredity that telescoped the biological and social sources of human behavior.[32]

The nosological edifice constructed by the degeneration theorists concerned the transmission of psychological as well as biological features, and the contemporary dynamism of the study of biological heredity was to have consequences for other related disciplines. In 1891, Dmitrii Dril' insisted that the laws of biological heredity served as a model for the transmission of other characteristics: "Via heredity man passes on his diseases, his facial features, beautiful and deficient aspects of his body. Why should he not also transmit a brain, anatomically and physiologically similar to his own and, consequently, his instincts, his passions, his vices?"[33]

Mental pathologists who wrote in the wake of Morel gradually elaborated and refined the process by which mental aberrations were inherited in degenerational syndromes. Jacques Joseph Moreau de Tours' *La psychologie morbide dans ses rapports avec la philosophie de l'histoire* (1859), Henri Legrand de Saulle's *La folie héréditaire* (1873), Théodule Ribot's *L'hérédité psychologique* (1873), J. Déjérine's *L'hérédité dans les maladies du système nerveux* (1886), Charles Féré's *Dégénérescence et criminalité* (1888), and Valentin Magnan and Paul Maurice LeGrain's *Les Dégénérés* (1895) were all in a direct line of descent from Morel. They extended the implications of degeneration more widely to include inherited "sentiments" and emotional states of a pathological type, and built up an impressive array of clinical anecdotes.

The principal features of the theory might be summarized as follows: there was no perceived distinction between mental and physical disorders; mental and physical functions were held to exist in an intimate relation with one another, and "pathologies" such as tuberculosis could not but have an effect on the psychological constitution of the individual sufferer. Likewise, the onset of moral insanity would frequently manifest itself in physical abnormalities. Deviations were far from constant and stable; they sometimes appeared with explosive ferocity, but often their effect was so slight as to be scarcely visible. They were also capable of striking one generation before melting away in the next, only to reappear in an entirely different guise in a third. The unpredictability of the syndrome and the unification of biological and psychological symptoms into expressions of a single "master pathology" afflicting the biopsychological organization of the degenerating individual were both to become primary assumptions underpinning the

32 Robert A. Nye, "Heredity, Pathology, and Psychoneurosis in Durkheim's Early Work," *Knowledge and Society: Studies in the Sociology of Culture Past and Present* 4 (1982): 111.
33 Dmitrii A. Dril', "Tiuremnyi mir," *Russkaia mysl'* (February 1891): part 2, 67.

work of a later generation of Russian degeneration theorists. Yet unpredictable though the individual manifestations of degeneration might be, they all shared a common telos: sterility and finally death, what Robert A. Nye has observed to be "Morel's concession to the continuing relative health of the population."[34]

The Rise of Degeneration Theory in Russia

Although discernable in the post-Emancipation era, the migration of the theory into the Russian Empire only became unmistakable from the 1880s onward, and then within the context of institutional psychiatry. It was precisely during this period that psychiatry was becoming established as a separate field within clinical medicine, gaining both a public profile and institutional recognition. Before the middle of the nineteenth century, there were only a few isolated practitioners in charge of asylums in Moscow and St. Petersburg and a few lackluster efforts to introduce insanity as a subject in the empire's medical schools. Only with the reforms of medical education in the wake of the defeat in the Crimean War (1854–55) did psychiatry really begin to flourish.[35]

In 1857, the government established the first department of psychiatry at the Medical-Surgical Academy in St. Petersburg, which was intended to ensure the availability of a steady supply of medical experts to staff the empire's growing number of asylums, and thereafter training programs continued to be introduced throughout the empire.[36] The transfer of responsibilities for care of the insane to the *zemstva*, the organs of local government set up in 1864 during the reform era, was codified by the mid-1870s in a mandate to require the institutional care of the insane. Julie Vail Brown has observed that by the 1890s, the majority of Russian universities had established programs in psychiatry and that the largest (in Moscow, Kazan, Kiev, and St. Petersburg) boasted professional societies and published a range of specialist journals in the disciplines of psychiatry and neurology.[37]

Russian psychiatrists were engaged in a constant struggle to acquire the status and prerogatives that they perceived their Western colleagues to enjoy. Their efforts were directed at the acquisition of control over both the terms

---

34   Nye, *Crime, Madness, and Politics*, 123.
35   Julie V. Brown, "Revolution and Psychosis: The Mixing of Science and Politics in Russian Psychiatric Medicine, 1905–13," *Russian Review* 46, no. 3 (1987): 286. For an extended discussion of these developments, see idem, "Social Influences on Psychiatric Theory and Practice in Late Imperial Russia," in *Health and Society in Revolutionary Russia*, ed. Susan Gross Solomon and John F. Hutchinson (Bloomington: University of Indiana Press, 1990), 27–31.
36   Julie V. Brown, "Psychiatrists and the State in Tsarist Russia," in *Social Control and the State*, ed. A. Scull and S. Cohen (Oxford: Blackwell, 1985), 269.
37   Brown, "Revolution and Psychosis," 285.

and technical content of their work. Yet as government policies were clarified toward the end of the nineteenth century, the ability of psychiatric physicians to control conditions within their institutions and access to those institutions was severely curtailed. For the remainder of the imperial period, relations between the state and psychiatrists remained at best uneasy and at worst antagonistic.[38]

The earliest example of a systematic treatment of degeneration theory in Russia is the 1866 study by Vasilii Markovich Florinskii (1833–1899), professor of obstetrics at the Medico-Surgical Academy in St. Petersburg, *The Improvement and Degeneration of the Human Race.* Florinskii acknowledged that the subject of his investigation in Russia was not "properly explored, one might even say, untouched," and although he neglected to cite any other authors, the influence of contemporary French theorists is not difficult to discern. Florinskii argued that heredity was a biological force subject to the inflections of the environment: "The environment has an influence over growth, the conditions of nutrition, development, and the exercise of the organs such that inherited features can develop in various directions. Although acknowledging that the influence of direct heredity was more commonly evident, Florinskii insisted that heredity was capable of skipping a generation or two and appearing only subsequently. He argued that pathological heredity was an excellent example of this phenomenon: in those cases in which "different pathological deformities in the build and hereditary diseases are passed on to the offspring, it is easier [than in the case of healthy heredity] to identify them and to follow the order of their origins."[39]

Florinskii's publication seems largely to have gone unnoticed in Russia, despite its relative sophistication and the degree to which it anticipated the principal tenets of degeneration theory as they became established two decades later. Translations of foreign publications on the theme were also small in number, presumably because interest in the subject remained confined to specialists conversant in the Western European languages in which works were originally written.[40] The shift from discussions in isolated treatises to

38   Brown, "Psychiatrists and the State," 267–68. For a more general examination of Russian medicine, see Nancy Mandelker Frieden, *Russian Physicians in an Era of Reform and Revolution, 1856–1905* (Princeton: Princeton University Press, 1981); and for the professions as a broad category, see Harley Balzer, "The Problem of Professions in Imperial Russia," in *Educated Society and the Quest for Public Identity in Late Imperial Russia,* ed. Edith W. Clowes, Samuel D. Kassow, and James L. West (Princeton: Princeton University Press, 1991), 183–98.

39   Florinskii, *Usovershenstvovanie i vyrozhdenie,* 5, 39, 50, 68.

40   1870 did see, however, the translation into Russian of the Swiss Eduard Reich's *Die Entartung des Menschen. Ihre Ursachen und Verhütung* (Erlangen: F. Enke, 1868) (Eduard Reikh, *Prichiny vyrozhdeniia cheloveka, nepolnota i nepravil'nost' ego telesnogo i dushevnogo razvitiia v nastoiashchee vremia,* trans. Oktavii V. Mil'chevskii (Moscow: A. I. Mamontov, 1870)). Reich's text was a compendium of different forms of physical and moral degeneration and their causes, and the discussion ranged over such diverse topics as different forms of cretinism and the influence of literature on public morals.

prominence within the intellectual production of the human sciences came in the 1880s. At the First Congress of National Psychiatrists, Sikorskii's closing speech was a declaration to the audience both within the chamber and the wider public beyond that the degeneration of the Russian population was a demonstrable fact and an issue of pressing medical concern. He contended that science was now well aware of the existence of "physical, mental, and moral degeneration" and that the dangers degeneration posed to the health of society were so serious that "research into the process of degeneration is a question of extreme importance, . . . and the investigation of measures against it should be acknowledged to be the most insistent, the most urgent demand of our time."[41] Indeed, a number of speeches to the congress by prominent psychiatrists had explicitly invoked degeneration theory as a heuristic device for the understanding of a range of psychological and moral disorders ranging from prostitution to suicide.[42]

It was also in the 1880s that degeneration theory began to figure prominently in textbooks of psychiatry and criminology. In 1886, Kovalevskii published a compendium of mental illness, entitled *General Psychopathology*, which drew extensively on the degenerative schema to explore a range of different social dynamics, from the Great Reforms and the inadequacies of the Russian education system to the effects of urbanization and alcoholism on the population.[43] In 1884, the young Dril' published his highly influential study, *Young Criminals*, which also made extensive use of degeneration theory to explain the destructive effects of pathological heredity and environmental vice on the moral and physical health of children.[44]

What then was the Russian reception of degeneration theory? Here something of a paradox emerged: widespread belief in the existence of degeneration as an empirically demonstrable medical, biological, or physical anthropological fact accommodated fierce disagreements over the *nature* of

41   Sikorskii, "Zadachi nervno-psikhicheskoi gigieny," 1055, 1057.
42   Ivan P. Merzheevskii, "Ob usloviiakh, blagopriiatstvuiushchikh razvitiiu dushevnykh i nervnykh boleznei v Rossii i o merakh, napravlennykh k ikh umen'sheniiu," *Trudy Pervogo s"ezda otechestvennykh psikhiatrov,* 15–38; and P. N. Tarnovskaia, "O nekotorykh antropologicheskikh izmereniiakh i fizicheskikh priznakakh vyrozhdeniia u privychnykh prostitutok," *Trudy Pervogo s"ezda otechestvennykh psikhiatrov,* 884–93. For an extended discussion of Tarnovskaia and her research, see Laura Engelstein, *The Keys to Happiness: Sex and the Search for Modernity in Fin-de-Siècle Russia* (Ithaca: Cornell University Press, 1992), 133–40; Susan Morrissey, *Suicide and the Body Politic in Imperial Russia* (Cambridge: Cambridge University Press, 2006), chap. 7.
43   Kovalevskii, *Obshchaia psikhopatologiia,* 176–202.
44   Dmitrii A. Dril', *Maloletnie prestupniki. Etiud po voprosu o chelovecheskoi prestupnosti, ee faktorakh i sredstvakh bor'by s nei* (St. Petersburg: A. I. Mamontov, 1884). Dril' went on to be Russia's leading criminal anthropologist, both popular and influential among his colleagues. See A. L. Shcheglov, "D. A. Dril' kak kriminalist-antropolog," *Obozrenie psikhiatrii, nevrologii i eksperimental'noi psikhologii* (January 1911): 1–16; Andrei Golosov, "Pamiati Dmitriia Andreevicha Drilia," *Vestnik psikhologii, kriminal'noi antropologii i gipnotizma,* no. 4 (1911): 80–94.

the disorder, its causes, trajectory, and possible responses to it. Morel bequeathed an ambiguous legacy to his Russian audience. The precise relationship between the environment and heredity remained contested, as did the relationship between degeneration and crime, madness, suicide, and other forms of social and moral deviance. The residual ambiguity left something of an interpretative vacuum into which subsequent commentators rushed with their own explanations of the precise mechanisms involved. Thus, at its broadest, degeneration theory offered a common language and a narrative structure into which contemporaries could inscribe their own assessments of the evolution of Russian society during the turbulent years of modernization and revolution from the 1880s until 1917. In the absence of verifiable knowledge, this flexible body of assumptions determined that, in the formulation of Charles E. Rosenberg, "social context, not empirical research or internal logic, determined the contours of nineteenth century hereditarian thought."[45] In the Russian case, this context comprised acute concerns about the normality of both the existing social order and its prospects for improvement.

Narratives of Heredity

A number of important studies have examined Charles Darwin's mounting influence in late Imperial Russia. Often within the framework of Darwinian evolutionism the medically established fact of biological heredity served as a model and empirical proof for the transmission of almost every conceivable human characteristic.[46] One of the cornerstones of degeneration theory was the intimate interrelation of mental and biological attributes. The enigma of apparently random and unpredictable psychological predispositions, reactions, and deviance acquired a sense of internal coherence when understood in conjunction with the biological information about a given person that clinical medicine could provide. In an article published in *Russkaia mysl'* in 1890, Dril' referred to "the contemporary development of psychology, or to be more precise, psychophysiology and psychiatry, which always approach any mental condition, any mental disturbance, however insignificant, from organic principles, from the organic processes which invariably accompany them."[47] Sikorskii agreed that a "broad range of facts had been established"

---

45   Charles E. Rosenberg, "The Bitter Fruit: Heredity, Disease, and Social Thought," in idem, *No Other Gods: On Science and American Social Thought* (Baltimore: John Hopkins University Press, 1961), 32.

46   On the reception of Darwin in Russia, see James Allen Rogers, "Russian Opposition to Darwinism in the Nineteenth Century," *Isis* 65, no. 4 (December 1974): 487–505; Vucinich, *Darwin in Russian Thought;* Todes, *Darwin without Malthus;* Francesco M. Scudo and Michele Acanfora, "Darwin and Russian Evolutionary Biology," in *The Darwinian Heritage,* ed. David Kohn (Princeton: Princeton University Press, 1985), 731–54.

47   Dmitrii A. Dril', "V chem zhe sostoiat uvlecheniia antropologicheskoi shkoly ugolovnogo prava?" *Russkaia mysl'* (June 1890): part 2, 134.

testifying to the nature of degeneration: "These facts can be briefly formulated in the form of the following psychophysical principle: *Clear thinking, a strong will, and a robust mood go together with the purity of the blood and fluids of the organism and exist in a strict correspondence with them.*"[48]

In a public lecture in 1887, Aleksandr Mikhailovich Dokhman (1804–92), a psychiatrist at the University of Kazan, celebrated the scientific advances of Darwinism and the fact that the struggle for existence did indeed lead to a process of "natural selection of the most worthy—the best and the strongest. . . . New physiological characteristics are gradually developed, which by means of heredity become established [*zakrepliat'sia*] in the species, and a given feature—which is still embryonic and incomplete in the forebears—becomes complete and developed in their offspring."[49] Dokhman went on to say that the two forces determining the essential characteristics were "heredity" and "adaptability": "Heredity is a conservative force; under the influence of it alone, the organism of an offspring would be identical to the organism of its parents. Adaptability is a progressive force; under its influence, the organism changes in accordance with the effects of the conditions that surround its external environment." Dokhman effectively argued that the process of adaptability was compatible with Darwin's general schema of survival of the fittest: "Changeability is a direct consequence of the inevitability confronting organisms: of extracting for themselves the means of existence from their external environments. Darwin calls the competition between organisms that is destined to emerge from this situation *the struggle for existence.*"[50] Dokhman saw the same mechanism of adaptability, confirmed by a process of hereditary transfer, at work in the degenerative model. He cited Edwin Ray Lankester to the effect that degeneration was the Darwinist evolutionary process thrown into reverse: "Degeneration can be understood to be a gradual change in the constitution, by which an organism adapts to less diverse and less complicated conditions of life."[51]

---

48   Ivan A. Sikorskii, "Biologicheskie voprosy v psikhologii i psikhiatrii," *Voprosy nervno-psikhicheskoi meditsiny,* no. 1 (1904): 113.

49   Aleksandr M. Dokhman, *Nasledstvennost' v nervnykh bolezniakh* (Kazan: Tipografiia gubernskogo pravleniia, 1887), 5.

50   Ibid., 6. Rüting has noted that the translation of the *Origin of Species* into Russian in 1864 was accompanied by an influential interpretation of the text by the nihilist critic Dmitrii Pisarev (1840–1868) in the journal *Russkoe slovo.* Pisarev's popularizing discussion "explained the expediency of the animal kingdom as the ability to adapt to the environment by determination and effort of will. The thesis of the heredity of acquired characteristics was then absolutely necessary in order to allow the process to affect the development of species and to be able to explain evolution. In this manner, Pisarev popularized a Lamarckian Darwinism in Russia." Rüting, *Pavlov und der Neue Mensch,* 63.

51   Ibid., 39. At the time, Lankester was professor of zoology at University College, London, a personal friend of Charles Darwin, and the author of *Degeneration, a Chapter in Darwinism* (1880). For a discussion of this work, see Pick, *Faces of Degeneration,* 216–18. Tutyshkin offered a slightly inflected version of neo-Darwinian genetics in support of the degenerative schema, arguing that natural selection could work negatively, accomplished by

Yet many of Dokhman's colleagues did not share his view of heredity as a conservative force. They argued, on the contrary, that heredity did not merely effect the transfer of disorders from one generation to the next, but that its transformative capacities ensured that each transmission accelerated the degenerative syndrome. In 1897, Orshanskii argued that "pathological heredity" differed from normal heredity in that "[normal] heredity [*nasledstvennost'*] is, for the most part, direct . . . and consists of the transfer of a type and likeness; pathological [*patologicheskii*] [heredity] for the most part expresses itself in a transformative transfer, and principally consists of a predisposition, which is closer to the [pure form of the] disease from which the parents suffered."[52] Bekhterev applied this model of transformative heredity to an assessment of the health of the Russian population in an address at the Third National Congress of Psychiatrists held in St. Petersburg in 1910: "It is well-known that hereditary transfer does not simply establish the diseased afflictions [*porazhenie*] of the parents' nervous system in the offspring, but also serves to extend their development. It has been demonstrated that mild nervous disorders observed in both parents lead to more acute nervous and mental diseases in the offspring."[53] Sikorskii was even more pessimistic. Once the degenerational syndrome was set in motion, it revealed itself not merely in purer or more acute manifestations of a given disorder, but rather each generational transfer would bring the species a step closer to annihilation. As Sikorskii argued, "The symptoms of degeneration, however slight they may initially appear, contain that deposit or kernel of subsequent changes. Frequently from behind weak harbingers in one generation, the serious symptoms of degeneration suddenly burst forth in the next; the process of degeneration usually leads to serious conditions and the extinction of the species."[54]

The insistence on the transformative power of the syndrome did not go unchallenged. In a review of an 1890 study by Dril', *Psychophysical Types and Their Relationship with Crime and Its Different Forms,* published in the liberal journal *Vestnik Evropy,* Dmitrii Nikolaevich Anuchin (1843–1923), professor of anthropology at Moscow University, claimed that fears of an acceleratory degenerative heredity were exaggerated. Citing Dril''s assertion of a "gradually progressing heredity [that] establishes a particular type of constantly increasing physiological impoverishment," Anuchin countered,

---

biologically and psychologically unfit individuals breeding together: "In the case of pathological selection, accidental harmful features accumulate and lead to the formation of more acutely expressed degenerative types." Tutyshkin, *Rol' otritsatel'nogo otbora,* 5, 36.

52   Isaak G. Orshanskii, *Rol' nasledstvennosti v peredache boleznei* (St. Petersburg: Prakticheskaia meditsina, 1897), 25.

53   Vladimir M. Bekhterev, "Voprosy nervno-psikhicheskogo zdorov'ia v naselenii Rossii," *Trudy Tret'ego s''ezda otechestvennykh psikhiatrov* (St. Petersburg: Tipografiia pervoi Sankt-Peterburgskoi trudovoi arteli, 1911), 60.

54   Sikorskii, "Biologicheskie voprosy," 97.

The expression: "gradually progressing heredity" can scarcely be permitted: heredity is a conservative force; if it were not, then species and breeds would have diversified into a mass of all conceivable variations. Heredity consists in the transmission to the offspring of the fundamental forms of the race [*rodichi*]; due to heredity, the features of the parents are repeated and individual deviations return to the original form in the offspring.[55]

Anuchin's view was a reassuring one. Not only did hereditary transfer apply the brakes to the degenerative syndrome in its passage from one generation to the next, it was even therapeutic, capable of curing the illnesses which had developed in a particular lifetime. Rather than turning to the "laws of heredity" for an explanation of the production by an alcoholic parent of an alcoholic child, Anuchin suggested that attention be directed to the latter's "conditions of development, the influence of the family and society."[56]

Responding to the article a month later in *Russkaia mysl'*, Dril' clarified his understanding of hereditary transformism. Conceding that he was guilty of an infelicitous turn of phrase, he insisted that he had not meant to speak of "progressing heredity as such, but only of progressive stages of organic impoverishment which are transferred via heredity." Dril' elaborated as follows:

> Under the influence of unfavorable living conditions, individual A grew poorer and physiologically weaker [*obednelo i oslabelo fiziologicheski*]. He passes on this acquired impoverishment via heredity to his children who, as a result of certain unfavorable peculiarities which their constitutions have received, are less capable of a successful struggle for survival and will be predisposed to find themselves in disadvantageous living conditions and, consequently, to further impoverishment. Heredity will then ensure the transfer of this impoverishment to the next generation, which in its turn will be predisposed to repeat the same thing.[57]

Dril' effectively shifted the understanding of hereditary transformism by arguing that each intensification of the disorder from one generation to the next was a result of a mutually reinforcing conjunction of hereditary and environmental forces.

The Acquisition of Pathologies

Even in its most circumscribed incarnation, the theory of transformative heredity was predicated on the existence of acquired pathologies. The latter

---

55   Dmitrii N. Anuchin, "Izuchenie psikhofizicheskikh tipov," *Vestnik Evropy* (May 1890): 342.
56   Ibid.
57   Dril', "V chem zhe sostoiat uvlecheniia," 144.

provided the conceptual link between an individual's disorders and the wider environment he or she inhabited. Many clinicians and theorists, who considered degeneration as Darwinian evolution thrown into reverse, continued nonetheless to view acquired pathologies as central to the development of the degenerative syndrome. Indeed, Darwinian ideas in *fin-de-siècle* Russia continued to be inflected by neo-Lamarckian understandings of acquired characteristics. During the 1880s and 1890s, the eagerness with which Russian medical and social experts seized upon Morel's theories reflected what Alexander Vucinich has termed "a revival of Lamarckian ideas [which] became a strong component of the general upsurge in [Russian] biological thought."[58] Vladimir Vladmirovich Vagner (1849–1934), professor of zoology in St. Petersburg and the founder of comparative psychology in Russia, argued that neo-Lamarckism and neo-Darwinism were "two branches of the same tree, two orientations built on Darwin's theory."[59]

Although neo-Lamarckism certainly underpinned the Russian receptivity to degeneration theory, discussions of acquired pathologies rarely, if ever, explained the actual mechanism by which environmental factors became "established" in the organism. Dril', for example, explained the impact of the environment in the following terms: "Unfavorable conditions of the surrounding environment always . . . produce more or less long-lasting and more or less stable negative conditions in the human organism."[60] Dril' did not find it necessary to elaborate on this mechanism, as he took for granted the existence of adaptive pathologies.

As a consequence, most accounts of the degenerative syndrome compressed biological and environmental factors and ignored the distinction one intuitively assumes to have prevailed. Writing in 1886, Kovalevskii argued that "the intellectual and moral organization of the individual was subordinate to, and conditioned by, the following two factors: heredity and the influence of the surrounding environment." These two factors enjoyed identical weighting, and the perfection of human nature depended equally on both. Yet this close interdependence meant that both factors could operate in concert to destroy as well as to improve human nature: "even if only one of these [forces] is defective, it can be reinforced by the effect of the other." The consequences of disturbances in the realm of either heredity or the environment were pernicious, and individual health was effectively

---

58   Vucinich observed that in Russia classical Lamarckism had three general characteristics: first, rather than constituting a systematic theory based on elaborate experimental research, it found expression in scattered and fragmented ideas; second, it displayed a conciliatory attitude toward Darwinism; and third, it emphasized the direct influence of the environment on the transformation process and the inheritance of acquired characteristics rather than "the internal impulse for perfection." Vucinich, *Darwin in Russian Thought*, 157, 161–62.

59   Vladimir V. Vagner, "Novye i starye puti v biologii," *Novoe slovo*, no. 11 (1896): 97, cited in Vucinich, *Darwin in Russian Thought*, 169.

60   Dril', "V chem zhe sostoiat uvlecheniia," 134.

besieged on two fronts: "Deviations and disturbances in heredity and edu-cation will produce deviations and disturbances in the organization of the central nervous system and its functioning—mental activity." As a result, any individual constituted a psychophysical document that could be scru-tinized for evidence of hereditary or environmental abnormalities: "These disturbances will be directly proportional to the degree of disturbances of either factor: in some cases they produce instability and vacillation, in others a predisposition to illness, and in still others the disease itself, and so on."[61]

The chief architect of the rise of neo-Darwinism in the 1890s, the German biologist August Weismann (1834–1919), contended that his research into the apparent immutability of germ plasma refuted neo-Lamarckian claims of the hereditary transfer of acquired characteristics. Weismann's conclusions prompted some Russian clinicians to reassess the belief that characteristics acquired over the course of an individual lifetime could be transmitted to subsequent generations.[62] Russian pathologist Vladimir Valerianovich Pod-vysotskii (1857–1913), for instance, followed Weismann in insisting that the role of such adaptive pathologies was far more limited:

> Only those diseases can be inherited which appear in the organism of the produc-ers in the first period of their gestation. . . . During this period, all the harmful substances acting upon the embryo can be transferred to the future reproductive glands and consequently to any future offspring.[63]

The implications of such a model were at best ambiguous. On the one hand, it held that a healthy child might develop pathologies over the course of its lifetime and its own offspring would be unscathed. Yet on the other, it de-termined that something only needed (perhaps exceptionally) to go awry in those first delicate weeks of the offspring's gestation to result in the onset of a degenerative syndrome in a child with otherwise healthy heredity.

Such a model could, in the final analysis, be accommodated within the degenerative schema, because it did not refute, but merely circumscribed, the central claim concerning the inscription of external factors into the psychophysical constitution of the individual. Yet many theorists appear to have taken this model of hereditary transfer as an extension of their gen-eral views of adaptive pathologies. One of the mechanisms for unleashing the syndrome then lay in the "circumstances" to which the fetus was ex-

61   Kovalevskii, *Obshchaia psikhopatologiia*, 178.
62   Vucinich, *Darwin in Russian Thought*, 165–69. On the nature and significance of Weismann's research, see Frederick B. Churchill, "From Heredity Theory to *Vererbung*: The Transmission Problem, 1850–1915," *Isis* 78, no. 3 (September 1987): 336–64.
63   Vladimir V. Podvysotskii, *Osnovy obshchei patologii*, 2 vols. (St. Petersburg: K. L. Rikker, 1894–96), 1:35–36.

posed. Sikorskii, who was convinced that pathologies acquired over an entire lifetime could indeed be passed on to children, nonetheless agreed with Podvysotskii that the experiences of the fetus might go a long way toward explaining certain forms of degenerative transfer: "Such a proposition would square with the fact that certain poisons, particularly volatile gaseous ones (for example, ethyl alcohol, ether), penetrate easily into tissue. By virtue of their volatility, they can have a harmful effect on the most immediate offspring of the drunkard freely reaching and affecting the centers of the reproductive cells."[64] Sikorskii was effectively employing the model of pathologies acquired in the womb as a specific and well-established instance of the acquisitive mechanism he held to exist in all forms of heredity.

Accounting for the onset of degeneration in this way had, in principle, the advantage of providing a far more precise etiology of the disease because it limited the decisive influence of external factors to a matter of a few weeks of gestation. A similarly precise diagnosis centered on the circumstances of conception. The psychiatrist Pavel Iakovlevich Rozenbakh (1858–1918) argued that observers had long concentrated on the circumstances of conception in order to explain the development in individuals of a wide range of debilitating conditions: "For example, scrofula in children was attributed to the dampness of the premises on which they were conceived, or gout to a conception that occurred after binge drinking."[65] Rozenbakh claimed that contemporary science had refined such notions to provide a more precise understanding of the mechanism of transmission: "It has been confirmed by innumerable observations that the inebriation of one of the parents at that moment [of conception] exerts a ruinous influence on the health of their offspring.... Frequently, the result of a conception which occurred in a drunken state is idiocy in the children."[66]

Individuals became living artifacts testifying to the conditions in which both they and their forebears had lived. If properly interrogated by a discerning questioner, the condition of an individual's health could reveal the recent history of a family, a class, or even an entire people. Yet since the establishment of the degenerative condition could range over the experiences of possibly several generations, a precise determination of its etiology remained frustratingly elusive. The determination of those experiences transmitted from one generation to the next was far more precise when the etiology of the degenerative syndrome was understood to reside not in characteristics acquired since the birth of the parents but rather in their specific condition at the moment of their child's conception.

64   Sikorskii, "Biologicheskie voprosy," 89–90.
65   Pavel Ia. Rozenbakh, "Nasledstvennost' boleznei i vyrozhdenie," *Entsiklopediia semeinogo vospitaniia i obucheniia,* part 9 (1899): 41.
66   Ibid.

The Degenerate and the Body Social

The precise relationship between heredity and environment remained, therefore, a matter of speculation and dispute. As Lesevich observed in 1887, heredity could only account for the transmission and exacerbation of the syndrome, never for its original cause: "In the case of psychiatrists . . . who see the sole cause of mental degeneration in heredity, we still have to ask ourselves: Where is the point of departure for this pathological heredity if the normal, healthy [human] type is not a figment of the imagination?"[67] Lesevich argued that for the proponents of degeneration theory, this "is the essential question, because once the process of degeneration is started, the progressive laws of heredity take care of the rest."[68] Kovalevskii agreed that heredity was an important factor in the etiology of psychopathology but that "it is undoubtedly the case that heredity itself basically comprises the social conditions under which people live."[69]

Indeed, the role degeneration theory accorded to the environment, with or without the intermediary of heredity, lent a logical impetus to examinations of the wider social context in which the degenerate had emerged. Both popular and scientific discussions of degeneration abounded with claims that the deviant could be examined as a body of scientific data that illuminated the wider conditions of his or her existence in the present or in the recent past. Drawing on Lamarckian heredity social theorists across Europe effectively placed the individual and society on a continuum wherein acquired individual characteristics could be fixed and then stored in the social organisms.[70]

Writing in *Russkaia mysl'* in 1890, Dril' argued that the frequently posited dichotomy between biological and sociological causalities was a false one. Given the power of the environment to inscribe itself in the psychophysical constitution of an individual, he argued that "the very biological organization of the individual is itself a social expression."[71]

Yet the intervention of heredity in the dynamic between individuals and their societies complicated the picture. Writing at the turn of the twentieth century, Kovalevskii argued that it was naïve of the classical jurists to argue that man really possessed free will and that he was, by nature, the straightforward reflection of his own society's moral norms and therefore responsible for any deviation from those norms. In fact the picture was more complicated than a synchronic view of social conditions might suppose:

67 Lesevich, "Ekskursii v oblast' psikhiatrii," 26.
68 Ibid., 24.
69 Kovalevskii, *Obshchaia psikhopatologiia*, 179.
70 Nye, "Sociology and Degeneration," 50.
71 Dril', "V chem zhe sostoiat uvlecheniia," 135.

History makes its influence, its reflection, its effects felt in the present and leaves on the individual those features that, in conjunction with current events, create for him the particular and distinctive character of the present. Consequently, not only the current conditions and forces of life but also those of a previous life influence the character of an individual.[72]

In such a view, each individual and, by extension, each society was a prisoner of the past. Perhaps specific to Russia, in ways not witnessed in the more developed industrial nations of Western Europe, the strong hereditarian component in degeneration theory served to mediate fears that Russia's "backwardness" would undermine any attempt to bring about the modernization of the country. In his study of degeneration and atavism, Orshanskii lamented "how often the distant past revives itself against the wishes and will of people, brutally invades the present, gives the latter its own coloring, its direction, sometimes completely smothering it, even dragging it backwards."[73] Or, in Dril''s more neutral formulation, "undoubtedly the past participates in the creation of the future."[74] Such a view necessarily inflected the perception of the individual degenerate, who was, in the opinion of the Ekaterinoslav psychiatrist Ivan Ivanovich Stelletskii (1869–?) in 1911:

the product of historical and social relations; he comprises the entire evolutionary experience of humanity, transmitted by heredity; the contemporary social order expresses itself in him, and at the same time he carries within him the germ of that individual who will realize social ideals. All the elements of the past, the present, and the future of humanity lie in the organization of contemporary society, and they all are encountered in distinctive combinations in each individual.[75]

Within such an evolutionary model, the study of an individual was a way of apprehending the titanic and enigmatic forces of history.

---

72   Pavel I. Kovalevskii, *Vyrozhdenie i vozrozhdenie. Genii i sumasshestvie. Sotsial'no-biologicheskie ocherki* (St. Petersburg: M. I. Akinfiev and I. V. Leont'ev, 1899), 17.

73   Orshanskii, *Rol' nasledstvennosti*, 87. Earlier commentators had observed that the reform period had disrupted the "normal" workings of the Russian body social. A journalist writing for *Otechestvennye zapiski* in 1872 described the process of reform as a form of vivisection which threatened the health of the patient: "The sudden reforms are very similar to excruciatingly painful surgical operations or amputations." "Nashi obshchestvennye dela," *Otechestvennye zapiski*, no. 7, (1872): 83–84, cited in Irina Paperno, *Suicide as a Cultural Institution in Dostoevsky's Russia* (Ithaca: Cornell University Press, 1997), 82.

74   Dmitrii A. Dril', "Zadachi vospitaniia i rol' nasledstvennosti," *Vestnik psikhologii, kriminal'noi antropologii i gipnotizma*, no. 10 (1906): 15. After 1917, the author's meditation on the inescapability of the past was to enjoy a particular resonance.

75   M. [*sic*—Ivan] I. Stelletskii, "K voprosu o vyrozhdenii. (Teoriia degeneratsii)," *Zhurnal nevropatologii i psikhiatrii*, nos. 5–6 (1911): 802.

Yet the individual and, by extension, the individual deviant were more than simply a document to be examined by the trained eye of the medical professional, as Stelletskii remarked. He argued that the relationship between the individual and society was a dynamic of mutually reinforcing conditioning: on the one hand, "the struggle of social elements always has a parallel in the struggle of the basic characteristics of the individual's soul." Yet on the other hand, "those tendencies that a person or a group of individuals manifest give direction to the development of social relations. The tendencies and strivings of individuals determine the course of social life down the path of either progress or regress."[76]

Consequently, degenerates were also agents of social change and represented a motive force in two senses. First, the syndrome was, by its very definition, accelerating, and afflicted individuals would transmit a set of defects to their offspring. (However difficult the prediction of their exact nature, there was a consensus that such defects would be transmitted.) Kovalevskii claimed, for example, that even if it were accepted that only three out of every one thousand people in St. Petersburg were mentally ill, "that would at the present time constitute *a psychopathic army of more than 3,000 individuals!* If we accept that of those individuals, fifty percent are married and every such woman has three children, then it means that in the future Petersburg will have 4,500 invalids who carry in themselves degeneration and are destined to die out."[77] Second, beyond the power to multiply degenerates, the syndrome impelled change in a more general sense, as Dril' explained in 1906: "In combination with a more or less significant number of degenerates, society itself changes and becomes corrupted in its manifestations of life, affected in the person of its members by the process of degeneration."[78]

The degenerate was thus both a portent and an agent of social change on a grand scale. Stelletskii elaborated this wider impulse: "Social life flows from the mental features of the individual and the progressive or regressive course of this current determines the character of these features. In individual psychology, and only in it, is it possible to find those embryonic forms of social development and degeneration that are lodged in the human soul from the moment of his birth [*zarozhdenie*]."[79] In such a view, degenerates were more than simply an unfortunate deviation from an existing social norm; they were evolutionary outriders, more advanced along the path of contemporary social change than their healthy contemporaries.

76   Ibid., 802–3.
77   Kovalevskii, *Vyrozhdenie i vozrozhdenie*, 30.
78   Dmitrii A. Dril', "Iavleniia vyrozhdeniia i usloviia obshchestvennoi sredy v sviazi s voprosami vospitaniia," *Vestnik psikhologii, kriminal'noi antropologii i gipnotizma*, no. 10 (1906): 270.
79   Stelletskii, "K voprosu o vyrozhdenii," 803.

Diagnostic Anxieties

Dowbiggin has argued that degeneration theory in France appealed to psychiatrists because it offered them a loosely defined yet appealing explanatory model around which they could forge an intellectual consensus concerning the relevance of their work to wider society. It also enabled them to draw upon the authority of contemporary biological science and thereby make influential interventions into the pessimistic discourses that characterized nineteenth-century currents of French thought.[80] Much of this analysis is relevant to the Russian context, in which medicine in general, and psychiatry as a fledging subdiscipline, were engaged in a struggle for public recognition and professional autonomy.[81] As the next chapter examines, with its explicit claims of a link between the condition of deviant individuals and the wider health of society, degeneration theory provided an excellent means by which to assert the importance and relevance of psychiatry to the interests of both state and society in the post-Emancipation period.

Yet to reduce the elaboration and deployment of degeneration theory within the psychiatric profession in Russia to an instrument for the advancement of institutional interests would be to ignore much of the theoretical uncertainty which pervaded the writing on the subject. Studies by psychiatrists reverberated with a palpable sense of disquiet at the elusive nature of the syndrome, its destructive powers, and clinical medicine's apparent powerlessness to track adequately its development and to combat its spread. Beneath the bold claims of psychiatry's ability to determine the general existence of the syndrome and its central role in the etiology of a number of moral, physical, and mental disorders afflicting contemporary society, there lurked deep insecurities over how this knowledge could usefully be employed in terms of either therapeutics or prophylactics in any given instance.

All degeneration theorists agreed, for example, on the primary role of heredity in the transfer of the degenerative disorder from one generation to the next. Yet this notion of heredity, which formed the cornerstone of the degenerative model, was unstable and shifting. In a 1904 survey, Sikorskii identified four different possible hereditary permutations:

1. *Direct heredity* is the transfer to the offspring of the features of the father and mother.
2. *Indirect heredity* is the transfer of the type and the characteristics not of the father or mother but of relatives in a horizontal lineage (e.g., uncles, aunts, first cousins, and so on).

80 Dowbiggin, "Degeneration and Hereditarianism," 189.
81 Frieden, *Russian Physicians;* Brown, "Russian Psychiatrists."

3. *Restorative heredity* applies when the features skip a generation in their transmission (e.g., from the grandfather or grandmother to the grand-children). If the features are transmitted from more distant predecessors, that particular form of heredity is known as atavism.

4. *Heredity by means of influence* consists in the appearance in offspring of a given individual of the physical and moral features of his or her first spouse, for example when a widow remarries and children are born to the second husband with the external features and the character of the first husband (who died before conception).[82]

Although Sikorskii's views were not uncontentious—many theorists firmly rejected, for example, the notion of atavism—they do highlight the disturbingly elusive nature of hereditary pathologies. Hereditary features could draw sustenance from family members removed from the immediate family of the individual concerned. They could disappear from view, incubated by parents and transmitted to their offspring; they could indeed lie dormant for generations only to resurface without warning in a particular individual. The degenerative syndrome could even be transmitted to offspring from an originator to whom they were neither related nor with whom they were even acquainted. These "laws" of heredity thus contrived to spin a web of potential conditions in which every individual was hopelessly enmeshed.

The invisible persistence of pathological heredity was explained in terms of a latent predisposition. The concept of a "pathological predisposition" accounted for the absence of a stable and predictable correlation between unfavorable environmental conditions and an individual's psychophysical constitution. It accommodated the spectrum of different ways in which individuals were affected by the same environment and explained why, in certain circumstances, a mildly unfavorable set of environmental conditions could serve as a trigger mechanism for the onset of the degenerative syndrome in certain individuals while leaving the majority *apparently* unaffected, as criminologist Susanna Al'fonsovna Ukshe (1885–?) explained: "The individual . . . seems to be healthy, but a diseased predisposition of his nature, inherited or acquired, swiftly manifests itself in psychopathic phenomena as a result of a more or less significant event in his life."[83]

Kovalevskii argued that an individual with a predisposition to degeneration was especially vulnerable to the depredations of the environment. He or she was, therefore, a particularly sensitive register of environmental conditions: "The subject has such a brain that the slightest bad influence in his or

---

82   Sikorskii, "Biologicheskie voprosy," 85. Kovalevskii mentioned the same range of forms of transmission of heredity in the expanded edition of his *Dushevnye bolezni: kurs psikhiatrii dlia vrachei i iuristov,* 5th ed. (St. Petersburg: Vestnik dushevnikh boleznei, 1905), 210–11.

83   Ukshe, "Vyrozhdenie," 802.

her life can provoke symptoms of disease. . . . But if the subject lives well, and does not encounter any particular physical or moral shocks, trouble, and unpleasantness, then he or she might not manifest any mental illness or any other symptoms of disease."[84] Echoing Kovalevskii's position in an article in the *Encyclopedia of Family Education,* Rozenbakh noted that the existence of a predisposition would explain why, in many cases, "the subject was healthy until a certain age, and only then did the transmission of diseases become apparent."[85]

Although a cure seemed, at this stage, beyond the capacities of contemporary medical science, judicious and rational counsel might ensure that the victim remained potential rather than actual. Assertions of the existence of a predisposition, which could be activated by exposure to a certain environmental context, constituted a prophylactic call to arms, an appeal to intervene to save the individual degenerate from a sin immanent yet not quite inevitable. Far from encouraging the social quietism with which they are commonly associated, hereditarian theories of deviance could, in fact, generate sanctions for radically interventionist policies on the part of the state—as I argue in chapter three.

Yet even this medicalized moral and social activism did not escape the burden of anxiety. Kovalevskii noted that although a healthy environment might prevent the onset of the degenerative syndrome in one generation, it offered no safeguards to the next: "It does not mean that he escapes passing on his inclinations, his predisposition to diseases to his children."[86] This peculiar combination of interventionist injunctions and bewildered, almost defeatist, resignation continued to inform the development of degeneration theory throughout the revolutionary period.

Yet the positing of a predisposition did more than simply endorse an interventionist agenda; it effectively blurred the distinction between the healthy and the diseased, for absence of evidence could never be taken to mean evidence of absence. The children of healthy parents or, indeed, of a family which had enjoyed good health for generations, could suddenly be struck down by an almost supernatural malevolent force that paradoxically took no account of the *apparent* heredity of the parents. The fear of latent threats obscured from view was the corollary of a deep skepticism at the condition of apparent health.

Compounding the invisibility of the disorder, no stable criteria existed with which to predict and anticipate the transmission of the syndrome. The afflictions of the offspring, and their similarity to the conditions suffered by the parents, could vary significantly depending on the specific nature of the degeneration under investigation. Kovalevskii identified two different forms

---

84   Kovalevskii, *Dushevnye bolezni,* 209–10.
85   Rozenbakh, "Nasledstvennost'," 31.
86   Kovalevskii, *Dushevnye bolezni,* 210.

of heredity. In some cases, he contended, "the children inherit the very same diseased mental symptoms as their parents had. Thus, alcoholic parents give birth to children with an inclination for alcohol; epileptic parents give birth to epileptic children, etc. This is singular, homogenous heredity." Yet more elusive and disturbing was "variegated, heterogeneous heredity," through which "alcoholic parents have children who are epileptics, idiots, melancholics, born criminals, and so on." Indeed, the experience of individual families defied a predictable taxonomy of pathologies: "In some cases all the children of sick parents manifest symptoms of disease; in others, only some do and the others appear healthy. It can also happen that one child is an idiot, another epileptic, a third deaf and dumb, a fourth hysterical, a fifth melancholic, and so on."[87] In such a model, individual disorders were held to represent facets of a deeper degenerative condition, what Moreau de Tours had termed the "empire of the law of inheritance," merely "different branches of the same trunk."[88] So although the transformative transfer of degenerational syndromes threatened subsequent generations with an inexorably deteriorating condition, its specific incarnation could not be foreseen.

This lack of predictability in the manifestation of the syndrome from one generation to the next constituted one of the abiding concerns of Russia's degeneration theorists. The apparently random nature with which the syndrome could strike at certain members of a family while leaving others apparently untouched encouraged deep fears of shadowy threats. The ability of degeneration to conceal itself from view only heightened anxieties concerning the power of medicine and psychiatry to identify, categorize, and ultimately control it. The degenerative syndrome was thus in part engaged in a guerrilla war against moral and physical health, delivering deadly blows before melting away into the psychophysical constitution of subsequent generations, only to reappear subsequently without warning in their offspring.

If the unpredictability of the degenerative condition often confounded prognosis, it also rendered diagnosis of the condition all the more difficult because the absence of a stable and clear genealogy in the family obscured the hereditary laws at work. Were the manifestations of relatively mild symptoms such as melancholy a temporary state—induced, for example, by exposure to specific external circumstances such as bereavement—that would pass without trace; or did melancholy herald the onset of a deep-seated pathological syndrome? There was grave concern over the determination of the symptoms of degeneration themselves.

Indeed, the taxonomy of biological, moral, and mental aberrations that Morel and his contemporaries identified was bewilderingly broad in scope.

87   Ibid.
88   Jacques-Joseph Moreau de Tours, *La psychologie morbide dans ses rapports avec la philosophie de l'histoire* (Paris: V. Masson, 1859) 99 cited in Pick, *Faces of Degeneration*, 50.

Pick has summarized them as follows: ". . . from hernias, goitres, pointed ears, absence of secondary teeth, stunted growth, cranial deviations, deaf and dumbness, blindness, albinism, club-feet, elephantitis, scrophula, tuberculosis, rickets, and sterility to the effects of toxins like alcohol, tobacco, and opium; [Morel] explored disturbances of the intellectual faculties, and the noxious tendencies of certain forms of romanticism which resulted in languorous desire, effeteness, reveries, impotence, suicidal tendencies, inertia, melancholy, and apathy."[89] Morel's seemingly encyclopedic taxonomy of disorders notwithstanding, Russian theorists were concerned that he had been too conservative in his identification of signifiers of degeneration. Even the mildest symptoms could be the harbingers of grave threats, as Sikorskii explained: "In its most acute manifestations, the process of degeneration is extremely typical/stable, but it is far less clear in atypical forms. However, if we consider that often as yet undeveloped forms . . . manifest themselves in *nervous* disorders, then we must of course concede that the forms of degeneration perhaps extend well beyond what are the acute or obvious signifiers."[90] On the basis of more than 10,000 cases of sufferers, Sikorskii identified three different kinds of indicators of degeneration: (1) physical indicators such as bodily deformity; (2) physiological indicators such as defective speech; and (3) mental indicators.[91] Addressing the last of these categories, mental degeneration (*psikhicheskaia degeneratsiia*), Lesevich agreed that the acute manifestations of the disease "are obvious as soon as we look through the collection of pictures in Morel's famous work." He cautioned, however, that the "basis of mental degeneration remains after all the organization of the brain and its functions and for this reason its external manifestation can sometimes be deceptive to the eyes of the ordinary observer."[92] Zhukovskii agreed that distinguishing between "mild degrees of degeneration and the normal person is extremely difficult. These deviations are so negligible and unnoticeable that drawing a line between the norm and abnormality appears impossible."[93] Rozenbakh also pointed to the vast twilight zone between "extreme expressions of degeneration, [which] are idiots, incapable of reproducing," and those "degenerates with completely developed mental faculties." The latter might not have been "insane in the strict sense of the word but were distinguished from normal individuals by certain mental deviations . . . such as blunted moral feelings, strange unconquerable urges, perverted sexual feelings, obsessions, etc."[94]

Sikorskii argued that although the symptoms of mental degeneration usually revealed themselves at an early stage in an individual's life, their

---

89   Ibid.
90   Sikorskii, "Biologicheskie voprosy," 91.
91   Ibid., 108–9.
92   Lesevich, "Ekskursii," 13.
93   Zhukovskii, "Morel'," 652.
94   Rozenbakh, "Nasledstvennost'," 46–47.

manifestations could be very subtle: "Their real nature is frequently only determined with complete certainty in subsequent generations, where the process of degeneration becomes completely evident and where it is possible to find ripened and fully developed the basic psychopathic characteristics that had been germinating in previous generations. Here we encounter the fact of a gradual growth of familial diseases, mental aberrations, and deficiencies of character, in a word, the process of mental degeneration [*psikhicheskoe vyrozhdenie*]."[95] Diagnostic clarity would only come then with the development of the disorder (and by definition its spread to subsequent generations) to such an extent that the possibility of effecting a cure had all but evaporated. Degeneration theory accounted for generational contamination and the almost mystical power of a heredity suddenly endowed with destructive capacities to strike down any and every family without discernible warning.

Seen from this perspective, practitioners of the human sciences were admitting the defeat of their diagnostic capacities in the face of a superior force. The irreversible decline of morality and civilization was now ensured by the cast-iron laws of medical science. Seemingly minor and remediable conditions in the present were in fact harbingers of terrible destruction. Clinical medicine had the effect of offering a persuasive commentary on the devastation without being able to offer a cure or even the power to circumscribe or retard its progress. Essentially reduced to the station of a prophesier of doom, medicine could only warn of impending calamity, powerless to prevent its occurrence. The Darwinian optimism of progress and enlightenment appeared to be thrown into reverse; human civilization was now threatened by precisely the same titanic and mystical forces that had originally lifted man from the swamp.

This deep pessimism did not, however, lead to a sense of defeatism, for which the moral and social activism of the human sciences was perhaps too dynamic. True, the theory offered a paradox in which medicine could *identify a mechanism* for transmission that was so variegated and unpredictable that it *defied identification in any specific instance*. Yet what emerged from this diagnostic frustration was a radical expansion of the focus and interest of "medical" investigation: the failure to agree upon a specific stable set of criteria by which to identify the syndrome demanded an intensive scrutiny of all historical aspects, both biological and social, of the (prospective) individual deviant. The intensity with which the human sciences now brought their analytical gaze to bear on the individual subject would logically, if deployed prophylactically, target each and every citizen, not just those guilty of crimes or a violation of social norms, as a "prospective" deviant. Diagnostic frustrations, cultural pessimism, and resolute medical activism thus

95   Sikorskii, "Biologicheskie voprosy," 110.

combined in paradoxical ways to argue in favor of a move away from a strategic targeting of individual deviants to a general systematic and permanent surveillance of the psychophysical and moral health of the population.

Elusive Normality

Embedded in the narrative structure of degeneration theory was a profound tension or contradiction regarding the status of the individual degenerates, who were simultaneously internal and external to the society they inhabited. On the one hand, degenerates were examples of evolutionary abnormality; their identification and the narration of their "fall from grace" by clinicians were part of an attempt to draw a boundary between society's healthy and diseased constituencies. Implicit in this urge to locate, identify, and categorize, as will be shown in discussions of criminality in chapter three, were proposals for the deviant's isolation within, or even excision from, the body social. Prophylaxis was thus seen as a legitimate necessary instrument for the renovation (*ozdorovlenie*) of society.

On the other hand, this representation of the degenerate as radically other coexisted with a far more disconcerting image: the degenerate as the incarnation of existing or historical social conditions. The explicitly theorized links between individual deviance and broader, pathological environmental conditions impelled the scrutiny of social health in general. The life histories of individual degenerates would come to be supplemented with the study of the history of an individual's family and class; in so doing, they became microhistories of society's own abnormalities, its own "fall from grace." The suspicion lurked in the discussions about degeneration that society had quite literally given birth to these creatures, that they were in a sense a biopsychological avant-garde illuminating the empire's trajectory in the post-Emancipation era.

The dual representation of the degenerate encoded in most elaborations of the theory meant that the greater the insistence upon an individual's abnormality, the greater the underlying indictment of the social body that found distilled expression in his or her biopsychological constitution. Within this structure of contradiction, the anxieties expressed by clinicians over the difficulties involved in any attempt to draw a line "between mild degrees of degeneration and the normal person," to repeat Zhukovskii's formulation, might strike us in revealing ways.[96] The indeterminacy or even invisibility of the syndrome's symptoms were in this sense a mediated expression of fears not that the degenerate could appear normal, but that society as a whole was pervaded by the abnormal. What made individual degenerates so

96 Zhukovskii, "Morel'," 652.

difficult to identify was the very degree to which they were representative of the society which had given birth to them, nurtured them, and shaped them in its own image. As a consequence, repositories of normality and health in Russian society were not to be found within any social "mean" determined by the moral and social conduct of the majority of the empire's subjects. Such a healthy majority did not, perhaps, exist at all. Instead, health and normality were to be located in a transformative vision of a future social order, one over which the human sciences would themselves wield considerable influence.[97] Anxieties over the dual status of the degenerate as the carrier of a disorder external to society and the incarnation of disorders internal to that society were thrown into particular relief in discussions of the causes of degeneration. The study of syndrome's etiology could not but constitute a call for social change.

97   In her study of legal culture, Jane Burbank has observed that the tutelary attitude of Russia elites was strengthened by the absence of representative political institutions: "Unhampered by electoral institutions that might have expressed an empirewide will, Russian intellectuals certainly asserted their own notions of what 'the people' wanted. Elites' assignment of their—various—desires to the population was enabled by the empire's practice of differentiated governance and the absence of even representative . . . all-empire bodies until 1906." "An Imperial Rights Regime: Law and Citizenship in the Russian Empire," *Kritika* 7, no. 3 (Summer 2006): 429.

2 The Etiology of Degeneration

> The laws of nature are immutable and woe is he who violates them.
>
> —Pavel I. Iakobii, 1881

By the end of the nineteenth century, a consensus of sorts had emerged within the human sciences in Russia that degenerates did not constitute a separate species of humanity. Rather, they were the fallen, or the children of the fallen, firmly embedded in the matrix of sociohistorical forces that had shaped both their milieu and their heredity.[1] The absence of obvious environmental causes of degeneration in a given generation did not mean that they had not played a role in the onset of the disorder. As Pavel Kovalevskii had pointed out in 1886, even the hereditary component in the theory was little more than the accumulated and transmitted aggregate of social conditions in the recent past, "the existence of the parents and their social position."[2] Heredity was then essentially a medium for the transmission of environmental factors from one generation to the next.

Theorists usually understood the environmental agents of degeneration to be self-inflicted wounds; "social" rather than "natural" in the sense that they were shaped by human agency. They were evidence of damaging human intervention into the equilibrium of the natural world and sometimes of a biological or psychological pollution that had accompanied industrial modernity.

---

1   See, for example, Boris Ivanovich Vorotynskii, "Psikho-fizicheskie osobennosti prestupnika-degenerata," *Uchenye zapiski Kazanskogo Universiteta*, no. 3 (1900): 87–106.
2   Pavel I. Kovalevskii, *Obshchaia psikhopatologiia* (Kharkov: Kaplan and Biriukov, 1886), 179.

As a consequence, clinical discussions of the etiology of degeneration inevitably harbored a prophylactic impulse. Biopsychological salvation could be achieved through the diagnosis and elimination of those factors understood to foster the degeneration of the population.[3]

Discussions of the etiology of degeneration both reflected and shaped the changing concerns of educated Russia in the post-Emancipation era. Many clinicians viewed serfdom as a kind of original sin that had initiated degeneration in both the exploited and the privileged estates. Although in the 1860s they still cherished the hope that the Great Reforms would constitute a series of prophylactic measures, by the 1880s they were a good deal more pessimistic. Many clinicians now understood the reforms themselves, combined with the empire's industrialization drive of the 1880s, to have overlaid and intensified the original injustices of serfdom. They were increasingly perturbed by the negative effects of increased competition and by the overcrowding and daily stress that accompanied Russia's rapid urbanization in the thirty years or so that spanned the turn of the century.

Claims within the profession to the effect that the status quo was inimical to the health of the population were therefore already well established before the 1905 Revolution. In the wake of the revolution, however, clinical assessments of the etiology of degeneration became increasingly trenchant in their criticisms of capitalism and of the tsarist state that defended the interests of the industrialists and landowners. As degeneration was, by its very nature, intensifying (minor aberrations in one generation would lead to far more serious disorders in the next), the theory militated against the acceptance of either the permanent social and moral disorders of a nonregulated capitalist economy or the sacrifice of one particular generation in the interests of the collective health of its successors. Embedded in the contemporary understanding of degeneration was a powerful call for a utopian project of economic, political, and social transformation that would forever cure society of its ills. It might then appear that studies of degeneration offered a theoretical endorsement of revolution.

Discussions of the etiology of degeneration were not, however, without their contradictions. In a number of studies of the experience of the Paris Commune and military conflict in general, psychiatrists had come to the view that exposure to trauma could unleash the syndrome. The explosion of violence in 1905 concentrated psychiatric minds on the widespread effects of such trauma on Russian society as a whole. As a result, the perception of revolutionary activity altered in the period from 1880 to 1914; political

---

3   For the argument that degeneration theory constituted a secularization of the Christian concern with perdition and salvation, see Heidi Rimke and Alan Hunt, "From Sinners to Degenerates: The Medicalisation of Morality in the Nineteenth Century," *History of the Human Sciences* 15, no. 1 (2002): 59–88.

violence came to be seen not simply as a symptom but also an important cause of degeneration.[4]

Far from encouraging theoretically legitimated calls for revolution, the experience of 1905 made most liberal and progressive clinicians think twice about the viability of revolution as an instrument for transforming Russia. What ensued was a paradox: the spread of degeneration in the late imperial period demanded radical intervention into the operation of the market and the structure of society, yet the instability and violence to which radicalism might lead were themselves widely seen as an important factor in the etiology of degeneration. Psychiatric discussions of the causes of degeneration both reflected and reinforced the swift disillusionment of many Russian progressives with the capacity of the revolutionary movement to achieve any more than anarchy and destruction in Russia. As a theoretical reflection of the liberal intelligentsia's ambivalence toward both tsarism and revolution, degeneration theory constitutes an important, and overlooked, window onto the paralysis of Russian progressive thought on the eve of the 1917 Revolution.

"Parasitism" and Its History: The Tsarist Social Order

Since the days of Alexander Radishchev's *Journey from St. Petersburg to Moscow* in 1790, Russian intellectuals had been disturbed by the vastly unequal distribution of wealth and privilege in the empire.[5] The extreme poverty of the village had been an important motif in the writings of liberal and radical critics of the tsarist regime throughout the nineteenth century. It was a central plank of intelligentsia criticisms of the status quo that were championed by Alexander Herzen in the 1840s, radicalized by Nikolai Chernyshevskii and his followers in the 1860s, and inspired the "going-to-the-people" movements of the 1870s.[6] The misery of peasant life also featured prominently in Russian literature throughout the nineteenth century, from Ivan Turgenev's *Sketches from a Hunter's Album* (1847–51) to Anton Chekhov's short story *Peasants* (1897), and in some of the century's most celebrated paintings, such as Il'ia Repin's *The Volga Barge Haulers* (1873). Cathy Frierson has analyzed the prominent sense of moral guilt

---

4   Irina Sirotkina, *Diagnosing Literary Genius: A Cultural History of Psychiatry in Russia, 1880–1930* (Baltimore: John Hopkins University Press, 2002), 117–44.

5   Alexander N. Radishchev, *Puteshestvie iz Peterburga v Moskvu* (St. Petersburg: Tipografiia Radishcheva, 1790).

6   Franco Venturi, *Roots of Revolution: A History of the Populist and Socialist Movements in Nineteenth Century Russia*, trans. Francis Haskell (1960; London: Phoenix Press, 2001), 498–506.

and responsibility toward, and acute perception of a terrible gulf of separation from, the peasant population, among educated Russians who felt themselves tainted by the crimes of exploitation and abuse characteristic of Russia's pre-Emancipation socioeconomic order.[7]

Social inequalities formed one of the primary concerns of Russian writers on degeneration. The proximity of the theory to evolutionary biology and zoology allowed degeneration theorists to argue that society was an edifice built on a natural order. Although human beings might differ in their innate capacities, the task of a social system was to equalize rather than to accentuate those differences in the name of collective health. Social structures that facilitated and encouraged the exploitation and repression of some members of society by others were not simply immoral and prejudicial to the welfare of a particular social constituency. They were in fact pernicious to the collective health of the entire body social. Degeneration theory served to medicalize the precepts of the French Revolution; the call for *liberté, égalité, fraternité* became supplemented by a fourth injunction, *ozdorovlenie!*

The very first Russian study of the phenomenon of degeneration, Vasilii Florinskii's path-breaking *The Improvement and Degeneration of the Human Race,* published in 1866, cited Russia's social order, with its extremes of wealth and poverty, as a causal factor in the etiology of degeneration. Florinskii argued that social inequalities served to maintain the state of material and spiritual impoverishment in which the lower orders found themselves. Subject to ruthless exploitation by their social superiors, they were deprived of the opportunity to improve their situation and thereby reverse the dynamic of degeneration in which they were caught up: "The more equal the distribution of national wealth and the rights and privileges of the various estates, the fewer the number of exploiting parasites there will be in society, the greater the harmony, the greater the success with which the people's strengths will develop, the more the estates will be defended from weakening and from degeneration [*vyrozhdenie*]." If the "serf estate" suffered from the serf owners, neither nature nor fate were to blame but the bloodthirsty tendencies of man himself."[8]

Yet it was not just the weak who began to degenerate under such an iniquitous feudal system. Russia's privileged classes were insulated from any form of genuine physical or mental exertion—fully provided for as they were by the labors of those they either owned or employed. Such a state of

---

7   Cathy A. Frierson, *Representations of Rural People in Late Nineteenth-Century Russia* (Oxford: Oxford University Press, 1993), 9. See also Andrew Donskov, *The Changing Image of the Peasant in Nineteenth-Century Russian Drama* (Helsinki: Soumalainen Tiedeakamatemia, 1972); Taisa Ganzhulevich, *Krest'ianstvo v russkoi literature XIX veka* (St. Petersburg: Obshchestvennaia pol'za, 1913).

8   Vasilii M. Florinskii, *Usovershenstvovanie i vyrozhdenie chelovecheskogo roda* (St. Petersburg: Riumin, 1866), 154–55.

affairs explained why Russia's aristocracy had effectively squandered the culture and ideals that had been transmitted down through the generations of their estate:

> The level of intellectual progress among the privileged classes, the lineage of their civilization notwithstanding, is lower than the other strata of society. With their privileged life style and in the absence of mental work, the brain quite naturally does not perfect itself but, on the contrary, atrophies. This circumstance is one of the reasons for the degeneration of aristocratic families, even of entire nations, if, having subjugated the humble people, they begin to live on the mental and physical labors of the latter and turn into parasites.[9]

Florinskii's early text already demonstrated the capacity of degeneration theory to offer scathing criticisms of the social order in a language of evolutionary biology and medicine. Yet writing in the midst of the Great Reforms, Florinskii was still optimistic that the emancipation of the peasantry and its fusion with the biopsychological material of Russia's privileged classes would lead to a "revival of the nation."[10]

This hopeful tone had all but evaporated by the end of Alexander II's reign, for the 1870s and 1880s were a period of mounting pessimism.[11] As Rotislav Sementkovskii commented in 1894, "a 'dark' mood seized the intelligentsia everywhere . . . disappointment and diseased skepticism are so often observed."[12] The reasons for this new mood were manifold: the stagnation of the Great Reforms in the last years of Alexander II's reign and their reversal under his successor; the failure of either the emancipation of the serfs or Populism to bring about the spiritual and material emancipation of the peasantry; the terror campaign culminating in the assassination of the tsar in 1881; and the social dislocations and suffering entailed by industrialization. Reflecting this sense of gloom, the writings of degeneration theorists in the 1880s were infused with an increasing sense of urgency and disquiet. Pursuing the biomedical criticisms of the tsarist social order first elaborated by Florinskii, theorists argued that many disorders in Russian life were traceable to an iniquitous social system that fostered the degeneration of the population. The theory wielded an explanatory power capable of articulating and explaining the "dark mood" identified by Sementkovskii.

9   Ibid., 79.
10   Ibid., 2.
11   Rosamund Bartlett and Linda Edmundson, "Collapse and Creation: Issues of Identity and the Russian *Fin de Siècle*," in *Constructing Russian Culture in the Age of Revolution: 1881–1940*, ed. Catriona Kelly and David Shepherd (Oxford: Oxford University Press, 1998), 165–224.
12   Rotislav I. Sementkovskii, "Nazad ili vpered?" foreword to Russian edition of Maks Nordau, *Vyrozhdenie*, trans. under ed. R. I. Sementkovski (St. Petersburg: P. P. Soikin, 1894), iv.

In a public lecture delivered in 1887, Aleksandr Dokhman was anxious to identify the credibility of the term "degeneration" as one which "not only correctly summarizes a series of observed phenomena, but also completely corresponds to facts established in zoology, where the study of the constitution and degeneration of animals is more obvious."[13] Dokhman went on to apply the celebrated metaphor of Darwinian evolutionary biology: "From a zoological perspective, we know that any new constellation of circumstances in which the acquisition of food and security by a creature becomes extremely easy as a rule leads to degeneration. In the same way, individuals who stand, by virtue of their birth and property rights, outside of the struggle for existence [*bor'ba za sushchestvovanie*] are subject to degeneration."[14]

Far from being insensible to the contemporary social implications of his statements, it seems probable that Dokhman was invoking zoology as a foil with which to deliver a ringing indictment of the tsarist social order. Indeed, zoological definitions of "parasitism" proved expedient in discussions of the social order in late Imperial Russia. On the one hand, they were clearly loaded with negative moral connotations that accorded well with criticisms of the apathy and decadence of the privileged; on the other, they enjoyed a scientific legitimacy born of their close proximity to the biological sciences.

Perhaps the most trenchant example of the artful invocation of "parasitism" to sustain social criticism was Vladimir Lesevich's extensive review of degeneration theory published in *Russkaia mysl'* in 1887. In his discussion of the etiology of degeneration, Lesevich cited the English popularizer of Darwin, Edwin Ray Lankester, to the effect that "any new combination of conditions that offer a creature the opportunity to provide for itself sufficient nutrition for its survival without any particular effort usually puts this creature on the path of degeneration." Having established the zoological credentials of this view, and recalling the arguments of Florinskii, whom he cited in his article, Lesevich explained that "with reference to human beings, parasitism . . . will always inevitably exert a pernicious and morally destructive influence. The parasite [*parazit*] loses normal bonds with his surroundings, to which he no longer needs to adapt; the exercise of his mental powers becomes superfluous to his requirements." Such a process had far-reaching implications for the whole of society and was not confined to the biopsychological health of the individual. Societies had themselves only evolved as morally structured entities as a result of the human need to adapt to external conditions in the interests of survival: "Even at the earliest stages of the development of sociability, the question of the relationship between the individual and the environment was the point of departure for embryonic morality. As societies developed further, the bonds linking them

---

13   Aleksandr M. Dokhman, *Nasledstvennost' v nervnykh bolezniakh* (Kazan: Tipografiia gubernskogo pravleniia, 1887), 41.
14   Ibid.

with individuals became more complex, demanding ever greater attention, ever greater exertion on the part of the individual."[15]

The parasite stood outside of this process of normal societal development; his life "did not demand any exertions of the will, no concentration was required." As a consequence, it was "scarcely surprising if the parasite degenerates [*degenerirovat'*] in the most fatal manner if from the first moments of his awareness of his own parasitism he becomes, as it were, excluded from society, alien to the people around him; he does not live with the same common feelings as they do, he does not share their work and concerns, he is completely consumed with his own egotistical interests and only lives by and for them." Such a moral corruption would have biopsychological consequences: "The natural consequence of such antisocial instincts and such abnormal conditions of life is the abnormality of the individual himself: the activity of his higher, controlling [*zapravliaiushchie*] centers of his nervous system weakens, the coordination of his mental elements diminishes, a psychological disorganization begins."[16]

In Lesevich's account, parasitism was clearly an undesirable and unhealthy state, but what were its origins? If biological definitions of the natural order provided one vehicle by which clinicians could voice criticisms of contemporary society, history provided another. In pursuing his inquiry into the phenomenon, Lesevich turned to the work of a Russian psychiatrist, Pavel Ivanovich Iakobii (1842–1913), whose monograph *Études sur la selection chez les hommes* had been published in Paris some six years earlier. The volume was a monumental survey of the effects of power and talent on the history of European dynasties from Ancient Rome to the eighteenth century. Lesevich praised Iakobii's "excellent essay," especially "those wonderful pages, in which the talented author depicts the deterioration of moral strength and energy of an individual placed in the condition of a parasite."[17] Lesevich went on to give fulsome quotations, translated into Russian, from the concluding paragraphs of Iakobii's study, which comprised a radical criticism of social stratification as inherently inimical to the interests of collective welfare:

> Men appear to have been organized . . . with equality in mind. Any division into classes—political, economic, intellectual—and any form of selection that logically and naturally follows from this division, is equally pernicious for humanity, both for the elect and for all the other people. This division generates on the one hand an insufficiency and on the other an excess of that quality on which the division is built. As soon as one part of humanity possesses too great a quantity of material and moral goods, the remainder will necessarily be left with too little of the same goods and both parts suffer equally, the one from

---

15   Vladimir V. Lesevich, "Ekskursii v oblast' psikhiatrii," *Russkaia mysl'* (February 1887): 23–24, 18.
16   Ibid.
17   Ibid., 24–25.

a shortage and the other from excess. But nature will, as it were, avenge this violation of its laws and will severely punish the elect, the happy, into their fourth and seventh generations. . . . Any privilege appropriated by man is a step toward degeneration, mental illness, and the death of the race.[18]

Iakobii's text demonstrated how psychiatric theories of degeneration reformulated traditional moral objections to social stratification in a language of natural laws. The contemporary social edifice in many European societies constituted a violation of this natural law, for which all classes would be punished. The relevance of such explicit criticisms of the social order could not have been lost on a Russian audience, which probably explains why Iakobii's work was never translated into Russian. Lesevich went on to formulate the conclusions from Iakobii's work in the unlikely event that they remained unclear to his readership. The art of building a society lay in reducing the inequalities between its members: "If such a goal will ever be achieved, it will be the result of a struggle with natural conditions, the result of the *art* of overcoming them, the fruit of the strategic application of conscious moral strength, striving to abolish the influence of the width, length, and topographical material of heredity itself. . . . Such a victory could only be achieved against the grain of those natural conditions that currently obtain, i.e. by means of their conquest and change."[19] In Lesevich's view, the task of human societies was not to construct a social edifice which magnified inherited differences but rather to perfect the natural order by generating social structures that capitalized on the natural state of moral equality and improved it by making adjustments for those discrepancies that appeared at birth. This amounted to an invocation of the "natural order" as giving shape to the arrangement of human affairs, coupled with an acknowledgement that human intervention into that order was required in the service of a just society.

The decline of Ancient Rome proved a popular image in the writings of degeneration theorists. In his address to the Second Congress of National Psychiatrists, which took place in Kiev in September 1905 (hereafter, the Kiev Congress) against the backdrop of revolution, Vladimir Bekhterev cited the decline of Ancient Rome, where "the higher orders of society became corrupted by wealth and the rapture of power, while the lower orders were beggars and slaves with all the moral features and vices common to them." Unfortunately, he noted, the collapse of the Roman Empire "has not served as a good example for the states of Europe, and the same thing has been happening in them in recent times."[20]

18   Ibid. For the original French, see Paul Jacoby, *Études sur la selection chez les hommes, Études sur la selection chez les hommes* (Paris: G. Baillière, 1881), 606–8.
19   Lesevich, "Ekskursii v oblast' psikhiatrii," *Russkaia mysl'*, pt. 2 (March 1887): 75.
20   Vladimir M. Bekhterev, "Lichnost' i usloviia ee razvitiia i zdorov'ia," *Trudy Vtorogo s''ezda otechestvennykh psikhiatrov, proiskhodivshego v g. Kieve c 4-go po 11-oe sentiabria 1905 goda* (Kiev: S. V. Kul'zhenko, 1907), 33. The speech was also published as a separate pamphlet, *Lichnost' i usloviia ee razvitiia i zdorov'ia* (St. Petersburg: K. L. Rikker, 1905).

A year later, Dmitrii Dril' also invoked the decline of Ancient Rome to offer a scarcely veiled criticism of the state of contemporary Russia. He cited the opinion of the French historian Henri Baudrillart, who in his monumental *Histoire de luxe privé et public depuis l'antiquité jusqu'à nos jours,* first published in 1878–80, had argued that "enormous accumulations of wealth and slavery—this is the source of Roman corruption." Dril' explained that such polarizations of wealth and poverty resulted from the separation of labor from property: "thanks to property, society becomes sharply divided into two parts: the lower, downtrodden, and impoverished mass of people, sinking in the filth of vulgarity, and financial nobility, weakened organically and spiritually, coddled, thirsting for crude sensuous satisfactions, and for this reason thirsting for profit by any means." Dril' concluded, "the physical and mental-moral degeneration of the species" was intimately connected to a society's "economic foundations."[21]

Although the thrust of the analysis of Bekhterev and Dril' did not differ substantially from that of their predecessors, the respective contexts in which they wrote certainly altered the resonance of their arguments and the sharpness of their critique of existing conditions. Theorists and clinicians in the 1880s might have sounded warnings at the long-term prospects for Russia's health if the vast inequalities in the social order were allowed to persist unchallenged. In the midst of the 1905 Revolution, the reflections of Bekhterev and Dril' on the same theme were now those of pathologists offering a determination of the causes of Russia's recent collapse into civil conflict. Moreover, the new atmosphere of liberalism that followed the promulgation of the Fundamental Laws by Nicholas II emboldened Dril' to hint at the relevance of his observations on Rome: "the latifundia, *understanding the word in its broadest sense,* destroyed Italy, but her alone?"[22]

Dril' was not, however, entirely pessimistic. He maintained that scientific advances had equipped contemporary societies with a knowledge of which their Ancient Roman predecessors had been ignorant, a knowledge that would enable them to avoid that "extreme of physical and mental-moral degeneration into which the misfortunate Ancient Rome had descended to the detriment of all its citizens." Yet scientific expertise was not the same as political will, and the conviction that society now possessed the knowledge "to create a virtual paradise on our sinful earth" only enabled Dril' to "hope that the higher culture of contemporary humanity will enable it finally to rework the current iniquitous order in the genuine interests of the common good."[23]

21   Dmitrii A. Dril', "Iavleniia vyrozhdeniia i usloviia obshchestvennoi sredy v sviazi s voprosami vospitaniia," *Vestnik psikhologii, kriminal'noi antropologii i gipnotizma,* no. 10 (1906): 280. See Henri Joseph Léon Baudrillart, *Histoire de luxe privé et public depuis l'antiquité jusqu'à nos jours,* 4 vols. (Paris: Hachette, 1878–80).
22   Dril', "Iavleniia vyrozhdeniia," 294.
23   Ibid.

The identification of Russia's social inequalities as a causal factor in the degeneration of the population nurtured an imperative to intervene to alter the social structure. The diagnostic powers of contemporary social and medical science had identified the impermissibility of the current social stratification, and their rational precepts delineated the kind of social structure required to save the population from degeneration. In the analyses presented above, the extremity of Russia's social inequalities was seen as a hangover from its feudal past, recently embodied in the institution of serfdom. The fact that Dril' chose to cite the *latifundia* of Ancient Rome underlined the degree to which he saw the vestiges of feudalism corrupting the health of Russian society. Yet the reasonable expectation that clinicians and theorists who accused the feudal order of fostering degeneration would celebrate those social and economic processes associated with the rise of industrial modernity was confounded. Imperfect, unsteady, and hesitant though the changes to Russia's social order were in the wake of the Great Reforms, there was a general consensus that change was indeed taking place. The decline of the nobility, the rise of the legal and medical professions, the rise of the *raznochintsy* (educated individuals drawn from a range of different estates), and the expansion of the country's commercial and industrial sectors were all, in part, the result of the reforms of the 1860s.[24] Far from welcoming these trends as a part of the remedy for the pathologies of serfdom and the bifurcation of the population into extremes of wealth and poverty, many of the same clinicians voiced grave misgivings over the impact of the reforms on the health of society.

Modernity and Its Discontents

In his 1886 textbook *General Psychopathology*, Kovalevskii reflected on the profound changes to which Russian society had been subject over the previous twenty years: "Following the Crimean campaign and the emancipation of the serfs . . . the aristocracy began to disappear and its ranks became filled with the *raznochintsy*. The children of priests, bureaucrats, merchants, traders, and even people from the 'lowest orders' began to swell the thinning ranks of the landed gentry. . . . The aristocracy of the blood began to cede to the aristocracy of the mind." Although Kovalevskii welcomed the reforms, he insisted that there was also a "reverse side of the coin": the secular culture of materialism and individualism to which they had given rise. Thousands of youths who had received primary and

24   W. Bruce Lincoln, *The Great Reforms: Autocracy, Bureaucracy, and the Politics of Change in Imperial Russia* (DeKalb: Northern Illinois University Press, 1990); Ben Eklof, John Bushnell, and Larissa Zakharova, eds., *Russia's Great Reforms, 1855–1881* (Bloomington: Indiana University Press, 1994).

secondary education but neither a solid moral upbringing nor any capital "hurled themselves into the embrace of Mammon. Thirst and greed for money became the primary impulse in their lives." This unbridled pursuit of profit was not without its costs for these young Russians in the form of "an extreme demand on their energies and labor: endless sleepless nights, extraordinary mental labor, insufficiency of means, false shame, false pride, frequent deception of their conscience."[25] In his speech opening the First Congress of Russian Psychiatrists in Moscow in January 1887, its chairman, Ivan Pavlovich Merzheevskii (1838–1908), also hailed the "emancipation of millions of people from their enslaved and downtrodden condition, from their mental lethargy and passive position."[26] Yet he argued that by facilitating the spread of commerce and industry throughout the empire, the Great Reforms had unleashed an avalanche of social change that was damaging to the mental and physical welfare of the population: "The development of trade and industry [and] the establishment of new financial and commercial institutions have given rise to a drive for profit, for swift enrichment, engendering a multitude of crises, bankruptcies, and disappointments. They have acted as the source of powerful moral shocks which encourage the development of mental and nervous illnesses."[27] Another delegate to the 1887 congress, Ivan Sikorskii, was keen to point out the negative effects of mechanization in the workplace: "The age of steam and the telegraph, as we like to call our century, has wrested a mass of physical labor from human hands; what was previously accomplished by human muscle is now performed by a dead machine, and the former seamstress is now directed by the inexorable demands of life to intellectual work."[28]

Merzheevskii argued that the difficulties were magnified by the speed of the reforms, which exceeded the capacity of human heredity to adjust to the demands of the new environment. The changes had been "sudden, without any preliminary preparation of minds," with the result that the "stimulation of minds and feelings elicited by the reforms produced a reaction which was incompatible with the habitual activity of the brain and in some cases disturbed the correctness of its regulation."[29] The failure of individuals to

25   Kovalevskii, *Obshchaia psikhopatologiia*, 184–85 (ellipses in original).
26   Ivan P. Merzheevskii, "Ob usloviiakh, blagopriiatstvuiushchikh razvitiiu dushevnykh i nervnykh boleznei v Rossii i o merakh, napravlennykh k ikh umen'sheniiu," *Trudy Pervogo s''ezda otechestvennykh psikhiatrov proiskhodivshego v Moskve s 5 po 11 ianvaria 1887 g.* (St. Petersburg: M. M. Stasiulevich, 1887), 22.
27   Ibid., 8. In his public lecture in 1887, Dokhman had also spoken of "the contemporary social order, with its dramas on both the stage and in life that harrow the nerves, with its fits and thirst for all that is new, with its passionate impulses." See Dokhman, *Nasledstvennost'*, 52.
28   Ivan A. Sikorskii, "Zadachi nervno-psikhicheskoi gigieny i profilaktiki," *Trudy Pervogo s''ezda*, 1055.
29   Merzheevskii, "Ob usloviiakh," 7.

adapt adequately to a social world that was undergoing rapid and profound change was one of the enduring themes of degeneration theory.[30] The social and economic changes associated with modernization could proceed at such speeds that they did more than simply leave individuals or certain social constituencies behind. Rather, they could overwhelm the limited capacity of humans to adjust to their changing environments and so trigger the onset of the degenerative syndrome.

Theorists and clinicians struggled to make sense of the social and moral disorder that seemed to accompany Russia's modernization in the late nineteenth century. In 1886, Kovalevskii's vision was not without hope, and he still held out the possibility that "anomalies such as pauperism, with its corresponding physical and moral degeneration," simply pointed to the fact that "civilization was not yet achieved"; it was still a work in progress.[31] Yet writing a decade later, he was readier to accept that modernity entailed living conditions far more challenging to the mental and physical health of the population than had Russia's earlier social order. He argued that contemporaries were justified to term the nineteenth century "the nervous century."[32] According to Kovalevskii, nervous illnesses in Russia revealed two characteristics: "They are on the increase, and the vast majority of them assume the form of degeneration." The pace of contemporary life had increased markedly. "A thirst for swift profit; extreme competition; a whole series of failures, misfortunes, and shocks; impossibly tense, extreme, and unendurable activity; hesitation, anxiety, and expectations, connected with the struggle [for existence]—all this leads to exhaustion and excessive tension." He was at pains to stress that the conditions of existence were peculiar to the contemporary period and are "very different from previous ones."[33]

Contemporary Babylons

Nineteenth-century writers ranging from celebrated novelists such as Nikolai Gogol, Fedor Dostoevskii, and Lev Tolstoi to *feuilletonists* had identified the city as a particular site of moral concern.[34] Vsevolod Vladimirovich Krestovskii (1840–95) introduced the Russian reading public to a world of

---

30   As I will discuss in chapter five, the ability to adapt to the new social world acquired a special and pernicious resonance after 1917.
31   Kovalevskii, *Obshchaia psikhopatologiia,* 181.
32   Pavel I. Kovalevskii, *Vyrozhdenie i vozrozhdenie. Genii i sumasshestvie. Sotsial'no-biologicheskie ocherki* (St. Petersburg: M. I. Akinfiev and I. V. Leont'ev, 1899), 30.
33   Ibid., 12.
34   The status of the city, notably St. Petersburg, as a site of moral and spiritual corruption is marked in Gogol's short story Nevsky Prospect (1835), Dostoevskii's *Crime and Punishment* (1866) and *The Idiot* (1868), and Tolstoi's *Anna Karenina* (1873–77).

beggars, drunks, prostitutes, and criminals in his novel *Slums of Petersburg,* which was published several times from 1867 onward.[35] In his 1882 chronicle of contemporary life in the capital, *Plagues of Petersburg,* Vladimir Mikhnevich also set about sketching the "picture of contemporary morality in the capital." Mikhnevich presented St. Petersburg as a veritable Sodom, overwhelmed by rampant crime, prostitution, suicide, and vice, the evidence of a "decrepit, emaciated social organism living though an exhausting period of agony."[36] Anatolii Aleksandrovich Bakhtiiarov's (1851–1916) celebrated *The Belly of Petersburg,* first published in 1887, offered a graphic depiction of the arduous life of the city's laboring classes by exploring the physical deprivation and immorality to which they were exposed.[37] Hubertus F. Jahn has argued that these journalists emphasized the proximity of sites of moral and disorder, such as the Haymarket, to centers of wealth and privilege, such as the shopping arcades and palaces of Nevskii Prospekt. This "cultural geography" of the capital stood as a "symbol for the dangers of the modern age."[38] Roshanna Sylvester has detailed how in journalistic descriptions of poor working-class neighborhoods in Odessa "darkness as a trope, in both its literal and metaphorical senses, permeated most dispatches about the urban depths." Even crusading journalists "perpetrated fears of 'the street' as an immoral force capable of massive corruption."[39]

By the turn of the century, Russian literature and the theater had also begun to address the fate Russia's urban poor.[40] Perhaps the most celebrated work was Maksim Gor'kii's play *The Lower Depths.* It was a great success when first performed at Stanislavskii's Moscow Art Theatre in 1902, stirring up controversy for pushing the limits of acceptable social criticism in its uncompromising depiction of life in Moscow's slums. Set in a flophouse,

35 Vsevolod V. Krestovskii, *Peterburgskie trushchoby: Kniga o sytykh i golodnykh,* 2 vols. (Leningrad: Khudozhestvennaia literatura, 1990). The work had originally appeared in installments in the journal *Otechestvennye zapiski* and the tabloid newspaper *Peterburgskii listok* from 1864 to 1867.

36 Vladimir O. Mikhnevich, *Iazvy Peterburga. Opyt istoriko-statisticheskogo issledovaniia nravstvennosti stolichnogo naseleniia* (St. Petersburg: Limbus Press, 2003), 43, 53. The work was first published as a book in 1886.

37 Anatolii A. Bakhtiiarov, *Briukho Peterburga: Ocherki stolichnoi zhizni* (St. Petersburg: Fert, 1994). The volume brought together the author's articles on life in the capital that had been published between 1885 and 1887 in *S.-Peterburgskie vedomosti, Novosti,* and *Peterburgskaia gazeta.*

38 Hubertus F. Jahn, "Der St. Petersburger Heumarkt im 19. Jahrhundert: Metamorphosen eines Stadtviertels," *Jahrbücher für Geschichte Osteuropas* 44, no. 2 (1996): 169. See also Daniel R. Brower, *The Russian City between Tradition and Modernity, 1850–1900* (Berkeley: University of California Press, 1990); Michael F. Hamm, ed., *The City in Late Imperial Russia* (Bloomington: Indiana University Press, 1986).

39 Roshanna P. Sylvester, *Tales of Old Odessa: Crime and Civility in a City of Thieves* (DeKalb: Northern Illinois University Press, 2005), 46–47. See also Joan Neuberger, *Hooliganism: Crime, Culture, and Power in St. Petersburg, 1900–1914,* (Berkeley: University of California Press, 1993), 235–55.

40 There were, of course, similarly unflattering portrayals of village life, notably Anton Chekhov's short story *Peasants* (1897) and Ivan Bunin's *The Village* (1910).

"a cellar, which looks like a cave," the play generates a searing indictment of a society prepared to abandon an entire class of its population to squalor and poverty, turning them into human derelicts, thieves, and prostitutes.[41] Clinicians also sought to capture in prose the entwined wonder and peril of the burgeoning urban centers. Writing in 1904, Dril' declared,

> In our time the environmental conditions in which man lives, develops, and acts are becoming ever more complex, and social life begins to evolve under increasing pressure. Humanity is progressively increasing and settles the planet ever more densely. . . . Enormous commercial-industrial centers multiply, expand, and swarm toward the skies. They bring with them great tedium and their peculiar conditions of tense and fussy life, which demand significant expenditures of energy and frequently squeeze a person like a lemon. As a result of the aggregate of these conditions, so-called social refuse accumulates relatively quickly.[42]

Writing in the literary journal *Novoe slovo* in 1909, Pavel Rozenbakh identified cities, with their overcrowding, bustle, noise, and squalor, as "contemporary Babylons" that, by way of respite from the working day and consolation for defeats in the struggle for existence, offered the population "a huge number of noisy, tempestuous entertainments that go on into the late night and that deprive it of a significant portion of the time intended for daily rest."[43] As Laura Goering has noted, a number of psychiatrists, including Kovalevskii and Vladimiar Fedorovich Chizh (1855–1914), argued that St. Petersburg was a particularly unhealthy environment, an artificial city constructed in defiance of the elements, and sustained only by the influx of hapless migrants from the countryside.[44] St. Petersburg might have been the most striking example of the artifice of the modern city, but it was by no means alone. For Bekhterev, the modern urban existence was in general one in which "physical exhaustion and moral deprivation lead to the excessive use of different forms of stimulants, which are, as we know, the real 'intellectual poisons,' with destructive effects on the organism, and engender the onset of degeneration."[45]

41   The immorality of the characters is reflected in their failing health, and they repeatedly complain of a variety of ailments. Maksim Gor'kii, "Na dne," *Polnoe sobranie sochinenii*, 25 vols. (Moscow: Akademiia Nauk SSSR, 1968–76), 7:109, 112, 115.

42   Dmitrii A. Dril', "Zadachi vospitaniia i rol' nasledstvennosti," *Vestnik psikhologii, kriminal'noi antropologii i gipnotizma*, no. 10 (1906): 4–5.

43   Pavel. Ia. Rozenbakh, "O prichinakh sovremennoi nervoznosti i samoubiistv," *Novoe slovo*, no. 11 (1909): 42.

44   Laura Goering, "'Russian Nervousness': Neurasthenia and National Identity in Nineteenth-Century Russia," *Medical History* 47, no. 1 (2003): 44.

45   Vladimir M. Bekhterev, "Voprosy nervno-psikhicheskogo zdorov'ia v naselenii Rossii," *Trudy Tret'ego s''ezda otechestvennykh psikhiatrov* (St. Petersburg: Tipografiia pervoi Sankt-Peterburgskoi trudovoi arteli, 1911), 60.

"Intellectual Poisons"

The most prominent of these "intellectual poisons" was alcohol. The majority of clinicians dealing with the problem believed conception that occurred when either of the parents was drunk (or even more damagingly, when both were drunk) would result in the degeneration of their offspring. In 1899, Rozenbakh noted that "the inebriation of either parent at the moment of conception has damaging effects on the health of the offspring and . . . frequently the result . . . is idiocy in the children."[46] Five years later, Sikorskii elaborated on the role of alcohol in the etiology of degenerative illness: "The hereditary effect of alcohol is to render the vasomotor system of the offspring of alcoholics excessively sensitive to any kind of stimulation. It is as if the paralysis of the vessels acquired by alcoholics is fully transferred to the offspring in the form of a hereditary physiological deficiency."[47]

The apparent power of alcohol to unleash the degenerative syndrome convinced economist and prohibition campaigner Dmitrii Nikolaevich Borodin, writing in 1910, that "alcohol at the present time is the principal agent of degeneration among peoples of the white race. The destruction caused by alcohol poisoning in the body and in the nervous system is transferred by means of heredity and in accordance with its laws."[48] In the same year, Ivan Vasil'evich Sazhin (1868–?) agreed that "alcohol today is one of the leading causes of the spiritual and physical degeneration of offspring. By virtue of its toxic effects, it constitutes the degenerative agent *par excellence*."[49] In the late imperial period there was a widely held view in educated society that rates of alcoholism had, to use Bekhterev's formulation, "achieved a gigantic growth in contemporary society."[50]

Many denounced the modernizing, secularizing, urbanizing, and industrializing movements in Russia at the end of the nineteenth century and beginning of the twentieth as causes of alcoholism. All strata of society who were engaged in temperance activity, from the followers of Tolstoi to the

46   Pavel Ia. Rozenbakh, "Nasledstvennost' boleznei i vyrozhdenie," *Entsiklopediia semeinogo vospitaniia i obucheniia*, no. 9 (1899): 41.

47   Ivan A. Sikorskii, "Biologicheskie voprosy v psikhologii i psikhiatrii," *Voprosy nervno-psikhicheskoi meditsiny*, no. 1 (1904): 104. Similar remarks were made in 1906 by Dr. Piotr S. Alekseev (1849–?), a physician from Riga and expert on alcoholism who claimed that alcohol was swiftly absorbed into the bloodstream and passed to some glands and genital secretions. Piotr S. Alekseev, "Kriminogennoe svoistvo alkogolia," *Vrachebnaia gazeta*, no. 36 (1906): 958–62; no. 37 (1906): 982–85.

48   Dmitrii N. Borodin, *P'ianstvo sredi detei* (St. Petersburg: Vilenchik, 1910), 74.

49   Ivan V. Sazhin, *Alkogol' i nasledstvennost'* (St. Petersburg: Ia. Trei, 1910), 18. Sazhin wrote widely throughout the late imperial period on the degenerative effects of alcoholism. See, for example, his *Vliianie alkogolia na razvivaiushchiisia organizm* (St. Petersburg: Tipografiia Shtaba otdela korpusa zhandarmov, 1902); *Alkogolizm i nervnaia sistema* (St. Petersburg: P. P. Soikin, 1907); and *Nasledstvennost' i spirtnye napitki. Rol' i znachenie spirtnykh napitkov v oblasti dukhovnogo i fizicheskogo vyrozhdeniia* (St. Petersburg: P. P. Soikin, 1908).

50   Bekhterev, "Lichnost'," 29.

Russian Orthodox Church, from Octobrist Duma deputies to the socialists, condemned the the status quo.[51] Such condemnation came unavoidably to be directed at the tsarist state. The state vodka monopoly introduced in 1896 by Minister of Finance Sergei Iulevich Witte (1849–1915) meant that the state itself became complicit in fostering what was widely recognized across the entire political spectrum and all strata of society to be a grievous social ill. The income generated by the monopoly for the state's coffers was so substantial (some twenty percent of state revenue) that any attempt to deal decisively with the problem would always be resisted by vested interests in the treasury. In response to mounting public disquiet, however, the tsarist state did establish its own temperance organization, the Guardianship of Public Sobriety. Contemporaries were quick to seize on the hypocrisy of the state's being the sole purveyor of alcohol while piously proclaiming moderation in drink.[52]

Indeed, the manifest hypocrisy of the state's position enabled critical voices to use the issue as a platform for the indictment of the entire tsarist order. P. N. Davidov was one of many clinicians to accuse the state of cynicism: "It would be a vain dream to expect a definitive elimination of alcohol while the people are sunk in poverty and in the most vulgar ignorance; while the low price of alcohol makes it readily available to everyone, and thousands of capitalists have a direct interest in poisoning the population with alcohol; while the Ministry of Finance, seduced by the prospect of fulfilling more than a quarter of our annual budget, does not shy away from making use of liquor for fiscal purposes."[53] Writing in 1913, Nikolai Iakovlevich Novombergskii (1871–1949), professor of jurisprudence at Tomsk University, also decried the "state budget, which has won the justifiable sobriquet 'the drunken budget' and which is maintained by a national vice, the alcoholization [alkogolizatsiia] of the population."[54] The prominence of alcoholism within the broader narrative of societal degeneration served as a two-fold indictment of the tsarist government. First, the alcohol monopoly exposed the cynicism of the government's calls for temperance and its readiness to prioritize revenue above the moral, physical, and mental well-being of its population. Second, the economic policies pursued by the regime resulted in appalling living and working conditions in Russian cities that were driving many to drink.

---

51   Patricia Herlihy, *The Alcoholic Empire: Vodka and Politics in Late Imperial Russia* (Oxford: Oxford University Press, 2002), 9, 147. See also W. Arthur McKee, "Sobering Up the Soul of the People: The Politics of Popular Temperance in Late Imperial Russia," *Russian Review* 58, no. 2 (April 1999): 212–33.

52   Herlihy, *Alcoholic Empire*, 7.

53   P. N. Davidov, "K voprosu o vyrozhdenii russkogo naroda ot p'ianstva," *Trudovaia pomoshch'*, no. 1 (1906): 93. See the same objection in Bekhterev, "Voprosy nervno-psikhicheskogo zdorov'ia," 54.

54   Nikolai Ia. Novombergskii, *Po puti k vyrozhdeniiu. Sotsial'no-gigienicheskie ocherki* (St. Petersburg: A.M. Lassman, 1913), 13.

It was perhaps a sign of a broader shift of emphasis within the etiology of alcoholism that in his address to the Kiev Congress in 1905 one of Russia's most eminent students of alcoholism and campaigner for its prohibition, Fedor Egorovich Rybakov (1868–1920) of the Moscow University Psychiatric Clinic, concentrated exclusively on hereditary factors in the development of alcoholism.[55] Yet only five years later, he was keen to stress that an acknowledgement of the "enormous role of heredity in the development of alcoholism" did not "minimize the significance in the matter of various external influences, including socioeconomic, hygienic, and other factors, which drive the population to alcoholism."[56] He concluded that "for a rational struggle with alcoholism, what is needed above all is an improvement in the country's socioeconomic conditions."[57] A vociferous article written by Susanna Ukshe in 1915 elaborated the nature of these conditions. Citing the left-wing physician and editor of *Meditsinskii vestnik*, Vladimir Vladimirovich Sviatlovskii (1851–1901), who had written widely on the effects of factory labor on the health of workers, Ukshe denounced "the contemporary conditions under which workers labor" and argued that they "directly drive workers to alcohol." Sviatlovskii had observed that "the nervous system of factory workers was so dulled by the deleterious working conditions that even vodka had become an insufficient stimulant, and they are driven to mix peppers and other spicy substances into it."[58] Alcoholism was another of the features of factory life to which Bekhterev referred when declaring in 1911 that "there can be no doubt that factories lead to the degeneration of the population."[59]

Indifference and Repression: The Tsarist State

By the 1905 Revolution, however, psychiatrists were accusing the government of more than simply turning a blind eye to the degenerative effects of alcoholism; they increasingly denounced the tsarist political system itself for engendering the degeneration of the population. In his address to the Kiev

55   Fedor E. Rybakov, "Alkogolizm i nasledstvennost'," *Trudy Vtorogo s"ezda*, 651–64.
56   Fedor E. Rybakov, "Nasledstvennost' i alkogolizm," *Zhurnal nevropatologii i psikhiatrii*, no. 1 (1910): 346–47.
57   Ibid., 348.
58   Susanna A. Ukshe, "Vyrozhdenie, ego rol' v prestupnosti i mery bor'by s nim," *Vestnik obshchestvennoi gigieny, sudebnoi i prakticheskoi meditsiny* (June 1915): 816. Sviatlovskii (1851–1901) published widely on the medical effects of factory labor on the working classes. See, e.g., his *Sukonnoe i sherstomoinoe proizvodstvo v sanitarnom otnoshenii* (Chernigov: Zemskii vrach, 1890); and *Priadil'noe proizvodstvo v sanitarnom otnoshenii* (Moscow: Russkaia Tipografiia, 1891).
59   Bekhterev, "Voprosy nervno-psikhicheskogo zdorov'ia," 57.

Congress in 1905, Bekhterev dwelt at length on Russia's recent and disastrous war with Japan, claiming that "the clash of peoples, or wars, are a form of social crisis in which the meaning of individuals is illuminated in the most expressive manner." He pointed to Russia's overwhelming numerical advantage in population and asked how it could have happened that the Japanese emerged victorious. The answer, he claimed, "was on everyone's lips," and he cited a recent newspaper article discussing the war: "'Battles between nations [narody] are won by those who breathe freedom as their native air.' . . . A nation that is comprised of weakly developed individuals . . . is not able to defend itself from exploitation by nations comprising more highly developed individuals." Bekhterev went on to denounce the various factors impeding the development of the individual in Russia. Many of these factors "are known under the term degeneration and consist of deleterious conditions of the conception and development of the human species." With the exception of the Japanese, who had defeated Russia because their society showed respect for individual initiative, "the vegetative existence [*proziabanie*] of the nations of the East serves as the best evidence that the absence of self-government and the despotism of those in power ruin the individual personality itself as the active unit of society." Thus, the decline of Russian power was intimately linked to the deteriorating health and vigor of the population.

Lack of self-government and despotism could only be arrested through a complete transformation of the political system. The autocracy was, directly or indirectly, responsible for famine, alcoholism, dreadful working conditions in the factories, the repression of individual initiative, and the persistence of massive inequalities in the distribution of wealth, to name but a few. The intimate relation between Russia's political order and the ill health of its population meant that "the struggle for the freedom of the individual is, at the same time, a struggle for society's correct and healthy development, and the rights of the individual are an indicator of its development as a social unit."[60] Another delegate to the same congress, Mikhail Iakovlevich Droznes (1844–1912), also pointed to "the need immediately to remove an etiological factor that facilitates the rapid spread of nervous and mental illness in the population: the extremely oppressive [*gnetushchii*] bureaucratic regime that constrains the individual."[61] Two years later, Droznes was even more emphatic: "The prevention of the physical and mental degeneration of the population depends on fundamental political and economic reform of Russian life."[62] The clinician Aleksandr Sergeevich Sholomovich struck a similarly uncompromising note in 1907: "The conditions of our contemporary political existence constitute

---

60   Bekhterev, "Lichnost'," 33, 39–42.
61   Mikhail Ia. Droznes, "Vazhneishie zadachi sovremennoi prakticheskoi psikhiatrii," *Trudy Vtorogo s''ezda*, 213.
62   Mikhail Ia. Droznes, *Zadachi meditsiny v bor'be s sovremennoi nervoznost'iu* (Odessa: Aktsionnoe Iuzhno-russkoe obshchestvo pechatnogo dela, 1907), 15.

a direct threat to the mental health not merely of those with a predisposition [to mental illness] but also those who are entirely healthy."[63]

One of the most radical members of the psychiatric profession, Petr Tutyshkin, was explicit in linking the government's reassertion of its political domination in the wake of 1905 with the degeneration of the population. At the Third Congress of National Psychiatrists in 1910, he denounced the "contemporary reaction" sweeping the empire. It had brought "economic and political disasters of a mass character," which in conjunction with the dreadful unhygienic conditions in which most of the population was forced to live, had

> significantly reduced the average reserves of physical and mental energy in individual Russian citizens of all strata of society. This decline in the mental energy of the average person chiefly manifests itself in a weakening of willpower; on the basis of this diseased lack of willpower, . . . a mass of neurasthenics, hysterics, and all kinds of failures appear who are unable to adapt to the difficult conditions of contemporary Russian reality.[64]

Russia's ruling classes were increasingly encouraging "vulgar and base instincts, the legacy of their animal nature," in the population. It was the encouragement of these instincts that generated the proliferation of brutality and disorder in Russian society: alcoholism, perversion, theft, suicide, and so forth. Tutyshkin characterized the psychology of Russian society in this period of reaction as one of "mass moral stupefaction, i.e., a certain step in the process of the evolution of moral insanity that, under favorable conditions, can lead to a deeper social degeneration [*sotsial'noe vyrozhdenie*] of certain strata of society."[65]

The "Lower Depths" of Russian Industry

One of the principal criticisms clinicians leveled at the state was its support for economic policies understood to foster the degeneration of the working classes. Bekhterev declared that "unfavorable economic circumstances exerted a substantial influence over the development of the individual, consistently leading to a physical weakening of the body, on the basis of which a series of physically exhausting illnesses can develop. These illnesses undermine the body's basic nutrition and disrupt the correct development of the

63   Aleksandr S. Sholomovich, "K voprosu o dushevnykh zabolevaniiakh, voznikaiushchikh na pochve politicheskikh sobytii," *Russkii vrach*, no. 21 (1907): 720.
64   Petr P. Tutyshkin, "Zadachi tekushchego momenta russkoi obshchestvennoi psikhiatrii," *Trudy Tret'ego s''ezda otechestvennykh psikhiatrov*, 736.
65   Ibid.

brain and, consequently, the personality." Rounding on the government, he pointed to the "terrible conditions in which our simple people find themselves," arguing that "the country's unsuccessful economic policies have turned [them] quite literally into half-starving beggars."[66] Sholomovich was even more forthright: "The political struggle is waged on the basis of the physiological starvation of tens of millions of people . . . [who] find themselves in nutritional conditions that are the most favorable for the development of all manner of diseases in general and mental diseases in particular.[67] Working conditions in Russian industry had become a topic of national debate by the turn of the twentieth century.[68]

Tat'iana Boiko's study of discussions of living and working conditions for Russian laborers in the pages of the conservative and liberal press of the period has illustrated the prominence of the topic. Conservatives favored a strengthening of religion and patriarchy in the factories; liberals the imitation of Western legislation to oblige factory bosses to take better care of those in their employ. Yet both sides agreed that current factory conditions were pushing workers toward physical exhaustion, mental illness, and moral perdition.[69] The conservative journal *Russkii vestnik* referred in 1902 to the factory as a "social disaster," especially for "the Russian common people, born farmers, wrenched from their native soil and good village life." Concerned with the effects of poverty on workers' morality, it argued in favor of raising living standards, because these would "be reflected in the psychology of the worker."[70] *Novoe vremia* also noted that "the worker question deserves the most serious attention, not simply from the perspective of law and order." In the interest of alleviating the severe economic position of workers, the newspaper suggested an entire range of steps the government could take in order to "promote the welfare of factory workers."[71] Liberals, meanwhile, argued that a more efficient and competitive

66   Bekhterev, "Lichnost'," 34.
67   Sholomovich, "K voprosu," 720. See the analogous arguments in Novombergskii, *Po puti k vyrozhdeniiu*, 12–13.
68   For descriptions of the working conditions of Russian printers, see Mark D. Steinberg, *Moral Communities: the Culture of Class Relations in the Russian Printing Industry, 1867–1907* (Berkeley: University of California Press, 1992), 28–29. For further information on late imperial working class conditions, see Reginald Zelnik, ed., *A Radical Worker in Tsarist Russia: The Autobiography of Semen Ivanovich Kanatchikov* (Stanford: Stanford University Press, 1986); Daniel R. Brower, "Labor Violence in Russia in the Late Nineteenth Century," *Slavic Review* 41, no. 3 (Autumn 1982): 417–31; Charters Wynn, *Workers, Strikes, and Pogroms: The Donbass and Dnepr Bend in Late Imperial Russia, 1870–1905* (Princeton: Princeton University Press, 1992).
69   Tat'iana V. Boiko, *Rabochie Rossii i kul'tura: Polemika na stranitsakh konservativnoi i liberal'noi periodiki nachala XX veka* (Moscow: RAN, 1997), 24–44.
70   "Vnutrennee obozrenie," *Russkii vestnik*, no. 12 (1902): 740, cited in Boiko, *Rabochie Rossii i kul'tura*, 32.
71   "Po povodu rabochikh besporiadkov," *Novoe vremia*, May 11, 1901, cited in Boiko, *Rabochie Rossii i kul'tura*, 35.

industry would result from improved educational and living standards among the workforce.

The Russian press also devoted a great deal of attention to workers' living conditions in the industrial centers. In 1899, *Russkie vedomosti* reported on the findings of a commission of inquiry set up by the Moscow City Council to look into apartments consisting of bunk-beds crammed into narrow berths in which thousands of factory workers, miners and artisans, railway workers, petty traders, and so forth lived: "The apartment is a terrible sight; it was crumbling; there were cracks stuffed with rags in the walls; it was dirty; the oven was falling to pieces. . . . There were no window frames, and so it was terribly cold. . . . Water was running down the walls, it was almost entirely dark. . . . The apartment was dirty. . . . The air was extremely stuffy, the building dilapidated."[72] A number of journalists and commentators offered graphic and indignant descriptions of the dreadful conditions in which many Russian workers were forced to exist. One observer called the barracks at the Briansk mines at the turn of the century dens of "parasites, filth, fetid air, and drunkenness," and another reported in 1913 that the miners still "drank more than factory workers, trying to erase all awareness of their hard and bitter lives with vodka." One crusading journalist described miners' lives underground as akin to

> a sentence of penal servitude, a place of hard labor, danger, and fines [for every minor infraction], while, above ground, there was only bad food and rotten, stinking barracks for these men. For unmarried men, there was homelessness and time spent in drunken stupor, with stinking, infected whores, and for those with families there was terrible overcrowding, deprivation, sick and querulous wives, and puny, emaciated children.[73]

Representations in the popular press of life in Russia's industrial centers illustrated that many contemporaries perceived an intimate relation between the biological and the moral welfare of Russian workers. Degeneration provided an interpretative apparatus through which clinicians and social scientists could conceptualize this relationship and explore its underlying coherence. In 1893, Dr Evstafii Mikhailovich Dement'ev (1850–1918) published a lengthy scientific tract examining the effects of factory labor on the working classes, *The Factory: What It Gives the Population and What It Takes from It.* Dement'ev scrutinized the effects of working with toxic substances in cramped conditions with no ventilation on the health and

72   "Zhilishcha moskovskoi bednoty [v 1899]," *Russkie vedomosti*, November 14, 1902.

73   Iu. I. Kur'ianov, *Rabochye iuga Rossii, 1914–fevral' 1917 g.* (Moscow, 1971), 103–4, cited in W. Bruce Lincoln, *Passage through Armageddon: The Russians in War and Revolution, 1914–1918* (Oxford: Oxford University Press, 1986), 223. For similar descriptions, see Sylvester, *Tales of Old Odessa*, chap. 2.

longevity of factory workers. Sustained over several generations, such conditions led to "a progressive extinction of 'the weakest' and a progressive deterioration of the physical qualities of the population, i.e., what is known as the degeneration of the race."[74] Writing a few years later in 1899, Rozenbakh argued that in the modern factory

> workers are frequently obliged to eke out their lives from earliest childhood under the intolerable burdens of labor, in the absence of the most elementary demands of hygiene, with insufficient and unbalanced nutrition, and without light or clean air. The offspring of the population of the factory quarters, chilled to the marrow under such dreadful conditions, constitute a sickly generation with a weak physical organism, predisposed to constitutional illnesses (rickets, scrofula, consumption, and so on), incapable of higher mental development. Here, the causes of degeneration afflict an entire class of society, generating results on a massive scale.[75]

The theory of adaptive pathologies offered a persuasive and alarming conceptualization of the relationship between unhygienic living and working conditions and the physical and moral debasement of those subject to them. Factories were always more than discrete centers of labor throughout the nineteenth century. They wielded an almost metaphorical power over the contemporary imagination, evidence of the awesome capacity of individuals both to manipulate their own environment and to exploit each other.[76] Accordingly, it was but a small step from discussion of factories in specifics to discussion of the more general system of which they were such a powerful expression.

The Naming of "Capitalism"

Historians of the late imperial period have frequently pointed to the disquiet and even enmity with which Russians had greeted the rise of capitalism in the West and its apparently irrepressible encroachment into the economy and society of the empire. Conservatives like Dostoevskii and the Slavophiles were excoriating in their rejection of the crippling influence of Western rationalism and individualism.[77] Andrzej Walicki has traced the anxious

74   E. M. Dement'ev, *Fabrika: Chto ona daet naseleniiu i chto ona u nego beret* (Moscow: I. N. Kushnerev, 1893), 225–40 (citation, 240).

75   Rozenbakh, "Nasledstvennost'," 46.

76   Iconic representations included, of course, Friedrich Engels, *The Condition of the Working Class in England* (1844) and Karl Marx, *Capital* (1867).

77   Andrzej Walicki, *The Slavophile Controversy: History of a Conservative Utopia in Nineteenth-Century Russian Thought* (Oxford: Oxford University Press, 1975); idem,

debates within the Russian Populist movement over the meanings of, and possible responses to, capitalism in Russia.[78] Marxism's paradoxical endorsement of capitalism as an unsavory necessity, an unavoidable antichamber to the socialist society of the future, was itself replete with images of desperate misery and exploitation.[79] Susan Morrissey has observed among commentators of the time a fundamental ambivalence regarding capitalism itself: ideals of equality, solidarity, and justice were often celebrated in opposition to negative images of both the free market—whether in labor or goods—and liberal individualism.[80]

Despite differences in liberal and conservative perspectives, a consensus was emerging among clinicians by the end of the nineteenth century that competition now governed the relations between human beings. Dril' noted that "personal, class, and international competition is increasing and intensifying, demanding wide-ranging initiative, applied dexterity, and well assimilated knowledge for success in the struggle for existence."[81] Kovalevskii also saw contemporary urban conditions in terms of a Social Darwinist "survival of the fittest" but contended that in reality, there were no winners:

> The struggle for existence is intensifying and becoming crueller. Both the victors and the vanquished suffer from the struggle. The victors become sickly and unstable, unable to exist without stimulants such as alcohol, tobacco, morphine, etc. and are extremely irritable, unstable, and prone to collapse at the slightest pressure. Their victory costs them very dearly and is achieved at the expense of their organism. The vanquished are already organically defective, bearing various . . . physical diseases such as syphilis, alcoholism, gout, rheumatism, neuroses—epilepsy, psychoses, and so on—acquired in life's struggle for existence.[82]

A History of Russian Thought from the Enlightenment to Marxism (Oxford: Oxford University Press, 1988); Leonard Schapiro, *Rationalism and Nationalism in Nineteenth-Century Russian Political Thought* (New Haven: Yale University Press, 1967); Richard Pipes, "Russian Conservatism in the Second Half of the Nineteenth Century," *Slavic Review* 30 (1971): 121–28; Wayne Dowler, *Dostoevsky, Grigor'ev, and Native-Soil Conservatism* (Toronto: University of Toronto Press, 1982).

78   Andrzej Walicki, *The Controversy over Capitalism: Studies in the Social Philosophy of the Russian Populists* (Oxford: Oxford University Press, 1969). See also Hans Rogger, *Russia in the Age of Modernisation and Revolution, 1881–1917* (London: Longman, 1983), 139–41.

79   Leszek Kowalski, *Main Currents of Marxism*, 3 vols. (Oxford: Oxford University Press, 1978), 2:14–15.

80   Susan Morrissey, *Suicide and the Body Politic in Imperial Russia* (Cambridge: Cambridge University Press, 2006), 323. In his study of the Russian printing trade in the late imperial period, Steinberg has suggested that even many Russian businesses had deep misgivings about the effects of unbridled competition on Russian industry. Steinberg, *Moral Communities*, 20.

81   Dril', "Zadachi vospitaniia," 5.

82   Kovalevskii, *Vyrozhdenie i vozrozhdenie*, 9–10.

Degeneration meant that a social struggle for survival would produce biologically and psychologically damaged "winners" who would subsequently pass on their defects to their offspring. The result was that a highly competitive social-economic environment was one that would necessarily jeopardize the health of all those operating within its structures.[83]

Degeneration in this account radically undermined the idea of a natural prophylaxis, which existed in many accounts of Social Darwinism. A number of scholars have pointed to the ambivalence with which Russian intellectuals responded to Darwinism in the second half of the nineteenth century.[84] Daniel P. Todes has examined the attempts by Russian commentators to reject the Malthusian implications of Darwin's celebrated metaphor, the "struggle for existence." Darwin's Russian audience accepted the term in the sense of a struggle with the environment in which an organism found itself, but reacted with hostility to what they perceived to be an attempt to import British enthusiasm for competition into evolutionary theory. The majority concluded "that Darwin had greatly exaggerated the role of the two parts most closely identified with Malthus: that is, of overpopulation as the generator of conflict and of intraspecific competition as its result."[85] Todes shows that Russian intellectuals from across the political spectrum shared anti-Malthusian views, identified Darwin's struggle for existence with Malthus, and rejected this Darwin-Malthus connection.[86] With its emphasis on the deleterious effects of intraspecific competition on the health of victors in the struggle for existence, degeneration theory offered a powerful challenge to Social Darwinist justifications for intraspecific competition as a necessary part of natural selection. Intraspecific struggle exacerbated environmental challenges and ensured that the "survival of the fittest" was unfortunately not the same as the survival of the fit.

By the turn of the century, psychiatrists, critical of the increasingly harsh conditions of the "struggle for existence" in the expanding industrial centers, invoked more frequently the term "capitalism" to denote the cultural, social, and economic processes they understood to cause degeneration. The growing popularity of the term undoubtedly reflected the growing influence

83   Morrissey has noted similar arguments in contemporary discussions of the causes of suicide. *Suicide and the Body Politic*, 317.

84   James Allen Rogers, "Darwinism, Scientism, and Nihilism," *Russian Review* 19, no. 1 (January 1960): 10–23; idem, "The Russian Populists' Response to Darwin," *Slavic Review* 22, no. 3 (September 1963): 456–68; Francesco M. Scudo and Michele Acanfora, "Darwin and Russian Evolutionary Biology," in *The Darwinian Heritage*, ed. David Kohn (Princeton: Princeton University Press, 1985), 731–54.

85   Daniel P. Todes, *Darwin without Malthus: The Struggle for Existence in Russian Evolutionary Thought* (Oxford: Oxford University Press, 1989), 3. Alexander Vucinich also has pointed to Russian's rejection of Social Darwinism in his *Darwin in Russian Thought* (Berkeley: University of California Press, 1988). There was, of course, an intellectual alternative to the status of competition as an engine of economic and social development: Petr Kropotkin's vision of mutual aid, which had engaged positively with Darwin. See Petr Kropotkin, *Mutual Aid as a Factor of Evolution*, (New York: McClure, Philips and Co., 1902).

86   Todes, *Darwin without Malthus*, 44.

of Marxism in Russia in the 1890s.[87] To critics, capitalism meant social inequality, intense competition, and dreadful conditions for workers in Russia's industrial centers. It represented both primary facets of modernity understood to promote the onset of degeneration. First, capitalism was a system of values and social goods that drove individuals to exceed their natural capacities and, second, it developed a modern urban environment, centered on the factory, that was profoundly damaging to the health of those living and working within its confines.

Isolated references to "capitalism" as a causal factor in the onset of degeneration had already begun to appear before the turn of the twentieth century. In his 1899 study *Degeneration and Regeneration*, Kovalevskii cited "drunkenness, perversion, prostitution, crime, poverty or pauperism, and possibly incredible wealth or capitalism" as "social deviations" that can cause degeneration.[88] In the wake of 1905, however, some clinicians elevated capitalism to a system that lay at the heart of all these social vices. At the Tenth Pirogov Congress of clinicians in Moscow in spring 1907, psychiatrist Sergei Ivanovich Mitskevich (1869–1944) decried it as the "fundamental evil of our era."[89] In 1907, factory physician Lev Borisovich Granovskii (1878–?) similarly argued that the expanding capitalist economy was responsible for the mounting incidence of alcoholism, tuberculosis, and syphilis in Russia.[90] In his public lecture to commemorate the opening of the Psycho-Neurological Institute in the St. Petersburg in 1908, Bekhterev turned to "the causes of degeneration in contemporary society." Bekhterev went further than his predecessors in identifying the capitalist system as the foundation of all these negative developments:

> The capitalist order in society today . . . leads to a ruinous struggle for existence [*pagubnaia bor'ba za sushchestvovanie*], it drives the nervous system of individuals to extreme tension, it reduces the working population to a state of extreme physical exhaustion, and it generates the need for recourse to the use of stimulants. It leads to the development of poverty on the one hand and criminal luxury on the other. . . . The capitalist order has come into being and lies at the source of the disharmony in the evolution of contemporary society, which leads inexorably to the degeneration of the population [*vyrozhdenie naseleniia*].[91]

87   Leopold H. Haimson, *The Russian Marxists and the Origins of Bolshevism* (Cambridge, MA: Harvard University Press, 1955); Andrzej Walicki, A *History of Russian Thought from the Enlightenment to Marxism* (Oxford: Oxford University Press, 1980), 406–48.

88   Kovalevskii, *Vyrozhdenie i vozrozhdenie*, 58.

89   Mitskevich, quoted in I. D. Ermakov, "Desiatyi pirogovskii s''ezd v Moskve, 25. IV–2.V.1907," *Zhurnal nevropatologii*, nos. 2–3 (1907): 551, cited in Sirotkina, *Diagnosing Literary Genius*, 135–36.

90   Lev B. Granovskii, *Obshchestvennoe zdravookhranenie i kapitalizm (Tuberkulez, alkogolizm, venerizm i nervnost' i usloviia bor'by s nimi* (Mocow: Obshchestvo russkikh vrachei v pamiat' N. I. Pirogova, 1907).

91   Vladimir M. Bekhterev, "Voprosy vyrozhdeniia i bor'ba s nim." *Obozrenie psikhiatrii, nevrologii i eksperimental'noi psikhologii*, no. 9 (1908): 520.

Selfish acquisitiveness lay at the heart of the capitalist system and the exploitation of man by man that flowed from it. At the Third Congress of National Psychiatrists in 1910, Bekhterev denounced "the golden idol, that terrible enemy of humanity, [which] paralyzes all striving for cooperation between people, setting them on each other."[92] Materialism fostered the ambition for personal gain, which distorted the traditional struggle for existence by making individuals disinclined to pursue cooperative forms of economic activity. Bekhterev's arguments amounted to a progressive attempt to wrest back a positive vision of the modern world from its destructive capitalist incarnation: "It should be clear to everyone that our 'nervous century' owes its name to the aggregate of conditions that are associated with contemporary civilization. But the foundation of our civilization is the significance of capital in the life of contemporary society, which leads to the struggle for survival familiar to everyone."[93]

The significance of such a synthesis of these features of contemporary urban industrial existence into a system that bore a name was profound. If modernity had appeared diffuse and bewilderingly incoherent in the changes it brought to late Imperial Russia, "capitalism" was an order, a system, one with principles and values that could be challenged. The term converted a range of discrete social issues into a single political one. The very name in this context implied a call to action, a call to intervene to alter the current trajectory of Russian society. Bekhterev made it clear that to understand capitalism as the underlying cause of degeneration was to understand that the response could not be piecemeal:

> The struggle with degeneration cannot be confined to a struggle with mental and physical exhaustion, with the spread of alcoholism, syphilis, and tuberculosis in the population; it cannot be confined to individual measures against the economic misfortunes of our lower orders, to the surgical removal of the reproductive capacity of the degenerates, and so on. Above all, it must also address the underlying cause of degeneration. Consequently, all our efforts in the sense of an effective struggle with the degeneration of the population, all our striving to achieve an improvement of human nature, should be directed at the removal of the capitalist order and at the gradual establishment of more correct norms of social life.[94]

Of course, not all clinicians agreed with Bekhterev's analysis. Ivan Stelletskii argued that one had to look deeper even than the capitalist order

92   Bekhterev, "Voprosy nervno-psikhicheskogo zdorov'ia," 59.
93   Ibid. In 1912, Bekhterev repeated the claim, declaring that "the basic cause of the evil is not contemporary industrialism but the capitalist order of contemporary society." Vladimir M. Bekhterev, *Ob''ektivno-psikhologicheskii metod v primenenii k izucheniiu prestupnosti* (St. Petersburg: V. Anderson and G. Loitsiatskii, 1912), 60.
94   Bekhterev, "Voprosy vyrozhdeniia," 520

to understand the underlying causes of degeneration: "We cannot possibly regard degeneration as a symptom of the capitalist order, just as we cannot view it as the cause of alcoholism, crime, mental illness, and so on. There are absolutely no grounds for attributing humanity's every step forward or backward to the effects of capitalism as if, prior to capitalism, humanity had no history." Yet Stelletskii's own diagnosis offered little comfort to the nation's capitalists. He averred that degeneration predated the development of the capitalist order and that the latter "in no way engendered degeneration, although in respect to other social diseases, it does represent the most propitious factor for the spread and intensification of the degenerative process, especially as a consequence of the acutely manifest division of labor under capitalism."[95] Stelletskii believed that the one-sidedness of most individuals' economic activity, which flowed from the division of labor, was the primary cause of degeneration. Such a division of labor had already existed in the precapitalist era, and so the conclusion one had to draw was not that capitalism was responsible for degeneration but rather that it was, as a system, founded upon principles that were responsible.

By the outbreak of the First World War, however, a number of clinicians were making increasingly outspoken attacks on capitalism as a central factor in the etiology of degeneration. In 1915, Ukshe used rhetoric clearly influenced by the Marxist language of class struggle. She decried "degeneration, this terrible scourge of humanity," arguing that it was, in a sense, natural retribution for the misdeeds of Russia's ruling classes. The disorder was "forcibly opening the doors of princely palaces and mansions, avenging centuries of caste-based segregation." The environmental and hereditary factors disseminating the disorder ensured, however, that once unleashed it did not remain with that parasitical class that was morally responsible for its instigation: "It is punishing entire generations of children for the crimes of their parents and manifests itself most fiercely among the lower orders, who have been baited by exploitation and need." Yet Ukshe was clear that responsibility for degeneration resided with those who enjoyed the power to fight it. She called on Russia's rulers to "destroy the underground flats, destroy the prisons, destroy human slavery, which is the result of an unequal class struggle, and then you will finally create sensible measures for the struggle with degeneration."[96]

What was the impact of the theory of degeneration on contemporary assessments of capitalism? Did the human sciences add anything novel to intelligentsia ambivalence at the forces that had been unleashed in the empire? Any period of primitive economic accumulation would inevitably entail suffering for the generation of workers unfortunate enough to live through it,

95   Mikhail [*sic*—Ivan] I. Stelletskii, "K voprosu o vyrozhdenii. (Teoriia degeneratsii)," *Zhurnal nevropatologii i psikhiatrii*, nos. 5–6 (1911): 807–8.
96   Ukshe, "Vyrozhdenie," 816.

but inscribed into the liberal capitalist notion of material progress was a teleological justification for this suffering. In a similar fashion, acceptance of capitalism implied acceptance of a number of permanent social and moral disorders. There would always be losers and exploited groups in a capitalist economy in which unemployment and competition would exert a downward pressure on wages and working conditions. The benefits to society as a whole in the shape of increased national prosperity, argued supporters of capitalism, outweighed the costs to those who were exploited in Russia's industries. These were the arguments Witte made in defense of industrialization and the hardship it entailed: Russia needed to exploit its workers in order to achieve a competitive edge over its Western rivals in the production of manufactured goods.[97]

However, one of the central planks of degeneration theory, the theory of hereditary transformism that had been elaborated in Morel's original schema, argued that disorders intensified in their passage from one generation to the next. It thereby undermined such utilitarian justifications of capitalism, effectively militating against the sacrifice of one generation in the interests of its successors.[98] Degeneration theory eroded the optimistic teleology that enabled contemporaries to rationalize the inequality and misery of the present. The disorder could not be dismissed as a temporary one that accompanied the progress of society from one stage of historical development to another. Less a symptom of progress, degeneration threatened to become a self-propelling and overwhelming dynamic itself—challenging, confounding, and even reversing the evolution of the human species as biological and social beings. The theory infused existing moral criticisms of the tsarist socioeconomic order with a pronounced sense of urgency by arguing that for each individual damaged physically or mentally by the deleterious conditions to which the capitalist economy subjected him or her, there would be countless offspring burdening the country's economy and medical and penal institutions, the source of a frightening array of vice and deformity, crime and sedition.

Bekhterev argued that the struggle against "the general social and economic conditions on which our contemporary civilization is based" was both "possible and necessary." Such an undertaking was necessary, however, not simply in order to arrest the spread of degeneration throughout society and so to safeguard the mental and physical welfare of the population, but also to preempt the country's slide into anarchy. Invoking historical parallels, Bekhterev intoned that "if Ancient Rome perished from slavery, if the social cataclysms at the end of the eighteenth century and the

97   "Dokladnaia zapiska Vitte Nikolaiu II," *Istorik-marksist* 2–3, nos. 42–43 (1935): 131–38. For a discussion of the document, see Theodore von Laue, *Sergei Witte and the Industrialisation of Russia* (New York: Columbia University Press, 1963), 1–3.

98   Bekhterev, "Voprosy nervno-psikhicheskogo zdorov'ia," 60. See also chap. 1.

first half of the nineteenth were due in large measure to the feudal structure of the state, then our economic slavery, which is conditioned by the
significance of capital in the life of contemporary society, threatens us with
no less disaster."[99]

Intervention was, however, deeply problematic. Although Bekhterev
called for steps "directed at the alleviation of the consequences of the current capitalist order . . . [and] at the prevention of the development of capitalism in the future," he appeared unprepared to draw revolutionary lessons
from his diagnosis of the deteriorating health of the body social. Indeed, his
proposals were decidedly idealistic: "This is possible by means of a series
of measures to restrict the concentration of capital in the hands of a few, by
means of the participation of laboring people in the receipt of a stake in the
income of their own enterprises, by means of the broadest possible development of artisanal and trade unions in the midst of the laboring elements of
the population."[100]

Bekhterev's moderation was shared by many of his colleagues. Even the
strident Ukshe acknowledged less than two years before the 1917 February
Revolution that "a change in social conditions is an ideal which belongs to
the distant future, and we need immediate measures in the struggle against
degeneration." Having called rhetorically for the abolition of an entire
socioeconomic system, she appeared to content herself with a number of
piecemeal measures intended to improve the lot of workers:

> Much can be done today, and indeed much is already being done in the West:
> improving sanitary conditions, improving housing conditions, restoring the lo-
> calities to health [*ozdorovlenie mestnosti*], increasing the average minimum
> wage of workers, establishing nurseries, orphanages, and sanatoria for work-
> ers, the improvement by legal means of the contemporary working conditions
> for workers, paying greater attention to the physical education of children, and
> introducing healthy individuals into degenerating families.[101]

Impassioned denunciation of the dreadful iniquities of Russia's capitalist
order coexisted with an apparent conviction that they could be alleviated
through the paternalistic pursuit of existing legal channels.

Although many of the proposals put forward by Bekhterev and Ukshe
would have sounded familiar and welcome to many within the Social Democratic movement, their apparent belief that the changes they proposed could
be achieved by nonrevolutionary means strains credulity. Which agency
under the existing political structures of the Duma Monarchy would be

99   Bekhterev, "Voprosy nervno-psikhicheskogo zdorov'ia," 65–66.
100   Ibid. Bekhterev repeated these proposals in 1912: Bekhterev, *Ob"ektivno-psikhologicheskii metod*, 60.
101   Ukshe, "Vyrozhdenie," 816.

either willing or able to undertake such fundamental improvements to the conditions of the empire's working classes, let alone a radical redistribution of wealth in Russian society in the teeth of entrenched and predictable resistance from industrialists and landowners, was left unaddressed. What Bekhterev and Ukshe betrayed was, on the one hand, an acceptance of the overwhelming medical need to reorganize the foundations upon which society rested and, on the other, a refusal to countenance revolution as a legitimate instrument of social change.

Reluctant Revolutionaries

Historians have differed in their accounts of the reactions of Russian psychiatrists to the events of the 1905 Revolution and its subsequent repression by government forces. Julie Vail Brown has argued that, with the exception of a few notable supporters of the autocracy such as Vladimir Chizh, 1905 served unambiguously to radicalize Russian physicians. Brown has noted that psychiatrists, frustrated by the government's obdurate refusal to grant them adequate funding and professional autonomy, had been critical of the autocracy throughout the post-Emancipation era.[102] She argues that in the wake of the 1905 Revolution, these criticisms became infused with a more urgent and trenchant tone. Psychiatrists began to notice the appearance of a new type of mental illness that had been induced by the trauma experienced by Russian citizens during the violence of the revolution and its bloody suppression by government forces. In the years that followed, spurred on by their own disappointments at the outcome of 1905 and the tsarist state's ruthless campaign of repression, psychiatrists increasingly denounced the tsarist order as a cause of the spread of mental illness and a threat to the physical well-being of the population. As a result, Brown believes, a radicalization of psychiatrists took place in the years following 1905 because they came to see revolution as the only means by which the mental health of the population could be restored.[103]

Indeed, there is ample evidence to support the claim that psychiatrists were deeply disturbed by the apparent increase in the incidence of mental illness during the period from 1905 to 1907. Many psychiatrists did become increasingly involved in opposition politics, and some, like Tutyshkin, even joined revolutionary parties in the years following 1905.[104] By the eve of

---

102   Julie V. Brown, "Psychiatrists and the State in Tsarist Russia," in *Social Control and the State,* ed. Andrew Scull and Stanley Cohen (Oxford: Blackwell, 1985), 267–87.

103   Julie V. Brown, "Revolution and Psychosis: The Mixing of Science and Politics in Russian Psychiatric Medicine, 1905–13," *Russian Review* 46, no. 3 (1987): 284, 300.

104   A. G. Ivanovskii, "P. P. Tutyshkin—vrach, uchenyi, revoliutsioner," *Zhurnal nevropatologii i psikhiatrii* 74 (1974): 1411–15.

the First World War, according to Brown, "many psychiatric hospitals had become centers of underground left-wing activity."[105]

Laura Engelstein, however, has painted a more cautious and ambiguous picture of psychiatric responses to 1905. She has noted that the 1905 Revolution left the medical profession politically divided. She argues that although many held to their radical views, others were disturbed by the increasing violence. They believed it to be an eruption of atavistic instincts that had lain dormant in the population for years, unchanneled by the rational precepts of a responsive and reforming government. As a consequence, more and more psychiatrists interpreted the revolution, with its chaotic nature, as a social pathology that threatened civilization and progress.[106] Engelstein argues that opposition to the tsarist regime and its repressive excesses did not necessarily translate into an endorsement of revolution.[107]

Irina Sirotkina has similarly pointed to divisions within the psychiatric profession in the wake of 1905 and noted that, as the revolutionary process developed, radical voices within the psychiatric profession were increasingly subdued.[108] She argues that a mistrust of spontaneous action was firmly embedded in the tracts penned by psychiatrists in this period; the clear preference was for the rational deployment of the will in the service of carefully conceived reform, not uncontrollable explosions of revolutionary activity. Sikorskii, for example, saw revolution as a triumph of crude instincts over willpower and rationality and argued that during revolutions, the weak will of the Russian people left them particularly vulnerable to political agitators: "Any fanatic could lead us easily, and that is why we fail to defend our personalities in a struggle with ourselves or with others whose will is stronger."[109]

Strengthening the individual's will, rather than dissolving it in a storm of revolutionary activity, was the best way to improve society. Sikorskii accused radicals of being "too self-confident in pronouncing loud words, operating with high principles, hoping to transform society without having done the most important thing, without transforming your own soul!"[110] Indeed,

---

105   Brown, "Psychiatrists and the State," 283.
106   Such a view of the ambivalence toward the prospects of a revolutionary overthrow of the autocracy in the wake of 1905 is neatly captured by the contrasting perspectives of two leading liberal politicians, Pavel Miliukov and Vasilii Maklakov. See Michael Karpovich, "Two Types of Russian Liberalism: Maklakov and Miliukov," in *Continuity and Change in Russian and Soviet Thought,* ed. Ernest J. Simmons (Cambridge, MA: Harvard University Press, 1955), 129–43.
107   Laura Engelstein, *The Keys to Happiness: Sex and the Search for Modernity in Fin-de-Siècle Russia* (Ithaca: Cornell University Press, 1992), 258, 256.
108   Sirotkina, *Diagnosing Literary Genius,* 138.
109   Cited in Ibid.
110   Ivan A. Sikorskii, "Uspekhi russkogo khudozhestvennogo tvorchestva: Rech' v torzhestvennom zasedanii II-go s"ezda otechestvennykh psikhiatrov v Kieve," *Voprosy nervno-psikhicheskoi meditsiny,* no. 3 (1905): 497, cited in Sirotkina, *Diagnosing Literary Genius,* 137–38.

even a convinced opponent of the autocracy, the Kadet Nikolai Bazhenov, reflected in a 1906 pamphlet entitled *Psychology and Politics* that the liberation movement had given birth to something of a Frankenstein's monster in the shape of the radical parties, particularly the Bolsheviks. He was disturbed by their readiness to engage in arbitrary popular violence in pursuit of millenarian designs for social transformation.[111]

Engelstein and Sirotkina both stress that while many in the profession believed that the revolution was a "healthy societal reaction" to abnormal political conditions, the same psychiatrists still understood revolutionary activity to be dangerously detached from the constraining and purposive voice of reason.[112] The following section explores how psychiatrists perceived the lasting effects of revolutionary disorder and how this perception fed into the reluctance of Bekhterev and others to offer a medical sanction to revolution. Psychiatrists had apparently sound *theoretical,* not just practical, reasons to fear a repeat of the revolutionary unrest that rocked Russia in 1905–06, even if the end result was a radical restructuring of the empire's socioeconomic structure, which many desired.

Before turning to this argument below, the social and political context within which psychiatrists formulated their responses to the revolutionary upheavals of 1905 must first be outlined. The reformist current in Russian medicine was well established: even in the midst of the 1905 Revolution, medical professionals still proposed moderate reforms to improve conditions in the urban centers and villages.[113] Brown has noted that due to their need for government funding of asylums and the fact that the government was the primary employer in their field, most psychiatrists were particularly dependent on the good will and financial assistance of the government.[114] A related constraint on radical pronouncements was censorship. Radical psychiatric congresses, such as the Kiev Congress in September 1905, could either be closed down by scandalized patrons or be subject to the interference of the authorities.[115]

Skeptics might also point to the fact that the majority of clinicians did not hail from the poorest strata of society and stood to lose their own property and privilege in a violent social revolution. A large number of commentators have noted that after the widespread attacks by peasants on gentry estates

111   Nikolai N. Bazhenov, *Psikhologiia i politika* (Moscow: I. D. Sytin, 1906), 7.

112   See, for example, Vladimir Ia. Iakovenko, "Zdorovye i boleznennye proiavleniia v psikhike sovremennogo russkogo obshchestva," *Zhurnal obshchestva russkikh vrachei v pamiat' N. I. Pirogova* 13, no. 4 (May 1907): 282.

113   Nancy Mandelker Frieden has emphasized this point in *Russian Physicians in an Era of Reform and Revolution, 1856–1905* (Princeton: Princeton University Press, 1981), 316.

114   Julie V. Brown, "Professionalization and Radicalization: Russian Psychiatrists Respond to 1905," in *Russia's Missing Middle Class: The Professions in Russian History,* ed. Harley D. Balzer (Armonk, New York: M. E. Sharpe, 1996), 161.

115   Sirotkina, *Diagnosing Literary Genius,* 137.

in autumn of 1905 and the violence of the Moscow Uprising in December of that year, many in the gentry called for stronger government action to combat revolution, even at the expense of their civil liberties.[116] The *Vekhi* symposium of essays published in 1909 was representative of a general revulsion at the actual manifestation of revolution in Russia. In the words of one contributor, the literary historian Mikhail Osipovich Gershenzon (1869–1925): "The intelligentsia should stop dreaming of the people—we should fear the people more than all the executions carried out by the government. Instead, we should hail this government, which alone, with its bayonets and its prisons, still protects us from the fury of the masses."[117] Expressing similar misgivings, *zemstvo* congresses, which had constituted prominent loci of opposition to the government in the years leading up to 1905, now denounced terrorism and even hailed as necessary and legitimate the government's campaign of repression. Physicians at one congress even offered toasts to the armed forces as "the firm support of the fatherland and order."[118]

In their theoretical writings and analyses of case histories, psychiatrists continued to betray real ambivalence toward the prospect of a second revolutionary upheaval. Although psychiatrists' writings on the etiology of insanity certainly accorded the repressive nature of the tsarist regime a significant causal role, their conclusions scarcely became what Brown has termed "a call to arms."[119] The 1905 Revolution and the government's subsequent campaign of repression did not serve as unalloyed engines of theoretical radicalization, whatever the practical actions of individuals within the profession. The experience of treating the psychiatric casualties of 1905 might have hardened the attitudes of the profession against tsarism; it also led them in their own published analyses firmly to reject revolutionary methods as an acceptable instrument for transforming the Russian state and society. Revolution did more than simply promote mental illness in those unfortunate enough to experience its violence and chaos. The trauma of revolution could initiate the degenerative syndrome capable of inseminating

116   See, for example, Roberta T. Manning, *The Crisis of the Old Order in Russia: Gentry and Government* (Princeton: Princeton University Press, 1982), 329.
117   Mikhail Gershenzon, "Tvorcheskoe samosoznanie," in *Vekhi. Intelligentsiia v Rossii: sbornik statei, 1909–1910,* 2nd ed. (Moscow: V. M. Sablin, 1909), 89. On the background of the volume and the debates it provoked, see Christopher Read, *Religion, Revolution, and the Russian Intelligentsia, 1900–1912: The "Vekhi" Debate and Its Intellectual Background* (London: Macmillan, 1979); Aileen M. Kelly, "Which Signposts?" in idem, *Toward Another Shore: Russian Thinkers between Necessity and Chance* (New Haven: Yale University Press, 1998), 155–200.
118   Manning, *The Crisis of the Old Order,* 329; John F. Hutchinson, "'Who Killed Cock Robin?': An Inquiry into the Death of Zemstvo Medicine," in *Health and Society in Revolutionary Russia,* ed. Susan Gross Solomon and John F. Hutchinson (Bloomington: Indiana University Press, 1990), 6–7.
119   Brown, "Revolution and Psychosis," 284.

the entire body social. The clinical experience of the first Russian Revolution all but obliterated psychiatrists' enthusiasm for a second.

The Effects of Trauma

The 1905 Revolution was not a watershed in terms of illuminating the relationship between trauma and mental illness. The siege of the Paris Commune in 1871 had provided French clinicians with ample evidence of the effects of trauma on the inhabitants of the city and, by the 1880s, Russian degeneration theorists were discussing their findings.[120] In 1887, Dokhman cited the work of Henri Legrand du Saulle (1830–86) and Désiré Magloire Bourneville (1840–1909), conducted eight to nine months after the siege, which had demonstrated that "a certain kind of mental state in the parents [at the moment of conception] influences the development of the fetus's nervous system." More generally, Dokhman added, "unfavorable conditions during pregnancy undeniably can lead to the appearance of diseased changes in the nervous system of the child."[121] Moreover, the effects of such trauma were not confined to the period of pregnancy: "Under unfavorable circumstances, . . . the most minor nervous disorders lead to serious illnesses, . . . which in their turn are passed on by heredity and, becoming concentrated, lead to the gradual degradation of physical and mental health."[122]

It was not, however, simply the fetus that was at risk. In 1886, Kovalevskii also pointed to "political events and military service" as leading to a significant increase in mental illness in adults.[123] At the turn of the century, Petr Petrovich Viktorov's (1853–?) *Study of the Personality and Moods* also cited the experience of the Paris Commune as evidence that "oppressive and suffocating feelings and sensations influence the physical and mental degeneration of an individual."[124] The intimate relation posited by contemporary psychiatry of mutual dependence between physical and mental conditions enabled Viktorov to affirm that "psychological trauma, psychological shock such as, for example, fear produces . . . a functional disruption of the general nervous system, under which both mental and nervous and physical

---

120   Daniel Pick, *Faces of Degeneration: A European Disorder, c. 1848–c. 1918* (Cambridge: Cambridge University Press, 1989), 70.

121   Dokhman, *Nasledstvennost'*, 34. See, e.g., Henri Legrand du Saulle, *Le délire des persécutions* (Paris: H. Plon, 1871); Désiré Magloire Bourneville, *De la contracture hysterique permanente* (Paris: Delahaye, 1872). For this current in French thought, see William Schneider, "Toward the Improvement of the Human Race: The History of Eugenics in France," *Journal of Modern History* 54, no. 2 (June 1982): 268–91.

122   Dokhman, *Nasledstvennost'*, 55.

123   Kovalevskii, *Obshchaia psikhopatologiia*, 205.

124   L. L. [*sic*—P. P.] Viktorov, *Uchenie o lichnosti i nastroeniiakh* (Moscow: Knizhnoe delo, 1903), 69.

functions of our bodies are afflicted by irritable weakness, i.e., they become easily agitated and just as easily exhausted."[125]

Although these studies suggest that the 1905 Revolution provided less of a new departure than Brown has suggested, the explosion of revolutionary violence and the concomitant increase in psychiatric casualties certainly did thrust the issue of the relationship between trauma and mental illness (ultimately leading to degeneration) to the top of the profession's agenda. The first article to register concerns about the effect of Russia's revolutionary violence on individuals who witnessed it was Rybakov's study "Mental Disorders in Connection with the Current Political Events," published in *Russkii vrach* in December 1905.[126] Rybakov argued that political unrest was leading to the development of mental illness in individuals with no evidence of a hereditary predisposition to psychiatric problems: "This circumstance suggests that a mental wound which has its origin in the current political events is so great that it can of itself, without any preparatory ground, sometimes disrupt the psychological balance of a hitherto healthy individual."[127]

Rybakov's article prompted a great deal of discussion in psychiatric circles. Some, like Sergei Osipovich Iaroshevskii (1856–1907) in 1906, also reported a number of cases of individuals who, following some form of traumatic shock, become mentally ill in the apparent absence of any hereditary condition.[128] Sholomovich also noted, "It is clear that the political struggle, in which physical and mental reasons are so closely and inextricably entwined, is undermining the mental health even of people without any hereditary defects."[129]

Others disagreed with the proposition that individuals with a healthy heredity, and not simply those with a predisposition, could also fall ill under the experience of trauma. Naum Izraelevich Skliar (1869–1957) disagreed with Rybakov, arguing that in his clinical experience, mental illness only appeared in those with a hereditary weakness.[130] Mikhail Zhukovskii asserted that many of those who had developed mental illness as a result of the unrest were in fact themselves degenerates: "Their

---

125   Viktorov cited the work of the Parisian chemist Armand Gautier (1837–1920), whose research suggested that "under certain conditions, processes of organic oxidization do not take place properly and, as a result, insufficiently oxidized and insufficiently metabolized substances accumulate in the body. These so-called toxic metabolites [*leukomainy*] . . . could lead to a poisoning of the organism, in particular of the nervous system and of the parenchymal organs, such as the liver, the kidneys, etc." Ibid., 70.

126   Brown, "Revolution and Psychosis," 287.

127   Fedor E. Rybakov, "Dushevnye rasstroistva v sviazi s tekushchimi politicheskimi sobytiiami," *Russkii vrach*, no. 51 (1905): 1593–95.

128   Sergei O. Iaroshevskii, "Materialy k voprosu o massovykh nervnopsikhicheskikh zabolevaniiakh," *Obozrenie psikhiatrii, nevrologii i eksperimental'noi psikhologii* 11, no. 1 (January 1906): 1–9.

129   Sholomovich, "K voprosu," 719–20.

130   Naum I. Skliar', "Eshche o vliianii tekushchikh politicheskikh sobytii na dushevnye zabolevaniia," *Russkii vrach*, no. 15 (1906): 448–49.

psyche, which is unstable and easily affected, quickly becomes disoriented under the influence of those causes that cannot but have physical and mental ill-effects on a body that has hitherto been healthy."[131]

Still other psychiatrists, like Viktor Petrovich Osipov (1871–1947) in a lengthy review article "On Political or Revolutionary Psychoses" published in 1910, argued that the dichotomy was a false one. Although an individual might require some form of predisposition in order to be affected so adversely by trauma, that predisposition could be *acquired,* rather than simply inherited, in the extremely stressful and exhausting circumstances in which many patients had found themselves for sustained periods during the revolution.[132]

In a sense, the debate over whether an inherited predisposition to mental illness was the inevitable precondition of the onset of mental illness resulting from trauma, that is, whether the trauma constituted a self-sufficient cause or merely a trigger mechanism, masked a broader agreement among Russian psychiatrists. Despite differences in their understanding of the precise etiology, psychiatrists were almost unanimous in their view that the political unrest was seriously damaging to the mental health of the Russian population. Even those who were skeptical about the ability of trauma directly to provoke the onset of mental illness in adults were far less sanguine when it came to the effects on unborn children. For example, Aleksandr Nikolaevich Bernshtein (1870–1922), a psychiatrist, gave clear expression to this fear:

Are the revolutionary shocks and the severe adversities—prison, tense sleepless nights, hunger, unemployment, prolonged heightened fear and sudden terror, the shift away from joyful hope to bleak despair that accompanies them—capable of influencing the mental sickness rate endogenously? Will the Russian Revolution effect the sickness rate among the generation that was conceived under the crash of cannon fire and the crack of whips and that in their mothers' wombs felt the same shocks as one and the same being? Our children will have to answer these questions.[133]

Bernshtein's analysis was significant for its explicit claim that subsequent generations could be damaged by the traumatic experiences of their parents.

---

131   Mikhail N. Zhukovskii, *O vliianii obshchestvennykh sobytii na razvitie dushevnykh zabolevanii* (St. Petersburg: P. P. Soikin, 1907), 37. Similar arguments were made by I. S. German, "O psikhicheskom rasstroistve depressivnogo kharaktera, razvivshemsia u bol'nykh na pochve perezhivaemykh politicheskikh sobytii," *Zhurnal nevropatologii i psikhiatrii,* no. 3 (1906): 321.

132   Viktor P. Osipov, "O politicheskikh ili revoliutsionnykh psikhozakh," *Nevrologicheskii vestnik* 17 (1910): 479. The article was also published as an eponymous pamphlet (Kazan: Tipografiia Imperialisticheskogo Universiteta, 1910).

133   Aleksandr N. Bernshtein, "Psikhicheskie zabolevaniia zimoi 1905–1906 g. v Moskve," *Sovremennaia psikhiatriia* (March 1907): 67. As I will explore in Chapter 5, the children would be alive and seeking to answer these questions in the 1920s.

The expanded fifth edition of Kovalevskii's *General Psychopathology* published in 1905 cited trauma—whether in the form of a physical injury or a moral shock—as one of the "etiological factors of neuroses or the psychoses of degeneration."[134] Ukshe agreed that "trauma was a cause of degeneration" in those cases of "individual degeneration, when the subject, in the absence of any hereditary or uterine influences, manifests clear symptoms of degeneration."[135]

By neglecting the perceived relationship between mental illness and degeneration, Brown's implicit assumption in her argument that the 1905 Revolution radicalized the psychiatric profession is that psychiatrists considered a temporary increase in insanity to be a price worth paying for the removal of the primary etiological factor in the spread of mental illness: the repressive tsarist regime. Yet the fact that revolutionary trauma was understood to threaten the biological and psychological welfare not only of present generations but also of their offspring constituted a powerful argument against the desirability of a revolutionary overthrow of the autocracy. Bekhterev gave expression to what had become the professional consensus in 1910 when he declared: "profound social shocks, like wars and revolutions, produce a significant increase in the number of nervous and mental illnesses." As a consequence, he argued, "the avoidance of extreme social crises and the end of wars should also be taken into account together with measures serving the preservation of the nervous and mental health of the population."[136]

The Etiological Catch-22

The inquiry into the etiology of degeneration in late Imperial Russia had identified two principal sources of the disorder: the first was the contemporary socioeconomic order, propped up by a repressive political system; the second was revolution itself. The evidence put forward by clinicians and theorists led to prophylactic impulses that resembled an intellectual Catch-22. The extent and proximity of the threat of degeneration demanded a radical transformation of the Russian socioeconomic order and the political institutions that governed it. On the other hand, another revolution would, in the eyes of many psychiatrists, only serve to exacerbate the very condition it sought to cure.

Torn between alarm at the effects of tsarist capitalism on the one hand and fear of the consequences of repeated revolutionary upheavals on the

---

134   Pavel I. Kovalevskii, *Dushevnye bolezni. Kurs dlia vrachei i iuristov*, vol. 1, *Obshchaia psikhopatologiia*, 5th ed. (St. Petersburg: M. I. Akinfiev and I. V. Leont'ev, 1905), 213–14.
135   Ukshe, "Vyrozhdenie," 802.
136   Bekhterev, "Voprosy nervno-psikhicheskogo zdorov'ia," 64.

other, degeneration theorists were representative of the voices of progressive Russia in the late imperial period. Sympathetic to many of the claims of the revolutionary movement, such as the need for a redistribution of wealth and property, many educated Russians nonetheless recalled with terror the indiscriminate destruction that had accompanied the 1905 Revolution, especially in the countryside. They struggled to articulate a coherent vision of Russia's future that would reform the worst excesses of inequality, exploitation, and repression characteristic of the autocratic order while holding at bay the dragon of social revolution. Degeneration theory not only offered a powerful interpretative apparatus for the exploration of this invidious dilemma, it infused the arguments for action with an acute sense of urgency, laying bare the paralysis of Russian liberalism. To steal a phrase from Trotskii, the progressives had argued themselves into "the dustbin of history." It would only be with revolution already a *fait accompli* that theories of degeneration would be free to offer radical prophylactic solutions to the problems of the moral, mental, and physical deterioration of the population.

Frustrated in the meantime by this theoretical impasse, practitioners of the human sciences turned their optimistic, rationalist attentions to those who had fallen victim to the iniquities of the status quo. Buoyed by their belief in the power of science to renovate Russia, they discussed changes not merely to its social structures but also to its human material.

3   "The Flesh and Blood of Society"

Young and adult criminals are born and live in the midst of society; they are its reflection; they are "the flesh of its flesh, and the bones of its bones."

—Dmitrii A. Dril', 1895

In 1913, the psychiatrist Samuel L'vovich Tsetlin (1878–?) reported in the influential *Sovremennaia psikhiatriia* on the case of a young man who had killed his father. Sergei Martionov had entered his father's room very early one morning in 1911 and stabbed the sleeping man to death with a dagger. Martionov made no effort to escape and returned to his own room in the house, where he was subsequently apprehended by the police, still in possession of the murder weapon. Tsetlin was explicit in approaching his examination of the crime "with the same methods with which one approaches the history of a disease, i.e., initially to identify the facts of the young man's heredity, his past, and the characteristics of Martionov's personality in the period leading up to the commission of the crime; a description of the crime and the events that followed; the facts of an examination of the accused in court; and, of course, the expert conclusions." Tsetlin then went on to note evidence of pathological heredity in the Martionov family: Sergei's brother manifested "acute symptoms of physical degeneration (with a misshapen skull and asymmetrical ears)."

Tsetlin's physical examination of Sergei showed that he also "had numerous physical signs of degeneration"; for example, "his skull was the wrong shape, with a sloping forehead with sharply prominent orbital ridges and acutely segmented upper parts." This defective heredity was exacerbated by his upbringing; in particular, his father's confused attempts to find him employment and alternative accommodation, both of which only worsened his condition. A psychological examination of the young man revealed "a clearness of consciousness and the absence of any delirium," and Martionov admitted that he had committed a crime and that it was wrong, "but his words conveyed no genuine sense of remorse or doubt." In conclusion, Tsetlin repeated that Martionov suffered from both "physical and mental degeneration" yet maintained that the symptoms of degeneration "were not so acute that they might not have been significantly alleviated had Martionov been exposed to more favorable conditions of education and family life."[1] In its unrelenting focus on the biopsychological characteristics of the murderer and their relationship with the forces of heredity and the environment, Tsetlin's article was typical of a substantial body of literature that emerged at the intersection of psychiatry and jurisprudence in late Imperial Russia and usually bore the name criminal anthropology.

This chapter seeks to excavate and explore the assumptions and arguments that underpinned Tsetlin's analysis. It does not seek to offer a comprehensive survey of the history of criminology in late Imperial Russia nor even of criminal anthropology as a specific subdiscipline. Rather, it shows how the application of degeneration theory to crime constituted a way of mediating between perceptions of social decline and individual deviance in the period.

Contemporaries themselves understood that criminal anthropology was inescapably a meditation on wider issues of societal health and disease. Writing in the official *Zhurnal grazhdanskogo i ugolovnogo prava* in 1891, criminologist Ignatii Platonovich Zakrevskii (1839–1906) argued that "the teaching [of the criminal anthropologists] is first and foremost sociological, seeking to determine, with the help of anatomy, psychiatry, history, and statistics, the origins and meaning of crime in a series of manifestations of social life. According to this school, since crime is to the social body what disease is to the human body, its teachings represent a kind of course of social pathology and therapy."[2]

Criminality was a key subject of public debate in the late imperial period.[3] The expansion of Russian cities and the cultural and social disorientation

---

1   S. L. Tsetlin, "Degenerativnaia psikhopatiia," *Sovremennaia psikhiatriia* (January 1913): 37, 44.

2   Ignatii P. Zakrevskii, "Ob ucheniiakh ugolovno-antropologicheskoi shkoly," *Zhurnal grazhdanskogo i ugolovnogo prava*, no. 9 (1891): 77.

3   Significant discussions of the topic include: Sergei S. Ostroumov, *Prestupnost' i ee prichiny v dorevoliutsionnoi Rossii* (Moscow: MGU, 1960); Richard Sutton, "Crime and Social Change in Russia after the Great Reforms: Laws, Courts, and Criminals, 1874–1894" (PhD diss., Indiana University of Maryland, 1981); Joan Neuberger, *Hooliganism: Crime, Culture, and Power in St. Petersburg, 1900–1914* (Berkeley: University of California Press, 1993); Jörg Baberowski, *Autokratie und Justiz: Zum Verhältnis von Rechtsstaatlichkeit und Rückständigkeit im ausgehenden Zarenreich* (Frankfurt am Main: Vittorio Klostermann, 1996); Stephen L. Frank, *Crime, Cultural Conflict, and Justice in Rural Russia, 1856–1914* (Berkeley: University of California Press, 1999).

associated with rapid urbanization and industrialization led to an increase in urban crime. The growth in the popular press and publishing in the wake of the Great Reforms, detailed by Louise McReynolds, brought the reading Russian public face to face with the "criminal class" with which they shared their cities. Newspapers reported avidly on trials of violent criminals, speculating on their motives and personal histories as well as detailing the psychiatric assessments of their mental health.[4] Joan Neuberger, Hubertus F. Jahn, and Roshanna F. Sylvester have all shown how journalistic *flâneurs* offered another important source of public knowledge of crime; they guided Russia's reading public into a seedy and yet exotic underworld of beggars, drunks, prostitutes, and criminals.[5] Vsevolod Krestovskii's novel *Slums of Petersburg* and Vladimir Mikhnevich's *Ulcers of Petersburg* were full of allusions to the corrupted moral and mental faculties of contemporary Russian criminals. Mikhnevich identified the "child criminal as the most terrible deformity and the most pernicious diseased symptom of all the moral anomalies and human deformities brought about by the current state of our social order." Recidivism among this group was a "common phenomenon, as it is among the adult and inveterate sons of vice and crime."[6]

At the turn of the twentieth century in Russia, press reports, court documents, and police records all indicated increases in a wide variety of crimes.[7] Psychiatrists confirmed that crime was on the increase. Writing in 1903, Pavel Kovalevskii noted that the Ministry of Justice had calculated that in the five years between 1889 and 1893, 284,073 crimes had been committed in European Russia: "such an incredible number of crimes in our society constitutes a great affliction and a terrible burden."[8] In the wake of the explosion of criminality that accompanied the 1905 Revolution, Vladimir Bekhterev inquired rhetorically:

Regarding the last few years, do we really need to turn to statistics to arrive at the conclusion that there has been an increase in crime in Russia? Anyone who

---

4   See the press treatment of two notorious murder trials in Louise McReynolds, *The News under Russia's Old Regime: The Development of a Mass-Circulation Press* (Princeton: Princeton University Press, 1991), 137–38, 141–44.

5   Hubertus F. Jahn, "Der St. Petersburger Heumarkt im 19. Jahrhundert: Metamorphosen eines Stadtviertels," *Jahrbücher für Geschichte Osteuropas* 44, no. 2 (1996): 169–77; Neuberger, *Hooliganism*; Roshanna P. Sylvester, *Tales of Old Odessa: Crime and Civility in a City of Thieves* (DeKalb: Northern Illinois University Press, 2005).

6   Vsevolod V. Krestovskii, *Peterburgskie trushchoby: Kniga o sytykh i golodnykh*, 2 vols. (Leningrad: Khudozhestvennaia literatura, 1990); Vladimir O. Mikhnevich, *Iazvy Peterburga. Opyt istoriko-statisticheskogo issledovaniia nravstvennosti stolichnogo naseleniia* (St. Petersburg: Limbus Press, 2003), 412, 419.

7   Neuberger, *Hooliganism*, 28.

8   Pavel I. Kovalevskii, *Vyrozhdenie i vozrozhdenie. Prestupnik i bor'ba s prestupnost'iu (Sotsial'no-psikhologicheskie eskizy)*, 2nd ed. (St. Petersburg: M. I. Akynfiev and I. V. Leont'ev, 1903), 258.

has followed recent events and is familiar with life in Russia can say without any statistics that . . . crime in its most terrible forms directed against both persons and property has perceptibly increased.[9]

In Bekhterev's influential assessment, "the roots of our civilization are being eaten away by the ulcer of crime, and if we do not cure this ulcer, which is destroying all around, then our contemporary civilization will not be able to make any claims for the stability of its future existence."[10]

Lombroso's *L'Uomo Delinquente* (1876) and the Rise of Criminal Anthropology

Concern over crime was a prominent feature of European societies in the second half of the nineteenth century, and a number of studies have highlighted the tremendous currency that discussions of the topic enjoyed in the public imagination in France, Germany, England, and Italy.[11] Like psychiatry, criminology in Russia was embedded in a pan-European dialogue with the intellectual development of the discipline in these other countries. Accordingly, the story of this chapter focuses to a great extent on the response of Russian clinicians and jurists to the development of criminal anthropology in the West, and particularly to its origins in Italy.

Medical research into the relationship between heredity and criminality began in earnest in the 1870s. At the beginning of the decade, a Scottish prison doctor, Bruce Thompson, published an article entitled "The Hereditary Nature of Crime" in the *Journal of Mental Science*. Thompson argued that a specific class of criminal existed that was characterized by physical and mental peculiarities.[12] Russian scholars were quick to discuss Thompson's article and to endorse his conclusions. In 1877, Leonid Efstav'evich Vladimirov (1845–1917), professor of law at the University of Kharkov, wrote an article in *Iuridicheskii vestnik* entitled "Psychological Peculiarities of Criminals in Light of the Most Recent Research." Vladimirov hailed Thompson's paper as

---

9   Vladimir M. Bekhterev, *Ob"ektivno-psikhologicheskii metod v primenenii k izucheniiu prestupnosti* (St. Petersburg: V. Anderson and G. Loitsiatskii, 1912), 10.

10   Ibid., 11.

11   Robert A. Nye, *Crime, Madness, and Politics in Modern France: the Medical Concept of National Decline* (Princeton: Princeton University Press, 1984); Daniel Pick, *Faces of Degeneration: A European Disorder, c. 1848–c. 1918* (Cambridge: Cambridge University Press, 1989); Ruth Harris, *Murderers and Madness: Medicine, Law, and Society in the Fin de Siècle* (Oxford: Clarendon Press, 1989); Eric A. Johnson, *Urbanization and Crime: Germany, 1871–1914* (Cambridge: Cambridge University Press, 1995); Richard Wetzell, *Inventing the Criminal: A History of Germany Criminology, 1880–1945* (Chapel Hill: University of North Carolina Press, 2000).

12   Bruce Thompson, "The Hereditary Nature of Crime," *Journal of Mental Science* 17, no. 75 (October 1870): 321–50.

pathbreaking: "The idea of the mental peculiarities of criminals in the current state of research should be disseminated as a hypothesis that is perhaps destined to offer great results in the study of crime and punishment."[13]

Vladimirov's wish was swiftly fulfilled by the impact of a study published in Italy a year earlier, Cesare Lombroso's *L'uomo delinquente*. Although Lombroso's status as pioneer in the field can be overstated, the publication of his study had such an impact on European criminology that no subsequent study over the following decades could ignore its precepts, even if only to condemn them.[14] Lombroso began his medical career as a military physician in the new national army and served in the military campaign against brigandage in Calabria. He developed an interest in psychiatry and became the head of a psychiatric ward in the hospital of Pavia in 1863. In 1876, he was appointed to a professorship at the University of Turin, where he taught and generated a prolific scholarly output until his death in 1909, holding chairs in forensic medicine, psychiatry and, eventually, criminal anthropology.[15]

During the 1870s, Lombroso revived the study of phrenology, initially pioneered by the German physicians, Franz Joseph Gall (1758–1828) and Johann G. Spurzheim (1776–1832), and extended it into an evolutionary theory of racial development. Gall and Spurzheim had argued that the brain was the organ of the mind and the states and contours of the latter lent shape to the former, which in turn could be identified by its imprint on the shape of the skull. Careful scrutiny of the skull could, therefore, shed light on the nature of the mind which it housed.[16] Lombroso applied this phrenology to a specific theory of evolutionary development that classified different social groups in a hierarchy of social "savagery."

The criminal's phrenology, which Lombroso identified in 1870, illuminated an evolutionary past quite different from those of his or her nondeviant contemporaries. Criminals languished in a primitive state of evolutionary

13   Leonid E. Vladimirov, "Psikhicheskie osobennosti prestupnikov po noveishim issledovaniiam," *Iuridicheskii vestnik*, nos. 9–10 (1877): 31. Thompson's research was also reviewed by Rudol'f R. Mintslov, "Osobennosti klassa prestupnikov," *Iuridicheskii vestnik*, no. 10 (1881): 223.

14   Cesare Lombroso, *L'uomo delinquente studiato in rapporta alla anthropologia, alla medicina legale ed alle discipline carcerarie* (Milan, 1876). On Lombroso and his legacy in Italy, see Mary Gibson, *Born to Crime: Cesare Lombroso and the Origins of Biological Criminology* (Westport, CT: Praeger, 2002); David Horn, *Social Bodies: Science, Reproduction, and Italian Modernity* (Princeton: Princeton University Press, 1994). On Lombroso's reception in Germany, see Mariacarla Gadebusch Bondio, *Die Rezeption der kriminalanthropologischen Theorien von Cesare Lombroso in Deutschland in 1880–1914* (Husum: Matthiesen, 1995); in France, see Laurent Mucchielli, ed., *L'histoire de la criminologie française* (Paris: Éditions l'Harmatten, 1994).

15   My reading of Lombroso's career and theoretical apparatus is drawn primarily from Pick, *Faces of Degeneration*, 113–39.

16   F. J. Gall and J. C. Spurzheim, *Observations sur la phrénologie, ou la connaissance de l'homme moral et intellectuel, fondée sur les fonctions du système nerveux* (Paris, 1810).

development and were throwbacks to a long-lost age of brutality, amorality, and anarchy, a state he termed "atavism." Later editions of Lombroso's work updated his definitions of biological deviance. In the third edition, published in 1884, he incorporated the concept of "moral insanity" developed by the British psychiatrist James Prichard in the 1830s, and later editions also made reference to degeneration as a cause of crime, although Lombroso never clarified his understanding of the relationship between it and atavism.[17]

Daniel Pick has offered a stimulating contextualist reading of Lombroso's criminal anthropology, arguing that it spoke to two principal concerns of educated Italian contemporaries. First, it offered an explanation for the persistence of "savagery" in the form of lawlessness, violence, and brigandage in the south of Italian during and after the Risorgimento; second, it provided a visible taxonomy of the forces that threatened to subvert social and political stability in Italy: "The naivety, but also the force, of this positivism lay in its attempt to deny the presence of metaphor, to imagine that by caging its shadowy images within rigid, visible taxonomies, subversion could be staved off from civil and political society. Presences designated as subversive were thus ritually conjured in order to be objectified and denounced: exorcised in language and exorcised from power."[18]

Just as the wider intellectual context shaped the resonance of Lombroso's ideas in his native Italy, his reception in Russia was similarly inflected by the local and immediate concerns of educated contemporaries.[19] Russian criminologists and psychiatrists responded positively to Lombroso's insistence that the criminal, rather than simply the crime, should be the object of legal and medical attention. Many of them also accepted that a link existed between physical and moral deformity and that individuals with inherited criminal urges, as posited by Lombroso, did exist.

Yet this broad acceptance of certain features of Lombroso's theory coexisted with an uncompromising rejection of others. With the exception of a few dissenting voices, Russian experts were extremely skeptical about the existence of a separate criminal class characterized by atavistic biological and psychological features. They were, from the outset, also reluctant to accept that criminality was biologically encoded in the individual and would manifest itself in destructive and illegal acts independently of the social environment. In terms of its historical narrative, the notion of atavism

17   Wetzell, *Inventing the Criminal*, 30. For a scathing refutation of Lombroso's theories, albeit one which pays scant regard to the wider culture in which they were developed, see Stephen Jay Gould, *The Mismeasure of Man*, rev. ed. (1981; New York: Norton, 1996), 151–73.

18   Pick, *Faces of Degeneration*, 115.

19   Ironically, Lombroso's works were not translated into Russian until after his influence had begun to wane. The vast majority of Russian psychiatrists and jurists read his works, however, either in the Italian original or in French translation. See Chezare Lombrozo, *Prestuplenie*, trans. G. I. Gordon (St. Petersburg: N. K. Martynov, 1900).

abstracted the individual out of the social context within which the crimes were committed, thereby removing any responsibility from the shoulders of society. It cast criminals as evolutionary freight, surplus to society's requirements and beyond its influence. Such a theory sat uncomfortably with the liberal *mission civilizatrice* of Russian educated society, centered as it was on a belief in the power of education and material improvement to transform society and its members.

Degeneration versus Atavism

Lombroso was not, however, without his adherents in Russia. Writing in *Iuridicheskii vestnik* in 1881, Rudol'f Rudol'fovich Mintslov (1845–1904) offered a positive survey of Lombroso's theories of atavism, arguing that "it was proven that crimes are committed . . . by representatives of our primitive and unruly forebears who live among us."[20] Mintslov clearly subscribed to the contemporary belief in a hierarchy of racial development, observing that the skull of Lombroso's atavistic born criminal bore more than a passing resemblance to certain ethnic groupings within the Russian Empire: "In the development and general form of the skull, Lombroso has found a predominance of prognathic brachycephalism, i.e., an approximation of the type of Tartars, Kalmyks, Arakurants, and so on."[21] Following the Italian psychiatrist, Mintslov argued that this biological underdevelopment signified a moral underdevelopment that was tantamount to the possession of "criminal instincts": "There is no doubt that the intellectual and moral underdevelopment of criminals has been proven and that . . . it entails an inevitable weakness if not the complete disappearance of their will or at least the total absence of those altruistic feelings that play such a prominent role in a normal person."[22] A similar position was put forward in 1884 by Stepan Aleksandrovich Beliakov (1858–?) of the Psychiatric Department of the Moscow Military Hospital: Beliakov hailed Lombroso's study as "a capital work."[23]

Yet even in these early discussions of Lombroso's theories, Russian clinicians were anxious to emphasize the role of the environment in the etiology of crime. For Mintslov, atavism was one of a range of factors that could cause criminality: he also included pathological heredity on the basis of degeneration and social factors.[24] Beliakov insisted, meanwhile, that the

---

20   Mintslov, "Osobennosti klassa prestupnikov," pt. 3, *Iuridicheskii vestnik*, no. 12 (1881): 586.
21   Mintslov, "Osobennosti klassa prestupnikov," pt. 1, no. 10 (1881): 219.
22   Ibid., 234.
23   Stepan A. Beliakov, "Antropologicheskoe issledovanie ubiits," pt. 1, *Arkhiv psikhiatrii, neirologii i sudebnoi psikhopatologii* 4, no. 1 (1884): 33.
24   Mintslov, "Osobennosti klassa prestupnikov," no. 10, 223.

forms of pathological heredity that set criminals apart from the majority of healthy human beings were firmly rooted in the material and spiritual environment that had shaped the criminals themselves and their ancestors. Acknowledgment of "heredity as the primary driver of criminality" did not relieve society of its obligations to "come to the aid [of criminals] and, with the help of rationally organized schools, to remove from the environment the poverty and corruption . . . from which criminals are recruited and the particular caste of robbers and vagabonds are constituted."[25] Atavisitc born criminals were a subspecies of criminals; they were not a genus.

Indeed, the early reception of Lombroso's theories of atavism and the born criminal already reveal the contours of the intellectual debates that were to frame later biopsychological discussions of criminality. When still a young scholar, Dmitrii Dril' wrote an extensive review of Lombroso's *L'uomo delinquente* in 1882. Dril' chafed at the immobilizing fatalism of Lombroso's conviction that crime was a feature of the natural order: "Crime and punishment, [Lombroso] argues, are essentially inevitable and inherent in the very nature of man. Yes they are inevitable, we would respond, but only given the existence of a particular kind of society—the kind in which the living conditions act destructively on the organism and clearly generate crime."[26] Criminal anthropology in Russia was to retain this strong emphasis on the normative influence of societal forces throughout the remaining years of the autocracy. Atavism was increasingly rejected in favor of a degenerative model that argued that biological and psychological differences between deviants and the healthy majority might be significant, but they did not exist out of space and time.

Even Russian criminologists and psychiatrists who had considerable sympathy with Lombroso's arguments tended to sublimate the notion of atavism, if they accepted it at all, into a wider spectrum of psychopathologies that did have environmental causes as their origin. Degeneration could manifest itself as a reversal of human evolution, and those afflicted by the syndrome might, over the course of several generations, come to resemble more primitive forms of humanity that *appeared* to herald from a different age altogether. Yet Russian experts were unwilling to place the criminal, born or otherwise, outside of the stream of history. In the first major Russian study of criminal anthropology, *Young Criminals,* published in 1884, Dril' argued that

the transfer of anatomical and psychophysical peculiarities is not confined to the law of heredity. Different forms of mental illness and different deformities

---

25   Beliakov, "Antropologicheskoe issledovanie ubiits," pt. 2, *Arkhiv psikhiatrii, neirologii i sudebnoi psikhopatologii* 4, no. 2, 51.

26   Dmitrii A. Dril', "Prestupnyi chelovek," *Iuridicheskii vestnik* (December 1882): 514.

in the psychophysical organization of the individual—whether a result of conditions of corrosive poverty and the spiritual poverty frequently associated with it or whether under the influence of corrupting inertia and luxury, as one might indeed expect—are passed on to the offspring and create from them the multiple forms of degeneration of the race that abound in the so-called dangerous classes of society, the population of prisons, and institutions for the mentally ill.[27]

These important modifications of Lombroso's theory by his Russian audience were far from unique to Russia. A number of scholars have traced the mounting opposition to Lombroso's theories of atavism from within the French psychiatric and legal professions. Already at the First International Congress of Criminal Anthropology, held in Rome in November 1885, the Italian psychiatrist and his followers encountered fierce resistance from French legal theorists and psychiatrists who took exception to the Italian school's apparent willingness to discount altogether the force of the environment.[28] Russian opponents of Lombroso frequently cited the authority of their French counterparts.[29]

By the end of the 1880s, Russian objections to the term "atavism" were becoming ever more voluminous. In a substantial 1889 review of Lombroso's *L'uomo delinquente*, the psychiatrist Alexander Efimovich Shcherbak (1863–1934) found that Lombroso's "atavistic theory of crime remains simply a hypothesis without foundation. . . . All the peculiarities of criminals can be explained in the absence of any atavism in terms of arrested or diseased development."[30] Indeed, the intellectual tide had now turned firmly against the theory, and a broad consensus had emerged on the primacy of acquired pathological heredity within the etiology of crime. Even Vladimir Chizh, an opponent of reform and staunch supporter of the autocracy, showed little enthusiasm for a theory of criminality that, in evolutionary terms, placed the person of the criminal far beyond the responsibility of contemporary society. On the contrary, Chizh argued that "the children of individuals

---

27 Dmitrii A. Dril', *Maloletnie prestupniki. Etiud po voprosu o chelovecheskoi prestupnosti, ee faktorakh i sredstvakh bor'by s nei* (Moscow: A. I. Mamontov, 1884), 274.

28 One of the leading French figures at the conference, Alexandre Lacassagne (1843–1924), challenged Lombroso's imprecise use of terms such as "atavism" or "Darwinism" and advocated instead a more nuanced vision of criminality as the product of a perpetual dynamic interaction between biological and environmental forces. In his celebrated Pasteurian formula, he countered: "The social milieu is the cultural broth of criminality; the microbe is the criminal, an element that gains significance only at the moment it finds the broth that makes it ferment." *Actes du premier congrés international d'anthropologie criminelle, biologie et sociologie* (Turin, 1886–87), 166, cited in Pick, *Faces of Degeneration*, 140. See also Nye, *Crime, Madness, and Politics*, 103–6.

29 Zakrevskii, "Ob ucheniiakh ugolovno-antropologicheskoi shkoly," 103; Petr N. Obninskii, "Illiuzii pozitivizma," *Zhurnal grazhdanskogo i ugolovnogo prava* (March 1890): 1–2.

30 Aleksandr E. Shcherbak, *Prestupnyi chelovek po Lombrozo (Vrozhdennyi prestupnik—nravstvenno-pomeshannyi epileptik)* (St. Petersburg: P. I. Shmidt, 1889), 50.

who have lived their entire lives in damp, dark apartments, malnourished, working with materials that are harmful to their health, such as mercury or lead, are frequently blessed with imperfect constitutions."[31] In his defense of Lombroso published in 1900, Bronislav Vorotynskii conceded that "the view of Lombroso and his disciples of crime as a symptom of atavism proved unfounded."[32]

One objection frequently raised to the concept of atavism was that, in the formulation of future Bolshevik leader Khristian Georgievich Rakovskii (1873–1941) in 1900, "savages are not similar to criminals. The criminal is one thing; primitive man quite another. A savage is a healthy man mentally and physically while a hardened criminal is someone sick and exhausted."[33] Reviewing the reception of Lombroso's theory of atavism a decade later, Bekhterev argued that the manifest differences between criminals and savages were also to be found in their respective behavior toward other members of their social group:

> Lombroso's premise that the criminal type is atavistic, or represents a return of man to the primitive state of a savage, cannot be accepted as fundamentally correct because the savage, and the child that is frequently compared with savages, are not criminal by nature. The savage is hostile toward members of other tribes, but he is not an enemy of his own and in his own environment he is in no way similar to a criminal.[34]

31   Vladimir F. Chizh, *Prestupnyi chelovek pered sudom vrachebnoi nauki* (Kazan: Tipografiia Imperatorskogo Universiteta, 1894), 23. Indeed, the traditional representation of Russian criminologists and psychiatrists as divided between left and right, and their theoretical investigations as overdetermined by their political affiliation stands in need of revision. Supporters of the autocracy such as Chizh were quite prepared to accept the normative power of the environment in the formation of degenerative criminality, and liberals such as Dril' did not shy away from the heredity component of the disorder. Beneath the debates that seemed to rage between them, Russian criminologists actually demonstrated a great deal of consensus over the shape, nature, and origins of the disorder. For a traditional account of the relationship between politics and psychiatry, see Julie Vail Brown's essays: "Psychiatrists and the State in Tsarist Russia," in *Social Control and the State,* ed. Andrew Scull and Stanley Cohen (Oxford: Blackwell, 1985), 267–87; and "Professionalization and Radicalization: Russian Psychiatrists Respond to 1905," in *Russia's Missing Middle Class: The Professions in Russian History,* ed. Harley D. Balzer (Armonk, NY: M. E. Sharpe, 1996), 143–67.

32   Bronislav I. Vorotynskii, "Psikho-fizicheskie osobennosti prestupnika-degenerata," *Uchennye zapiski Kazanskogo Universiteta,* no. 3 (1900): 101.

33   E. Stancheva (Khristian Georgievich Rakovskii), *"Neschastnen'kie": o prestupleniiakh i prestupnikakh. Ocherk po obshchestvennoi patologii i gigiene* (St. Petersburg: Sever, 1900), 29.

34   Bekhterev, *Ob"ektivno-psikhologicheskii metod,* 16. Although a matter of speculation, it is perhaps worth noting that the resistance to Lombroso's conflation of savages and criminals was entirely consonant both with the paternalistic sense of guilt felt by many educated and privileged Russians toward the peasantry and with the continuing Populist idealization of the village as a relative site of moral simplicity, harmony, and purity. The profound

Russian criminal anthropologists were, however, anxious to salvage the credibility of their discipline from the onslaught against Lombroso. Some, like Dril', pointed out that Lombroso did not entirely ignore the influence of social factors in the etiology of crime; he simply subordinated them to the force of heredity.[35] Lombroso did discuss, Dril' noted, a range of social factors, from boredom and alienation in the cities to the poor quality of food. Moreover, his suggestions for the treatment of crime included a number of adjustments to the social order.[36] Dril' bemoaned the resultant division of criminal anthropology into two mutually hostile camps: "the organic, with Lombroso at its head, which, it is claimed, completely ignores the influence of social conditions, and the sociological, which on the contrary places them at the center of the analysis. What a strange misunderstanding!"[37] He argued that such mutual hostility ignored the essential compatibility of both theoretical positions.[38]

Yet most commentators remained unconvinced by these protestations.[39] In an excoriating critique of Lombroso's work published in *Russkaia mysl'* in 1895, Ivan Ivanovich Dobrovol'skii rejected the arguments of Dril', pointing out that although Lombroso may have made some minor tactical concessions to environmental factors at the Second and Third International Congresses of Criminal Anthropology, which took place in Paris in 1889 and in Brussels in 1893, respectively, even the later editions of his *L'uomo delinquente* in no way retracted its central claim that "'the real cause of criminality is to be found in atavism.'"[40]

A more promising form of defense mounted by the criminal anthropologists was to distance themselves from Lombroso's theory of atavism but to insist on the fundamental correctness of his contention that an awareness of the biopsychological nature of the criminal was essential for understanding the genesis of crime. In his reflections on the 1893 Brussels congress, at which

ambivalence toward industrial modernity examined in the previous chapter might logically have dissuaded Russian clinicians and theorists from an equation of material and cultural underdevelopment with malevolence.

35   Dmitrii A. Dril', "Antropologicheskaia shkola i ee kritiki," *Iuridicheskii vestnik* 4, no. 4 (December 1890): 589.

36   Dmitrii A. Dril', "Chto govoril os' na mezhdunarodnom ugolovno-antropologicheskom kongresse v Briussele," pt. 1, *Russkaia mysl'* (February 1893): 96. A similar defense continued into the twentieth century. See Aleksandr Shcheglov, "Prestupnik, kak predmet izucheniia vrachebnoi nauki," *Vestnik psikhologii, kriminal'noi antropologii i pedologii*, no. 1 (1913): 7–8.

37   Dmitrii A. Dril', "Chto govoril os'," pt. 2, *Russkaia mysl'* (March 1893): 95.

38   These synthetic arguments continued well into the twentieth century. See Shcheglov, "Prestupnik," 9.

39   Vladimir V. Lesevich, "Ekskursii v oblast' psikhiatrii," *Russkaia mysl'* (February 1887): part 2, 26.

40   I. D-ov [Ivan Ivanovich Dobrovol'skii], "Tsezar' Lombrozo kak uchenyi i myslitel'," *Russkaia mysl'* (July 1895): part 2, 13.

he had been a delegate, Dril' emphasized that Lombroso's contribution to the discipline of criminology did not stand or fall by the existence of the born criminal or the accuracy of Lombroso's stigmata but by his explanation "of the importance of the physical peculiarities of the criminal."[41] Chizh similarly hailed "Lombroso's immortal achievement, [which] consisted of bringing a scientific-historical method to bear in the study of the criminal."[42]

Both Dril' and Chizh were anxious not to throw the criminal baby out with the Lombrosian bathwater. Chizh raised the familiar objection of the criminal anthropologists: "Jurists themselves cannot deny that the influence of the 'environment' can explain the general quantity of crime, but it cannot explain why one individual, and not another, commits crime. Without denying the significance of the 'environment,' the medical study of the criminal examines why the environment acts on certain individuals and in such a way that their entire life is a series of criminal acts."[43] Dril' meanwhile declared that "although without environmental influence there is no crime . . . nevertheless, the physiological factor or, more accurately, the psychophysical factor, is always the driver and immediate cause."[44] This theoretical response to attacks on criminal anthropology continued into the twentieth century. According to the psychiatrist Lev Isaevich Sheinis (1871–?) in 1905, the principal achievement of criminal anthropology was that "it made a break with the metaphysical notion of free will and addressed the real nature of the crime, it made a serious attempt to link the criminal with the conditions of reality—in particular with the peculiarities of the psychophysical organization of the criminal himself—and to extend in this way the law of causality to the phenomenon of crime."[45] In 1913, Aleksandr L. Shcheglov still found it necessary to make the same point.[46]

Amid the mounting international opprobrium assailing the theory of atavism, degeneration theory provided criminal anthropologists with a theoretical structure within which environmental forces could be accommodated and, indeed, accorded an etiological primacy of sorts, and yet enabled them to retain their emphasis on the biopsychological constitution of the criminal. Zakrevskii endorsed the displacement of atavism with degeneration:

> There is no doubt that the majority of people who find themselves in the dock, in prison, and in asylums do indeed carry such [criminal] stigmata, but in fact

41   Dril', "Chto govorilos'," pt. 1, 91. Even Lombroso's Russian opponents, such as Zakrevskii, conceded the same: Ignat'ev P. Zakrevskii, *Ugolovnaia antropologiia na Zhenevskom Mezhdunarodnom Kongresse* (St. Petersburg: Tip. Pravitel'stvuiushchego Senata, 1897), 16.
42   Chizh, *Prestupnyi chelovek*, 6.
43   Ibid., 39–40.
44   Dril', "Chto govorilos'," pt. 1, 99.
45   Lev I. Sheinis, "Prestupnost', ee evoliutsiia i sotsial'noe znachenie," *Vestnik znaniia*, no. 9 (1905): 59.
46   Shcheglov, "Prestupnik," 6. <see note 36.>

these indicators do not testify at all to the influence of atavism generating, as it were, in certain people the zoological instincts of primordial man. On the contrary, they point to diseased changes in the original healthy human form under the harmful influence of the environment, insufficient nutrition, damp dwellings, exhaustion induced by excessive labor, unhygienic living conditions over a series of generations, alcoholism, mental fatigue; in a word, as a consequence of all the negative conditions of contemporary life.[47]

Writing in 1891, Isaak Orshanskii agreed that the demonstration of pathological changes from a normal type over the course of a number of generations amounted to a stark refutation of Lombroso's theory of atavism: "There is no reason to see in that unfortunate group of people standing at the frontier of health and illness a mystical return to the past, so-called atavism. Rather, we should see in them a socially diseased group . . . [that] in essence is the debris of our culture and contains the victims of the harmful sides of civilization and the offspring of these victims."[48]

However, not all Russian psychiatrists and legal theorists rejected atavism out of hand. Some sought to redefine it in terms of a subcategory of degeneration that amounted to regression to a more primitive stage of human evolution. In 1904, Ivan Sikorskii argued that "a recognizable criterion [for the determination of physical degeneration] was the reversibility of a given stigmata, i.e., that it belongs to features that have already long disappeared phylogenetically: for example, mammary glands of large dimensions, large quantities of body hair."[49] A few years later, Orshanskii modified his earlier rejection of atavism, now stressing that the anatomical deformities with which atavism was frequently associated were not "'nature's tricks,' 'the product of chance,' 'deformity,' and 'anomalies' but completely logical phenomena, the return to long-outlived forms, that is, the features of atavistic heredity."

Yet although Orshanskii imposed a conceptual coherence on the broad range of deformities associated with a return to a more primitive evolutionary state, he still insisted that the onset of this process was grounded in the empirical experiences of the individual concerned. It was, therefore, essentially the same process as degeneration: "The symptoms of degeneration and atavism are linked by their common genesis. Syphilis and alcoholism of the parents elicit degeneration in some of the offspring, in others simply deviations in their body that have an atavistic character; in some of the children

47   Zakrevskii, "Ob ucheniiakh ugolovno-antropologicheskoi shkoly," 113.
48   Isaak G. Orshanskii, *Nashi prestupniki i uchenie Lombrozo* (St. Petersburg: E. Arnol'd, 1891), 17.
49   Ivan A. Sikorskii, "Biologicheskie voprosy v psikhologii i psikhiatrii," *Voprosy nervno-psikhicheskoi meditsiny*, no. 1 (1904): 103.

we find degeneration and atavism at the same time."[50] The important consequence of this position was that it effectively stripped the notion of atavism of its primordial separateness and offered a contextual explanation for the appearance of individuals who looked like their long dead forebears. Individuals with atavistic characteristics did not stand outside of the temporal parameters of a given society; they were still very much its children.

Reading the Stigmata of the Criminal

A rejection of atavism in favor of degeneration did not, however, necessarily imply a rejection of the existence of the criminal stigmata to which Lombroso attached such significance. Indeed, many physicians subscribed to the view that criminal deviance did find expression in a range of physical deformities that could be identified and classified as part of the detection of individual criminals. The virtue of the stigmata was their visibility, their stable (if expansive) taxonomy of deviance, and their underlying coherence. All manner of threats to society, ranging from prostitution to suicide, violent crime to terrorism, were revealed to have a common origin in the mal-development of their perpetrators. The conceptual exorcism of diseased elements from a healthy body social was possible on the basis of the careful scrutiny and detection of them. The socially unstable, unfit, and destructive could be identified and isolated in the interests of collective health. Such a view accorded well with positivist minds convinced of the power of science to render fundamentally intelligible not just the natural but also the social world.

Like Mintslov, Dril' enthusiastically endorsed Lombroso's attempt "to establish a stable correlation between the peculiarities of the [body's] organization in a general sense of the term and psychological peculiarities."[51] He supported Lombroso's use of phrenology as a means of investigating this correlation: "Anyone who wants to study the moral and mental features of a given category of individuals should necessarily start with the study of the form and development of the different parts of their head."[52] Other scholars agreed. Beliakov endorsed Lombroso's identification of criminal stigmata:

> Physically, they are tall with dark hair, premature balding, sparse facial hair. A head of large dimensions is found more commonly among criminals than among the mentally ill; small heads are found significantly less often among the mentally sound than among criminals; asymmetry of the skull, flatness of the

50   Isaak G. Orshanskii, *Atavizm i vyrozhdenie* (Moscow: I. N. Kushnerev, 1910), 5, 7.
51   Dril', "Prestupnyi chelovek," *Iuridicheskii vestnik* (November 1882): 403.
52   Ibid. (December 1882), 515.

forehead, the pronounced development of the eye sockets, the abnormal configuration of the ears, slanted eyes, asymmetry of the pupils, strabismus, mydriasis, nystagmus, prognathism, a heavy body with reduced muscular power; the skull of murderers is brachycephalic.[53]

Such assessments of Lombroso's theory coincided with the zenith of the Italian's international influence in the mid-1880s, manifest at the Rome congress in 1885 in which the Italian delegates, largely supporters of Lombroso, dominated.[54]

Yet at the Paris congress in 1889, Lombroso's insistence on the existence of criminal stigmata was subject to a mauling by other delegates, especially the French. Nye has remarked that the Paris congress of 1889 was the occasion of a "stunning public reversal" in the fortunes of the Lombrosian theories. Prominent French anthropologists like Léonce Manouvrier (1850–1927) and Paul Topinard (1830–1911), both of the École d'anthropologie in Paris, compared Lombroso's theories to Gall's phrenology, dismissed Lombroso's criminal type of being a sort of "ideal harlequin," and subjected the Italian efforts at statistical analysis to a rigorous examination. Methodological objections centered on Lombroso's failure to collect measurements within discrete series according to race, sex, and class and to compare his statistics on criminal anomalies with broad samples of "honest" men.[55]

Russian scholars were quick to seize on and contribute to these objections. Writing a few months after the Paris congress, Shcherbak cited Topinard's arguments to dismiss Lombroso's contention that savages and criminals shared the same anthropological features.[56] Zakrevskii objected to Lombroso's failure to adequately differentiate between various "races," declaring "however much I looked in Lombroso's atlas, I could not find a common anthropological type. There were simply rather unpleasant faces and nothing more."[57] By 1894, Chizh was lamenting the fact that the Italian's dubious attempt to revive phrenology as a means of mapping the criminal had dealt a serious blow to the credibility of criminal anthropology as a discipline: "When checked, almost all Lombroso's conclusions on the subject proved to be mistaken, which gave his opponents grounds to dismiss his entire theory."[58] Still others, however, were far more skeptical about the existence of any correlation between physical and moral deformity. In his highly critical review of Lombroso in 1895, Dobrovol'skii ridiculed the notion that the stigmata had any meaning whatsoever: "On careful and

53   Beliakov, "Antropologicheskoe issledovanie ubiits," vol. 4, no. 1, 33.
54   Pick, *Faces of Degeneration,* 140.
55   Nye, *Crime, Madness, and Politics,* 106.
56   Shcherbak, *Prestupnyi chelovek po Lombrozo,* 50.
57   Zakrevskii, "Ob ucheniiakh," 94.
58   Chizh, *Prestupnyi chelovek pered sudom vrachebnoi nauki,* 27.

sometimes even a casual inspection, almost every honest person you care to meet ... has some kind of defect or even a great many of them."[59] One year later, Professor Dmitrii Nikolaevich Zernov (1843–1917) of Moscow University similarly asserted that "atavistic anomalies ... are a purely anatomical concept."[60]

Yet the discrediting of Lombroso's own particular visible taxonomy of deviance did not sap the positivist impulse to detect physical anomalies in criminals and to scrutinize their meaning.[61] Whatever the shortcomings of Lombroso's clumsy methods, Chizh was clearly reluctant to break with the belief that a correlation existed between physical and moral states:

> Even if it were established that the born criminal did not differ at all in terms of his physical organization from honest people, it would in no way prove that their physical organization really did not differ at all from the normal. Rather, it would simply demonstrate that with our crude methods of analysis we are unable to determine the signifiers of this organization, just as we are unable to detect anomalies in the physical organization in case of many forms of mental illness.[62]

59   I. D-ov (Dobrovol'skii), "Tsezar' Lombrozo kak uchenyi i myslitel'," *Russkaia mysl', July 1895,* part 2, p. 18.

60   Dmitrii N. Zernov, *Kriticheskii ocherk anatomicheskikh osnovanii kriminal'noi teorii Lombrozo* (Moscow: Universitetskaia tipografiia, 1896), 54.

61   Indeed, Eugene M. Avrutin has noted that scrutiny of criminal stigmata came to inform policing practices in Russia in the first decade of the twentieth century. Faced with the growing problems of recidivism and political terrorism, the Ministry of the Interior "began to rely on the techniques established by Alphonse Bertillon to detect criminals based on anthropometric measurements of the body and forensic photography. The Bertillon system, as it came to be called, was premised on the principle that all human measurements were racially fixed and obeyed objective, statistical norms. In the inter-revolutionary period, the St. Petersburg police received taxonomic charts based on the Bertillon system; in their descriptions of the criminal body, police officials were instructed to pay particular attention to physiognomic indicators that served as important clues to criminal identity: nose, ear, mouth, and race if the suspects were colored [*esli tsvetnokozhii*]." Avrutin cites a number of police manuals such as *Kratkoe rukovodstvo dlia antropologicheskikh izmerenii s tsel'iu opredeleniia retsidivistov, sostavlennoe po sisteme Bertil'ona (izdano po rasporiazheniiu S.-Peterburgskogo gradonachal'nika)* (St. Petersburg: Tipografiia Kantseliarii S.-Peterburgskogo gradonachal'nika, 1891). See his "Racial Categories and the Politics of (Jewish) Difference in Late Imperial Russia," *Kritika* 8, no. 1 (Winter 2007): 38.

62   Chizh, *Prestupnyi chelovek pered sudom vrachebnoi nauki*, 27. Other clinicians did indeed persist in the endeavor to isolate individual physical deformities that testified to the existence of mental anomalies. In 1899, Viktor V. Vorob'ev argued that although Lombroso's stigmata had failed to accommodate racial and class differences, "deformity in the ear" pointed to the "existence of subtle deformities in the functioning (and the construction) of the central nervous system." See his "K voprosu ob osobennostiakh fizicheskogo stroeniia dushevnobol'nykh. O 'degenerativnom ukhe,'" *Vorposy nervno-psikhicheskoi meditsiny* 4, no. 4 (1899): 526. At the same time, Vorob'ev dismissed claims of a difference in the cranial structure between "healthy" and "degenerate" individuals. See Vorob'ev, "K voprosu o tak nazyvaemom zatylochnom tipe stroeniia cherepa vyrozhdaiushchikhsia dushevnobol'nykh," *Zhurnal nevropatologii i psikhiatrii*, no. 2 (1901): 384–99.

Indeed, the majority of Russian clinicians accepted the existence of physical stigmata among criminals; they simply disputed Lombroso's interpretation of their origins. In a major study published in 1890, *Psychopathological Types and Their Relationship with Crime and Its Different Forms,* Dril' explained that degeneration could account for all the atavistic features of Lombroso's born criminal: "All the organs of the body are afflicted with degeneration. . . . Hypertrophy, atrophy, and the arrested development of individual organs and their complete disappearance [produces] deformities; those anatomical-physiological stigmata appear, on the basis of which Lombroso discerns 'the born criminal.'"[63]

Another physician, Praskov'ia Nikolaevna Tarnovskaia (1848–1910), published a series of influential studies on female crime from the 1880s to the 1900s. Tarnovskaia was sympathetic to Lombroso's insistence on the primary importance of pathological heredity in the etiology of crime and endorsed his identification of a wide range of physical deformities as particular to a criminal type. Indeed, she developed her own exhaustive compendium of stigmata based on her anthropometric studies of female prostitutes and murderers "belonging exclusively to the Slavic race, and the White Russian group." Yet she attributed these stigmata to the effects of degeneration, not atavism, and cited the role of parental tuberculosis, syphilis, and alcoholism in producing deformity in the children.[64]

The attribution, however, of physical deformity to physical degeneration elicited by unhealthy environmental conditions suggested for many a correlation with moral deformity and criminal propensities, themselves understood to originate in the same milieu. Clinicians seized on this correlation in their bid to retain a legibility of deviance. Rakovskii affirmed that

> the facial features of the criminal are often particularly coarse and deformed. How can this be explained? . . . This is because criminals are degenerate individuals. Both the tendency to commit crime and bodily deformity manifest

---

63   Dmitrii A. Dril', *Psikhofizicheskie tipy i ikh sootnoshenii s prestupnost'iu i ee raznovidnostiami* (Moscow: A. I. Mamontov, 1890), 15.

64   Praskov'ia N. Tarnovskaia, *Vorovki. Antropologicheskoe issledovanie* (St. Petersburg: Kudozhestvennaia pechat', 1902), 18. Tarnovskaia was the daughter of the prominent advocate of women's medical education, Nikolai Kozlov. Laura Engelstein has noted Tarnovskaia's conclusion "that biological deformity was the result of ills attributable to poor living conditions" in her *The Keys to Happiness: Sex and the Search for Modernity in Fin-de-Siècle Russia* (Ithaca: Cornell University Press, 1992), 138. The psychiatrist Kesar' Aleksandrovich Belilovskii (1859–1934) of the Imperial Military-Medical Academy in St. Petersburg argued that the stigmata were, in those cases in which they did not simply represent racial or individual peculiarities, "essentially the symptoms of acquired degeneration: diseases, poor nutrition, life style, occupation, etc." Belilovskii maintained therefore that "whatever the origins of these physical stigmata, not one of them enjoys an organic link with the mental activity, with the intellectual life of the individual." Kesar' A. Belilovskii, *K voprosu ob antropologicheskom tipe prestupnika* (St. Petersburg: Ia. I. Liberman, 1895), 121.

themselves in the individual for the same reason: because of physical exhaustion, and such exhaustion proceeds from a life of hardship, from poverty.[65]

A few years later, the psychiatrist Lev Gregor'evich Orshanskii (1866–?) similarly argued that the factors leading to deformity in the skull were "an abnormal uterine position of the infant, rickets in the mother, syphilis, alcoholism, blows suffered during pregnancy, and arduous physical labor. And precisely these are the conditions that virtually constitute the everyday life of the lower orders of the people."[66]

In 1911, Ivan Stelletskii was even more explicit than his colleagues in his interpretation of the stigmata. The physical deformities of the deviant were not simply transmuted evidence of unhealthy and destructive environments; they constituted a map of the deformities of the body social: "Those stigmata, divisions, asymmetries, and deformities, which Lombroso mistakenly believed to be the features of beasts or savages, were in fact nothing more that the imprint of the extreme division of contemporary society into all manner of partitions."[67] The stigmata offered not merely a legibility of deviance; to the discerning eye they were the very incarnation of social disharmony.

Lombroso's Russian audience thus offered a radical reinterpretation of his criminal stigmata. For Lombroso, they amounted to a marker of biological distinction, indisputable proof of the criminal's fundamental otherness. As signifiers of atavism, the stigmata served to jettison the criminal not merely out of the framework of normal society in the present but also out of the historical trajectory along which that society had traveled. For Lombroso's Russian audience, by contrast, it was precisely deformity that demonstrated the empirical links binding the individual together with the wider society of which he or she was a part. The stigmata served to highlight the status of the deviant as a contemporary of modern Russia. Degeneration theory could thus satisfy the appetite of positivistic minds for intelligibility and legibility in the social world while avoiding the metaphysics of Lombroso's atavistic theories.

The Born Criminal and the "Struggle for Existence"

The rejection of the notion that criminals constituted a separate evolutionary species and the insistence on the empirical links between individual criminals and the wider social order that had shaped them still coexisted,

---

65   Stancheva [Rakovskii], "*Neschastnen'kie*," 29.

66   Lev G. Orshanskii, *Kriminal'naia antropologiia i sudebnaia meditsina* (St. Petersburg: G. Pozharov, 1903), 10. For the same argument, see Nikolai S. Lobas, *Ubiitsy. (Nekotorye cherty psikhofiziki prestupnikov)* (Moscow: I. D. Sytin, 1913), 72–138.

67   M. [sic—Ivan] I. Stelletskii, "K voprosu o vyrozhdenii. (Teoriia degeneratsii)," *Zhurnal nevropatologii i psikhiatrii*, nos. 5–6 (1911): 822.

however, with a representation of certain criminals as radically other. This otherness, almost a form of exotica, continued to exert a marked fascination over the minds of contemporary Russians. In a review of Émile Laurent's *Les habitués des prisons,* which had been published in Paris in 1890, Dril' represented the prison population as a form of Darwinian refuse governed by diseased heredity: "A significant part of all that which did not cope with today's severe struggle for life, all those who became maimed and corrupted by it, who became deflected from the correct path, and in so doing frequently, hereditarily deflected from it—they all accumulate in the prison and constitutes its peculiar and unfortunate population."[68] Dril' referred to some prisoners as "born criminals." The term was a controversial one, contaminated by Lombroso's atavistic theories of evolutionary distinctiveness, and had been the subject of sustained attacks at the Brussels congress in 1893.[69]

Like the majority of his Russian colleagues, Dril' was keen to distance himself from Lombroso's assertion that atavistic criminals were "naturally" predisposed to criminal acts. He pointed out that criminality was a juridical concept subject to change, whereas Lombroso's arguments were biological and medicinal, and that these very different categories should not be conflated. Moreover, in challenging Lombroso Dril' noted that "we must understand the concept of the born criminal to be an individual who under all and any imaginable conditions will necessarily become a criminal."[70] In 1900, Rakovskii reformulated the "inevitability" in terms of a probability greater than that which would obtain for a healthy individual. Although in his opinion no inevitable causality existed to link the degenerative condition with the criminal act, "bodily and spiritual degeneration do open up the path to crime. . . . Degeneration does not determine that an individual will commit a crime; it only makes him weaker."[71]

This weakness, in the form of mental and moral defects such as pathologies of the will, amounted to a predisposition to crime, as Vorotynskii explained in a public lecture delivered at the University of Kazan in 1900: "Hereditary degenerates . . . as predisposed natures carry in themselves the features of a pathological organization, which under corresponding unfavorable circumstances can either put them on the path of criminal activity or make them candidates for insane asylums."[72] Kovalevskii likewise argued that born criminals did indeed exist in the sense that degenerate children had "inherited a corrupted biopsychological constitution, a diseased heredity"

68   Dmitrii A. Dril', "Tiuremnyi mir," *Russkaia mysl'* (February 1891): part 2, 63.
69   Dril', "Chto govorilos'," pt. 1, 90–5.
70   Ibid., 98.
71   Stancheva [Rakovskii], *"Neschastnen'kie,"* 43.
72   Bronislav I. Vorotynskii, "Biologicheskie i sotsial'nye faktory prestupnosti," *Zhurnal Ministerstva Iustitsii* (September 1901): 11.

that made them capricious, of low intelligence, insensible to affection, and unable to perform successfully at school.[73] What degeneration theory promoted, therefore, was the idea of a class that distinguished itself not by the inevitability of its criminal acts but by its intensified predisposition to them. In Kovalevskii's view, they were set apart "because their moral capacities reveal significant and acute deviations, which do indeed set them apart from the rest of society and unite them into a particular class of people, what is known as a criminal class."[74]

As chapter one demonstrated, however, Russian physicians held persistent doubts about medicine's capacity to discharge its positivist mission to detect and scrutinize a morphology of deviance. They continued to fear that criminals might give the appearance of normality while harboring a defective moral and mental constitution that would lead them to commit crimes. Pathologies of the will, which weakened the criminal's ability to resist the satisfaction of his or her immediate and irrational impulses, were one example of such a defect.[75] The publication in 1884 of Théodule Ribot's (1839–1916) influential study, *Les maladies de la volonté*, which was immediately translated into Russian, heralded the rise to prominence of the theory of will pathologies within psychiatry and criminology. Ribot argued that consciously directed willpower was the last of the mental qualities appropriated phylogenetically in mankind's slow evolution from savagery. Consequently, it was the most fragile of his mental powers and the first to disappear in individuals afflicted by mental disorders of an organic (that is, degenerate) type.[76] For Ribot, the will was the crucial element that enabled normal individuals to inhibit their automatic urges and adapt positively to the environment.[77]

By the 1890s, will pathologies had become a staple part of discussions of degenerative criminality. In 1894, Chizh observed that "an underdevelopment of the higher feelings, a weakness of the mental powers and the will

---

73   Kovalevskii, *Vyrozhdenie i vozrozhdenie*, 241–45.

74   Ibid., 248. Orshanskii agreed, "It is precisely degeneration that unites people who are quite different in terms of blood and background, but who are related by the process of disintegration, degeneration. Degeneration and heredity, as the internal foundations of the criminal, and social, i.e., economic and political-moral as the external conditions, this is the ground on which what we term crime takes place!" Orshanskii, *Kriminal'naia antropologiia*, 32.

75   Mintslov had already advanced this argument in his essay of 1881: "There is no doubt that the proven intellectual and moral underdevelopment of the criminal entails an inevitable weakening, if not the complete disappearance, of their will and more or less the complete absence of those altruistic impulses that play such an important part for the normal person." Mintslov, "Osobennosti klassa prestupnikov," 234.

76   Théodule Ribot, *Les maladies de la volonté* (Paris: G. Ballière, 1883). The Russian translation was Teodul' Ribo, *Bolezni voli*, trans. from the French under ed. Dr. B. V. Tomashevskii (St. Petersburg: S. S. Riabchenko, 1884). Philippe Pinel (1745–1826) had explored diseases of the will in his *Traité medico-philosophique sur l'aliénation mentale, ou la manie* of 1801, which was translated into Russian as F. Pinel', *Vrachebno-filosofskoe nachertanie dushevnykh boleznei* (Moscow: I. Roshetnikov, 1829).

77   Ruth Harris, *Murders and Madness: Medicine, Law, and Society in the Fin de Siècle* (Oxford: Oxford University Press, 1989), 40.

are entirely indicative features of the defective mental organization of many criminals."[78] A year later, Dril' also made reference to that dangerous group of individuals "who are usually distinguished by . . . the intensified development of their emotional impulses, *which dominate over their will and do not enable them to balance and accommodate their interests with the interests of their environment and, on the contrary, drive them to resist the development and flourishing of the latter.*"[79] Particularly disturbing about these will pathologies was their coexistence with other mental faculties that appeared completely in order, as Vorotynskii explained in 1900:

> Different affections of the will can exist independently of affections of reason, referring to the existence of a particular form of insanity, "manie sans délire," i.e., of a mental disturbance in which the stricken are capable of correct, logical, and sensible reasoning but at the same time perpetrate a whole series of insane, impermissible, and criminal acts.[80]

For it was the resultant social deviance that concentrated minds on the phenomenon of will pathologies. In an article published in *Russkaia mysl'* in 1912, Pavel Liublinskii agreed that degeneration led to a weakening of willpower and an increased susceptibility to vice: "The majority of the representatives of this class are not susceptible to moral or intellectual pressures and are deprived of willpower and the capacity to restrain themselves, such that even knowing of the criminal nature of their actions, they are unable to resist."[81] Three years later, Susanna Ukshe echoed these comments, affirming the existence of

> a group of degenerates who are unbalanced in the area of willpower and who frequently enter into conflict with the law. There can be no doubt that the power of an individual to resist negative external conditions is directly proportionate to the degree of perfection of his psychophysical organization [*psikhofizicheskaia organizatsiia*] and that a person who is sick and unbalanced will find it extraordinarily difficult to orient his activities in accordance with the law.

For Ukshe, the quality of an individual's "psychophysical organization" was the most eloquent indicator of his or her prospects of leading a life of normality and legality.[82]

78   Chizh, *Prestupnyi chelovek pered sudom vrachebnoi nauki*, 12.
79   Dmitrii Dril', *Prestupnost' i prestupniki (ugolovno-psikhologicheskie etiudy)* (St. Petersburg: Ia. Kantorovich, 1895), 177.
80   Vorotynskii, "Psikho-fizicheskie osobennosti," 93.
81   Pavel I. Liublinksii, "Novaia mera bor'by s vyrozhdeniem i prestupnost'iu," *Russkaia mysl'*, no. 3 (1912): part 2, 53.
82   Susanna A. Ukshe, "Vyrozhdenie, ego rol' v prestupnosti i mery bor'by s nim," *Vestnik obshchestvennoi gigieny, sudebnoi i prakticheskoi meditsiny*, no. 42 (June 1915): 808, 800.

The notion of a criminal predisposition allowed Russian criminologists and psychiatrists to soft-pedal the claim of radical otherness that underpinned Lombroso's understanding of the deviant. Criminals were indeed distinct from the mass of healthy individuals, but the differences might often remain latent unless catalyzed into action by social forces. When attempting to explain the conversion of a predisposition to criminality into its active pursuit, theorists often invoked Darwin's metaphor of the "struggle for existence." Kovalevskii observed in 1903 that the children of those afflicted with the degenerate condition were born with "weak, defective, debilitated psychophysical constitutions. When they . . . take part in the struggle for existence . . . they are unable to find sufficient strength within themselves for a determined struggle for the right to live, and so they swiftly embark on the slippery path of vice and crime."[83] Orshanskii explained that "criminals suffer from all the diseases that erode the health of the mass of the people, but they suffer to such an extent that they necessarily become unable to adapt to the given order of things."[84]

Degeneration theory thus invested the criminal with an ambiguous status. On the one hand, a defective biopsychological constitution marked the criminal out from the normal and healthy majority of society; on the other hand, the sources of the defectiveness were irreducibly social. The criminal class delineated the contours of a healthy body social by embodying all the biopsychological disorder of which society wished to cleanse itself. Yet the forms of threatening abnormality were firmly embedded in the social order in a dual sense. Society bore a historical responsibility both for the original genesis of criminal predispositions and for allowing conditions to obtain that then converted this predisposition into criminal activity. In 1890, Dril' remarked, "Under the influence of harmful education and unhealthy living conditions, the terribly unfortunate and organically hapless permanent population of the prison gradually emerges and takes shape in an environment of diseased clans and families who are, in their turn, *for the most part* the inevitable product of societal currents, injustice, and evil . . . that facilitate the physical and moral degeneration of the breed."[85]

Society's Children

Within the theoretical elasticity of the degenerative schema, emphasis was everything. Heredity might be the incarnation of current social conditions or it might incubate the effects of social conditions that obtained in a more

---

83 Kovalevskii, *Vyrozhdenie i vozrozhdenie*, 287.
84 Orshanskii, *Kriminal'naia antropologiia*, 25.
85 Dril', *Tiuremnyi mir*, 79.

distant past. The force and scale of the hereditary component thus served as an inverse projection of the force and scale of society's immediate responsibility for its own criminal class. Broad subscription to the view that crime was the product of both biopsychological and environmental factors left a great deal of interpretative space for the practitioners of the human sciences to concentrate on either the diseased heredity of criminals or the pathological social environment that had spawned them. In the Russian case, a broad if uneven consensus emerged that individual pathologies had empirically verifiable social origins. If the defective biopsychological constitution of the criminal was ultimately traceable to defects in the organization of the social order, crime itself became a symptom of broader social pathologies, as Dril' evocatively wrote:

> Young and adult criminals are born and live in the midst of society; they are its reflection; they are "the flesh of its flesh, and the bones of its bones." Under the influence of peculiarities in the living conditions created by society, their peculiar natures are prepared and develop, pushing them, under certain circumstances to crime.[86]

Indeed, implicit in the entire body of criminological writings discussed in this chapter was the notion that social forces were to blame for the genesis of criminal impulses. Yet the "buffer" of heredity enabled many theorists to sidestep the direct question of contemporary society's complicity in the existence of criminality. References to social hardship or the challenges of industrial modernity were discussed, but without the identification of a particular agency that could mitigate them. By the turn of the century, however, clinicians were ever more explicit in their articulation of a language not simply of social causation but of social responsibility. Kovalevskii insisted, for example, upon the essential indivisibility of the criminal and the social order in language that reflected this shift in emphasis:

> We are the flesh of our parents' flesh, we are the blood of the society's blood in which we lived and were raised. . . . It is true that criminals are guilty of violating society's interests. But are not the parents guilty who gave birth to them with a nervous system that expressed a malevolent will? Is not the society guilty which permitted their education in an environment of corruption, drunkenness, poverty, prostitution, thievery, and so on?[87]

Bekhterev agreed that the individual criminal was little more than a biopsychological distillation of the environmental forces that had shaped his birth

---

86   Dril', *Prestupnost' i prestupniki*, 247.
87   Kovalevskii, *Vyrozhdenie i vozrozhdenie*, 238.

and upbringing: "All of society, or more precisely its entire structure of life, its system of socioeconomic conditions, its precepts, customs of a moral and legal character, and the conditions of cohabitation . . . are responsible for the crimes of individuals."[88]

The shift in emphasis here from an analysis of the power of the environment to inscribe itself in the biopsychological constitution of the individual to impassioned denunciation can perhaps be captured by the treatment of the "Jukes" family history in Russian criminology. In 1877, Richard Louis Dugdale (1841–83) published his influential book *The Jukes: A Study in Crime, Pauperism, Disease, and Heredity*.[89] Dugdale had spent a year investigating county jails for the New York Prison Association and identified a certain family, which he gave the fictitious name "Jukes," as being pervaded by criminal instincts and hereditary degeneracy. An alcoholic mother, Ada, had spawned a line of criminals, alcoholics, and drunks who were notorious within the New York State penitentiary system. Dugdale's study achieved international standing and was repeatedly cited by criminologists as evidence of the primacy of heredity over environment in the etiology of crime.[90] In his study of 1884, Dril', for example, hailed Dugdale's excellent work as "the most striking example of heredity criminality, poverty, and corruption."[91] Yet by the end of the period under investigation here, the story of the Jukes family received a very different interpretation. Writing in 1915, Ukshe took "the classical example of Ada Jukes, which caused such a sensation and strengthened calls for repressive measures in the struggle with degeneration."

> What was the cause of the degradation of that family? Let us assume that, on the basis of the alcoholism of its progenitor, grandmother Ada, they were degenerates and the entire family constitutes a degenerative type. But even independently of the hereditary influence, socioeconomic factors played their part here: if Ada Jukes was an alcoholic, a thief, and a vagrant, it is not difficult to imagine the conditions in which her children were born and raised, what kinds of mental and physical torments they had to endure from earliest childhood. . . . And the result is obvious: beggars, prostitutes, and thieves. . . . On the basis of this example, it is difficult to ascertain which factor played a greater part: the individual or the social. They are so closely related: one factor supplements the other, the one is elicited by the other.[92]

88   Bekhterev, *Ob'ektivno-psikhologicheskii metod*, 56.
89   Richard Dugdale, *The Jukes: A Study in Crime, Pauperism, Disease, and Heredity* (New York: Putnam, 1877).
90   For a discussion of Dugdale's research and its subsequent influence, see Charles E. Rosenberg, "The Bitter Fruit: Heredity, Disease, and Social Thought," in Rosenberg, *No Other Gods: On Science and American Social Thought* (Baltimore: Johns Hopkins University Press, 1961), 45–46.
91   Dril', *Maloletnie prestupniki*, 295.
92   Ukshe, *Vyrozhdenie*, 815.

Although individual and social factors might be indistinguishable in the case of a particular individual's reasons for committing crime, Ukshe found no difficulty in identifying the original cause in broader terms: "Even if it seems that a particular crime was committed exclusively because of the psychological anomalies [of the criminal], here too on the basis of degeneration socioeconomic forces play their part, for degeneration is elicited principally by negative socioeconomic conditions: illness, hunger, the absence of hygiene, intoxication . . .—these are the chief factors of degeneration, and their fundamental and primary cause is want and the contemporary social order."[93]

The startling paradox was that Lombroso's identification of pathological heredity, which had originally distinguished criminal deviants from any social context in which they acted, had now become converted into an indictment of the social order, even when the social factors promoting degeneration were no longer at hand. Heredity had effectively become little more than the mediated expression of social factors.

Crime in an Era of Social Reform

Several factors explain this concentration on social influences at the root of biopsychological anomalies in the criminal. First, there was a discernible theoretical impulse within degenerational accounts of deviance to investigate the relationship between individual disorders and the wider society in which they had emerged. Second, the widespread ambivalence regarding the empire's experience of modernization tended to generate arguments that expressed dissatisfaction or disdain for the social conditions of contemporary Russia. These grew louder over the course of the late imperial period as the forces of capitalism and urbanization began to change the face of Russian society and generated concentrations of poverty and squalor in Russia's cities.

Perhaps most important, however, society's responsibility for crime also signaled its power ultimately to eliminate crime. Nye has noted that the French rejection of atavism was championed by clinicians who, as a result of a neo-Lamarckian perspective, could not accept that progressive evolution had completely come to an end for an entire class of humanity.[94] In his internationally influential work of 1888 *Dégénérescence et criminalité*, the psychiatrist Charles Féré (1852–1907) had argued that unhealthy social environments, to which individuals necessarily adapted in pathological ways, could be improved such that they would come to exert a positive and healthy influence over their inhabitants. The rejection of atavism in

93   Ibid., 816.
94   Nye, *Crime, Madness, and Politics,* 125.

favor of degeneration resulted in the application to crime of the etiological arguments discussed in the previous chapter. Russian clinicians declared the contemporary social order to be the source of the disease of crime; and social reform the cure. In his attack on the Lombrosian school in 1890, Petr Narkizovich Obninskii (1837–1904) condemned the "hopeless theory of born criminality" and contended optimistically that the new emphasis on the crimonogenic properties of the environment was

> a bright and cheerful [theory], which once again opens up to the confused practitioners [of the legal system] who had been condemned to inaction a broad range of possibilities of fruitfully taking measures against the factors and stimulants of criminality. The latter have now been born out of the narrow immobile sphere of the physical imperfections and deviations of a given criminal type and into a realm of extrapersonal and social phenomena with which it is possible to conduct a strategic and deliberate struggle and which it is possible to eliminate.[95]

Writing a decade later, Kovalevskii articulated the nature of this struggle. Parental and social responsibility for the actions of criminals conferred not merely "a duty on society to ensure that these people did not harm it, that they were removed from its midst; society's obligation is also to correct those unfortunate individuals and to turn them into law-abiding and useful citizens. But a greater, a higher, and an even more binding obligation was the renovation [*ozdorovlenie*] of society itself, so that it did not give birth to and raise such deformed and unfortunate members."[96]

The application of degeneration theory to the genesis of crime thus held out the possibility of its eventual eradication. If all criminal deviance was understood ultimately to be the result of an unhealthy social environment, the theory contained an important utopian urge for prophylactic improvement; it signposted boundless possibilities for the elimination of crime. That the theory should enjoy such purchase in the minds of contemporary Russian scientists, legal theorists, and clinicians is not surprising given the ethos of the professional disciplines in the post-Emancipation era.

Support for strategic reform of the social order in the interests of a biopsychological improvement of its constituent members was central to the essential Enlightenment belief in human improvement that characterized so much of Russian progressive thought in the second half of the nineteenth and early twentieth centuries. To condemn an entire criminal class of Russians to moral and social oblivion would have been an admission, at least in part, of the limited possibilities of social reform.

---

95 Obninskii, "Illiuzii pozitivizma," 2.
96 Kovalevskii, *Vyrozhdenie i vozrozhdenie*, 239.

It was this optimistic commitment to a transformist perspective that informed the response in Russia to another measure of social defense pioneered in the State of Indiana in the United States and enacted into law in 1907: the forced sterilization of degenerate criminals.[97] The overwhelming majority of Russian commentators expressed deep unease at the policy. Discussing "the Indiana project" in *Pravo* in 1908, prominent liberal jurist Vladimir Nabokov warned that "the advocacy of sterilization might easily lead penal policy to a state of complete savagery. . . . If we brush aside the ethical criteria that have been developed over centuries, we will swiftly return to those measures to which our practical forebears had recourse."[98] The criminologist Aleksandr Aleksandrovich Zhizhilenko (1873–?) was similarly unequivocal: "It goes without saying that the pure measures of sterilization in connection with [dangerous criminals], such as their castration, introduced in Indiana in 1907 should be unequivocally rejected."[99]

Indeed, the vast majority of jurists and psychiatrists remained implacably opposed to the use of forced sterilization as a means of combating degenerate criminality. Writing in *Sovremennaia psikhiatriia* in 1912, the psychiatrist Sergei Aleksandrovich Preobrazhenskii (1878–?) condemned sterilization, countering with an

> understanding of degeneration as a complicated phenomenon, the roots of which lie in the particularities of contemporary culture and its economic foundations. . . . In accordance with such an understanding, the struggle with

97   On the history of sterilization in the United States, see Philip Reilly, *The Surgical Solution: a History of Involuntary Sterilization in the United States* (Baltimore: Johns Hopkins University Press, 1991), 41–55; Edward Larson, *Sex, Race, and Science: Eugenics in the Deep South* (Baltimore: Johns Hopkins University Press, 1995), 18–39. For an informative treatment of the eugenics movement in Russia, see Mark B. Adams, "Eugenics in Russia, 1900–1940," in *The Wellborn Science: Eugenics in Germany, France, Brazil, and Russia*, ed. Adams (New York, Oxford University Press, 1990), 153–216.
98   Vladimir D. Nabokov, "Poslednee slovo kriminalistiki," *Pravo* no. 13 (1908): 807. In 1911, Nikolai N. Lebedev gave a scathing account of measures of forced sterilization in the state of Indiana. "Bor'ba s prestupnost'iu v Amerike. Operativnyi sposob uluchsheniia roda chelovecheskogo," *Vestnik obshchestvennoi gigieny, sudebnoi i prakticheskoi meditsiny* (January 1911): 1–11.
99   Aleksandr A. Zhizhilenko, "Merysotsial'noi zashchity v otnoshenii opasnykh prestupnikov," *Pravo*, no. 37 (1910): 2171. One of Zhizhilenko's colleagues was, however, decidedly equivocal in his discussion of sterilization. Liublinskii had been invited to Indiana to attend one of the sterilization operations undertaken in the state penitentiary and was at pains to stress that the operation had nothing to do with castration, was extremely brief and painless, and a large number of convicts willingly underwent it. Liublinskii cast himself in the role of a dispassionate observer who summarized the ethical arguments both for and against sterilization but was clearly sympathetic to the vigor and sense of purpose with which the United States was pursuing its struggle with degenerate criminality, in contrast to the vacillation of its European counterparts. Russia, for example, merely opined endlessly about the dangers of degeneration without implementing any measures to combat it. Liublinskii, "Novaia mera bor'by s vyrozhdeniem," 56.

degeneration depends on an amelioration of social conditions. The latter can be arranged such that they can prevent the appearance of mass morbid symptoms [*massovye boleznennye simptomy*] such as degeneration. The prophylactics of degeneration [*profilaktika vyrozhdeniia*] should be social and should not boil down to a form of social hygiene [*sotsial'naia gigiena*], to a struggle with the mass of sick individuals, by means of coercive sterilization.[100]

Sterilization foreclosed on the possibility of reform and left unaddressed the risks the criminal posed to the rest of society. Furthermore, it amounted to an acknowledgement of the state's limited power to forge change on the human material of its own population except by the crudest of means. Yet coercion had many faces; it could mean the physical alteration of a deviant's body or the reconstitution of his psychology.[101] For there was another policy option that retained the intelligentsia's tutelary ethos and offered the benighted delinquent an opportunity for self-improvement: social isolation and corrective detention.

The "Socially Dangerous"

The theoretical reinforcement of the optimistic impulse to reform still left an important issue unaddressed. Criminology necessarily had to confront the problem of what to do with those individuals whose moral and mental faculties were so degraded that they posed a threat to the health of society. Not only did these deviants threaten to inseminate broader society with their diseased heredity, they also posed an immediate danger to the well-being of their contemporaries. Across the continent, classical deterrence theory, which posited an essentially rational criminal making calculations based on self-interest before engaging in criminal activity, gradually gave way to a theory of punishment based on the concept of "social defense," which was pioneered in Germany in the 1890s.

Richard Wetzell has traced the increasing influence of a utilitarian idea of protecting society that was championed by a reformist movement of the German legal establishment. Pioneered by the law professor Franz von Liszt (1851–1919), the movement charged that the existing German penal system, with its fixed prison sentences prescribed by the penal code, was ineffective in protecting society from crime. Liszt and his fellow reformers argued that this goal could best be achieved by a criminal justice system in which the punishment fit the criminal rather than the crime. Accordingly,

---

100   Sergei A. Preobrazhenskii, "Khirurgicheskaia profilaktika vyrozhdeniia," *Sovremennaia psikhiatriia* 6, no. 2 (February 1912): 115.
101   For the classic statement of this argument, see Michel Foucault, *Discipline and Punish: The Birth of the Prison*, trans. Alan Sheridan (New York: Random House, 1977).

they proposed a system of individualized punishments in which first-time offenders would receive suspended sentences for the purpose of specific deterrence, repeat offenders who seemed both in need of and capable of rehabilitation would be subject to a prison sentence for the purpose of reha-bilitation; and repeat offenders who seemed incorrigible would be subject to indefinite detention for the sake of incapacitation.[102]

Liszt's influence in Russia was substantial; his works were translated and eagerly discussed by Russian criminologists and psychiatrists.[103] In 1901, for example, Vorotynskii summarized Liszt's findings that existing penal policy made no impact on the rate of recidivism and even encouraged it: "Such neg-ative results from the application of the existing system of penal repression flow from the fact that we currently judge and punish the crime rather than the criminal according to his crime, as the new positive school demands."[104]

It should not be surprising that Lombroso's disciples were themselves at the forefront of calls for the introduction of social defense.[105] More surpris-ingly, however, as Nye and Harris have each noted, the idea of social de-fense became very popular and influential in France, where the medico-legal establishment had spearheaded the onslaught against Lombroso's ideas of fixed hereditary criminality in the 1880s and 1890s.[106] In Russia, a similar paradox emerged in which the very psychiatrists and jurists who had em-braced degenerational accounts of the etiology of crime endorsed social de-fense not merely as an unsavory social necessity but as something positively in the interests of the deviant.

The pan-European context that saw the rise to prominence of the idea of social defense coincided with the upsurge of social disorder and political vio-lence that accompanied Russia's entry into the twentieth century. Neuberger

102   Wetzell, *Inventing the Criminal*, 75.

103   Frants von List [Franz von Liszt], *Nakazanie i ego tseli* (St. Petersburg: I. Iurovskii, 1895); idem, *Prestuplenie kak sotsial'no-patologicheskoe iavlenie* (St. Petersburg: A. V. Orlov, 1903); idem, *Uchebnik ugolovnogo prava. Obshchaia chast'*, trans. from 12th German ed. by R. El'iashchevich (Moscow: A. I. Mamontov, 1903). See also the enthusiastic review of Liszt's ideas of social defense in Vladimir V. Przheval'skii, *Prof. Frants List i ego vozzreniia na prestuplenie i nakazanie* (St. Petersburg: M. M. Stasiulevich, 1895).

104   Vorotynskii, "Biologicheskie i sotsial'nye faktory prestupnosti," 21–22.

105   In his influential *Criminal Sociology*, first published in 1897, Enrico Ferri (1856–1929) declared that "punishment ought not to be the visitation of a crime by retribution, but rather a defense of society adapted to the danger personified by the criminal." Enrico Ferri, *Criminal Sociology* (New York: D. Appleton, 1897), 208. Ferri's major works were translated into Russian and his research was generally understood to be more sophisticated than that of his mentor, Lombroso, because Ferri struck more of a balance between social and biological factors in his analysis of the etiology of crime. See, for example, A. Likhachev, "Novye raboty v oblasti ugolovnoi statistiki i antropologii. Teoriia Ferri," *Grazhdanskoe i ugolovnoe pravo*, no. 3 (1883): 1–24. For translations of Ferri's work see, for example, Enriko Ferri, *Prestuple-nie i prestupniki v nauke i v zhizni* (Odessa: N. Leinenberg, 1890); idem, *Ugolovnaia sotsi-ologiia*, with a foreword by E. Ferri and D. Dril', trans. from 4th Italian ed. (St. Petersburg: Prosveshchenie, 1910–12).

106   Harris, *Murderers and Madness*, 3; Nye, *Crime, Madness, and Politics*, 191.

has examined the "moral panic" surrounding the issue of hooliganism in the period from 1900 to the outbreak of the First World War. Educated Russian society was shocked by the combination of easy violence and lack of social deference that they encountered on the streets of their towns and cities at the hands of lower class men.[107] Politically motivated crime also increased enormously, beginning with the revival of the terrorist campaign directed against servitors of the state by a collection of left-wing extremists and culminating in the inchoate violence of the 1905 Revolution and the bloody years of virtual civil war that raged across the empire until 1907.[108] Anna Geifman has calculated that during a one-year period beginning in October 1905, a total of 3,611 government officials of all ranks were killed and wounded throughout the empire.[109]

Such an explosion of criminality concentrated minds in Russia, as elsewhere in Europe, on the question of whether the existing legal system was adequate to the task of containing the disorder.[110] Criminal anthropology set great store by its transcendence of the notions of retribution and punishment and its concern with what Dril', in 1893, had termed "the necessity of protecting society from the evil of crime."[111] Vorotynskii declared that the great achievement of the criminal anthropologists was that they "positively demonstrated that we should not see crime as an abstract juridical concept but a pathological feature of social life." A medicalized understanding of criminal deviance logically invoked a medical language of prophylactics when identifying the penal measures society might take to protect itself from a particularly inveterate criminal class:

> No one argues any longer that there do exist criminals with morally corrupted natures, individuals who are mentally deformed from birth. Their criminal activities are determined by their unfortunate heredity, their deformed psychophysical constitution. These individuals should not be punished but rather corrected or cured; they should not be terrorized with severe penalties but simply isolated, as it were, removed from everyday life with a view to protecting society from their harmful influence.[112]

---

107   Neuberger, *Hooliganism*.

108   For descriptions of the massive levels of violence and social disorder, see Abraham Ascher, *The Revolution of 1905: Russia in Disarray* (Stanford: Stanford University Press, 1988).

109   Anna Geifman, *Thou Shalt Kill: Revolutionary Terrorism in Russia, 1894–1917* (Princeton: Princeton University Press, 1993), 21. See also Jonathan Daly, "Political Crime in Late Imperial Russia," *Journal of Modern History* 74, no. 1 (March 2002): 62–100.

110   For an institutional history of the Russian penal system, see Peter H. Solomon, ed., *Reforming Justice in Russia, 1864–1994: Power, Culture, and the Limits of Legal Order* (New York: M. E. Sharpe, 1996); Bruce F. Adams, *The Politics of Punishment: Prison Reform in Russia, 1863–1917* (DeKalb: Northern Illinois University Press, 1996).

111   Dril', "Chto govorilos'," pt. 2 (March 1893): part 2: 60.

112   Vorotynskii, "Psikho-fizicheskie osobennosti," 101. Such discussions were, of course, accompanied by detailed arguments identifying the scale of a criminal's responsibility

As a consequence, Vorotynskii argued a few years later, "the struggle with crime should express itself primarily in terms of measures of a preventive character [*predupreditel'nogo kharaktera*]."[113] Kovalevskii agreed that the fight against crime should not only be directed at the removal of social causes of degeneration such as poverty and alcoholism. "Born criminals with inherited diseased natures" should, "in view of the extreme danger they pose to the wider society, be isolated from the entire world in special institutions, in special prisons."[114]

Isolation was generally framed in paternalistic terms as a removal of the deviant from the unhealthy or demanding environment that fostered the sustenance—and the genesis—of the diseased criminal condition. In an article published in 1912, Gustav Vladimirovich Reitts (1876–?), a doctor at the hospital of St. Nikolai the Miracle Worker in St. Petersburg, argued that the existing prison system was in no position to deal with pathological criminals because "the source of their conflict with society lay within them and is hereditary, unresponsive to external influences; the current penal system is designed with normal, psychologically healthy individuals in mind, not the ill and half-deranged." The answer, for Reitts, was the construction "of a specific and artificial environment, adapted to the individuality of the criminal, in which all the harmful influences of contemporary life would be removed and in which the subject could exist without harming either himself or others." Yet, paradoxically, it was precisely such a benevolent approach to the treatment of the individual deviant that justified "not a brief but a prolonged period of residence in this environment."[115] Even Bekhterev, one of the most eloquent critics of the iniquities of the tsarist social order, affirmed in 1912 that although society's culpability for the genesis of deviance deprived it of the right to punish criminals, it was entitled to "isolate" those who posed a major threat to its well-being:

> In some cases in the interests of education and in others in the interests of treatment, but under no circumstances in order to punish, . . . if there is nothing from which the criminals can be cured or nothing about which they can be educated, as in the case of political crimes, then isolate them if it is helpful, but do not hang them and execute them: you do not have the right![116]

---

for his or her actions, a question that had been problematized since the profession's acceptance in the 1870s of various forms of diminished responsibility such as moral insanity. See Bekhterev, *Ob"ektivno-psikhologicheskii metod*, 62; Vladimir F. Chizh, *Uchebnik psikhiatrii* (St. Petersburg—Kiev: Sotrudnik, 1911), 318; Dril', *Prestupnost'*, 286.

113   Vorotynskii, "Biologicheskie i sotsial'nye faktory prestupnosti," 24.

114   Kovalevskii, *Vyrozhdenie i vozrozhdenie*, 327, 356.

115   Gustav V. Reitts, "Patologicheskaia prestupnost' i umen'shennaia vmeniaemost'," *Sovremennaia psikhiatriia* (June 1912): 439.

116   Bekhterev, *Ob"ektivno-psikhologicheskii metod*, 64.

Zhizhilenko argued in a lengthy article entitled "Measures of Social Defense Relating to Dangerous Criminals," published in the weekly legal journal *Pravo* in 1910, that the degree of the individual's legal responsibility was, in the terms of this new criminal policy, only of consequence in as much as it could "testify to the natural impulses within the criminal. Of particular interest therefore are the criminal's way of life and the conditions under which his activity has occurred." Although Zhizhilenko did concede that such measures had to take account of the right of the individual to freedom, the intellectual force of his argument was decidedly draconian and illiberal: the release of the criminal "cannot be determined by the fact that he might be forgiven but only by the fact that he no longer poses a danger." Essentially, therefore, "protective measures should not be of a fixed term, as they are in the case of punishment, as it is impossible to discern in advance when the danger will cease."[117]

Some were alive to the risks of such a policy. In 1910, Nabokov cautioned against the indiscriminate use of the term "socially dangerous" in the absence of a strengthened *Rechtsstaat* in Russia. He reminded his audience that Russians were all too familiar with the state's penchant for labels such as "unreliable," "individuals harmful for public peace," and the "harmful and corrupt members of village societies." "We know," he declared, "what preventive measures can turn into when applied to individuals deemed by certain institutions to be 'dangerous.'" As a consequence, the notion of "socially dangerous" could not be allowed to shape penal policy in the absence of a consolidation of individual rights within society, otherwise the result would be "a deformed deviation from the functioning of a *Rechtsstaat*."[118] Yet even Nabokov remained convinced that the strategic, precise, and measured use of the term "socially dangerous" would minimize the opportunity for its abuse and would represent a significant advance on the current clumsy and indiscriminate penal policy, which fostered recidivism in the empire's prisons on a massive scale.[119]

Indeed, part of the ethical justification for indefinite preventive detention was paradoxically a continuing belief in the essential reformability of deviants. Zhizhilenko proposed the construction of labor colonies "in which dangerous recidivists could be accommodated. Inasmuch as these individuals show themselves to be accessible to corresponding forms of influence, we should not lose hope that they might be restored to an honest way of life, and therefore the regime in these institutions should be organized such that it allows for their possible correction."[120] In the final analysis, for all

---

117   Zhizhilenko, "Mery sotsial'noi zashchity," 2169, 2168.
118   Vladimir D. Nabokov, *Ob "opasnom sostoianii" prestupnika kak kriterii mer sotsial'noi zashchity* (St. Petersburg: Obshchestvennaia pol'za, 1910), 29–30.
119   Ibid., 36–37.
120   Zhizhilenko, "Mery sotsial'noi zashchity," 2171.

the Russians' rejection of the fixed biological determinism of Lombroso's atavistic theories of criminality, their identification of a criminal disposition, which in conjunction with an unhealthy or challenging environment drove an individual to crime, resulted in calls for very similar penal policies. The difference between the Italian school and the Russian criminal anthropologists and psychiatrists lay in the question of the reformability of the deviant. For Lombroso and many of his disciples, the two options available to lawmakers were an expression of fatalism: either capital punishment or deportation.[121] By contrast, the Russian commitment to social reform extended to the fervent belief that virtually no criminals were immune to healing influences, coercive or otherwise. Although these influences might never effect a complete moral or psychological cure, they would at least be able to inhibit the conversion of a criminal predisposition into action.

Strategies of Social Hygiene

Criminal anthropology in the Russian *fin-de-siècle* embodied the tension within contemporary discourse between prophesies of impending disaster on the one hand and a validation of the power of science and reason to avert calamity on the other. The human sciences conjured visions of biopsychological demons threatening society and then optimistically pointed the way to defeat them. The way forward comprised two important theoretical impulses. The first was an attempt to identify threats to social stability and progress, represented by those whose biopsychological predisposition impelled them to engage in criminal acts detrimental to the well-being of the body social. The second was an acknowledgement that society was ultimately the source of these disorders, and so the body social, which Russian psychiatrists and criminologists sought to defend from deviance, had itself spawned the criminal delinquents that threatened it. These arguments resulted in calls for two related measures, each indebted to an abiding belief in the capacity of rationality and science to reorder not simply the structures of society but also the biopsychological material that constituted its population. The first measure, examined in chapter two, was reform of the socioeconomic conditions that were understood both to unleash the degenerative syndrome and then to drive biopsychologically weakened individuals to acts

---

121   In 1897, Ferri offered a Darwinian justification for capital punishment: "In agreement with natural laws . . . human society should make an artificial selection, by the elimination of anti-social and incongruous individuals." Ferri, *Criminal Sociology*, 170. The Russian rejection of the Malthusian overtones of Darwin's "struggle for existence" meant that such justifications were unlikely to gain much traction in debates over penal policy. Daniel P. Todes, *Darwin without Malthus: The Struggle for Existence in Russian Evolutionary Thought* (Oxford: Oxford University Press, 1989), 44.

of crime. The second measure was the isolation of those with a criminal predisposition in the interests of collective health and the introduction of preventive detention, which was justified in a language of medical prophylactics and therapy. Both theoretical urges, the reform of society and the isolation of the deviant, would, as I will argue, find their apotheosis in the revolutionary project of the Bolsheviks.

4   "Microbes of the Mind"

> In the secrets of the human soul, beyond the sphere of conscious-
> ness, there are hidden mental foundations, capable, in the pres-
> ence of the necessary conditions, of manifesting themselves in life.
>   —Vladimir K. Sluchevskii, 1893

Lev Tolstoi's *War and Peace,* published in 1869, contains an arresting scene
depicting the lynching of a young man. Vereshchagin stands accused of disseminating defeatist literature in Moscow as Napoleon's army sweeps east-
ward. On the eve of the city's fall in September 1812, a crowd of fearful
and panicked Muscovites assembles in front of the residence of the city's
governor, Count Rostopchin. Disconcerted by the crowd's unpredictable
and riotous potential, Rostopchin pronounces the prisoner responsible for
Moscow's surrender and orders his dragoons to cut Vereshchagin down in
front of the crowd. Yet events quickly run out of control:

> "Sabre him!" the dragoon officer almost whispered.
> And one soldier, his face all at once distorted with fury, struck Vereshchagin
> on the head with the blunt side of his sabre.
> "Ah!" cried Vereshchagin in meek surprise, looking round with a frightened
> glance as if not understanding why this was done to him. A similar moan of
> surprise and horror ran through the crowd. "O Lord!" exclaimed a sorrowful
> voice.
> But after the exclamation of surprise that had escaped from Vereshchagin
> he uttered a plaintive cry of pain, and that cry was fatal. The barrier of human
> feeling, strained to the utmost, that had held the crowd in check, suddenly
> broke. The crime had begun and must now be completed. The plaintive moan
> of reproach was drowned by the threatening and angry roar of the crowd. Like

the seventh and last wave that shatters a ship, that last irresistible wave burst from the rear and reached the front ranks, carrying them off their feet and engulfing them all. The dragoon was about to repeat his blow. Vereshchagin with a cry of horror, covering his head with his hands, rushed towards the crowd. The tall youth, against whom he stumbled, seized his thin neck with his hands and, yelling wildly, fell with him under the feet of the pressing struggling crowd.

Some beat and tore at Vereshchagin, others at the tall youth. And the screams of those that were being trampled on and of those who tried to rescue the tall lad, only increased the fury of the crowd. It was a long time before the dragoons could extricate the bleeding youth, beaten almost to death. And for a long time, despite the feverish haste with which the mob tried to end the work that had been begun, those who were hitting, throttling, and tearing at Vereshchagin were unable to kill him, for the crowd pressed from all sides, swaying as one mass with them in the centre and rendering it impossible for them to either kill him or to let him go.

"Hit him with an axe, eh! . . . Crushed? . . . Traitor, he sold Christ . . . Still alive . . . tenacious . . . serve him right! Torture serves a thief right. Use the hatchet! . . . What still alive?"

Only when the victim ceased to struggle and his cries changed to a long-drawn, measured death-rattle, did the crowd around his prostrate, bleeding corpse begin rapidly to change places. Each one came up, glanced at what had been done, and with horror, reproach, and astonishment, pushed back again.[1]

In the last two decades of the nineteenth century, extensive citation and discussion of this scene became almost *de rigueur* in examinations by criminologists, psychiatrists, and psychologists of crowd psychology. In 1882, Nikolai Mikhailovskii cited the scene in full, declaring that he knew of "no other historical or artistic description of the moment when a crowd was stimulated by example that might be compared with these two pages in terms of the expressiveness and subtlety of the work."[2] A decade later, the criminologist Vladimir Konstantinovich Sluchevskii (1844–1926) similarly hailed "one of the most magnificent scenes, depicted in graceful prose, of the life of a crowd." In an 1893 article entitled "The Crowd and Its Psychology," Sluchevskii drew attention to "the powerful rendition of the excitability of the crowd, its credulity, and its bloodthirsty instincts, unleashed under the influence of the victim's cry and the sight of suffering and blood."[3] In 1898,

---

1   Leo Tolstoy, *War and Peace*, trans. Louise Maude and Aylmer Maude (London: Wordsworth Classics, 1993), 705.
2   Nikolai K. Mikhailovskii, "Geroi i tolpa" (1882), *Sochineniia*, 6 vols. (St. Petersburg: Russkoe Bogatstvo, 1896–97), 2:100.
3   Vladimir K. Sluchevskii, "Tolpa i ee psikhologiia," *Knizhki nedeli*, no. 4 (1893): 32.

Vladimir Bekhterev declared that the scene represented a "clear example of the influence of suggestion on the crowd."[4] Finally, in 1903 Nikolai Bazhenov cited the murder of Vereshchagin as "a depiction, superb in its clarity and power, of a mental contagion [*psikhicheskaia zaraza*], intellectual and emotional, which initially appears in one individual, and then seizes an entire group . . . in accordance with psychological law."[5] Sirotkina has demonstrated that the invocation of literary material in psychiatric analyses was a common practice in *fin-de-siècle* Russia.[6] Yet the insistence with which medical and social scientists returned to this particular scene in Tolstoi's *War and Peace* suggests that it had struck a nerve. What was it in this depiction of collective irrationality and destructiveness that contemporaries found so compelling?

The power of the crowd was both real and symbolic. In reality, it was capable of wreaking devastation in the countryside in the form of peasant riots; it could lay waste to entire sections of cities; it could transform itself into a revolutionary mob able to overthrow the existing political and social order. Symbolically, it constituted a distilled expression of mass society—a psychological organism in which, briefly and often violently, the subconscious and irrational sinews unifying populations as a whole were laid bare. For many contemporaries, then, crowds were central constituent phenomena of the modern age, thrust into the intellectual limelight by the French Revolution and Europe's often chaotic and violent experience of the rise of mass politics throughout the nineteenth century.[7] Indeed, the French Revolution, the 1848 revolutions, and the Paris Commune struck many observers as inseparable from the broader evolution of modern societies. They provoked anxiety on the part of educated Europeans, but also a desire to understand the mechanisms by which ideas and feelings spread throughout large agglomerations of human beings.[8] In the second half of the nineteenth century, the disciplines of psychiatry, criminology, and social psychology gradually extended their explanatory models of crowd behavior

---

4   Vladimir M. Bekhterev, *Vnushenie i ego rol' v obshchestvennoi zhizni* (St. Petersburg: K. L. Rikker, 1898), 166.

5   Nikolai N. Bazhenov, *Psikhiatricheskie besedy na literaturnye i obshchestvennye temy* (Moscow: A. I. Mamontov, 1903), 99–100.

6   Irina Sirotkina, *Diagnosing Literary Genius: A Cultural History of Psychiatry in Russia, 1880–1930* (Baltimore: Johns Hopkins University Press, 2002).

7   Colin Lucas, "The Crowd and Politics between *Ancien Régime* and Revolution in France," *Journal of Modern History* 60, no. 3 (September 1988): 421–57; John Plotz, "Crowd Power: Chartism, Carlyle, and the Victorian Public Sphere," *Representations* 70 (Spring 2000): 87–114; Christopher E. Forth, "Intellectuals, Crowds, and the Body Politics of the Dreyfus Affair," *Historical Reflections* 24, no. 1 (1998): 63–91; Gal Gerson, "Liberalism, Welfare, and the Crowd in J. A. Hobson," *History of European Ideas* 30 (2004): 197–215.

8   For this interpretation of the development of mass psychology in France and Italy, see Roger L. Geiger, "Democracy and the Crowd: The Social History of an Idea in France and Italy, 1890–1914," *Societas* 7, no. 1 (Winter 1977): 47–71.

to the seemingly unpredictable, spontaneous, and destructive power of riots, strikes, and the forces of revolution in the age of mass politics.[9]

The study of social psychology enjoyed a particular resonance in late Imperial Russia, when educated society was discussing both the nature of the empire's modernization and the cultural and political forms that might prove adequate to its direction and maintenance. Caught between the apparently endemic threat of violent social revolution and the obduracy of the tsarist state, the empire's liberal modernizing elites struggled to articulate a vision of a harmonious and stable society, in part by identifying the forces impeding its emergence. In this context, theories of social and psychological interaction between individuals should be understood from their very inception as protopolitical metaphor and commentary, increasingly explicit in its deployment, on the challenges and perils of social and political change.

Recognition of the status of moral contagion as a disturbing and prevalent feature of human interaction accommodated a wide range of opinions about the precise mechanism involved in the transmission of mental states from one individual to another and, crucially, about the etiology of phenomenon. In the early 1880s, discussions of moral contagion focused on the spectacular instances of mass hysteria and violence manifest in religious sectarianism and rural unrest. Psychiatrists and psychologists emphasized the backwardness and superstition of the peasant population in order to advance a campaign of national enlightenment and renewal. The phenomenon of moral contagion, or a least its worst manifestations, were frightening but eradicable. However, under the impact of French and Italian studies, which directed clinical attention to the transformative powers wielded by crowds over their constituents, more pessimistic voices began to caution that susceptibility to moral contagion was an inalienable constituent feature of the human condition, to be limited but in no way eliminated by the power of enlightenment. The status of France in particular as the cradle of the Enlightenment and the engine room of the political transformations that had shaken Europe throughout the nineteenth century invested the French experience of urbanization and the rise of mass politics with a special significance for Russian contemporaries. Whereas Russian commentators could hopefully posit a future development for their nation in which the forces of progress would dispel what appeared to be a residue of backwardness, the experience of France was very disconcerting. As French commentators turned their attention to the power of crowds and mobs in both the French Revolution and the Paris Commune, they seemed to be delineating Russia's

9   The disquiet and alarm with which these psychologists and criminologists responded to the rise of the crowd was an expression of their determination to subject it to critical analysis in the interests of both epistemic and actual control of society. See Robert A. Nye, "Two Paths to a Psychology of Social Action: Gustave Le Bon and Georges Sorel," *Journal of Modern History* 45, no. 3 (September 1973): 423.

own future in an age of modernization and revolution. From this perspective, the appropriation of French theories and their integration into Russian domestic concerns is a fascinating context in which to track the intellectual traffic linking late Imperial Russia with its Western neighbors.

Indeed, in the 1890s and partly under the influence of these foreign studies of mass psychology, a tendency emerged to extrapolate a general theory of social interaction from the study of crowds and mobs. The fragmentary and localized nature of rural and feudal society had historically dissipated the transmission of subconscious and irrational forces keeping them (by and large) confined within certain regions of the countryside.[10] Yet the very experience of modernization was generating population concentrations in the urban centers, bound together by the structures of a mass society and mass politics, which facilitated the spread of emotions and states of mind across large expanses of territory, often mediated by the printed word. Seen in these terms, the creation of a modern unified society itself and the rise of mass politics were unavoidably beholden to dark, irrational human instincts. Some medical and legal experts began to believe that far from being the conjoined prize of the progressive intelligentsia, reform and democracy were in fact antithetical. The specter of popular revolt, which had long haunted theories of moral contagion, would find its most emphatic and revealing manifestation in the 1905 Revolution.

Theories of moral contagion provide a fascinating lens through which to trace the mounting despair of an influential group of Russian intellectuals with not just the obstacles to modernity in Russia but also its very promise. The established intelligentsia discourse of national enlightenment in the service of social cohesion began to cede ground to a new discourse that stressed the necessity of circumscribing and containing human freedom. In their intersection with theories of degeneration, clinical discussions of moral contagion were part of the dark underbelly of the optimistic and secular discourse of rational enlightenment, reflective of lingering doubts that reason and order might prove not just elusive, but also illusory.

The Emergence of Social Psychology in Russia

Disciplinary boundaries were decidedly fluid within the late imperial human sciences. The clinicians and theorists who made a significant contribution to the contemporary understanding of moral contagion were drawn from the intersecting fields of psychiatry, criminology, law, and psychology. For this reason, tracing the evolution of theories of moral and mental contagion and their various clinical applications necessarily overruns any particular

---

10   There were of course spectacular exceptions to this rule, such as the Pugachev uprising of the 1770s.

institutional setting or history of discipline-building. For the sake of concision, I have used the term "social psychology" throughout this chapter to designate a series of overlapping disciplinary contributions.

Russian theories of social psychology developed as clinicians and social scientists critically assimilated the principles of Western positivism developed by figures such as Auguste Comte, Herbert Spencer, and John Stuart Mill.[11] The belief that psychological reciprocity constituted the essential and irreducible dynamic of social interaction enjoyed great currency among Russian sociologists at the end of the nineteenth century. Many Russian clinicians and social scientists came to the conclusion that identifying the role of psychological forces was the key to an understanding of both society and history and accordingly turned their attention to the means by which ideas, emotions, and actions pass from one individual to another.

An epidemiological construction of mass psychology developed in parallel with the model of bacteriological epidemiology.[12] In the latter, it was common to separate the process by which an illness is spread from the conditions—hygienic and meteorological—that facilitate contagions. Similarly, educational conditions, alcoholism, religious creeds were said to be factors that could facilitate the contagion of ideas. Indeed, the sciences of bacteriology and epidemiology served as a model for mass psychology, as the former enjoyed great influence following the discovery of a coherent and testable description for the contagion of illnesses. According to the epidemiological approach, the suggestion of ideas, attitudes, or behavioral patterns, whether normal or pathological, is just another instance of contagion. The literature thus mentions not only a *contagium vivum*, but also a *contagium psychicum*, analogous to organic agents of contagion such as microbes, which cause a person's mind to be contaminated with ideas, habits, and attitudes of another person.[13]

11   See, for example, Viktor Kh. Kandinskii, *Obshcheponiatnye psikhologicheskie etiudy* (Moscow: A. Lang, 1881), 168. This argument has been made by Vladimir A. Alekseev and Mikhail A. Maslin, *Russkaia sotsial'naia filosofiia kontsa XIX—nachala XX veka: Psikhologicheskaia shkola* (Moscow: Issledovatel'skii tsentr, 1992), 5–7. See also David Joravsky, *Russian Psychology: A Critical History* (Oxford: Blackwell, 1989). On Western positivism, see J. W. Burrow, *The Crisis of Reason: European Thought, 1848–1914* (New Haven: Yale University Press, 2000); Maurice Mandelbaum, *History, Man, and Reason: A Study in Nineteenth-Century Thought* (Baltimore: Johns Hopkins University Press, 1971); J. D. Y. Peel, *Herbert Spencer: the Evolution of a Sociologist* (London: Heinemann, 1971).

12   Alexandre Métraux, "French Crowd Psychology: Between Theory and Ideology," in *The Problematic Science: Psychology in Nineteenth-Century Thought*, ed. William R. Woodward and Mitchell G. Ash (New York: Praeger, 1982), 285. On the development of bacteriology in Russia, see John F. Hutchinson, "Tsarist Russia and the Bacteriological Revolution," *Journal of the History of Medicine and Allied Sciences* 40, no. 4 (1985): 420–39.

13   The first reference to mental contagion was a thesis by Prosper Lucas entitled *De l'imitation contagieuse ou de la propagation sympathique des névroses et des monomanies* (Paris, 1833). The theme was again picked up by Prosper Despine, who wrote a pamphlet against the current press reporting of crimes, *De la contagion morale. Faits démontrants son existence* (Marseilles: E Camoin, 1870). Despine used the term as an explanation for the spread of identical symptoms of mental illness from a diseased individual to a healthy one.

Writing in 1881, the psychologist Viktor Khrisanfovich Kandinskii (1849–89) was explicit about the analogy of physical and mental epidemics: "Like a contagion [*kontagii*] of smallpox or typhus, a mental disease [*dushevnaia zaraza*] is transmitted from one person to another to a third . . . spreading with ever more power, afflicting an ever greater mass of people, as long as it finds fertile soil. In the past, smallpox and the plague have carried off thousands and tens of thousands of victims and devastated entire countries. Mental epidemics are no less harmful."[14]

Although epidemiology now became the lens through which the phenomenon of mental contagion was seen, the putative referent of 'mental contagion' remained notional since the *contagium psychicum* had not been discovered. In other words, the epidemiological approach only defined the causal agent of mental contagion formally, but not materially.[15] From the late 1880s until the outbreak of the First World War, paradigms of "mental contagion" came to inform theories of mass psychology.

Not only did the mechanism of transmission of psychological states remain elusive, the very terms used to denote it remained unstable and shifting.[16] This conceptual slippage was in part a result of the diverse origins of epidemiological models of crowd behavior. One concept, that of "imitation," was developed from Spencer's conception of primitive learning and Walter Bagehot's explanation of mental unity within sovereignty. The use of imitation—conceived of as an "automatic" instinct—to explain the transmission of social facts became widespread in sociology and social psychology.[17] The related concept of "suggestion" and "suggestibility," which was drawn from the scientific lexicon of hypnosis, was used to denote "unconscious imitation."[18] Initially, then, imitation and suggestion had separate origins from the strictly pathological application of mental contagion. However, and this is essential to the development of this discourse in Russia, the distinctions between the

14   Kandinskii, *Obshcheponiatnye psikhologicheskie etiudy,* 153–54.

15   Alexandre Métraux points here to perhaps the decisive weakness in the epidemiological approach and the reason why its interpretative power ultimately ceded ground to the sociological and psychiatric. Métraux, "French Crowd Psychology," 286.

16   George Dumas, "Contagion mentale: épidémies mentales, folies collectives, folies grégaires," *Revue Philosophique* 71 (January–June 1911): 225.

17   Rick Rylance, *Victorian Psychology and British Culture, 1850–1880* (Oxford: Oxford University Press, 2000), 203–50; Susanna Barrows, *Distorting Mirrors: Visions of the Crowd in Late Nineteenth-Century France* (New Haven: Yale University Press, 1981), 116–17.

18   The concept of "suggestion" originally was intimately associated with *hypnos* and was introduced in the mid-nineteenth century by Alexandre Bertrand in France and James Braid in England as an explanation of hypnotic phenomena. It thus replaced the theory of animal magnetism and other fluidistic theories. Suggestion became a universally recognized psychological concept during the famous controversy between the schools of Salpêtrière and Nancy in the 1880s and 1890s. As long as the term "suggestion" was used exclusively in connection with hypnosis, it related to functionally rather homogenous phenomena. Yet by the 1880s, social scientists found it useful to incorporate the hitherto predominantly medical concept of suggestion into their theories of social interaction. Sociologists such as those named above regarded suggestion as the basic mechanism in the social process.

two terms became blurred, largely because of the indiscriminate use made of them by collective psychologists to account for the thoughts and actions of groups of all sorts: crowds, publics, and political groupings.

Some sociologists, psychologists, and criminologists used the term "contagion" in a narrow sense of "automatic imitation," the unconscious and reflexive imitation of the psychological states of others.[19] Yet others assimilated the idea of suggestion and imitation into a broader conception of mental contagion.[20] The broad application of the term "suggestion" in Russia in the 1890s was manifest in an article that defined its meaning written by Pavel Rozenbakh in Brokgauz and Efron's authoritative *Entsiklopedicheskii slovar'*: ". . . understanding 'suggestion' [*vnushenie*] in its broadest sense as a definite influence of external factors on the concrete substance of an individual's mental life, 'suggestion' must be acknowledged as a powerful factor that constitutes the essence of reciprocal influence [*vzaimodeistviie*] between society and the individual."[21]

Authors did not respect the separate origins of mental contagion and imitation or suggestion, with the result that they came to use them almost interchangeably. In 1898, for example, Bekhterev produced precisely this blurring of the categories. Noting that some authors used the expression "mental contagion" (*psikhicheskii kontagii*) instead of suggestion (*vnushenie*) to denote unconscious imitation (*podrazhanie*), he objected that in reality "suggestion and mental contagion were so closely bound up with each other that they could not be easily separated."[22] Since the actual degree of consciousness involved in imitative emotion or action could never be determined, the very vagueness of the concepts of "moral contagion," "suggestion," and "imitation" facilitated their gradual extension to a wide range of essentially disparate social phenomena.

The Rise of the Epidemiological Model

One of the earliest discussions of mental contagion in Russian was an anonymous article, "The Contagiousness of Mental Delusions," which appeared

19   Viacheslav A. Manassein, *O znachenii psikhicheskikh vliianii* (St. Petersburg: L. F. Pantaleev, 1877), 35.

20   Kandinskii, *Obshcheponiatnye psikhologicheskie etiudy*, 178. Dumas, "Contagion mentale," 225–27, cites the French edition of Bekhterev's study of suggestion: Vladimir M. Bekhterev, *La Suggestion et son rôle dans la vie sociale* (Paris, 1910), 24.

21   Pavel Rozenbakh, "Vnushenie," in *Entsiklopedicheskii Slovar'*, ed. F. Brokgauz and I. Efron, 43 vols. (St. Petersburg: F. A. Brokgauz and Efron, 1890–1907), 11:690.

22   Bekhterev, *Vnushenie*, 16. The second edition was published in 1903; citations here are from the expanded 1908 edition (citing A. Vigoroux and P. Juquelier, *La contagion mentale* [Paris: Doin, 1905]). Anticipating Bekhterev's position, the influential French sociologist Gustave Le Bon (1841–1931) treated imitation as only a "simple effect" of mental contagion in his *Psychologie des foules* (Paris: F. Alcan, 1895), 114.

in the popular scientific journal *Znanie* in 1871. Comparing mental with physical epidemics, the author argued, "In different countries and at different times, we have been able to observe the appearance of epidemics that have utterly changed the moral nature of human beings."[23] The author distinguished between the spread of manias such as the desire to emigrate or asceticism and the spread of a different form of moral epidemics that, although generally affecting a smaller number of people, were capable of wreaking far greater havoc in society. "We are speaking of that irresistible attraction that, possessing an individual like a disease, forces him to commit some type of crime."[24] The horrors of the French Revolution were a persuasive example of the epidemic qualities of certain forms of crime: "All the conditions conducive for the spread of a mania of murder came together here. Violent political changes, extreme poverty among the people, the gradual loss of respect for human life in general, self-defense, fear, diseased imitation [*boleznennaia podrazhatel'nost'*]—all this inevitably led to those horrific scenes to which Europe bore witness at the end of the last century."[25]

In the early accounts of imitation and mental contagion, commentators were content to describe the fact of the contagiousness of certain states of mind without subjecting the actual mechanism of transmission to any particular scrutiny. Writing in 1877, the criminologist Leonid Vladimirov affirmed that "insanity in a healthy individual is infectious; it can seize entire masses of the people and become, in a word, epidemic." His explanation of the dynamic was brief and superficial: as all healthy individuals, unlike unhealthy ones, shared essentially the same "roots of passion," disturbance in one individual might elicit disturbances in others.[26]

The first substantial treatment of the mechanism of transmission was Kandinskii's 1881 study *Psikhologicheskie etiudy,* the second part of which was entitled "Nervous-Mental Contagion and Mental Epidemics." In language reminiscent of the *Znanie* article, Kandinskii claimed that in addition to physical diseases, "diseases of the mind [*bolezni dushi*], mental disorders, often also assume an epidemic character."[27] Kandinskii's elucidation of the mechanism of transmission was beguilingly simple, indebted originally to Alfred-Victor Espinas's (1844–1922) influential study of collective behavior in animals, *Des sociétés animales: étude de psychologie comparée* published in 1877, which seemed to offer a physiological basis for mass psychology.[28]

---

23   "Zarazitel'nost' umstvennykh zabluzhdenii," *Znanie* (November 1871): 93.

24   Ibid., 94.

25   Ibid., 109.

26   Leonid E. Vladimirov, "Psikhicheskie osobennosti prestupnikov po noveishim issledovaniiam," *Iuridicheskii vestnik,* nos. 9–10 (1877): 31.

27   Kandinskii, *Obshcheponiatnye psikhologicheskie etiudy,* 153–54.

28   Alfred Victor Espinas, *Des sociétés animales: étude de psychologie comparée* (Paris: G. Baillière, 1877). On Espinas' contribution to crowd psychology, see Barrows, *Distorting Mirrors,* 115–19.

Kandinskii offered an example favored by social psychologists of the time: the act of yawning. "The sight of a person yawning produces an irresistible desire to yawn. . . . Consciousness and the will are irrelevant here, because the person infected with yawning performs the act not only bypassing his will but often in spite of it, or absolutely unconsciously."[29]

More complicated emotions or states of mind could be communicated in an essentially identical manner: "In the case of fury, the circulation becomes significantly impeded; breathing becomes difficult; the face reddens or becomes deathly pale; the nostrils flare and quiver; the voice breaks, becomes hoarse and shrill or disappears altogether; the teeth grind convulsively; the entire body, with muscles tensed, straightens or leans forward sometimes trembling; the eyes flash and become bloodshot; the hands tightly clenched into fists are raised, as if to deliver a blow to an opponent."[30] Kandinskii maintained that less striking emotional states were transmitted from one individual to another in exactly the same way, however subtle, and that when it came to the transmission of *feelings* and *motives,* the notion of "mental contagion" (*dushevnaia kontagioznost'*) was more accurate than that of imitation (*podrazhatel'nost'*).[31]

Discussions over the precise mechanism involved in the transmission of psychological states from one individual to another changed little over the subsequent years. Indeed, the speculative and ill-defined models at the heart of the social psychological paradigm betray almost an indifference to the question of transmission on the part of practitioners of the human sciences. Many studies made no mention whatsoever of the actual process of transfer, content simply to invoke it as a demonstrable fact. Clinicians expended far greater analytical energy on the question at the heart of criminal anthropology and its related fields of inquiry: Why did certain individuals appear more prone than others to the contagions of irrationality?

Evolutionary Hierarchies

Many believed that the answer lay, at least in part, in the existence of hierarchies of racial or cultural development.[32] That such an answer should wield persuasive power in late nineteenth-century Russia is not surprising in the

29   Ibid., 177. Kandinskii's conceptualization of the mechanism of transmission was shared by many other European psychologists, sociologists, and criminologists in the final decades of the nineteenth century.

30   Ibid., 184.

31   Ibid., 182. This physiological theory was refined in 1883 by the French psychiatrist Jean Rambosson in his study *Phénomènes nerveux, intellectuels et moraux, leur transmission par contagion,* which was repeatedly cited by Russian commentators throughout the rest of the century. See, for example, Pavel F. Kapterev, "O podrazhatel'nosti v psikhologicheskom i pedagogicheskom otnosheniiakh," *Obrazovanie,* nos. 7–8 (1893): 26.

32   On this phenomenon in general in the nineteenth and early twentieth centuries, see Stephen Jay Gould, *The Mismeasure of Man,* rev. ed. (1981; New York: Norton, 1996),

context of arguably the single most important concern of the contemporary Russian intelligentsia: the peasant question. The village remained in the last decades of the Romanov dynasty an object of anthropological and literary fascination and moral and political anguish.[33] Narratives of cultural underdevelopment enabled progressive practitioners of the human sciences to articulate a scientifically grounded plea for national enlightenment in order to rescue their rural brothers and, by extension, the rest of Russian society, from the depredations of destructive irrationality.[34]

A few years before Kandinskii's study, in 1877, Viacheslav Avksent'evich Manassein (1841–1901), professor of medicine at the Medical-Surgical Academy in St. Petersburg, published his lectures on mental influence. Manassein argued that there was a relationship between evolutionary development and imitation; the unconscious and uncontrolled traffic between individuals was more typical of primitive races than of their developed counterparts: "More characteristic of lower types of people than higher types is their tendency to replicate the movements and noises produced by others; they manifest this tendency in the form of an involuntary habit, which, according to travelers, they are unable to resist." For Manassein, such behavior was not "significantly different from automatic actions, and we might expect it to be weakened together with a strengthening of the capacity to direct oneself [*upravliat' soboi*]."[35] In other words, imitation was a function of an underdeveloped mind and would diminish as evolution progressed.

In Kandinskii's evolutionary hierarchy as well, primitive groups of individuals were more susceptible to imitation or spiritual contagion than were developed ones: "In general we can say that the tendency to imitate instinctively diminishes with the development of the mind, and the reason for this is clear. . . . Instinctive imitation [*podrazhatel'nost'*] depends on the nervous-mental organization itself, on the coordinated acts of the automatic mechanisms of the brain. . . . Emotional impressions, perceived by the higher centers of the brain, elicit the activity of the mind, thoughts. In this way, the reaction to emotional impressions can be not simply actions but thoughts as well."[36] This mental activity acted as a sort of buffer between the actions or moods of one individual and another witnessing them. More primitive

30–69. On theories of race in late Imperial Russia, see the collection of contemporary essays in *Russkaia rassovaia teoriia do 1917 goda*, ed. V. B. Avdeev (Moscow: Feri-V, 2002); Eugene M. Avrutin, "Racial Categories and the Politics of (Jewish) Difference in Late Imperial Russia," *Kritika* 8, no. 1 (Winter 2007): 13–40.

33   Stephen L. Frank, *Crime, Cultural Conflict, and Justice in Rural Russia, 1856–1914* (Berkeley: University of California Press, 1999). Uncompromising literary representations of peasant society include Anton Chekhov's short story *Peasants* (1897) and Ivan Bunin's *The Village* (1910).

34   Christine Worobec, *Possessed: Women, Witches, and Demons in Imperial Russia* (DeKalb: Northern Illinois University Press, 2001), 151.

35   Manassein, *O znachenii psikhicheskikh vliianii*, 36–37.

36   Kandinskii, *Obshcheponiatnye psikhologicheskie etiudy*, 179.

societies lacked, however, sufficient development of this cognitive apparatus and were unable to mediate their responses to emotions. For Kandinskii, the intimate relationship between ideas and the emotions they elicited meant that the transmission of the latter served as a model for the transmission of the former: "An intellectually undeveloped, ignorant, or half-educated society willingly embraces a new idea without any criticism, without any attempt to assimilate it properly or to develop its logical consequences."[37] The equation of primitiveness with group behavior unmediated by the censorious capacities of reason and the will would become an abiding theme of a later series of studies of mass psychology in the 1890s.[38]

Yet elsewhere, Kandinskii was skeptical about the capacities of reason and willpower to mediate social interaction rationally: "Any impartial observer would come to the conclusion that it is not reason and the will that are the immediate drivers of human behavior but rather desires, feelings, and passions." Kandinskii cited Comte to the effect that reason does not prompt us to action but merely controls our impulses and restrains our passions: "In general, in relation to actions, if one can so express it, reason plays the role of the police, a role which can be summarized by the term 'it is not allowed.' Just as in a well-ordered state the police should be well organized, so should reason and the will be sufficiently developed in a well-ordered mental life; but in the average person this mental police is not strong and active, and therefore a great deal happens without its knowledge or in defiance of it."[39] Kandinskii was drawing an analogy between disorder within a state and disorder within a mind. Yet the obvious parallel betrayed a more disturbing relationship between individual and social instability: How could individuals with such imperfect control over their own emotions and states of mind serve as adequate agents of social control in a state?

Kandinskii's understanding of the shortcomings of the will suggested, moreover, a deeply pessimistic view of the capacity of human rationality to organize the world and thus to enjoy substantive freedom: "Only a conscious logical process of thought, the independent assimilation of external impressions, which has as its goal the final result of a conscious exercise of the will, makes a person free." Yet although uneducated and ignorant individuals were incapable of such an attempt, "even a person with a high level of intellectual and moral development can never *entirely* avoid the effects of nervous-mental contagion [*nervno-psikhicheskii kontagii*]. . . . The facts demonstrate clearly that the contemporary high level of knowledge in no

37   Ibid., 181.
38   See Worobec's examination of psychiatric discussions of shriekers, or *klikushi*, at the turn of the twentieth century, which revealed a similar nexus of assumptions about cultural backwardness, infused with beliefs about women's sexuality predisposing them to irrational thought and behavior. *Possessed*, 148–87.
39   Kandinskii, *Obshcheponiatnye psikhologicheskie etiudy*, 169.

way safeguards even the educated [*intelligentnyi*] layer of society from mental epidemics (it suffices to recall that there are many scholars among the spiritualists)."[40]

These misgivings notwithstanding, early psychologists concentrated their analytical energies on the intimate relationship between underdevelopment and susceptibility to moral contagion. In 1889, an article appeared that examined an epidemic of hiccuping among the peasant population of a particular district in Podolsk Province. The local doctor, Ksenofont Platonovich Sulima (1855–?), insisted that psychological and physical ill-health provided an ideal breeding ground for mental epidemics: "Our villages abound with a mass of mentally ill individuals, and we frequently have to observe the most exquisite forms of nervous and mental illness." Therefore, "it is unsurprising that neuroses and psychoses can assume an epidemic character: unconscious imitation [*bessoznatel'naia podrazhatel'nost'*] or, following [George Henry] Lewes, the capacity of one person unconsciously to enter into unison with another, is more present in individuals with primitive mental activity and weakly developed and expressed individuality."[41] Sulima cited the German psychiatrist Theodor Meynert (1833–1898) to the effect that "the less the mind and individuality depend on their own logical combinations, the stronger the urge to direct thoughts and the actions associated with them toward the imitation of the psychological combinations taken from other people; the lower the mind, the less developed the individuality." Sulima pointed out that "this was the reason for the appearance of mental epidemics and such a high degree of infectiousness of nervous and mental illness in the Middle Ages."[42] The fundamental equation here of mental illness and backwardness was to form the nexus of the clinical understanding of mass psychology throughout the late imperial period. The backwardness of the village impeded both the psychological individuation of its members and the development of a robust, independent, and critical cognitive apparatus in each member.[43]

Ivan Sikorskii put forward an alternative reading of the relationship between rural poverty, backwardness and the spread of moral contagion in a study of a mass suicide that had occurred in Ternovskie Khutora, a village in

40   Ibid., 234.
41   Ksefont P. Sulima, "Epidemiia ikoty (Singultus) v selenii Ketrosy, Iamol'skogo uezda, Podol'skoi gubernii," *Vestnik obshchestvennoi gigieny, sudebnoi i prakticheskoi meditsiny* 4 (October–December 1889): 36. On George Henry Lewes, see Rylance, *Victorian Psychology,* 251–330.
42   Sulima, "Epidemiia ikoty," 36.
43   A few years later and in more abstract language, Kapterev also identified "the most favorable condition for the development of imitation is the instability, the insufficiency of the imitating organism's formation. While the organism is not properly formed and finds itself in a process of education, it is the most predisposed to imitation as it is unable to resist in any significant way external influences." Kapterev, "O podrazhatel'nosti," 34.

Kiev Province in 1892. Sikorskii investigated the case of more than twenty Old Believers who, inspired by their leader Kondratii Malevanyi, took a shortcut to immortality by burying themselves alive with small children—an act apparently motivated by fear that interference by the authorities into their liturgical practices threatened to compromise their salvation.[44] Sikorskii argued that "the phenomenon rightly deserves to be called a mental epidemic," which had "swiftly overwhelmed the peasant population in a number of villages."[45]

Sikorskii maintained that the susceptibility of the peasantry to religiously inspired mental epidemics was because "the mass of the people wait and thirst for spiritual renewal. They search for the savior and . . . they find him in the insane Kondratii Malevanyi! It is impossible to ignore that the epidemic of Malevanyi is a cry of despair from an ailing population and a prayer for emancipation . . . for the improvement of education and sanitary conditions."[46] In other words, responsibility for the peasants' self-destruction and their readiness to follow a madman into the grave lay with the tsarist social order, which had locked them down in such extremes of degradation and ignorance that they were unable to distinguish salvation from oblivion. It was the spectacular irrationality of the peasants' behavior that advanced not merely the conflation of backwardness and madness but also the marking out of them as radically other, removed from anything approaching the psychology of educated Russia.

In 1897, Sikorskii published an extended study of mass suicides in Kiev Province entitled *Epidemic Voluntary Deaths and Murders at Ternovskie Khutora* in which he also emphasized the role of insanity in Malevanyi's followers. Sikorskii argued that these acts of self-immolation presented society "with a *pathological* phenomenon [*patologicheskoe iavlenie*] that was related to a series of *mental epidemics* [*psikhicheskie epidemii*]."[47] In the hands of its leader, Vitalii, one Ternovskie Khutora sect became "an instrument of *pathological selection* [*patologicheskii podbor*] and the most dangerous source of mental contagion [*psikhicheskaia zaraza*]." Returning to the 1892 suicides, Sikorskii identified something new in the understanding

---

44   Such self-immolation may also be viewed as part of a countervailing discourse within Christianity stressing that stigma, sin, and depravity were indications of holiness, martyrdom, and asceticism. Indeed, the stigma of depravity was presumed by every true Christian as part of his or her post-lapsarian condition. Some saw the "salvation" offered by the Orthodox Church as a satanic interference with a necessary stigma or vice that should be accepted as gifts by true martyrs. Self-immolation was thus an effective measure to sabotage the unholy and secularized sanctions of the state-owned Church. On the appropriation of Sikorskii's work by the Orthodox Church, see Daniel Beer, "The Medicalization of Deviance in the Russian Orthodox Church, 1880–1905," *Kritika* 5, no. 3 (Summer 2004): 451–83.

45   Ivan A. Sikorskii, *Psikhopaticheskaia epidemiia 1892-go goda v Kievskoi Gubernii* (Kiev: Universitet Sviatogo Vladimira, 1893), 1.

46   Ibid., 46.

47   Ivan A. Sikorskii, *Epidemicheskie vol'nye smerti i smertoubiistva v Ternovskie Khutora* (Kiev: I. N. Kushnerev, 1897), 83.

of the sources of moral contagion—the psychopathologies of the leader. Malevanyi was "suffering from a typical form of insanity," and "the number of the mentally ill in Malevanyi's sect was greater than that in the rest of the population, which did not take part in the religious ferment." This constituency provided a critical mass of psychopathology, which when triggered by Malevanyi overwhelmed the sanity of sections of the remaining population: "The religious ferment was sustained in the population around Kiev District (*uezd*) while Malevanyi was in a psychiatric asylum in Kiev. When he was released into the care of his family and appeared among the ignorant rural population, the ferment intensified significantly and affected many districts in Kiev [Province] and contiguous provinces: pilgrimages to see Malevanyi began, and first in one place and then in another, epidemics of hysteria with convulsions, hallucinations, and delirium broke out among the hitherto healthy population."[48]

Sikorskii's pamphlet attracted a great deal of attention among fellow psychiatrists and spawned a series of reviews and derivative studies.[49] One such example was Pavel Iakobii's article of 1903 entitled "Religious-Mental Epidemics," in which the author saw the tragic events at Ternovskie Khutora as evidence of a "mental contagion [*psikhicheskaia zaraza*] of a significant number of people, who had undoubtedly been infected [*zarazhennye*] by some mentally-ill person."[50] Reviewing the mass suicide in a text published in 1905, *Hypnotism and Mental Contagion*, Fedor Rybakov combined the language of backwardness and a language of psychopathology in his analysis of events. He identified two types of "carriers of mental infection: (1) a psychopathic type of subject and (2) a type of subject who is insufficiently enlightened, insufficiently developed in a spiritual and an intellectual sense. Both of these types are well known. The first is found in all strata of society, but the second primarily among the lowest class: it personifies that elemental force which bears the name of the dark masses."[51] Rybakov's analysis suggested a fundamental equivalence between backwardness and insanity, thereby uniting the principal explanations of susceptibility to moral

---

48   Ibid., 93.
49   Vladimir Ia. Iakovenko, "Epidemiia istericheskikh sudorog v Podol'skom uezde, Moskovskoi gub.," *Vestnik obshchestvennoi gigieny, sudebnoi i prakticheskoi meditsiny* 15, no. 3 (March 1895): 93–109; E. A. Genik, "Vtoraia epidemiia istericheskikh sudorog v Podol'skom uezde, Moskovskoi gubernii," *Nevrologicheskii vestnik* 6, no. 4 (1898): 146–59; N. V. Krainskii, *Porcha, klikushi i besnovatye* (St. Petersburg: M. I. Akynfiev and I. V. Leont'ev, 1900); V. Ia. Iakovenko, "Psikhicheskaia epidemiia na religioznoi pochve v Anan'evskom i Tiraspol'skom uezdakh Khersonskoi gub.," *Sovremennaia psikhiatriia* (March 1911): 191–98; (April 1911): 229–45; E. A. Genik, "Tret'ia epidemiia isterii v Moskovskoi gubernii," *Sovremennaia psikhiatriia* (August 1912): 588–604.
50   Pavel I. Iakobii, "Religiozno-psikhicheskie epidemii," *Vestnik Evropy*, no. 11 (1903): 119–20.
51   Fedor E. Rybakov, *Gipnotizm i psikhicheskaia zaraza* (Moscow: V. Rikhter, 1905), 124.

contagion: "a psychopathological subject who is also uncultured represents the most suitable material for induced insanity."[52]

Not that backwardness was a prerequisite for mental illness. The relationship between mental illness and susceptibility was one that featured in a large number of psychiatric studies. Pavel Kovalevskii's textbook on psychiatry published in 1886 made repeated references to instability (*neustoichivost'*) to describe susceptibility to abnormal mental states and mental illness. Observing a high incidence of mental illness among students, he remarked, "What are the causes? Where is the basis for this mental instability?" and suggested that parents of psychopaths, criminals, and drunkards had passed on a "predisposition to instability and wavering [*kolebaniia*] to their offspring."[53] Pavel Fedorovich Kapterev (1849–1921) also identified instability as the *sine qua non* of imitation: "A subject lacking established and carefully thought-out concepts and views, with an unstable mood, with ever-changing desires and urges, easily falls prey to imitation."[54]

Given its apparent irrationality, suicide was usually cited as the example of moral contagion that most clearly revealed the psychopathologies of the imitating subject.[55] It was here, above all, that the theories of degeneration and psychopathology intersected with an epidemiological understanding of social influence. Rybakov inquired, "What sort of subject is it who sacrifices his life simply out of imitation? If a psychiatric examination of this subject were undertaken, it would not be difficult to conclude that it is a degenerate and psychopathological individual. In a healthy person, the instinct for self-preservation always dominates over spontaneous influences, whatever they might be."[56]

The Psychology of the Crowd

Visions of the unpredictability and irrationality of interaction between individuals, unmediated by the constraints of the will and reason, found their most concentrated manifestation in discussions of the crowd. The crowd temporarily, but often with destructive consequences, replicated the lack

---

52   Ibid.

53   Pavel I. Kovalevskii, *Obshchaia psikhopatologiia* (Kharkov: Kaplan and Biriukov, 1886), 161, 165.

54   Kapterev, "O podrazhatel'nosti," 34.

55   Irina Paperno has noted that in the period between the 1905 Revolution and the outbreak of the First World War, "the notion of 'epidemic' [as it related to suicide] now received attention from scientists. Read in its direct, not metaphoric sense, the notion implied a medical explanation." *Suicide as a Cultural Institution in Dostoevsky's Russia* (Ithaca: Cornell University Press, 1997), 96. See also Susan Morrissey, *Suicide and the Body Politic in Imperial Russia* (Cambridge: Cambridge University Press, 2006), chaps. 10–11.

56   Rybakov, *Gipnotizm*, 125.

of individuation found among the peasantry and represented an atavistic return to more primitive human instincts. Peasants continued to feature prominently in studies of the crowd, but the emergence of crowd psychology as a distinct subdiscipline in the 1890s enjoyed a much more expansive scope of application. This subdiscipline came to be deployed in studies of all human agglomerations and the functioning of society as a whole in the age of mass politics.

A number of scholars have traced the significance of the crowd in late nineteenth-century European thought.[57] Roger L. Geiger has noted that with its connotations of uncontrolled energy, explosive violence, and revolutionary potential, the crowd symbolized the temporary abandonment of civilization's constraints on human behavior.[58] Serge Moscovici has argued that theories of crowd psychology developed in reaction to the power France's lower classes acquired after 1850.[59] Susanna Barrows has similarly observed that fear of crowds was indeed a constituent feature of the cultural anxiety that beset France in the *belle époque*.[60]

The elaboration of crowd psychology in the Russian *fin-de-siècle*, informed by theories of imitation and moral contagion, was similarly representative of a profound unease at the potentially destructive forces that could be unleashed from below. The developments in the theory in Russia were, however, far from simply an appropriation, however creative, of theories first elaborated in Western Europe. Russian psychologists and sociologists had already addressed the issue of crowd behavior in the 1880s before the publication of the major French and Italian studies of the topic at the end of that decade. In his 1881 study, Kandinskii had commented that the "effects of mental contagion are particularly manifest in a mass of people and all the more manifest the larger and more compact that mass and the less the individuals comprising it are accustomed to governing their actions in accordance with the dictates of reason." The herd-like mentality with which most crowds were invested conferred tremendous power on any leader able to direct them by example: "Whoever is able to act in the necessary way on a crowd will be able to lead them wherever he likes—into fire, into water, into the murderous combat of a battle." Indeed, one of the examples of crowd psychology repeatedly invoked to demonstrate the power of example was that of soldiers at war: "The word of a leader able to inspire soldiers can turn them into heroes and brings victory in a battle that had already

57   Jaap van Ginneken, *Crowds, Psychology, and Politics, 1871–1899* (Cambridge: Cambridge University Press, 1992); Serge Moscovici, *The Age of the Crowd*, trans. J. C. Whitehouse (Cambridge: Cambridge University Press, 1985).
58   Geiger, "Democracy and the Crowd," 47.
59   Serge Moscovici, "Bewußte und unbewußte Einflüsse in der Kommunikation," *Zeitschrift für Sozialpsychologie* 12 (1981): 94.
60   Barrows, *Distorting Mirrors*, 2.

appeared lost. By contrast, the example of one or two cowards infects an entire regiment and causes them to flee shamefully."[61]

A year after the publication of Kandinskii's study, the relationship between leaders and crowds was the subject of a lengthy article by Mikhailovskii.[62] "The Hero and the Crowd" discussed notions of suggestion and the spread of ideas and emotions in crowds and masses of people in general. Mikhailovskii clarified that he did not mean "hero" in the positive sense but rather in terms of the individual who was able to prompt the crowd to follow his or her example. In the case of Vereshchagin's lynching, he identified the dragoon who had delivered the initial blow with the blunt edge of his saber: "Vereshchagin was killed by the unrestrained striving of the crowd, with its disposition to imitate the hero. In this case, the hero was the dragoon who either out of bravery or cowardice delivered the first blow."[63] As early as in this 1882 study, Mikhailovskii noted the expansive explanatory potential of theories of imitation: "The power of imitation lies in the fact that it manifests itself at virtually every step, in an innumerable quantity of slight instances."[64] A decade later, the generalization of this explanatory model to the study of societies as a whole would become a feature of studies of moral contagion.

Throughout the 1880s, discussions of crowd psychology remained, however, confined to isolated articles. Interest in the subject intensified as Russian psychologists discussed Hippolyte Taine's (1828–1893) monumental *Les origines de la France contemporaine*, published between 1875 and 1893, which devoted long passages to descriptions of the revolutionary crowds in 1789. In Taine's account, "the laws of mental contagion" could, within a crowd, bring about the transformation of an individual into an irrational savage: "Mutual contagion inflames the passions; crowds . . . end in a state of drunkenness, from which nothing can issue but vertigo and blind rage."[65] The work was subsequently translated into Russian in a number of editions between 1880, when the early volumes began to appear, and the first decade of the twentieth century, and Taine's work was widely discussed in Russian literary and scientific journals throughout the 1890s.[66] Barrows has argued

61   Kandinskii, *Obshcheponiatnye psikhologicheskie etiudy*, 185–86.
62   Mikhailovskii's contemporaries intensively discussed his writings on social psychology. See, for example, A. I. Krasnosel'skii, *Mirovozzrenie gumanista nashego vremeni: Osnovy ucheniia N. K. Mikhailovskogo* (St. Petersburg: B. M. Vol'f, 1900), 7–14; M. M. Kovalevskii, "N. K. Mikhailovskii kak sotsiolog," *Vestnik Evropy*, no. 4 (1913): 192–212.
63   Mikhailovskii, "Geroi i tolpa," 103. These early studies of the relationship between crowds and their leaders (or heroes) anticipated Le Bon's influential treatise on the same subject, *La psychologie des foules*.
64   Ibid., 113.
65   Hippolyte Taine, *Les origines de la France contemporaine*, 6 vols. (Paris: Hachette, 1876–94), vol. 2, *La Révolution*, 133.
66   See, for example, Ippolit Ten, *Proiskhozhdenie obshchestvennogo stroia sovremennoi Frantsii*, vol. 1 (St. Petersburg: I. I. Bilibin, 1880); idem, *Proiskhozhdenie obshchestvennogo*

that Taine came to stand as "the hero and model for crowd psychologists," yet he "simply stated that passions were contagious without asking why they were."[67] Like Tolstoi's depiction of the murder of Vereshchagin, Taine's *Les origines* provided abundant material for the exploration of this question in the language of social psychology.

Domestic events also contributed to the rise of crowd psychology as a discernible subdiscipline within the fields of psychiatry and psychology. In the wake of the rioting that had accompanied the Russian cholera epidemic of 1892, psychologists, criminologists, and psychiatrists began to address the subject in significant numbers.[68] As the legal scholar Leonid Egorovich Obolenskii (1845–1906) observed in 1893, "the cholera riots of last year have elicited intensified interest in the issues of 'the criminal crowd' and the 'psychology of the masses.'"[69]

The speed with which the unrest had spread prompted some to inquire into the conditions that made it possible. Sluchevskii argued that the cholera riots had shown that all a crowd required was a mobilizing myth or fable to galvanize it to action: "Without any factual basis, the tales, for example, of doctors poisoning the people during the development of the cholera riots occurred not only in our country but also in Paris and Sicily during the cholera epidemic that ruled there during the 1830s." He was adamant that certain common conditions must first obtain, providing a platform for the collective sentiment that could then become catalyzed into the unity of a crowd: "Without the presence of this unity of feelings and thoughts, that bond which fuses people into a single crowd and invests it with a single soul will not exist." Sluchevskii's language revealed the impulse to generalize implicit in his discussion of the crowd, which identified in no uncertain terms the location of the threat. When he invoked Taine's *Les origines* as evidence of the behavior of crowds, he switched to discussion of "the people" (*narod*) in general: "The people are unable to distinguish or reason; they think in simple schemes [*par blocs*]; facts and dreams appear to them compatible and united together." He invoked the specter of peasant revolt, familiar to

---

stroia sovermennoi Frantsii, 5 vols., trans. A. V. Svyrov (St. Petersburg: M. V. Pirozhkov, 1907). For examples of the discussion of Taine's work, see V. Ger'e, "Ippolit Ten i ego znachenie v istoricheskoi nauke," *Vestnik Evropy*, no. 1 (1890):. 5–65; no. 2 (1890): 463–500; K. K. Arsen'ev, "Novyi istorik sovremennoi Frantsii," *Vestnik Evropy*, no. 1 (1891): 313–42; no. 2 (1891): 784–814; no. 4 (1892): 913–51.

67   Barrows, *Distorting Mirrors*, 85–86.

68   On the riots in Tashkent, see Jeff Sahadeo, "Epidemic and Empire: Ethnicity, Class, and 'Civilisation' in the 1892 Tashkent Cholera Riot," *Slavic Review* 64, no. 1 (Spring 2005): 117–39.

69   Leonid E. Obolenskii, "Noveishaia psevdo-nauka," *Russkaia mysl'* (November 1893): 122. On psychiatric interest in the riots see also Pavel N. Obninskii, "*Contagion morale* i kholernye besporiadki," *Zhurnal grazhdanskogo i ugolovnogo prava*, no. 1 (January 1893): 1–14.

educated Russians since the reign of Catherine the Great: "The harshness of living conditions in the time of Stenka Razin and Pugachev, as the historical sources of that period testify, created for [these rebels] a crowd of adherents everywhere they appeared and where the people gathered under the banner they had raised."[70] He concluded his article with a plea for the improvement of the condition of the peasantry:

> The significant majority of those individuals who enter the crowd belong to the lower orders of society, who live under harsh conditions of obtaining the basic means to survive and whose proud dreams never go beyond the desire expressed in those lines by Nekrasov:
> "If only someone would call me
> 'Ivan Moiseich' just once!"
> And suddenly this humble man, downtrodden by everyday living conditions, hears that people are hailing Ivan Moseich, he sees that they pay him a great deal of attention, and feels that people are only concerned with him, people serve him. . . . Is this not a reason to become swept away, to lose all control over oneself?[71]

Faith in the power of Enlightenment rationality to dispel the ignorance and poverty that provided the breeding ground for mental epidemics also characterized a speech by Ardalion Ardalionovich Tokarskii (1859–1901), a member of the faculty at Moscow University, to a gathering of psychiatrists at the university in October 1893. Tokarskii argued that "ignorance in all its forms" rendered individuals susceptible and that the two causes of mental epidemics were, first, the "dominant ideas and external events" and, second, "imitation, mental contagiousness, suggestion, and the provocative influence of the masses."[72] Speaking in the immediate aftermath of the cholera riots, Tokarskii could scarcely avoid mentioning them. Referring to the "senseless acts of evil" that had accompanied the disturbances, he suggested that the "basic reason for senselessness and savagery of any kind of mass movement is to be found in the ignorance of the masses; such incidents can only be prevented by the timely dissemination of the largest possible quantity of knowledge and sound principles among the people."[73]

At the beginning of 1890s, then, many discussions of crowd psychology continued to identify the same two principal factors in the spread of collective deviance: backwardness and insanity. The view that peasant ignorance, superstition, and poverty predisposed the masses to mental epidemics was obviously a disconcerting one. It suggested that the majority of the Russian

---

70   Sluchevskii, "Tolpa i ee psikhologiia," 11, 13, 26.
71   Ibid., 38.
72   Ardalion A. Tokarskii, *Psikhicheskie epidemii* (Moscow: I. N. Kushnerev, 1893), 4.
73   Ibid., 23.

population was yet to be inoculated against the depredations of irrationality, panic, fear, and the spread of violence through education and civilization. Yet such a view nevertheless affirmed the ultimate power of reason and progress to overcome these "remnants of the Middle Ages," as Sulima had called them.

These analyses all claimed to locate the source of moral contagion within the psychological condition of those caught up in its tide, shaped by either cultural backwardness or mental illness. An alternative focus of analysis, however, argued that the key to understanding collective deviance lay not merely within its individual practitioners but also within the psychological structures of the collective itself, in other words, within the crowd.

The Fragility of Reason

West European studies of crowd psychology wielded a catalytic influence over the contemporary Russian understanding of the robustness of human reason and moral and mental development in the spread of emotional states. Whereas the initial equation of irrationality and backwardness had served effectively to endorse both the necessity and potential of enlightened rationality; far more disturbing was the view, hinted at in some of the earlier discussions, that the susceptibility to moral contagion was in fact embedded deep in the psychological constitution of all human beings and was an inalienable part of their condition. The rise of this second explanation owed a great deal to the writings of French and Italian criminologists working in the field of collective psychology. Their research lent impetus to this reconfiguration of moral contagion not simply as the engine of isolated acts of deviance, such as an epidemic of suicide or murder, but as the mainspring of the social order. The crowd was simply an environment which illuminated to a striking degree the subconscious forces that determined human behavior in a more diffuse manner in everyday coexistence in communities. The first step in this line of argument was to point out the "democratic" appeal of the crowd in the sense that it could activate and accentuate impulses in all humans, not just the backward or pathological.

Almost any person, so the argument ran, would unconsciously surrender their individuality and deliver themselves to the collective impulses of the crowd. To take a couple of influential examples: 1890 saw the publication of Gabriel Tarde's *La philosophie pénale*, which argued that although crowds could easily be dangerous, most of them were not composed of naturally vicious deviants: "The majority of these men had assembled out of pure curiosity, but the fever of some of them soon reached the minds of all, and in all of them there arose a delirium. The very man who had come running to oppose the murder of an innocent person is one of the first to be seized with the *homicidal contagion,* and, moreover, it does not occur to him to be astonished at this."[74]

A year later, the publication of young Italian criminologist Scipio Sighele's (1868–1913) *La folla delinquente,* which was translated into Russian in 1893, further elaborated the normalization of the members of a deviant crowd.[75] Anthropologists and legal authorities, cautioned Sighele, must differentiate between two kinds of collective crime: premeditated offenses by groups like the Mafia and spontaneous destruction by a crowd. For born criminals and for organized groups of bandits, anthropological factors predominated; crowds, like casual offenders, were most conditioned by social factors.[76] All crowds, even those of decent men and women, were predisposed to evil: "The microbes of evil develop very easily, good ones almost never."[77] These studies of urban crowds tended to militate against the equation of rural superstition with a predisposition to moral contagion; they suggested on the contrary that the disorder had the power to affect all individuals, not just the unenlightened.

Adherents of certain Russian ideological orientations were predisposed to challenge the framing of discussions of moral contagion within an

74   Gabriel Tarde, *Philosophie pénale,* 2nd ed. (Paris: A. Storck, 1891), 324. Tarde's (1843–1904) prolific output during the 1890s eventually brought him to the chair of Modern Philosophy at the College de France (1900). In Russia, his influence was extensive; his works were immediately translated into Russian and avidly discussed in the pages of Russian journals. See his *Zakony podrazhaniia* (St. Petersburg: F. Pavlenkov, 1892); *Prestupleniia tolpy,* trans. I. F. Iordanskii (Kazan: N. Ia. Bashmakov, 1893); *Publika i tolpa,* trans. F. Laterner (St. Petersburg: Ivanov, 1899); *Obshchestvennoe mnenie i tolpa,* trans. P. S. Kogan (Moscow: A. I. Mamontov, 1902); *Lichnost' i tolpa. Ocherki po sotsial'noi psikhologii,* trans. E. A. Predtechenskii (St. Petersburg: A. Bol'shakov and D. Golof, 1903). For Russian discussions of his work, see Aleksei A. Kozlov, *Tard i ego teoriia obshchestva* (Kiev: Tipografiia Imperatorskogo Universiteta Sviatogo Vladimira, 1887); Leontii Danilovich, *Espinas i Tard ob obshchestve* (Moscow: I. N. Kushnerev, 1902). Tarde was also the subject of an extensive entry in the *Entsiklopedicheskii slovar'.*

75   In works such as *La folla delinquente,* Sighele established many of the founding principles that were subsequently codified in Le Bon's *Psychologie des foules:* the centrality of heterogeneous crowds in modern life, the inferior intelligence of collectives vis-à-vis individuals, the primacy of imitation and suggestion in crowd behavior, and the violent or criminal predisposition of human agglomerations.

76   Scipio Sighele, *La foule criminelle, essai de psychologie collective,* trans. Paul Vigny (Paris: F. Alcan, 1892), 28–29. Two Russian translations of the volume appeared in 1893: Skipio Sigele, *Prestupnaia tolpa: Opyt kollektivnoi psikhologii,* trans. A. P. Afanas'ev (St. Petersburg: F. Pavlenkov, 1893), and no trans. identified (Novgorod: N. S. Tiutchev, 1893). For a review of Sighele's work see I. D-ov [Ivan Ivanovich Dobrovol'skii], "Psikhologiia 'prestupnoi' tolpy," *Russkaia mysl'* (December 1894): 130–58.

77   Not all individuals were equally susceptible to the noxious "microbes" of the crowd. Those few individuals endowed with exceptionally strong wills could resist the infection of suggestion. The rest of mankind Sighele divided into two categories: (1) born criminals who profited from any occasion to break the law and (2) the majority of normally lawful citizens who under certain circumstances might be led into illegal actions. Only the morally weak, degenerate, or "criminaloid" person with an organic predisposition to evil could be hypnotized to commit truly heinous crimes. Sighele, *La foule criminelle,* 63, 137–44.

evolutionary or cultural hierarchy of development. With his populist sympathies, Mikhailovskii resisted indictments of the ignorance and spiritual poverty of the peasantry and argued that the crowd should not be conflated with "the people." Indeed, for Mikhailovskii, social station was of no consequence in determining how individuals behaved within a crowd: "If, therefore, people point, for example, to the recent cholera riots and say, "Such is the Russian people!"—we can confidently retort, "No, these are not features particular to the Russian people!" They can manifest themselves in any other European or Asiatic people. . . . This psychological process is not the exclusive preserve of the lower orders of society, usually denoted by the words "the people" (*narod*). In a word, the crowd is not the people, but an autonomous social-psychological phenomenon, in need of specific study."[78] In effect, Mikhailovskii was arguing that the crowd was representative of all people, rather than simply "the people" (*narod*). Such an impulse to generalize crowd behavior led contemporaries to a number of disturbing conclusions about the stability of contemporary society and the status of rationality within it.

Even those clinicians like Sluchevskii who appeared at times to argue that educational and material improvement would render the peasant population resistant to the forces of moral contagion were riven by doubts. Referring to the studies of Mikhailovskii, Tarde, and Sighele, in "The Crowd and Its Psychology," Sluchevskii painted a disturbing picture of irrational forces that remained latent within all human beings until they were unleashed within a crowd:

> In every person, invisible to him and all the more so to an external observer, there lies in the sphere of unconscious mental activity the potential for a gradually accumulated structure of mental forces. These mental forces manifest themselves in the life of a crowd. . . . It is they that give the crowd the character of an organism, living its own mental life, just as they transform for a time the souls of its members.[79]

Although the emergence of a crowd might be subject to empirically discernible sociological and psychological factors, once formed it extended a profound and incomprehensible power over its members: "In the secrets of the human soul, beyond the sphere of consciousness, are hidden mental foundations, capable, in the presence of the necessary conditions, of manifesting themselves in life."[80] Sluchevskii's article reverberated with anxiety at the potentially destructive forces of human irrationality that lurked not

---

78   Mikhailovskii, "Eshche o tolpe" (1893), *Sochineniia* 2:415.
79   Sluchevskii, "Tolpa i ee psikhologiia," 10, 16.
80   Ibid., 37.

just beneath the surface of contemporary Russian civilization but within each individual.

Early studies of crowd psychology in the 1880s had proposed a correlation between the psychological predisposition, shaped by insanity or backwardness, of the members of a crowd and its collective behavior. Such a view persisted in the following decade but gradually began to cede ground to an alternative explanation, championed by Tarde and Sighele, that emphasized the transformative capacities of crowds to alter radically the behavior of the men and women who comprised them. Morality was a precarious social virtue, constantly threatened by the power of crowds or, as many commentators came to conclude, by the power of human association in a far more general sense.

Civilization and the Expansion of "the Crowd"

The crowd was a cauldron of psychological transformation. What, however, did "the crowd" actually signify? Where did the frontiers of its transformative powers lie? Was the crowd simply the most striking and distilled expression of a much broader, more subtle psychological dynamic? Having eroded the stability of individual rationality within social interaction, studies of the crowd necessarily harbored an impulse to articulate a disturbing vision of human association in general.

The extrapolation from crowd behavior to a general theory of social interaction began in the 1890s. It was then that Tarde published a study, *Les lois de l'imitation,* which argued that imitation, or unconscious social influence, was the key to an understanding of societies: "The social, like the hypnotic state, is only a form of a dream, a dream of command and a dream of action. Both the somnambulist and the social man are possessed by the illusion that their ideas, all of which have been suggested to them, are spontaneous."[81] A year later, Bazhenov endorsed Tarde's extension of the early studies "of the activities of individuals and masses" to the study of societies as a whole: "At the present time, one of the greatest thinkers of contemporary France, Tarde, has gone even further and has placed these ideas at the basis of an entire sociological theory. . . . Inasmuch as he is a social being, man is above all an imitator, and imitation is essential a feature of a social organism as heredity in individuals and vibration in the inorganic world. He identifies society as a collection of beings imitating each other."[82]

---

81 Gabriel Tarde, *Les lois de l'imitation* (Paris: F. Alcan, 1890), 87. Tarde had first advanced the idea in an article published six years earlier: Gabriel Tarde, "Qu'est-ce qu'une société?" *Revue philosophique* 18 (July–December 1884): 489–510.

82 Nikolai N. Bazhenov, *Oblast' i predely vnusheniia* (Moscow: I. N. Kushnerev, 1891), 16.

A number of commentators noted that social homogeneity facilitated the spread of emotions from one individual (or group) to another. Peasants and soldiers were good examples of such a dynamic.[83] Kapterev's analysis of imitation expressed a schizophrenic attitude to the binary of culturedness and unculturedness by expanding the argument about group homogeneity to embrace the emergence of a modern, unified society. Having declared that uneducated subjects were more prone to imitation than their sophisticated counterparts, Kapterev went on to radically subvert this view by suggesting that civilization itself was a bearer of dynamics that advanced the spread of moral contagion: "[The spread of] culture undoubtedly brings about the physical and mental leveling down of people. Particular religions, specific forms of daily life, original world views, and separate languages all disappear under the pressure of the dominant unifying ideas, beliefs, customs, languages. . . . An approximation takes place among people, an equalization takes place, and this equalization facilitates the development not of originality, but rather of imitation [*podrazhatel'nost'*]."[84] The entire reform project of the liberal and progressive intelligentsia, which strove for the integration of the peasantry into the emerging civil society of educated Russia, therefore threatened to intensify rather than diminish dangerous explosions of irrationality in society.

In early studies of the phenomenon, contagiousness was understood to reside in the deviant acts themselves; what their spread revealed about the nature of the social order had been far less clear. Under the impact of the studies of crowd psychology in the 1890s, however, social psychologists reconfigured suicide and crime as particularly horrifying instances of a far more disturbing vision of a society in the grip of the forces of pathological imitation. As societies developed, the web of relations between their members became ever denser, subjecting each individual to myriad influences and pressures that radically undermined autonomy and independent reasoning. Kapterev explained the dynamic as follows:

> The individual in society hears conversations, reads discussions of certain topics and of certain incidents in books; people in front of him praise certain principles and actions and condemn others; he encounters a certain mood, a certain rise or fall in spirits in society, he reads books with a certain orientation, with a certain tendency. All this unwittingly captivates him, directs his thoughts and

---

83   I. Kablits (I. Iuzov), *Osnovy narodnichestva* (St. Petersburg: A.M. Kotomin, 1882), 67–68. The military physician N. A. Ukhach-Ugorovich argued that the bonds of discipline within the army were something of a double-edged sword: "An organic dependence of the will of the soldiers on the will of the commander is created. This dependence expresses itself first and foremost in the fact that the energy, toughness, and determination of subordinates increases or weakens in accordance with the wavering willpower of the senior commander." *Psikhologiia tolpy i armii* (Kiev: S. V. Kul'zhenko, 1911), 34.
84   Kapterev, "O podrazhatel'nosti," 36.

mood, and subordinates his mind and his heart to the social or literary mental tendency and current of the day.[85]

Bekhterev's *Suggestion and Its Role in Social Life*, published in 1898, began with an even more alarming description of the vulnerability of all individuals to mental contagion: "Although [mental] microbes are invisible under the microscope, like genuine physical microbes they act everywhere and are transmitted by words, gestures, and movements surrounding the face, through books, newspapers, and so on. In a word, wherever we are in the society that surrounds us, we are subject to the effect of mental microbes and are consequently in danger of being mentally infected [*psikhicheski zarazhennye*]."[86] Kapterev and Bekhterev thus extended the scope of contagion to include not merely unmediated forms of imitation, such as panic, but a whole range of activities that formed the very fabric of the social world. The national press and literature became the carriers of pathological imitation and suggestion, capable of extending their influence throughout the whole of society.

In a sense, such an analysis had been implicit within even the earliest accounts of moral contagion. They had frequently cited the example of the reporting of murders or suicides in the press generating a wave of copycat crimes—producing a conceptual blur between imitation occurring between two individuals in physical proximity and imitation transmitted over space and time by word of mouth or the printed word.[87] The anonymous author of the 1871 article "The Contagiousness of Mental Delusions" in *Znanie* and Kandinskii had both cited the phenomenon of copycat killings following the publication of details of murders in the press.[88] Yet these analyses took note of the role of the press in the dissemination of certain forms of deviance; they did not scrutinize what its role revealed about society. By contrast, the studies of the 1890s and 1900s explicitly conceptualized a link between psychopathologies and moral contagion in terms of a latent predisposition to criminal acts that could be triggered by reporting in the press.

85   Ibid., 16.
86   Bekhterev, *Vnushenie*, 1.
87   Indeed, in his study of 1838, *Des maladies mentales considerées sous le rapport médical, hygienique et médico-légal*, the influential French psychiatrist Jean-Étienne Esquirol had noted the role of the press in fostering the spread of deviance. A disciple of Philippe Pinel, Esquirol (1772–1840) was one of the founders of French psychiatry and a strong supporter of the isolation of the mentally ill in psychiatric institutions. On Esquirol's career and influence, see Jan Goldstein, *Console and Classify: The French Psychiatric Profession in the Nineteenth Century* (Cambridge: Cambridge University Press, 1987), 128–47. In 1882, Mikhailovskii also cited Esquirol's remark that "Friends of humanity should demand that newspapers be prohibited from printing news of the motives and details of all suicides." Mikhailovskii, "Geroi i tolpa," 110.
88   "Zarazitel'nost' umstvennykh zabluzhdenii," 109; Kandinskii, *Obshcheponiatnye psikhologicheskie etiudy*, 190–91.

In 1906, Dmitrii Dril' drew on the precepts of degeneration theory to argue that suicide was frequently a result of the combined effects of diseased heredity and pathological imitation. Individuals with defective biopsychological constitutions were fatally susceptible to the influence of their environment. It might be the case that individuals were born with a particular predisposition to suicide, but their choice of means was often shaped by the examples to which they were exposed. Suicide was then a conjunction of "(1) the usually acute internal state of health and moods that are the result of certain deficiencies in the functioning of the organism and (2) the thought of taking one's life *as a means of escaping from these acute internal conditions, a means of bringing them to an end.*" Dril' maintained that although "the first factor might be inherited," the second could only come about "under the influence of an overheard conversation, reading the newspapers, books, and so on; in a word, from external influences."[89] Contemporaries celebrated the growth of the print media in postreform Russia as a feature of society's progress, because it helped to develop literacy and culture.[90] Yet in this particular context, the rise of the mass circulation press and the growth of publishing effectively provided the sinews of an enormous crowd, generating conduits for the transmission of pathological imitation from individuals in one time and location to individuals in quite another.

A number of clinicians concluded that society essentially functioned in the same way as a giant crowd; similarly governed by the contagions of emotions and moods, unstructured by reason. Bekhterev declared that "what we find in individually formed crowds, we also find, although to a much lesser extent, in every social milieu and also in large societies, especially in periods of heightened social passion." In such an environment, members of society "infect each other with their thoughts every minute."[91] On the eve of the First World War, the psychiatrist Aleksandr Nikanorovich Mumortsev (1879–?) was even more emphatic in his comparison: "The social organism is an enormous crowd. The laws of suggestion and suggestibility are the same for it as they are for the individual and for a typical crowd in the street."[92]

The specter of popular revolt haunted these theoretical writings on moral contagion. Clinical visions of the crowd combined with long-standing convictions about the underdevelopment of rural Russia to generate significant reservations about the growth of mass society and its prospects for rationality and stability. In the wake the first Russian Revolution, such fears retrospectively also acquired a prophetic quality.

89   Dmitrii A. Dril', "Zadachi vospitaniia i rol' nasledstvennosti," *Vestnik psikhologii, kriminal'noi antropologii i gipnotizma,* no. 3, (1906): 18.
90   Louise McReynolds, *The News under Russia's Old Regime: The Development of a Mass-Circulation Press* (Princeton: Princeton University Press, 1991), 123–44.
91   Bekhterev, *Vnushenie,* 171.
92   Aleksandr N. Mumortsev, "O sovremennom pessimizme i samoubiistvakh," *Sovremennaia psikhiatriia* (November 1914): 879.

The "Traumatic Epidemic" of 1905

The violent disorder of the years 1905–07 provided ample evidence of the destructive power of crowds. Indeed, 1905 suddenly embodied the very social revolution that had long haunted educated Russian society and had been so vividly described in the pages of Taine's *Les origines*. Even long-standing opponents of the autocracy were disconcerted by the seemingly random and limitless nature of the violence.[93] Writing in 1906, Sergei Iaroshevskii described the revolution as impelled by "everything that had matured over decades and centuries in the deepest recesses of the people's collective soul, everything that had moved their hearts and minds and that had seethed and bubbled below the surface had broken through with unrestrained power." Iaroshevskii was decidedly ambivalent about the nature of this force that had been unleashed: "In this chaos of feelings, thoughts, desires, and urges, it is sometimes difficult for the observer to orient himself, to distinguish the good from the evil, the useful from the harmful, the realistic from the utopian, the true grain of culture and progress from those manifestations of atavism that sometimes recall the features of our distant and savage forebears."[94] The very indiscriminate nature of social and political action during the revolution and its estrangement from the structures of morality and reason invited the application of moral contagion as an explanatory framework capable of accounting for the spread of the violence. Faced with the explosion of disorder and the arbitrary nature of attacks on a bewilderingly wide variety of social constituencies, from government officials to impoverished Jewish communities, many clinicians deployed the theoretical apparatus elaborated over the previous two decades to understand events.

As discussed in chapter two, many clinicians considered the experience of trauma associated with revolutionary violence to play a significant role in the etiology of degeneration and mental illness. Traumatic experiences also psychologically destabilized individuals, rendering them more susceptible to the spread of moral contagions. Just as Dril' had maintained that the press reporting of suicide could trigger the onset of pathological imitation in those with a predisposition, Iaroshevskii noted that the experience of the trauma of revolution had a similar catalyzing effect on those

with an inherited or acquired instability of their nervous-mental apparatus. . . . In normal times, when social life flows peacefully without severe shocks, these unstable individuals can also lead their lives peacefully without revolt,

---

93   Laura Engelstein, *The Keys to Happiness: Sex and the Search for Modernity in Fin-de-Siècle Russia* (Ithaca: Cornell University Press, 1992), 254–98.

94   Sergei O. Iaroshevskii, "Materialy k voprosu o massovykh nervnopsikhicheskikh zabolevaniiakh," *Obozrenie psikhiatrii, nevrologii i eksperimental'noi psikhologii* 11, no. 1 (1906): 1.

as perfectly normal people, provided nothing happens in their individual lives capable of disturbing their mental equilibrium. But the vulnerability of these unstable natures is acutely revealed during political catastrophes. Just as physically unstable individuals receptive to a given infection, most easily become infected and fall ill during a given epidemic, so during historical catastrophes unstable minds most easily contract nervous and mental illnesses.[95]

In Iaroshevskii's opinion, although the empire was undoubtedly experiencing "a mental epidemic," yet to be properly diagnosed, its carriers were subjects with impaired or unstable nervous-mental constitutions.[96] Dril' suggested in a lecture delivered at the Pedagogical Department of St. Petersburg University in 1906 that revolutionaries were indeed recruited from the ranks of "degenerating generations . . . and frequently play, especially in periods of social unrest, one of the most important roles in the lives of entire peoples."[97] Mumortsev also believed that "if the role of suggestion as a social factor is so significant even in normal and healthy conditions of social life, what can we expect when this life begins to experience certain deviations when the mental equilibrium of every individual comprising that society or a whole people is disturbed?"[98] In these accounts, revolution was then both a prerequisite for and a function of moral contagion. Although its spread was sustained by the existence in Russian society of pathological subjects unable to mediate their responses to the social influences that surrounded them, the vulnerability of these subjects to contagion was only exposed under the traumatic effects of their revolutionary experiences.

The *zemstvo* physician Dmitrii Nikolaevich Zhbankov (1853–1932) explored the precise nature of these revolutionary experiences and their relationship with moral contagion in an influential series of articles written

---

95   Ibid., 1–2. Discussions of the need for a robust and disciplined willpower were nowhere more in evidence than in discussions of military psychology. Writing in 1905, the military psychiatrist Gerasim Egorovich Shumkov (1873–?) confirmed the "infectiousness of moods" in his observations of Russian soldiers at the front: "I saw fear on their faces. And the shouts and groans and prayers infected [*zarazitel'no deistvovali na*] my mood. . . . One has to be Napoleon or Alexander of Macedonia, possessing an iron will, in order not to submit to general influence." Gerasim E. Shumkov, "Rasskazy i nabliudeniia iz nastoiashchei russko-iaponskoi voiny (Voenno-psikhologicheskie etiudy)," *Voprosy nervno-psikhicheskoi meditsiny,* no. 1 (January–March 1905): 20. See also idem, *Psikhika boitsov vo vremia srazheniia* (St. Petersburg: B. I., 1909); Nikolai N. Golovin, *Issledovanie boia* (St. Petersburg: Ekonomiche-skaia tipografiia, 1907); Aleksandr S. Rezanov, *Armiia i tolpa: Opyt voennoi psikhologii* (Warsaw: Varshavskaia esteticheskaia tipografiia, 1910).
96   Ibid., 1.
97   Dmitrii A. Dril', "Iavleniia vyrozhdeniia i usloviia obshchestvennoi sredy v sviazi s voprosami vospitaniia," *Vestnik psikhologii, kriminal'noi antropologii i gipnotizma,* no. 10 (1906): 272.
98   Mumortsev, "O sovremennom pessimizme," 880.

between 1905 and 1907 and widely cited by his colleagues.[99] Zhbankov offered a compendium of the violence that was overwhelming the empire during the revolution, in which he discussed in detail press reports of terrorist killings, pogroms, and the government's bloody campaign of internal pacification. He termed the revolutionary violence "the traumatic epidemic in Russia" and argued that it had generated an atmosphere of "panic and terror that had paralyzed both the reason and the willpower of many people." Kept in a state of permanent anxiety and fear by the threat of government repression, "the entire peole [*narod*] and unfortunately the mass of educated society find themselves in such a mood of pathological excitement that the merest pretext is enough to cause them to lose self-control and bring about panic and disturbances."[100]

The anti-Semitic pogrom in the Bessarabian town of Kishinev in April 1903 was a case in point.[101] Zhbankov argued that it was not a "spontaneous hurricane but rather a systematically prepared massacre of neighbors by neighbors, of peaceful people by other peaceful people under the influence of the local administration" that had spread "microbes of misanthropy" and "created an atmosphere, full of excitement, of all kinds of gossip and rumors about what lay in store." In this atmosphere, "the beast inside man awakened; the air was heavy with the thirst for blood, violence, and vengeance." The events in the town constituted the origins of a moral contagion that "began to spread everywhere, intensified all the time by growing administrative repression, which suppressed the population and drove it to a state of panic, which [in turn] increased susceptibility to any kind of mental contagion."[102]

The reporting on the Russo-Japanese War of 1904 further strengthened the mood of violent hysteria, and then the real tipping point in the revolutionary violence came with the events of Bloody Sunday in January 1905, as a result of which "society and the people became debauched: they ceased to love life and to fear death." The national press became a vehicle for the

---

99 Dmitrii N. Zhbankov, "Travmaticheskaia epidemiia v Rossii (Aprel'–mai 1905 g.)," *Prakticheskii vrach* 4, nos. 32–35 (1905): 633–37; 656–61; 681–86; 703–6; "Travmaticheskaia krovavaia epidemiia v Rossii," *Prakticheskii vrach* 5, nos. 32–35 (1906): 533–36; 552–55; 569–71; 584–88; "Travmaticheskaia epidemiia v Rossii (fevral' 1905 g.—iiun' 1907 g.)," *Prakticheskii vrach* 6, nos. 34–38 (1907): 609–15; 624–25; 644–45; 661–64; 680–83. Bekhterev cited Zhbankov's article in the expanded third edition of his *Vnushenie i ego rol' v obshchestvennoi zhizni* (St. Petersburg: K. L. Rikker, 1908), 64. On Zhbankov's article, see also Morrissey, *Suicide and the Body Politic*, 301–5.
100 Zhbankov, "Travmaticheskaia epidemiia v Rossii (Aprel'–mai 1905 g.)," *Prakticheskii vrach* 4, no. 32 (1905): 633.
101 Edward Judge, *Easter in Kishinev: Anatomy of a Pogrom* (New York: New York University Press, 1992). On the pogroms more generally in the period, see Charters Wynn, *Workers, Strikes, and Pogroms: The Donbass and Dnepr Bend in Late Imperial Russia, 1870–1905* (Princeton: Princeton University Press, 1992).
102 Zhbankov, "Travmaticheskaia epidemiia," *Prakticheskii vrach* 4, no. 32 (1905): 635.

transmission of the contagion: "The newspapers reveled in the bloodshed and became bulletins about the course of the bloody epidemic: telegrams and reports about thousands killed and wounded in the [Russo-Japanese] war, telegrams and government reports about individual murders and the large-scale pogroms inside Russia."[103] The press thereby disseminated the horror of the violence, both military and civil, across the empire, influencing populations that had hitherto remained unaffected by the unrest directly. And so the contagion spread.

Zhbankov's views were widely shared. Pavel Rozenbakh argued in 1909 that the "persistent reports in the press of killings and executions created an abnormal atmosphere" and "under the influence of general suggestion on the minds and imagination of the population" the number of suicides had increased.[104] Bekhterev himself regarded the outbreak of revolutionary violence as, in large part, a product "of the influence of reciprocal suggestion [*vzaimovnushenie*] and social contagion [*sotsial'naia zaraza*]" and cited Kuz'min-Karavaev, a deputy in the first Duma: "When policemen are killed, when soldiers are killed at their posts, when children and schoolboys shoot guns and throw bombs, then it is obvious that we are confronting an epidemic phenomenon [*iavlenie epidemicheskoe*], a particular form of mass psychosis [*massovyi psikhoz*]."[105]

Zhbankov was unwilling, however, to stigmatize the entire revolutionary movement as driven by irrational and destructive forces and pointed to "a rise in the self-consciousness of certain groups who clearly understood the real situation and had proposed effective measures for a restoration of Russia's health, [without which] we would be threatened with complete impotence and the kinds of mass mental epidemics that broke out in the Middle Ages." Social elites of the left-liberal orientation, to which Zhbankov himself subscribed, had to exert a restraining influence over the "greater part of our society, which is knocked off track, stupefied by both external and internal events, and no longer able to resist outrageous impressions, loses its self-control and the voice of reason."[106] Yet where Zhbankov saw a possibility for the reinsertion of reason and morality into the course of the revolution, others identified only the indiscriminate subordination of the masses to those who claimed leadership.

Writing in the midst of the 1905 Revolution, Bazhenov declared that "the most striking feature of the masses is their suggestibility, their imitativeness, and this has perhaps never been more obvious than during the days

103   Ibid.
104   Pavel I. Rozenbakh, "O prichinakh sovremennoi nervoznosti i samoubiistv," *Novoe slovo*, no. 11 (1909): 46.
105   Bekhterev, *Vnushenie*, 64–65.
106   Zhbankov, "Travmaticheskaia epidemiia," *Prakticheskii vrach* 4, no. 32 (August 13, 1905): 634.

of the Russian Revolution." This fact was the mainspring of the revolutionary movement, not the ideas or ethical codes put forward by would-be leaders. Indeed, the particular forms of political organization championed by the various groups contending for power during the revolution were in fact of little consequence. The differences between them would effectively be obliterated "by the power of that psychological law in accordance with which the whole of humanity is divided into two entirely unequal groups—a smaller number of suggesters and the huge majority who are suggestible." The operation of this law determined that "any form of social and political structure, whatever name it bore—a despotism or a republic, unlimited or constitutional monarchy—in the final analysis boils down to one and the same form, to an oligarchy."[107]

In Rybakov's opinion, the unrestrained dominance of this psychological division of humanity into suggesters and the suggestible was compounded by the underdevelopment of political society in Russia. He equated political parties with a "herd instinct" (*stadnost'*) that served to channel the undiscriminating and unstable emotions of individuals and crowds toward certain forms of action and certain strategic goals. Parties thus served as a filter of popular emotions, exerting a civilizing influence necessary for the maintenance of social stability. The absence of an established party system in contemporary Russia left the crowds, and indeed the population as a whole, dangerously responsive to all manner of usurpers and demagogues:

> In the West, where social life is more extensively developed than ours, the herd-instinct manifests itself with greater power, but there it finds a more noble form: the form of a party outlook [*partiinost'*]; there every party firmly knows the leader it follows. . . . [This difference between Russia and the West] does not depend on the fact that the Russian public is in general less

---

107 Nikolai N. Bazhenov, *Psikhologiia i politika* (Moscow: I. D. Sytin, 1906), 13. Bazhenov's argument anticipates, in intriguing ways, the thesis on oligarchy advanced by the German syndicalist, and later fascist, Robert Michels (1876–1936) in his influential *Zur Soziologie des Parteiwesens in der modernen Demokratie; Untersuchungen über die oligarchischen Tendenzen des Gruppenlebens* (Leipzig: W. Klinkhardt, 1911). Although Bazhenov made no mention of his work in this pamphlet, it is inconceivable that he was not well-acquainted with the writings of the influential French sociologist, Gustave Le Bon, whose treatise on crowd psychology appeared in several translations in Russia and was widely read in the original. Le Bon argued that crowds were an inalienable feature of the modern age and if they could not be removed, they needed to be tamed: "Crowds are somewhat like the sphinx of ancient fable; it is necessary to arrive at a solution of the problems offered by their psychology or to resign ourselves to being devoured by them." Le Bon offered Machiavellian advice to a would-be leader of the crowd. To seduce the masses, the leader had to enter the irrational minds of its members, pretending to sympathize with their plight, and using emotional and evocative slogans and images to attain control over them. Le Bon, *La psychologie des foules*, 90, 162–63. See, e.g., Gustav Lebon, *Psikhologiia narodov i mass*, trans. A. Fridman and E. Pimenova (St. Petersburg: F. Pavlenkov, 1896). On Le Bon, see Robert A. Nye, *The Origins of Crowd Psychology: Gustave Le Bon and the Crisis of Mass Democracy in the Third Republic* (London: Sage, 1975).

developed than in the West but rather on the fact that in our social life there are no established social organizations, the whole of our life is fragmented into individual parts, and when these elements are occasionally fused together, it is for the most part by chance, it is a fusion not of thought or of conviction but of place and time.[108]

The revolution represented, therefore, the eruption of mass politics unfettered by established parties.[109] The term *partiinost'* has traditionally been associated with Bolshevik sectarianism. First used by Lenin in 1895, the term became an important constituent feature of the Bolshevik mindset, denoting a series of political and social views inflected by tribal party loyalty and a Marxist-inspired vision of class conflict and social progress.[110] Yet Rybakov's encouragement of the development of *partiinost'* in contemporary Russian political culture suggests that it was not merely a manifestation of antidemocratic sectarian instincts. In Rybakov's opinion, the clinical analysis of the psychological forces impelling politics in the age of revolution revealed the need for a set of political institutions and practices capable of restraining the worst excesses of mass democracy. In these terms, *partiinost'* denoted fealty not to any particular party but to the party of reason and order.

The Democratic Surfeit

Moral contagion was a rich and flexible tool of sociopolitical analysis in late Imperial Russia. It now provides a fascinating lens through which to examine the evaporating faith of the liberal intelligentsia in its own tutelary

---

108   Rybakov, *Gipnotizm*, 129.
109   This reaction on the part of Russian progressives to the revolution of 1905 would be reprised just over a decade later in 1917. In November 1917, for example, the eminent scientist and Constitutional Democrat Vladimir Vernadskii wrote in his diary, "It is a tragic situation. Forces and layers of the people are now playing a role in determining our structure of life [*zhiznennyi stroi*], but they are in no condition to understand [this structure's] interests. It is clear that unrestrained democracy, the pursuit of which I set as the goal of my life, requires corrections." V. I. Vernadskii, *Dnevniki, 1917–1921*, 2 vols. (Kiev: Naukova Dumka, 1994), 1:88 (November 10, 1917), cited in Peter Holquist, *Making War, Forging Revolution: Russia's Continuum of Crisis, 1914–1921* (Cambridge, MA: Harvard University Press, 2002), 49. On Vernadskii, see Kendall E. Bailes, "Science, Philosophy, and Politics in Soviet History: The Case of Vladimir Vernadskii," *Russian Review* 40, no. 3 (July 1981): 278–99.
110   Lenin declared, "Materialism includes, so to speak, *partiinost'* [partyness], enjoining one in any judgment of an event to take directly and openly the standpoint of a definite social group." V. I. Lenin, "Ekonomicheskoe soderzhanie narodnichestva i kritika ego v knige g. Struve," *Polnoe sobranie sochinenii*, 55 vols. (Moscow: Gosizdatel'stvo politicheskoi literatury, 1958–65), 1:418–19. On the significance of the term, see Leopold Haimson, *The Russian Marxists and the Origins of Bolshevism* (Cambridge, MA: Harvard University Press, 1955); John Barber, "The Establishment of Intellectual Orthodoxy in the U.S.S.R, 1928–1934," *Past and Present* 83 (May 1979): 141–64; David Joravsky, *Soviet Marxism and Natural Sciences, 1917–1932* (London: Routledge, 1961), 25.

mission of national enlightenment. Three overlapping stages of disillusionment are discernible. Initially convinced of the correlation between psychological irrationality and cultural and social underdevelopment, liberal practitioners of the human sciences remained committed to the promise of reform and enlightenment to yield a free and autonomous society. Yet under the conjoined influence of Italian and French studies of the crowd, Russian clinicians began to register serious concerns that human agglomerations wielded disturbing transformative powers. Mass societies were able to alter the moral and intellectual nature of all their constituents, not just the unenlightened, from civilized and sensible individuals to violent and destructive animals. Finally, studies of moral contagion began to emphasize that essentially irrational forces governed all human beings. A series of institutional and political structures, capable of filtering out the baser impulses of human beings, was required in order to hold these forces in check.

The cumulative effect of these three related positions in the social and political context of contemporary Russia amounted to a profoundly ambivalent response to the rise and promise of mass politics. Practitioners of the human sciences, whatever their hostility to the autocracy, appeared to regard the advent of mass politics with deep unease, something to be contained and directed rather than unfurled and celebrated. In this view, the involvement of the mass of the Russian people in politics held the political community of the nation hostage to the unpredictable and uncontrollable instincts that lurked beneath the surface of the social order.

The disillusionment with the promise of mass politics in Russia in some measure actually preceded the 1905 Revolution; it was not born simply of educated European Russia's fear of a tsunami of anarchic peasant violence. Progressive Russian clinicians and social scientists were in fact registering serious doubts about mass politics *tout court*, not simply about the risks attendant upon its introduction in an underdeveloped peasant society. The year 1905 was less a watershed in liberal attitudes toward mass politics than a confirmation of fears long harbored; it had realized on a grand scale the potential for irrationality, barbarism, and limitless violence that Tolstoi had so deftly captured in *War and Peace*.

It was precisely in their Enlightenment concern with reason and order that the liberal elites within the human sciences found the irrationality, unpredictability, and chaos of mass politics disconcerting. Attempts to devise institutional and ideological structures within which the values of the Enlightenment might be defended from the vagaries of mass society constituted an initial step in the direction of a circumscription of democracy and the rise of political authoritarianism that was to culminate under the Bolshevik regime.

5 Social Isolation and Coercive Treatment after the Revolution

> If ancient Themis only listened to the description of an offense
> with her eyes bound and without ever looking at the actual
> person of the criminal, we biologists should not only regard him
> with our eyes completely uncovered but should also scrutinize
> him with all the means of investigation available to us.
> —Viktor V. Brailovskii, 1927

In 1927, the criminologist G. N. Udal'tsov published a study entitled "Criminal Offenses in the Armed Forces from the Perspective of Pathological Physiology" in the authoritative *Obozrenie psikhiatrii, nevrologii i refleksologii*. The study related the case of a student at a technical college. Actively religious before the revolution, he had been drafted into the imperial army in 1916 and in 1920 joined the Bolshevik Party. Recently the young man, who was described as "a passive rank and file worker," had been admitted to the clinic for mental illness at Leningrad's Military-Medical Academy. Udal'tsov's diagnosis of the student's condition is worth citing at length:

> He once again became religious, avidly read the Gospels, and distributed his possessions among his acquaintances. He began to preach against human injustice, emphatically rejecting the Party's program in particular, saying that truth could only be found in the Gospels. He spoke out against war and against all its instruments, especially the army, declaring military service to be potential participation in murder. He was arrested as a counterrevolutionary for his refusal to serve in the army and for his open dissemination of his views . . . [and] was sent to the clinic for examination. The clinical diagnosis was "dementia praecox." Here we have an interesting case, as a result of the dissolution of

restraints and under the influence of a pathological process, of the reappearance of old reflexes that had been strongly instilled in childhood—religiosity and conservatism.[1]

Leaving to one side the issue of its clinical accuracy, which here can be neither corroborated nor refuted, Udal'tsov's diagnosis is striking for its characterization of the subject's condition in terms of a failure to adapt to the ideological demands of postrevolutionary society. The student's exposure to a religious and conservative milieu under the *ancien régime* had instilled in him psychological reflexes or "social instincts," as they were often termed, which resulted in deviant and subversive behavior in the socialist state. Udal'tsov explained this failure of individual adaptation to a changing environment as a consequence of biopsychological deficiencies:

> As a result of phylogenesis, man receives a range of hereditary features, instincts, and unconditional reflexes, on the basis of which he constructs a conditional-reflexive system over the course of his life. A healthy [*polnotsennyi*—literally, "full value"] individual is characterized by a swift and complete adaptation to the surrounding milieu, based on the regulatory work of the higher nervous system.

Individuals with an "an easily-excitable and functionally unstable cortex" would, however, experience "an acute struggle between excitement and restraint that . . . in individuals with weak nervous systems would result in a disturbance in the cortical balance, an explosion in its cortical activity, and a neurotic condition."[2] The language of psychopathology was here integrated into a revolutionary narrative of societal change and individual adaptation. The persistence of a prerevolutionary system of beliefs and values into the Soviet Union of the 1920s resulted in behavior that could be diagnosed as mentally ill, "socially dangerous," and even counterrevolutionary.

It was in the wake of 1917 that criminology emerged as a distinct discipline within the human sciences with institutional grounding and regime funding.[3] The first criminological research center was founded in Petrograd in 1918. Adoption of the 1922 criminal code laid the foundation for extensive criminological research by recognizing the existence of criminality in Soviet society. As Louise Shelly has shown, criminologists of this period

---

1   G. N. Udal'tsov, "Pravonarusheniia v voiskakh s tochki zreniia patologicheskoi fiziologii," *Obozrenie psikhiatrii, nevrologii i refleksologii,* no. 2 (1927): 121.
2   Ibid., 124.
3   On the history of Soviet criminology, see Peter H. Solomon Jr., "Soviet Penal Policy, 1917–1934: A Reinterpretation," *Slavic Review* 39, no. 2 (June 1980): 195–217; idem, "Soviet Criminology: Its Demise and Rebirth, 1928–1965," *Soviet Union* 1, no. 2 (1974): 122–40; Louise Shelly, "Soviet Criminology after the Revolution," *Journal of Law and Criminology* 70, no. 3 (1979): 391–405; Aleksandr B. Sakharov, *Istoriia kriminologicheskoi nauki* (Moscow: MVShM, 1994).

were primarily interested in the personality of the criminal and tried to categorize personal motivations and characteristics according to particular types of criminality.[4]

During the mid-1920s, the State Institute for the Study of Crime and the Criminal was organized under the auspices of the NKVD with affiliates in Moscow, Leningrad, Saratov, and Rostov-on-Don. The Moscow headquarters had four sections: socioeconomic, penitentiary, biopsychological, and criminalistics. Other independent research institutes were based in Minsk, Kharkov, Odessa, and Kiev. Criminologists and psychiatrists were able to pursue their research in the period between the Civil War and the Cultural Revolution with both intellectual and institutional freedom.[5]

This period of tolerance came to an abrupt end, however, at the close of the 1920s. Some scholars have argued that these developments represented the victory of "sociological" over "biological" theories of deviance.[6] Yet it is easy to overplay the division between these approaches to crime and to neglect their well-established interaction and synthetic explanations. That criminology was effectively extinguished as a vibrant intellectual field at the end of the 1920s represents not so much the triumph of "Marxist" approaches to crime over others but the intellectual subordination of the entire discipline to a very narrow and ruthlessly practical agenda determined by the regime under the aegis of the Communist Academy.[7]

Building on the intellectual legacy of the prerevolutionary era, Soviet psychiatrists and criminologists grafted a working synthesis of socioeconomic and biopsychological analyses of criminality onto a Soviet Marxist analysis of class struggle and social change. Therein lay a dangerous potential for a radical expansion of biomedical explanations of deviance to all those constituencies believed to resist the regime's program of modernization and state-building. Peter Solomon argues that during the early 1930s "criminology's emasculation . . . was [due to] its irrelevance to the principal crime problem of those years—the repression of the so-called class enemies who threatened the success of the collectivization and industrialization drives. Criminologists were hardly needed to chronicle the growing application of terror to 'kulaks' and to alleged industrial saboteurs; ideologists rather than criminologists were best qualified to explain the appearance of these new threats to the regime's plans."[8] To the contrary, this chapter argues that

4   Louise Shelly, "Soviet Criminology: Its Birth and Demise, 1917–1936," *Slavic Review* 38, no. 4 (December 1979): 617.
5   Solomon, "Soviet Criminology: Its Demise and Rebirth, 1928–1965," 123.
6   Sharon A. Kowalsky, "Who's Responsible for Female Crime? Gender, Deviance, and the Development of Soviet Social Norms in Revolutionary Russia," *Russian Review* 62, no. 3 (July 2003): 370.
7   Shelly, "Soviet Criminology: Its Birth and Demise, 1917–1936,," 624–25; Solomon, "Soviet Criminology: Its Demise and Rebirth, 1928–1965," 125–29.
8   Solomon, "Soviet Criminology: Its Demise and Rebirth, 1928–1965," 129.

criminological and psychiatric theories lent an important sanction to the regime's modernization project, articulated cultural or ideological anxieties in a language of medical science and highlighted the threat posed to the regime by social constituencies understood to have failed in their adaptation to the new, postrevolutionary order.

Practitioners of the human sciences, many of whom had already established their careers in the last two decades of the tsarist period, continued to elaborate and refine theories of biopsychological deviance in the early years of the Soviet regime.[9] Unsurprisingly, a great deal of continuity characterizes their theoretical writings across the revolutionary divide; they continued to regard deviance as a fateful conjunction of both hereditary and environmental forces, a failure on the part of the individual to adapt to the new terms of the struggle for existence, and evidence of the ominous moral and social forces unleashed by Russia's plunge into modernity in the late nineteenth century.

What follows is not, however, merely a tale of overlooked continuity between two ostensibly dissimilar epochs. The enthusiasm with which criminologists and psychiatrists continued to develop theories of degeneration, psychopathology, and moral contagion was representative not simply of an enduring fidelity to a prerevolutionary scientific discourse. Neither were these theories merely a reflection of the enduring popularity of biological theories of social evolution that still wielded great influence across the European continent.[10] The freedom and energy with which Russian clinicians and scientists continued to pursue biomedical explanations of crime, social disorder, and subversion—and the endorsement of their work by the Soviet state—were in large measure due to the ability of the human sciences to offer a compelling meditation on the country's experience of revolution and the obstacles confronting the future development of society. With their sophisticated readings of the relationship between heredity and the environment, between criminals and their actions, and between social change and the generation of deviance, medical and legal experts were uniquely placed to narrate the revolution and the prospects for modernization in a backward country.

---

9   Sergei S. Ostroumov, *Prestuptnost' i ee prichiny v dorevoliutsionnoi Rossii* (Moscow: Izdatel'stvo Moskovskogo Universiteta, 1960).
10   On the voluminous literature dealing with the persistence of biomedical constructions of social change and deviance in the first half of the twentieth century, see Richard Wetzell, *Inventing the Criminal: a History of Germany Criminology, 1880–1945* (Chapel Hill: University of North Carolina Press, 2000); Michael Schwartz, "Biopolitik in der Moderne: Aspekte eines vielsichtigen Machtdispositivs," *Internationale wissenschaftliche Korrespondenz zur Geschichte der deutschen Arbeiterbewegung* 31, no. 3 (September 1995): 332–47; Mark Mazower, *Dark Continent: Europe's Twentieth Century* (London: Penguin, 2000), chap. 3; Edward Ross Dickinson, "Biopolitics, Fascism, Democracy: Some Reflections on Our Discourse about 'Modernity,'" *Central European History* 37, no. 1 (2004): 1–48.

As before 1917, these sciences encapsulated the hybrid mood of optimism and pessimism characteristic of the modern era. They elaborated the nature of the threats and obstacles confronting the Bolsheviks in their bid to build a new society; yet they also confirmed the belief that the obstacles could be overcome. Explorations of biopsychological deviance did not encourage a sense of powerlessness and defeat; they unfailingly pointed out strategies by which the forces of disorder could be contained and, ultimately, eliminated.

Bolsheviks were obsessed with their own "backwardness." Lenin's contempt for the Russian *oblomovshchina* is well known, and acute anxieties about the premature status of the revolution belied the bellicose pronouncements of the Party leadership.[11] The concept of heredity, initially elaborated as a biological term in the *fin-de-siècle* but seen increasingly in cultural or psychological terms, lent itself to a conceptualization of the imperial legacy as one that the new regime had either to assimilate or to destroy.

Similarly, environmental theories of human development were a double-edged sword in the first decade or so of Soviet power. On the one hand, the conviction that human material could be significantly reworked through a rationalization of the environment was a central feature of the Soviet revolutionary project. As Nikolai Bukharin remarked in 1928, "If we believed that racial or national peculiarities were so durable that they could only be changed over thousands of years, then our entire work would of course be absurd, built on sand."[12] Yet on the other hand, belief in the transformative powers of the environment raised all manner of disturbing questions concerning the quality of the human material that the Party had inherited from the period of capitalism and rapid modernization. This defective human material had been subjected to seven long years of war, revolutionary upheavals, famine, and epidemics. The resulting cumulative damage to the biopsychological health of the Soviet population challenged the optimism of all but the most determined builders of the new society. Finally, the theories of collective irrationality and societal instability examined in the previous chapter continued to wield interpretative power among contemporaries disturbed by the chaotic results of the revolution and civil war and the apparent indifference and hostility of large sections of the population to the Party's transformative program.

11   The term "oblomovshchina" connotes the indolence and apathy attributed by contemporaries to the Russian gentry in the nineteenth century and made notorious by Ivan Goncharov's novel *Oblomov* of 1859. Lenin wrote in 1920 that "*the old Oblomov is with us and for a long while yet he will still need to be washed, cleaned, shaken and given a good thrashing if something is to come of him.*" Vladimir I. Lenin, "O mezhdunarodnom i vnutrennem polozhenii," *Polnoe sobranie sochinenii*, 5th ed., 55 vols. (Moscow: Gosizdatel'stvo politicheskoi literatury, 1958–62), 45:13.

12   Speech by Nikolai Bukharin to the First Pedological Congress, reported in *Na putiakh k novoi shkole*, no. 1 (1928): 11–12, cited in Sheila Fitzpatrick, *Education and Social Mobility in the Soviet Union, 1921–1934* (Cambridge: Cambridge University Press, 1979), 141.

As in the late imperial period, the human sciences were therefore vehicles for the exploration of contemporary anxieties. They made available a complex of facts and theories that lent themselves to an analysis of Russia's experience of revolutionary change and the prospects of societal renewal. They were, however, in an important sense also enabling; they highlighted, consolidated, and legitimated new objects of medical and scientific concern. They facilitated the extension of a medicalized language of criminal deviance to all expressions of opposition, real and potential, to the Soviet regime. When the new regime sponsored these scientific attempts to articulate an explanatory language with which to analyse and master the social and political disorder fomented by the revolution, it found a ready vocabulary in the biopsychological theories of criminality. Theories of the hereditary and environmental etiology of deviance now partially structured the Bolsheviks' rudimentary attempts to reclassify society, with the result that entire social constituencies were invested with the dangerous moral defects of the prerevolutionary class of habitual criminals and psychopaths.[13] The consequence was a radical expansion of the range of deviant behaviors that the human sciences could now legitimately claim as objects of study and knowledge.

It is a truism, of course, that each society defines its own criminals and that these definitions shift from one time to another. In 1925, the criminologist Aleksandr Karlovich Lents (1882–1952) declared that

> crime is not in fact an absolute and permanent phenomenon. It is always bound up with the existence of a particular social group in a ruling order. If the ruling order changes, the range of criminal activities that incur punishment also changes fundamentally. Revolutionary propaganda was a serious crime according to the 1903 criminal code. In the criminal code of the RSFSR, such a crime no longer exists, because this form of activity has now become supportive of the existing order. Blasphemy and many other offenses have undergone a similar metamorphosis.[14]

Lents' point was well made, but he neglected to mention that the reverse was also true. In its first decade in power, the Soviet regime set about to discursively stigmatize and often legally criminalize vast areas of economic, social, and political activity that had been permitted and even encouraged by the

---

13   Sheila Fitzpatrick, "The Problem of Class Identity in NEP Society," in *Russia in the Era of NEP: Explorations in Soviet Society and Culture*, ed. Sheila Fitzpatrick, Alexander Rabinowitch, and Richard Stites (Bloomington: Indiana University Press, 1991), 12–33; idem, "Ascribing Class: The Construction of Social Identity in Soviet Russia," *Journal of Modern History* 65, no. 4 (December 1993): 745–70.

14   Aleksandr K. Lents, "Zadachi i plan sovremennoi kriminal'no-psikhiatricheskoi ekspertizy," *Sudebno-meditsinskaia ekspertiza. Trudy II Vserossiiskogo s"ezda sudebno-meditsinskikh ekspertov, Moskva, 25 fevralia—3 marta 1926*, ed. Ia. L. Leibovich (Ul'ianovsk: Izdanie Ul'ianovskogo Kombinata PPP, 1926), 113.

authorities before the 1917 Revolution. This amounted to the "production of deviance" on a massive scale.[15] The state now had to find a language in which to articulate its rejection of the values and practices of the old world, and it found that language in biomedical theories of crime. A Marxist language of class struggle provided the basic epistemological platform for the Party's program of modernization; yet the biomedical discourse furnished the categories of class with tangible and urgent threats. An intellectually fertile union of Marxism and the biomedical sciences was central to the development of a discourse that explained the origins of social disorder, moral and ideological deviance, and even political subversion and proposed the means to combat them.

In this discourse, Soviet criminologists and psychiatrists applied prerevolutionary understandings of criminality and psychopathology in ways that their forebears would have recognized. As the case of Udal'tsov's student shows, the concepts and language of psychopathology were decidedly elastic; their extension to religious, political, and social disorder was a matter of a definitional adjustments rather than imaginative leaps.

The Diseased Heredity of the Bolsheviks

The characterization of the 1920s as a decade of anxiety for the Bolsheviks has become an axiom of recent studies of the period. The years linking the end of the Civil War with the launch of the collectivization and industrialization campaigns were a period of uncomfortable compromise with the forces of small-scale capitalism during NEP. The period was marked by the dilemmas of how to deal with the prerevolutionary classes whose existence and influence were understood to be in conflict with the construction of the socialist society of the future.[16] Michael David-Fox has argued that the Cultural Revolution, a term traditionally applied to a discrete period of radicalism between 1928 and 1932 in the midst of the Great Breakthrough (the twinned campaigns of forced collectivization and industrialization), might more instructively be expanded to address continuities running through Bolshevik cultural policy from 1917 into the 1930s. Indeed, the Bolsheviks'

---

15   I have borrowed the phrase from Marie-Christine Leps, *Apprehending the Criminal: The Production of Deviance in Nineteenth-Century Discourse* (Durham, NC: Duke University Press, 1992).

16   Sheila Fitzpatrick, "The Bolshevik's Dilemma: Class, Culture, and Politics in Early Soviet Years," *Slavic Review* 47, no. 4 (1988): 599–613; Stuart Finkel, "Purging the Public Intellectual: The 1922 Expulsions from Soviet Russia," *Russian Review* 62, no. 4 (October 2003): 589–613; Golfo Alexopoulos, *Stalin's Outcasts: Aliens, Citizens, and the Soviet State, 1926–1936* (Ithaca: Cornell University Press, 2002); Eric Naiman, *Sex in Public: The Incarnation of Early Soviet Ideology* (Princeton: Princeton University Press, 1997); Anne E. Gorsuch, *Youth in Revolutionary Russia: Enthusiasts, Bohemians, Delinquents* (Bloomington: Indiana University Press, 2000).

revolutionary transformation of society during the 1920s was to a large degree defined in terms of overcoming the survivals of the past. Illiteracy, uncultured behavior, religiosity, and superstition were all to be challenged and eliminated through a continuous state-sponsored program of tutelary enlightenment.[17] The transformation of individual conduct was key to the success of this program. As Catriona Kelly and Lynne Attwood have commented, the Soviet "New Man" and "New Woman" were celebrated for playing a crucial role in the construction of a new reality which was to be characterized by the suppression of both larger social evils such as insubordination and corruption, and small ones such as superstition and unpunctuality.[18]

How did biomedical theories of deviance reflect and engage with the Bolsheviks' understandings of their own troubled inheritance? Steeped in the discursive tradition of the radical intelligentsia, which had long characterized the tsarist order as a disease-ridden and pathological order in a terminal state of degeneration, the now victorious Bolsheviks feared that they would be contaminated by its remnants. As the Party—that erstwhile "bacteria of revolution"—underwent a discursive mutation to the robustly healthy new proletarian state, it did so against the background of the old order's literal and metaphorical decomposition.[19] In June 1918, Lenin presented the dangers of contamination in vivid terms:

> Yes, a Great Wall of China does not separate the working class from the old bourgeois world. And when the Revolution arrives, things do not happen as with the death of a single person, when the dead is carried away. When the

17   Michael David-Fox, "What Is Cultural Revolution?" *Russian Review* 58, no. 2 (April 1999): 181–201; Sheila Fitzpatrick, Alexander Rabinowitch, and Richard Stites, eds., *Russia in the Era of NEP: Explorations in Soviet Society and Culture* (Bloomington: Indiana University Press, 1991); Daniel Peris, *Storming the Heavens: The Soviet League of the Militant Godless* (Ithaca: Cornell University Press, 1998); Catriona Kelly, *Refining Russia: Advice Literature, Polite Culture, and Gender from Catherine to Yeltsin* (Oxford: Oxford University Press, 2001), chap. 4; Jochen Hellbeck, *Revolution on My Mind: Writing a Diary under Stalin* (Cambridge, MA: Harvard University Press, 2006).

18   Lynne Attwood and Catriona Kelly, "Programs for Identity: The 'New Man' and the 'New Woman,'" in *Constructing Russian Culture in the Age of Revolution, 1881–1940*, ed. Catriona Kelly and David Shepherd (Oxford: Oxford University Press, 1998), 256.

19   In his polemic against the Economists in 1900, Georgii Plekhanov made repeated references to professional revolutionaries as a "revolutionary bacillus" (*revoliutsionnaia batsilla*) whose "entire task . . . consists in facilitating the development of the workers' consciousness." G. V. Plekhanov, "Predislovie k 'Vademecum' dlia redaktsii 'Rabochego Dela,'" *Sochineniia*, 24 vols. (Moscow: Gosizdatel'stvo, 1924–27), 12:26–28. It is worth recalling the extent to which the Bolsheviks' language of disintegration, putrefaction, and illness appeared to many an intelligible and accurate description of the processes underway in Russia during the years of the revolution and civil war. Moshe Lewin has written eloquently on the process he terms "archaization," the depletion of the cities, the dispersal of the proletariat and the countryside's return to an almost premodern condition. See his *The Making of the Soviet System: Essays in the Social History of Interwar Russia* (London: Methuen, 1985), 194–99, 296–300.

old society perishes, it is impossible to hammer the cadaver of the bourgeois society [*trup burzhuaznogo obshchestva*] into a coffin and put it in the grave. Decomposing in our midst, this cadaver rots and infects us [*On razlagaetsia v nashei srede, etot trup gniet i zarazhaet nas samikh*].[20]

Yet the Bolsheviks feared much more than simply the threat of contamination from outside the Party. Even more pernicious and difficult to neutralize was the disease implicit in the tsarist legacy the Bolsheviks had inherited. Anxieties surrounding the fate of the revolution during NEP were often expressed in terms of the diseased parentage of the infant state. The rector of Sverdlov Communist University, Martyn Nikolaevich Liadov (1872–1947), identified the "psychology of the petty-bourgeoisie" as one of the great obstacles to the successful development of communism in the Soviet Union. In a 1924 speech to Party cells, which was published a year later, Liadov used the term "heredity" to denote not the biological constitution passed on from parents to children but rather the complex of values and instincts that the former instilled in the latter: "A child is born healthy physically and morally. It is only by means of his upbringing that we inject him with our hereditary diseases [*privivaem emu nashi nasledstvennye bolezni*]."[21]

Liadov's pronouncement revealed the growing tendency to read cultural and psychological influences through a biologizing prism of "heredity," applying a biomedical model to an understanding of the harmful psychology that the Soviet state had to combat. He reinforced his contention with an imaginary conversation between a petty bourgeois and the new state: "'It is my child'—says the petty bourgeois—'and I will corrupt [*portit'*] him as I wish.' 'You gave birth to the child but he is not your property; he was born a member of a society that wishes to see him grow into a healthy, normal person, and that he inherits [*unasledovat'*] as little as possible your petty-bourgeois characteristics, your social diseases.'"[22]

The concept of heredity, as deployed in these examples, served the additional purpose of diluting contemporary responsibility for criminality. In

20   V. I. Lenin, "Doklad o bor'be s golodom," *PSS* 36:408–9. This metaphor of a corpse enjoys a long pedigree in the writings of Russian radicals. In 1862, the radical critic Dmitrii Pisarev proclaimed that the tsarist order was already diseased to such an extent that therapeutics could no longer save it: "The Romanov dynasty and the Petersburg bureaucracy must disappear. . . . That which is dead and decaying [*mertvo i gnilo*] will come crashing down into the grave on its own; our role is merely to give it the final push and hurl the stinking corpses [*smerdiashchie trupy*] into the mud." Dmitrii Pisarev, "O broshiure Shedo-Ferroti," *Sochineniia*, 4 vols. (Moscow: Khudozhestvennaia literatura, 1955–56), 2:126.

21   Martyn N. Liadov, *Voprosy byta* (Moscow: Kommunisticheskii universitet im. Sverdlova, 1925), 22, 28–29.

22   Ibid., 29. The term "social diseases" had, of course, been coined by the people's commissar for health, Nikolai Semashko, in September 1918: "The name 'social disease' was derived from the social conditions in a capitalistic state, as even the bourgeois medical service recognizes the fact that diseases such as phthisis and venereal diseases are an outcome of these conditions." *Sovetskaia Rossia*, (September 18, 1918).

1926, the criminologist Evgenii Konstantinovich Krasnushkin (1885–1951) was keen to locate the origins of much NEP criminality in the prerevolutionary era. Recidivist criminals and the "socially dangerous" "undoubtedly had their sociobiological origins in the prerevolutionary and in part the prewar eras. They were prepared both biologically and socially in the epoch of old tsarist Russia."[23] In the same year, the head of the Soviet Union's penal administration, Evsei Gustafovich Shirvindt (1891–?), wrote that there could be no question as to the origins of the country's criminality: "Banditry, speculation, bribery, moonshine, embezzlement, youth crime—all these forms of crime, which were born somewhere in the depths of the remnants of the order that has been overthrown, began to flare up again [after the revolution]."[24] Writing a year later on a prominent issue of the day, Lev Orshanskii also declared that the hooligan was "the offspring of the past; alien to the contemporary world."[25]

That a measure of comfort might be drawn from a vigorous assertion of the anachronistic status of the criminal is perhaps not surprising. The new regime had an enormous investment in narrating 1917 and the early Soviet years as a period of struggle against the vestiges of the old order. Discursively returning the criminal to the prerevolutionary era simultaneously reinforced the pathologies of that era and affirmed the transience of postrevolutionary criminality. As Krasnushkin remarked,

> For Soviet Russia, the claim that "there are a large number of defective natures among criminals" can in fact be reassuring, since the order that generated these defective natures and that led individuals to degeneration is now behind us. And in the light of contemporary science, degeneration is not at all that hopeless terminal disease that Morel believed it to be; it can be cured with the renovation [*ozdorovlenie*] of the socioeconomic life of the people along the path we have embarked on.[26]

This optimistic construction of deviance as a residue of the old order, anachronistic and at the same time dangerous in the new, framed the very project of Soviet modernity in terms of the purification or cleansing of society of its inherited disorders. The elimination of deviance, which for tsarist

23   Evgenii K. Krasnushkin, "Chto takoe prestupnik," *Prestupnik i prestupnost'*. *Sbornik I* (Moscow: Moszdravotdel, 1926), 28.
24   Evsei G. Shirvindt, "O problemakh prestupnosti," *Problemy prestupnosti*, no. 1 (1926): 5.
25   Lev G. Orshanskii, "Khuligan. Psikhologicheskii ocherk," in *Khuliganstvo i prestuplenie. Sbornik statei*, ed. Lev G. Orshanskii, A. A. Zhizhilenko, and I. Ia. Derzibashev (Leningrad and Moscow: Rabochii sud, 1927), 67. In 1926, the Party published a collection of Lenin's essays, the title of which, *Bor'ba s naslediem kapitalisticheskoi kul'tury* [Struggle with the legacy of capitalist culture] (Moscow: Gosizdatel'stvo, 1926), spoke for itself.
26   Krasnushkin, "Chto takoe prestupnik," 33

liberals had stood as a measure of successful societal reform, had now come to stand as a tangible measure of revolutionary progress.

Bequeathals of War and Revolution

Liberal practitioners of the human sciences in the late imperial period, however, had been decidedly ambivalent about the suitability of revolution as an instrument for the elimination of a pathogenic capitalist environment. Many specialists had feared that revolution would itself further weaken the biopsychological health of the population and unleash a range of psychological disorders that would only increase the level of crime in society. Their arguments, discussed in chapter two, now came back to haunt psychiatrists and criminologists in the first decade of Soviet power. Orshanskii acknowledged that the experience of revolution and war had not simply failed to "temper" the instincts of the old order; in certain cases it had reinforced them. The revolution had temporarily subsumed the destructive energies of many hooligans into the struggle against the old regime, but in its aftermath it was clear that "not everyone was able to maintain their heroic behavior in the everyday life that followed. A new psychological stage arrived: nervous and physical exhaustion, insufficiency of strength, and through this exhaustion the old ways began to reassert themselves. These old ways opened the way for a time to the forgotten disease of hooliganism."[27]

The exhausting nature of the revolutionary turmoil had unleashed barbaric energies simmering beneath the surface of late imperial society. The revolution was therefore Janus-faced: forward-looking and progressive in its reordering of the socioeconomic order; backward-looking and atavistic in the regressive and antimodern instincts it had unleashed in sections of the population. Indeed, the entire revolutionary era had arguably comprised a continuum of privation, hunger, and disease. In 1929, the criminologist E. A. Lisianskaia cast a troubled glance over the previous two decades: "The older representatives of the current generation bore the burden of unenlightened reaction, then a period of unprecedented imperialist war, then a period of revolution and civil war combined with displacement, epidemics, and famine. The younger representatives, who were still children at the time of the imperialist war, were witness to the kinds of events unheard of in the most fantastical tales."[28]

27 Orshanskii, "Khuligan," 62.
28 E. A. Lisianskaia, "Prinuditel'noe lechenie kak mera sotsial'noi zashchity," in *Dushevno-bol'nye pravonarushiteli i prinuditel'noe lechenie*, ed. P. V. Gannushkin (Moscow: NKVD, 1929), 41. For similar arguments, see Aleksandr M. Tereshkovich, "Vliianie voiny i revoliutsii na psikhicheskuiu zabolevaemost'," *Moskovskii meditsinskii zhurnal*, no. 4 (1924): 67–74. The effects of war on the genetic health of the population were a prominent topic of

Indeed, exposure to the violence and trauma of armed conflict was one of the central concerns of those investigating postrevolutionary criminality.[29] Many clinicians built on the analyses of the relationship between trauma and the onset of nervous, mental, and degenerative disorders undertaken by clinicians in the wake of the 1905 Revolution. In 1923, the criminologist Sergei V. Poznyshev (1870–?) identified a group of "criminaloid bandits," whose tendency was not necessarily to banditry but to "lower forms of activity." Poznyshev argued that this group included

> individuals who had become coarsened by long postings at the front, in an atmosphere of those terrible images of death and malign excitement that are characteristic of war and, in particular, of civil war; individuals who served as executioners, slaughterhouse workers, and so on. More or less prolonged work of such a nature leaves the kind of residue, especially in mental constitutions of individuals who had not received sufficient education, that facilitates the formation of a preference for violent actions. Sometimes this residue already forms in childhood.[30]

Writing in 1928, Ia. M. Lobach of the Department for the Study of Crime at the Law Faculty of Belorussian State University in Minsk cited Soviet public prosecutor Nikolai Vasil'evich Krylenko (1885–1938), who had referred to the experiences of young offenders during the years of the revolution and civil war in the following terms: "These were years of acute destruction, of the absolute maximum demands on all the physical and mental energies of the proletariat. . . . The growing generation only gained and really imbibed one inheritance [*nasledie*] from the revolution: its destructive instinct. The revolution smashed the tsarist order, the family order, and the

concern among Russian biologists involved in the eugenics movement in the early 1920s. See, for example, Lev S. Berg, "Brachnost', rozhdaemost' i smertnost' v Leningrade za poslednie gody," *Priroda*, nos. 7–12 (1924): 101–8; A. V. Gorbunov, "Vliianie mirovoi voiny na dvizhenie naseleniia Evropy," *Russkii evgenicheskii zhurnal* 1 (1922): 40–64; V. V. Bunak, "Novye dannye k voprosu o voine kak biologicheskom faktore," *Russkii evgenicheskii zhurnal* 2 (1922): 223–32. On Soviet eugenics, see Loren Graham, "Science and Values: The Eugenics Movement in Germany and Russia in the 1920s," *American Historical Review* 82, no. 5 (December 1977): 1133–64; Mark B. Adams, "Eugenics in Russia, 1900–1940," in *The Wellborn Science: Eugenics in Germany, France, Brazil, and Russia*, ed. Mark B. Adams (Oxford: Oxford University Press, 1990), 153–216; idem, "Eugenics as Social Medicine: Prophets, Patrons, and the Dialectics of Discipline-Building in Revolutionary Russia," in *Health and Society in Revolutionary Russia*, ed. Susan Gross Solomon and John F. Hutchinson (Bloomington: Indiana University Press, 1990), 200–23.

29   On contemporary German studies of the same phenomenon, see Doris Kaufmann, "Science as Cultural Practice: Psychiatry in the First World War and Weimar Germany," *Journal of Contemporary History* 34, no. 1 (1999): 125–44.

30   Sergei V. Poznyshev, "K psikhologii sovremennogo banditizma," *Zhurnal psikhologii, nevrologii i psikhiatrii* 3 (1923): 67. See the same point made by A. O. Edel'shtein, "Khuliganstvo kak bio-sotsial'naia problema i ego sotsial'no-psikhitricheskoe izuchenie," *Vestnik sovremennoi meditsiny*, no. 12 (1926): 22.

prerevolutionary factory order to smithereens. Our youth acquired a fair amount of this destructive energy."[31]

Such discussions of the tsarist past and the experience of the war and revolution came to a consensus that unfavorable, exploitative, and degrading conditions and trauma had a lasting effect on individuals unfortunate enough to suffer them.[32] The issue of how these effects could be identified and how they had come into being required further elaboration.

Heredity and Milieu in an Age of Materialism

After 1917, biomedical sciences proved highly adaptable to the narrative and explanatory paradigms of Soviet Marxism. They embraced and inflected materialist understandings of the social world, offering ever more detailed and sophisticated accounts on the relationship between human beings and their environments. As Krasnushkin was keen to point out in 1926, criminal anthropology had demystified the notion of individual free will, which had traditionally, in its neglect of the environmental pressures that drove individuals to commit crimes, thrown a veil over the prerevolutionary era's great disparities in wealth and living conditions. The significance of the environment could not be reduced to the proposition that it "exerts on these identical individuals an exclusively psychological influence. . . . Of course, the psychiatrist who thinks as a materialist is not inclined to analyze the influence of the socioeconomic environment on the individual in such a primitive way, . . . accustomed as he is to perceiving as a united entity both the mental and physical sides of human behavior. He seeks to arrive at a united understanding of the social and psychophysical life of the individual."[33] Shirvindt also made the point that "Marxist thought, which rejects the existence of anatomical or anatomical-biological peculiarities typical

---

31   Ia. M. Lobach, "O mekhanizme prestupnoi agressivnosti," *Sbornik po psikhonevrologii* (Rostov-on-Don: Severnyi Kavkaz, 1928), 551. On Krylenko's role and influence in the development of Soviet jurisprudence, see Eugene Huskey, "Vyshinskii, Krylenko and the Shaping of the Soviet Legal Order," *Slavic Review* 46, no. 3/4 (Autumn–Winter 1987): 414–28. It is striking that Poznyshev's analysis of the effects of the Civil War on soldiers and the political culture of those who fought in it prefigured the work of a much later generation of scholars. See, for example, Sheila Fitzpatrick, "The Civil War as a Formative Experience," in *Bolshevik Culture: Experiment and Order in the Russian Revolution,* ed. Abbot Gleason, Peter Kenez, and Richard Stites (Bloomington: Indiana University Press, 1985), 57–76; Stefan Plaggenborg, "Gewalt und Militanz in Sowjetrussland, 1917–1930," *Jahrbücher für Geschichte Osteuropas* 44, no. 3 (1996): 409–30; Josh Sanborn, *Drafting the Russian Nation: Military Conscription, Total War, and Mass Politics, 1905–1925* (DeKalb: Northern Illinois University Press, 2003), 165–200; Catherine Merridale, "The Collective Mind: Trauma and Shell-shock in Twentieth-Century Russia," *Journal of Contemporary History* 35, no. 1 (January 2000): 39–55.

32   It is regrettably the case that the sources upon which the monograph is based fall silent, for the most part, during the period 1914–1921.

33   Krasnushkin, "Chto takoe prestupnik," 9.

of criminals, perceives a direct connection between crime and the socio-economic conditions. It devotes ever greater attention to the pathological changes in a person that can arise on the basis of difficult conditions of labor, housing, food, and so on."[34] Seeking to establish the Marxist credentials of such a view, both Krasnushkin and Shirvindt went on to cite Friedrich Engels' celebrated 1845 study, *The Condition of the Working Class in England*, which had illuminated the effects of sustained exhaustion, poverty, and disease on workers in the factories of Manchester.[35]

A synthesis between Marxism and degeneration theory was not a new departure in the literature. Diane Paul has emphasized the compatibility of Marxist and biological conceptions of society in the nineteenth and twentieth centuries.[36] Indeed, already in 1903 Khristian Rakovskii had submitted a dissertation to the Sorbonne entitled *The Etiology of Crime and Degeneration*, which had deployed an explicitly Marxist framework and which was published in Russia for the first time in 1927.[37] Shirvindt declared Rakovskii's research pathbreaking and noted that the bourgeois specialists of the time had predictably passed over it in silence.[38] In 1926, Nikolai Pavlovich Brukhanskii (1893–?) also asserted that Rakovskii's 1903 study illuminated the ways in which permanent factors such as "competition, concentrations of capital, the impoverishment of the masses, women, and children, the extinction of the villages, the growth of the cities" combined with periodic circumstances such as "industrial crises and harvest failures" to play a "decisive role in the nervous-mental condition of the population's health." Postrevolutionary society, he explained, was still experiencing the consequences of

> the tension of the class struggle, the depletion of the villages, the disorganization of the family, the insufficiency of salaries, difficult living conditions, ignorance, intolerability in the organization of the rhythm of life in the big cities, exhaustion, prostitution, venereal disease, alcoholism, other social diseases, homelessness, and so on. As a consequence, on the one hand, they directly weaken individuals' nervous-mental resistance and can become the impetus

34   Shirvindt, "O problemakh prestupnosti," 12.
35   Krasnushkin, "Chto takoe prestupnik," 20; Shirvindt, "O problemakh prestupnosti," 12. For a general examination of the debates about the relationship between heredity and the environment in the Soviet period, see Mark B. Adams, "The Soviet Nature-Nurture Debate," in *Science and the Social Order,* ed. Loren Graham (Cambridge, MA: Harvard University Press, 1990), 94–138.
36   Diane Paul, "Eugenics and the Left," *Journal of the History of Ideas* 45, no. 4 (October–December 1984): 567–90; idem, "'In the Interests of Civilization': Marxist Views of Race and Culture in the Nineteenth Century," *Journal of the History of Ideas* 42, no. 1 (January–March 1981): 115–38.
37   Khristian G. Rakovskii, *Etiologiia prestupnosti i vyrozhdaemosti* (Moscow: Gosizdatel'stvo, 1927).
38   Shirvindt, "O problemakh prestupnosti," 3.

for the emergence of criminal actions; on the other, by means of hereditary predispositions, they indirectly influence the nervous-mental instability in all the subsequent generations.[39]

This explicitly materialist reading of degeneration led to attempts to revive the stigmata as a predictor of criminality, which Lombroso had pioneered and which had remained a feature (admittedly a controversial one) of criminal anthropology in the late imperial period.[40] As had been the case before 1917, degeneration theory allowed some clinicians to claim a visible mapping of deviance while steering clear of the metaphysics of Lombroso's atavistic criminal. In 1926, for example, Nikolai Nikolaevich Korganov (1891–?) adhered to the theoretical axis elaborated by his predecessors when he argued that degenerative disorders unified physical with mental deficiencies and that a correlation of sorts existed between the two: "*Antisocial behavior in children goes hand in hand with a greater incidence of degenerative stigmata; the latter, while they are not pathognomical symptoms in relation to any one individual, do serve as good external indicators of impaired biological or biosocial value [biosotsial'naia tsennost']*."[41]

A year later, Viktor Valerianovich Bunak (1891–1979) of the Moscow Anthropological Institute agreed it was still possible that "the study of external anomalies . . . might produce interesting theoretical and practical results in the study of certain criminals."[42] Professor Aleksandr Ivanovich Kriukov (1866–?) of the Department of Forensic Medicine at Moscow State University remained adamant that such a correlation did exist: "Study of the construction of skulls of the mentally ill, morally defective children, manifest degenerates, criminals, suicides . . . has without doubt established significant anatomical and physical anomalies in the skulls of such subjects."[43] In a textbook published in 1923, Poznyshev argued that "neurological and pathological constitutions and physical and moral degeneration" were "one of the most important endogenous factors in crime. . . . Many criminals exhibit the stigmata of nervous disorders, physical and mental degeneration. . . . Degeneration is a condition of greater or lesser deterioration [*upadok*] and regressive changes in the organism and in the psyche. It can manifest itself

39   Nikolai Brukhanskii, "Vvedenie v kriminal'nuiu psikhopatologiiu," in *Sudebno-meditsinskaia ekspertiza. Sbornik I*, ed. Ia. L. Leibovich (Moscow: Narkomzdrav, 1925), 41.
40   See, for example, Aleksandr M. Tereshkovich, "Nasledstvennost' u prestupnikov," *Russkii evgenicheskii zhurnal* 4, no. 2 (1926): 77.
41   N. N. Korganov, "K voprosu o znachenii biologicheskogo faktora v razvitii antisotsial'nykh detei," *Voprosy izucheniia prestupnosti na Severnom Kavkaze*, no. 1 (1926): 60.
42   Viktor V. Bunak, "Antropologicheskoe izuchenie prestupnika, ego sovremennoe polozhenie i zadachi," *Arkhiv kriminologii i sudebnoi meditsiny* 1, no. 3 (1927): 549.
43   Aleksandr I. Kriukov, "O degeneratsii cherepa," *Arkhiv kriminologii i sudebnoi meditsiny* 1, nos. 2–3 (1927): 706.

primarily either in physical stigmata or in changes in the mental activity."[44] Like his prerevolutionary predecessors, Poznyshev was keen to dissociate himself from any endorsement of Lombroso's born criminal: "A born predisposition to criminality is both psychologically and logically impossible." Yet he did affirm that a greater incidence of degeneration existed among criminals than among law-abiding citizens.[45]

Although the seductive potential of this reading of deviance lay in its appeal to the contemporary materialist view of the social world, the degenerative model itself could never offer more than a probabilistic correlation between outward deformity and malign intent. Yet it did offer a revelatory theory of a different kind. Studies of degeneration had long insisted on the indivisibility of biological and psychological features. As the modeling of *invisible* biological features came to be substantially refined in the 1920s, it had dynamic consequences for the understanding of psychological abnormality.

Advances in physiology, genetics, and endocrinology over the course of the 1920s served to divert medical attention away from the outward manifestations of abnormality to the defects that lurked unseen, inside the human body, in the nervous system.[46] Genetics now made an occasional, if subordinate, appearance in discussions of hereditary transfer. In 1927, Lents referred to "the laws of heredity revealed by Mendel" as explaining the sudden emergence of mental illness in offspring with apparently healthy heredity.[47] Genetics did not, however, appear to be in conflict with neo-Lamarckian explanations of acquired heredity. As David Joravsky has observed, in the 1920s Soviet biologists held a favorable view of genetics because it established clear natural laws of individual heredity, but they also criticized the discipline because they alleged that it could not explain the evolution of species and the role of the environment in it. As a consequence, "epigeneticists" or "mechano-Lamarckists" who attempted to determine the precise nature of environmental influences on heredity were in general viewed sympathetically.[48] Bunak argued that "every individual is linked with the members

44 Sergei V. Poznyshev, *Uchebnik ugolovnogo prava: Ocherk osnovnykh nachal obshchei i osobennoi chasti nauki ugolovnogo prava. 1. Obshchaia chast'* (Moscow: Narkomiust, 1923), 171.

45 Ibid., 187.

46 Pavlov's research into physiology also provided an apparently sound empirical basis for the relationship between environmental conditioning and physical and psychological changes in individuals. As Lents declared in 1927: "In questions of assessing the behavior of people and animals, thanks to the labors of our physiologist, I[van] P. Pavlov, his students and followers, we can ground [our research] in a strictly objective and scientific perspective." Aleksandr K. Lents, *Kriminal'nye psikhopaty (sotsiopaty)*, with a foreword by Vladimir P. Osipov (Leningrad: Rabochii sud, 1927), 16. On Pavlov in the 1920s and 1930s, see Torsten Rüting, *Pavlov und der Neue Mensch: Diskurse über Disziplinierung in Sowjetrussland* (Munich: Oldenbourg, 2002).

47 Lents, *Kriminal'nye psikhopaty*, 8–9.

48 David Joravsky, "Soviet Marxism and Biology before Lysenko," *Journal of the History of Ideas* 20, no. 1 (January 1959): 91. See also Yuri Slezkine, "N. Ia. Marr and the Origins of Soviet Ethnogenetics," *Slavic Review* 55, no. 4 (Winter 1996): 826–62.

of his tribe not only by external circumstances and experiences but also by a range of deposits inherited from their common ancestors; from his immediate forebears the individual gains both an accumulation of certain educational stimuli and a certain selection of genes, and the latter cannot be without influence over his behavior."[49] In 1925, the geneticists Gedalii D. Aronovich and Zinaida A. Bannikova argued that the study of genetics might finally illuminate the long opaque relationship between physical and mental deformity.[50]

Another explanatory paradigm, endocrinology, featured prominently in studies of deviance. As Kenneth Pinnow has found in his examination of the forensic use of endocrinology in pathological accounts of suicide, those engaged in the human sciences believed they had discovered a connection between skull deformities and dysfunctional endocrine systems, on the one hand, and disruptions in a person's internal equilibrium, especially the nervous system, on the other.[51] Endocrinology made similar inroads into the study of criminality. Korganov hailed "contemporary advances in endocrinology [that] have, to a considerable degree, revealed the formative forces shaping the organism; we now have a significant number of examples of the ways in which anomalies in the skeleton and the central nervous system develop on the basis of a pathological environment."[52] Udal'tsov also claimed that endocrinology offered a more sophisticated and empirically grounded explanation of the interaction between pathological environments and individual deviance. Hormonal changes led to the formation of certain unconditional reflexes or "instincts, on the basis of which a chain of reflexive conditioning is created that ends in specific actions. The condition of the cortex of the large cerebral hemispheres regulates relations [between the external environment and the individual's reactions]. Defects in either one of these components can induce anomalous reactions."[53]

---

49   Bunak, "Antropologicheskoe izuchenie prestupnika," 561. This apparent synthesis of genetics and theories of acquired heredity in discussions of the etiology of deviance reflected the sometimes uneasy coexistence of the two in Soviet biology in the 1920s. Genetics did manage to push Lamarckism onto the defensive in 1929, but its victory was short-lived. Maxim W. Mikulak has suggested that in the late-1920s "Western nations had simply exhausted most of the environmental factors for improving plant and animal stock, whereas in the Soviet Union environmental factors were still a fruitful area of manipulation for increasing agricultural yields." Maxim W. Mikulak, "Darwinism, Soviet Genetics, and Marxism-Leninism," *Journal of the History of Ideas* 31, no. 3 (July–September 1970): 368.

50   Gedalii D. Aronovich and Zinaida A. Bannikova, "Biogeneticheskii analiz (kachestvennyi i kolichestvennyi) fizicheskikh degenerativnikh priznakov u defektivnykh i zdorovykh detei," *Pedologicheskii zhurnal*, no. 3 (1923): 17. See the similar arguments made by Mikhail I. Astvatsaturov, "Biologicheskie osnovy klassifikatsii fizicheskikh degenerativnykh priznakov," *Nauchnaia meditsina*, no. 10 (1922): 40.

51   Kenneth Pinnow, "Cutting and Counting: Forensic Medicine as a Science of Society" in Bolshevik Russia, 1920–29," in *Russian Modernity: Politics, Knowledge, Practices*, ed. David L. Hoffmann and Yanni Kotsonis (Basingstoke: Macmillan, 2000), 120.

52   Korganov, "K voprosu o znachenii," 57.

53   Udal'tsov, "Pravonarusheniia v voiskakh," 120. Bunak also hailed the empirical data obtained by experiments into the power of endocrinology to affect the growth of the

These different explanatory frameworks each lay claim to a biological basis for the psychological life of individuals, effectively collapsing the two categories together. They thereby facilitated the extension of understandings of physical or biological change in an individual to the psychological sphere. Perhaps more significantly, however, they also led to assertions of the reverse: exposure to certain psychological environments could bring about lasting changes in the biological constitution of an individual. In 1927, Ian Pavlovich Bugaiskii (1895–?) published a study entitled *Hooliganism as a Sociopathological Phenomenon* in which he elaborated the process by which economic conditions inscribed themselves in the very biological and psychological composition of the individual. He pointed not only to the deleterious effects on workers of their unhealthy physical environment but also to the pernicious effects of their exposure to the *ideological* world of capitalism:

> According to contemporary science, even the purely psychological influences of the environment produce physical-chemical changes in the juices and tissue of the organism [*fizichesko-khimicheskie izmeneniia v sokakh i tkaniakh organizma*], which in turn have a harmful effect on the mind. All these environmental influences, acting from one generation to the next, result in radical biological changes to the individual, predisposing him to all kinds of mental illnesses [*dushevnye bolezni*]. . . . This is how "economics" crosses over into "biology."[54]

Krasnushkin made the same argument: "According to contemporary science, exclusively mental effects of the surrounding environment generate physiochemical changes in the juices and tissues of the organism, which then in turn affect the psyche."[55]

The Biologization of the Social

The establishment of a "materialist" understanding of criminal psychology enabled Soviet-era criminologists to divest themselves of any suggestion of Lombroso's discredited biological fatalism while actually retaining a

---

organism. Bunak, "Antropologicheskoe izuchenie prestupnika," 547. Dan Healey has pointed to the dynamism of endocrinology in the 1920s and Yvonne Howell has demonstrated its popular currency in one of the most important works of fiction written in the decade. Dan Healey, *Homosexual Desire in Revolutionary Russia: The Regulation of Sexual and Gender Dissent* (Chicago: University of Chicago Press, 2001), 170–71; Yvonne Howell, "Eugenics, Rejuvenation, and Bulgakov's Journey into the Heart of a Dog," *Slavic Review* 65, no. 3 (Fall 2006): 544–62.

54   Ian P. Bugaiskii, *Khuliganstvo kak sotsial'no-patologicheskoe iavlenie* (Moscow: Molodaia Gvardiia, 1927), 40.

55   Krasnushkin, "Chto takoe prestupnik," 12.

biopsychologically determined taxonomy of deviance that they could comfortably square with the discriminatory social mapping of Soviet Marxism. Poznyshev argued that

> the criminal type is determined by the peculiarities of his psychological constitution. . . . The criminal type is not anatomical-physical or anthropological but rather psychological; it represents the kind of psychological constitution in which the individual develops the urge to commit a particular crime under circumstances in which the overwhelming majority of people do not experience that urge, or at least not to the point of commission. A psychological constitution is a certain combination of more or less permanent psychological features of the individual, which have a particular organic base.[56]

Aleksandr Mironovich Tereshkovich (1881–?) argued along similar lines. Although it was impermissible to speak of a "direct hereditary transfer of criminal tendencies," an inherited tendency toward crime consists of the hereditary transfer of those psychological features that characterize a degenerative individual—instability, vagrancy, mendacity, failure to develop the normal, correct reactions to surrounding circumstances, inability to adapt to, and resist, difficult moral and material conditions that one encounters in life."[57]

Biological heredity thereby came to provide a cognitive model for apprehending the transfer of social instincts. Krasnushkin explained in 1925 that not merely the intellect but "in an even greater measure, instincts (inherited as ready mechanisms of behavior) and feelings (emotions and affects) which are the prompts for specific responses to an external stimulus" determined human behavior.[58] A year later, he declared that "heredity passes on instincts, the animal's innate apparatus of adaptation to the surrounding environment."[59] Bunak added his own voice to this consensus in 1927 when he observed that "crime is too complex a phenomenon, which does not conform to the concept of heredity," for the "existence of a particular criminal gene to be possible." He did, however, maintain that "it was possible to talk about the heredity of certain elements in the psychological structure that predispose an individual to antisocial behavior, but the latter feeds not only into crime but also into other forms, vagrancy, prostitution, and so on."[60]

Rather than scrutinizing degenerates for the evidence of physical signs of degeneration, contemporaries now focused their analytical energies on determining the existence and nature of predispositions to crime that were em-

56 Poznyshev, *Uchebnik ugolovnogo prava*, 193.
57 Tereshkovich, "Nasledstvennost' u prestupnikov," 77.
58 Evgenii K. Krasnushkin, *Sudebno-psikhiatricheskie ocherki* (Moscow: M. & S. Sabashnikovy, 1925), 104.
59 Krasnushkin, "Chto takoe prestupnik," 9.
60 Bunak, "Antropologicheskoe izuchenie prestupnika," 563.

bedded in the nervous system, inherited or acquired, of individuals. In 1923, Poznyshev affirmed that criminology needed to set itself the task of "identifying the absence or presence of certain [psychological] complexes" that were the "psychological forces determining the behavior of people . . . and different kinds of criminals."[61]

This biologization of the psychological life of individuals amounted to a substantial theoretical refinement of the relationship between an individual's past and present. Prerevolutionary theorists and clinicians had repeatedly pointed to the negative psychological effects of an environment on a given individual. Yet their elaboration of the precise mechanism involved had always remained rather vague. Advances in the study of both the nervous system and endocrinology, however, strengthened and consolidated interest in the psychological effects of environments, which, it now appeared, occurred on a verifiable empirical basis. Just as the physical body of the degenerate in the prerevolutionary period had become a distilled expression of the social order it inhabited, so now an individual's psychological predisposition could be scrutinized for information about the history of that individual's life and of the wider society he or she inhabited.[62]

In 1934, Bukharin boasted that the socialist project transformed workers, exploited and degraded by capitalism, "into persons, into collective creators and organizers, into people who work on themselves, into conscious producers of their own 'fate,' into real architects of their own future."[63] Jochen Hellbeck has suggested that therein lay an important reason for the Bolsheviks' scrutiny of psychological predispositions: "Under these revolutionary imperatives, Soviet citizens were judged upon the trajectories of their subjective lives."[64]

Revolutionary Adaptation

One of the chief consequences of a defective nervous system was the failure to adapt to the surrounding environment. This assessment was, of course,

61   Poznyshev, "K psikhologii," 65. Lents confirmed that "an enormous contingent of lawbreakers are individuals with unbalanced nervous systems, in other words, psychologically abnormal people." Lents, "Zadachi i plan," 116. For the same argument, see also V. V. Brailovskii, "O biologicheskikh korniakh prestupnosti," *Sbornik po psikhonevrologii*, 545–48.

62   On the Bolshevik obsession with narrating and fixing individual identities, see Anne E. Gorsuch, "Women's Autobiographical Narratives: Soviet Presentation of Self," *Kritika* 2, no. 4 (Fall 2001): 835–47; Sheila Fitzpatrick, "Making a Self for the Times: Impersonation and Imposture in 20th-Century Russia," *Kritika* 2, no. 3 (Summer 2001): 469–88; Igal Halfin, *From Darkness to Light: Class, Consciousness, and Salvation in Revolutionary Russia* (Pittsburgh: University of Pittsburgh Press, 2000); Igal Halfin, *Terror in My Soul: Communist Autobiographies on Trial* (Cambridge, MA: Harvard University Press, 2003); Hellbeck, *Revolution on My Mind*.

63   Nikolai I. Bukharin, *Tiuremnye rukopisi N. I. Bukharina*, vol. 1: *Sotsializm i ego kul'tura* (Moscow: "Airo-XX", 1996), 66, cited in Hellbeck, *Revolution on My Mind*, 7.

64   Hellbeck, *Revolution on My Mind*, 7.

familiar from prerevolutionary studies of criminality, which had stressed that biopsychologically impaired individuals were unable to compete in the struggle for existence within the confines of the law. Krasnushkin noted that "every living creature needs to adapt its constitution and its reactions to the surrounding environment, since this adaptation allows it to preserve itself in this environment. When this capacity to adapt is disturbed or weakened, a diseased condition comes into being."[65] Lents similarly maintained that "in order to adapt to the surrounding environment, an individual needs the constant formation in their cerebral cortex of those conditional reflexes and conditional inhibitors that are the organism's strategic responses to changes in the external circumstances." He defined psychopaths as "individuals with an unstable nervous system who have difficulty adapting to their social environment and easily come into all manner of conflicts with it. . . . Their chief characteristic is *social inadaptability.*"[66]

The concept of adaptation, however, had begun in the wake of 1917 to acquire an additional and powerful resonance. The revolution had radically redefined the terms on which society functioned and the nature of the struggle for existence within it. The issue of adaptability to the postrevolutionary environment thereby became a gauge by which to measure the danger posed by various social constituencies in Soviet society.[67] In 1926, the eminent psychiatrist of prerevolutionary standing Vladimir Osipov declared, "The October Revolution was an enormous leap forward that immediately and with dizzying speed propelled the country through a series of evolutionary forms. New demands on the behavior of citizens emerged together with the new order; the great majority of citizens accepted these demands, accepted them seriously and began to adapt to them, elaborating new [reflexive] combinations that were to force out and replace the old ones."[68] In a similar argument, Udal'tsov believed the entire revolutionary project rested upon its success or failure in facilitating the adaptation of individuals to the new social order. The construction of the army was analogous to this broader process:

---

65   Krasnushkin, *Sudebno-psikhiatricheskie ocherki,* 103.
66   Lents, *Kriminal'nye psikhopaty,* 52, 24. Korganov made the same point in 1926. "K voprosu o znachenii," 57.
67   It also enabled the human sciences to respond to the frustratingly elusive nature of class designations in the postrevolutionary era. Fitzpatrick has noted how the Party struggled to "reclassify" society in the wake of the upheavals of the revolution and civil war, which had led so many individuals, willingly or unwillingly, to abandon their prerevolutionary stations and professions only to reappear under an entirely different guise in the early years of the Soviet regime. The issue of revolutionary adaptation constituted a theoretical means of scrutinizing each individual Soviet citizen, of peering behind their current occupations to discern their "true" class affiliation, evidenced by their psychological reflexes and social instincts. Fitzpatrick, "The Bolsheviks' Dilemma"; idem, "Ascribing Class."
68   Vladimir P. Osipov, "O kontrrevoliutsionnom komplekse u dushevno-bol'nykh," *Obozrenie psikhiatrii, nevrologii i refleksologii,* no. 2 (1926): 91. At the time of writing, Osipov (1871–1947) was professor of psychiatry at Kazan University and the Military Medical Academy in Leningrad. One of the most influential psychiatrists in the Soviet Union, he went on to become a member of the Soviet Academy of Sciences in 1939.

The army draws recruits from a huge mass of people with the most diverse types of reaction. The same set of demands confronts them all. What is required is a swift and complete adaptation to new environmental conditions. . . . To a degree, the individuality of the person is suppressed and there are great demands for the development of a social reflex; the individual is sacrificed to the interests of the collective. As a result of both [the current revolutionary] break in the old, habitual foundations of human behavior, acquired over the course of a lifetime under the reactionary system [of tsarist Russia], and the attempt to generate a new knowledge, a new chain of conditional reflexes, . . . we encounter an entire series of emerging conflicts.[69]

Biopsychological explanations of mental illness and deviance came to provide a model for discussions of conventional criminality, revealing an explanatory scope that acknowledged no boundaries. In a study of swindlers published in 1927, Mikhail Aleksandrovich Chalisov (1898–1973) argued that their crimes were embedded in their biological constitutions: "A significant percentage are characterized by alcoholic heredity, instability, suggestibility, which means a certain defectiveness [*nepolnotsennost'*] that turns them into [Gustav] Aschaffenburg's 'socially unfit.'" This biological deficiency was only compounded by the experience of the early years of Soviet power:

After the Civil War with its devastation . . . people had to adapt to the new circumstances; material resources were not yet sufficiently extensive to satisfy all demands; NEP generated a whole range of seductions. In addition, after a long period in which the restraining influences dissipated, new ones had not yet managed sufficiently to establish themselves in order to direct tendencies and urges along a particular channel. Only individuals with sufficient biological resources were able to develop new restraining mechanisms relatively quickly; biologically deficient individuals, like our swindlers, were unable . . . to develop these useful mechanisms quickly enough.[70]

Individual adaptation was one issue; class adaptation another. Lents pointed out that the sustained influence of a given milieu, especially in early childhood, served to unify the biopsychology of members of a particular class: "From the first year of life, every one of us is subject to the formative influence of the people around us, especially parents and teachers. In games with other children, the growing child gains another wave of social influences, every one of which leaves a certain mark in the nervous system." As a consequence, "in each individual there are a certain fairly extensive group of

---

69   Udal'tsov, "Pravonarusheniia v voiskakh," 119–20.
70   Mikhail A. Chalisov, "Opyt bio-sotsial'nogo obsledovaniia rastratchikov v Rostove-na-Donu," *Voprosy izucheniia prestupnosti na Severnom Kavkaze*, no. 2 (1927): 74.

features that bind him together with people of the same sex, class, nationality, profession, and epoch."[71] Seemingly innocuous, such a view could easily shade into a blanket denunciation of the failure of certain social constituencies to adapt to the revolution. As Krasnushkin declared in the same year, "The offspring of the bourgeoisie of the tsarist era, déclassé by the revolution, are frequently biologically defective [*nepolnotsennyi*]."[72]

Such examples demonstrate that in the 1920s the languages of biomedical abnormality and class struggle were compatible and mutually reinforcing. The intuitive assumption that only "environmental" explanations of crime could be accommodated within the frame of Marxist theory is not borne out by the criminological scholarship of these years. The view that individual biopsychological constitutions were "social archives," that is, the accumulation of experiences common to a particular social constituency, could explain the persistence of a class struggle in the years after the revolution. Individuals who fatefully carried within them the instincts of their class would come into conflict with members of other classes, their emancipation from the exploitative structures of late tsarist capitalism notwithstanding. At the same time, the discriminatory power of the discourse about class in early Soviet Russia endorsed a kind of shorthand for assessing the biopsychological condition of individuals. As Sheila Fitzpatrick has noted, ascription to a particular class often had a more pronounced influence over an individual's social prospects than did his or her personal history.[73]

Moreover, a class-based assessment of revolutionary adaptation lent itself to an analysis not simply of conventional criminality but also of politically motivated opposition to the regime. A rejection of the values and practices of the new Soviet order could be interpreted as a biopsychologically determined failure to adapt to them, not unlike the adaptive failures of common criminals. Such was the view Osipov put forward in an article entitled "The Counterrevolutionary Complex in the Mentally Ill," published in 1926 in the authoritative *Psikhiatricheskoe obozrenie*. Like Orshanskii and Udal'tsov, Osipov observed that the experience of revolution had unleashed atavistic forces in those who had experienced its tumult and destruction:

> The turbulent early years of Soviet power represent a good touchstone against which to measure changes in the stability of the [individual's] cortical superstructure [*nadstroika*]. . . . Under the influence of the different conditions of that time, a great many people's psychological combinations, linked with their hereditary reflexes, began to dominate over their later cortical architecture, and they were reduced to their primitive state, revealing behavior of which even people who had known them would not have thought them capable. Those

---

71   Lents, *Kriminal'nye psikhopaty*, 9.
72   Krasnushkin, "Chto takoe prestupnik," 26.
73   Fitzpatrick, "Ascribing Class."

difficult times have changed, and together with them these people, although by no means all, once again acquired their cortical shape; yet many had sunk to such depths that they were no longer able to raise themselves to the necessary psychological level.[74]

The distinction between those who were able to recover psychologically and those who were not lay in their biological constitution: "Only physiologically, biologically sound people succeeded in preserving themselves in this purifying fire of revolution and emerged from the revolutionary flames even more stable than they had been before." Osipov invoked the authority of Pavlov to explain the psychophysiological responses of some individuals to the revolutionary changes: "When changes to the surrounding environment are too abrupt, the nervous system is deluged by an entire flood of new, unexpected, unfamiliar stimuli, which destroy the old orientation but which still require time in order to consolidate themselves." Osipov explained the opposition of certain social groups to the new order with reference to their biopsychological condition on the eve of revolution:

> Those who were ideologically well prepared for the revolution were not so adversely affected by the changes. Yet other people, whose old reflexive combinations had established themselves so firmly that the new reflexes differed from them too markedly, . . . required too long a period for their education; examples of these people are to be found in extreme conservatives. . . . Their inability to change their old combinations of psychological reflexes often expressed itself in counterrevolutionary behavior.[75]

Osipov's thesis was controversial, and a month later, a fellow psychiatrist, Isaak Izrailevich Rozenblium (1895–1991), challenged Osipov in the journal's discussion section, charging him with neglect of the class determinants of behavior.[76] Osipov responded to this criticism by invoking the authority of Karl Marx:

> I fully accept Marx's dictum that "life determines consciousness," but consciousness is inextricably bound up with those biological reactions that flow in our nervous system under the influence of the stimulants in the outside world that act upon it. . . . Various more or less stable and habitual reactions emerge under the influence of these stimuli. This is the essence of a biosocial approach to human behavior.[77]

74   Osipov, "O kontrrevoliutsionnom komplekse," 86.
75   Ibid., 86–87.
76   Isaak I. Rozenblium, "Po povodu kontrrevoliutsionnogo kompleksa u dushevno-bol'nykh," *Obozrenie psikhiatrii, nevrologii i refleksologii*, no. 3 (1926): 209–11.
77   Vladimir P. Osipov, "Otvet doktoru Rozenbliumu," *Obozrenie psikhiatrii, nevrologii i refleksologii*, no. 3 (1926): 212.

Osipov explained divergent political responses to the October Revolution with reference to the biopsychological condition of different social groups: "In the revolutionary period, a series of political configurations emerge— each social group assimilates the new stimuli insofar as its preparation, its [reflexive] combinations that have been established earlier, allow."[78] Political opposition to the October Revolution was thus a reflection of citizens' biopsychological conditioning by the capitalist values of the late imperial period. Osipov's thesis might have been controversial, but in an important sense it simply stretched to their logical conclusion the arguments put forward by the majority of his contemporaries: an individual's or group's experiences over a sustained period of time combined with their hereditary material to produce biopsychological changes in their constitution. These changes then determined their responses to environmental changes and enhanced or restricted their adaptive capacity.

Moral Contagions of the New Economic Policy

The contemporary story of 1920s criminality was not, however, simply one that described the adaptive failures of various social constituencies to the new order. Bolshevik leaders also developed grave concerns that the economic and cultural dynamics of NEP were in fact incubating the very social instincts that the new regime was seeking to eliminate.[79] In this context of discomfort, applications of the scientific explanatory model of moral contagion to the threats confronting Soviet society in the 1920s resonated against the background of the Party's use of a metaphorical language of contagion to stigmatize threats to its supremacy. To take one influential example: a pamphlet published by the Workers' and Peasants' Inspectorate in 1921, *On Checking, Reexamining, and Purging the Party,* set out instructions concerning elements to be expelled from the Bolshevik Party in its first purge. The document asserted that "Menshevism is a contagious disease [*prilipchivaia bolezn'*]; even those who sincerely strive to cure themselves of it do not always manage. These elements infect [*zarazhaiut*] not only our Party organizations, but also wider workers' organizations such as the trade unions."[80]

78   Osipov, "O kontrrevoliutsionnom komplekse," 87.
79   In Naiman's opinion, "NEP was itself a type of vaccination on an unprecedented scale. A limited amount of capitalism had been reintroduced into the Soviet economy, the argument went, so that communism could master its tools and use them for anti-capitalist ends." Naiman, *Sex in Public,* 263. Peter Holquist has noted the descriptions of banditry as "a dangerous epidemic" during the anti-insurgency campaigns in the Don region in 1920–21. "State Violence as Technique: The Logic of Violence in Soviet Totalitarianism," in *Landscaping the Human Garden: Twentieth-Century Population Management in a Comparative Framework,* ed. Amir Weiner (Stanford: Stanford University Press, 2003), 26.
80   *K proverke, peresmotru i ochistke partii* (Irbit: RKI, 1921), 3. An excerpt from the Cheka *Weekly* of August 1918 concerning the attempt on Lenin's life and the murder of

Epidemiological theories of deviance spoke directly to these fears of com-municable moral and social disorders, yet unlike the degenerative model of psychopathology, there was little change here in the evolution of their theo-retical base. Before 1917, epidemiological theories had been powerful and eloquent media through which liberal clinicians and scientists had explored and expressed ambivalence toward the rise of mass politics in the late impe-rial period. In the wake of the 1917 Revolution, however, they were used primarily to explore the mounting threat of social disorder in Russian cities amid the moral panic surrounding hooliganism in the 1920s.[81]

Practitioners of the human sciences under the Bolsheviks selectively ap-propriated the preconditions of mental contagion identified in the late impe-rial period. They continued to invoke the backwardness of certain groups within Soviet society as a significant factor in susceptibility to moral con-tagion. Orshanskii declared that hooliganism, "like banditry, or robbery, and so on, spreads like a kind of mental contagion [*psikhicheskaia zaraza*] throughout the country." He argued that it was contaminating the new order with the virus of the old; "one of those social phenomena that accom-pany the shift from one order to another." The susceptibility to the conta-gion reflected the backwardness that the new regime had inherited from its predecessor: "The phenomenon [of hooliganism] is explained by the great excitability of the Russian, his easily inflammable passions and great *sug-gestibility* and *imitativeness* [*vnushaemost' i podrazhatel'nost'*], and these are the characteristics of a young people and a low level of culture."[82]

Brukhanskii conducted a study of hysteria among peasants attending a wedding ceremony at a village in Moscow Province in 1926 and of the spread of various forms of mental illness among urban factory workers in which he made sustained reference to the "backward dark village" and "un-cultured working-class milieu." Yet Brukhanskii also turned his attention to

---

Uritskii framed the response in the following terms: "Measures have been taken to forestall this vile enterprise, and antidotes have been devised to stop the contagion, i.e., RED TERROR, massed against the bourgeoisie, the former gendarmerie, the constables, sheriffs, and other po-lice and officers guiding the counter-revolutionary element. All of Russia has been vaccinated." Published in a bound volume, no. 1, pp. a, b, KGB Archive, cited in *Revelations from the Russian Archives*, ed. Diane P. Koenker and Ronald D. Bachman (Washington, DC: Library of Congress, 1997), 14. This symbolic function of the leader's body was further in evidence in the subsequent representations of the assassination attempt. In Iaroslavskii's hagiography of Lenin, written after his death in 1924, the leader's bodily conquest of the allegedly poison-tipped bullets could be read as a metaphor for the Party's own battles with the diseases of NEP: "It turned out that he was wounded by bullets saturated in the most powerful poison [*sil'neishii iad*], and cut into at the tips, so as to inflict even greater and more painful injuries. Had Lenin not had such a strong nature, so much strength, he would not have been able to endure [such wounds]. . . . The robust health and revolutionary nature [*revoliutsionnaia priroda*] of Vladimir Il'ich was victorious." Emelian Iaroslavskii, *Vozhd' rabochikh i krest'ian* (Leningrad: Gosizdatel'stvo, 1924), 73–74.

81   Gorsuch, *Youth in Revolutionary Russia*.
82   Orshanskii, "Khuligan," 80, 61.

the destabilizing effects of revolutionary change on the psychological stability of those caught up in its flux, noting that "the existence of an increased susceptibility to mental contagion (mental epidemics) results from transitional epochs." Reflecting on the experience of the 1917 Revolution, he concluded that "mental contagion develops into fanaticism [*izuverstvo*] in the broadest possible sense, with an emphasis on mysticism among those social groups who have outlived their time; among the milieu associated with the old order; and among those social strata who have been called to action by the new social and political constellation but who remain essentially on the level of an individualist existence. It develops into anarchist actions, of course understood in the broadest sense of the word (for example, hooliganism)."[83]

If backwardness and accelerated social change were each important preconditions for the spread of mental contagion, the biopsychological damage inflicted by capitalism was another. Bugaiskii explained that individuals psychologically deformed and weakened by capitalism "have a particular susceptibility to what is known as mental contagion [*psikhicheskoe zarazhenie*], some features of which can be seen in acts of hooliganism."[84]

Conspicuous by its absence from these discussions of moral contagion was any suggestion of the fundamental, irreducible irrationality of human beings that had characterized the more skeptical judgments of prerevolutionary commentators. The revolutionary project in Russia was perhaps unwilling to part company with the conviction that human beings were entirely amenable, if properly enlightened, to the appeal of reason.

The "Socially Dangerous"

Theories of psychopathology and moral contagion thus combined to generate a thoroughgoing medicalization of criminality in the early years of the Soviet regime; they stressed both the destructive and the contagious properties of the deviant. The literature began effectively to graft clinical diagnoses of biopsychological disorders onto the study of social and political disorder in general. Tereshkovich argued that the etiology of crime shared a great

---

83   Nikolai P. Brukhanskii, *Ocherki po sotsial'noi psikhopatologii* (Moscow: M. and S. Sabashnikovy, 1928), 24–25. An earlier version of the study had been published as "K voprosu o psikhicheskoi zarazitel'nosti," *Obozrenie psikhiatrii, nevrologii i refleksologii* 24, nos. 4–5 (1926): 279–90.

84   Bugaiskii, *Khuliganstvo*, 44. In 1929, Timofei Segalov was similarly concerned by the spread of disorder in the cities of the new Soviet state: "The laws of imitation have been sufficiently studied to allow us to assert that . . . the masses are always infected by the example of someone's actions. The more unrestrained the action, the less it is inflected with the elements of reason and doubt, the more it is contagious." Timofei Segalov, "Prestupnoe khuliganstvo i khuliganskie prestupleniia," in *Khuliganstvo i khuligany. Sbornik*, ed. Vladimir N. Tolmachev (Moscow: NKVD, 1929), 71.

deal with the etiology of mental illness and that the models developed for understanding and treating the latter could also be fruitfully deployed in the case of the former.[85] The criminologist Timofei Efimovich Segalov (1881–?) argued that "the deprivation of freedom is understood in terms of isolation as a measure of social defense, and that naturally in such an understanding, isolation in a corrective-labor institution and isolation in an asylum are of equal value and meaning."[86]

In his 1923 textbook, Poznyshev elaborated the consequences of this medicalization of criminal dispositions. The balanced declaration that "crime is a product of either external factors or factors within the individual, exogenous or endogenous factors" was familiar from the work of prerevolutionary liberal clinicians.[87] Yet as the previous chapters have demonstrated, before 1917 practitioners' deep disquiet about the biopsychological damage inflicted by late tsarist capitalism had tended to mitigate the emphasis on individual biopsychological factors. Not only did sustained exposure to the depredations of the factory and the slum weaken individuals, but the brutal nature of the struggle for existence then denied them any opportunity to compete legally. In the arguments that flowed from this analysis, social defense was understood in terms of a holding operation intended to contain criminality while the essential project of transforming the social order and its capitalist economic foundations was undertaken. In the wake of the October Revolution, the second component of this general response to crime was deemed essentially accomplished; social transformation was already underway.

More important, by the 1920s the sympathy of the liberals for the plight of the economic and social losers under prerevolutionary capitalism had mutated into entrenched hostility to those who appeared marked by its influence. Deviants would no longer charitably be deemed unable to compete within a bruising and unequal struggle for survival. Failures to adjust to the new order were now evidence of an inability to adapt to the revolution itself, of an antipathy toward its values. Under these conditions, what had before 1917 amounted to a liberal plea for reform and tolerance based on a twinned strategy of social defense and social change was now reconfigured within the deeply discriminating discursive framework of Soviet Marxism. As the old institutional order was dismantled, the Civil War won, and the former ruling classes disenfranchised, exiled, or slain, statements to the

85   Tereshkovich, "Nasledstvennost' u prestupnikov," 77.
86   Timofei Segalov, "Mery sotsial'noi zashchity meditsinskogo kharaktera po UK 1926 g.," in *Problemy prestupnosti*, ed. E. Shirvindt, F. Traskovich, and M. Gernet, vyp. 3 (Moscow: NKVD, 1927), 174. For a discussion of the notion of "social danger" and its place in Soviet jurisprudence, see Iu. I. Liapunov, *Obshchestvennaia opasnost' deianiia kak universal'naia kategoriia sovetskogo ugolovnogo prava* (Moscow: VIuZSh, 1989); Paul M. Hagenloh, "'Socially Harmful Elements' and the Great Terror," in *Stalinism: New Directions*, ed. Sheila Fitzpatrick (London: Routledge, 2000), 288–90.
87   Poznyshev, *Uchebnik ugolovnogo prava*, 169.

effect that criminality flowed from both endogenous and exogenous factors increasingly focussed on the former at the expense of the latter.

Of course, NEP had its imperfections, and as the foregoing discussion has noted, studies of contemporary criminality in the 1920s made sustained reference to survivals of the old order in the belly of the new Soviet state. Yet whereas prerevolutionary studies had voiced alarm at the unavoidability of moral and physical corruption, the postrevolutionary scholarship was far less sympathetic. Wellsprings of pathology did of course remain, but they now required the active connivance of individual deviants if they were really to wield transformative powers.[88] In a study of youth crime published in 1923, Pavel Liublinskii, as before the revolution a professor of law at Petrograd State University, argued that individuals who had failed to respond to the curative powers of the revolution or had become corrupted in its wake could no longer expect the indulgence of the authorities: "Already developed defectiveness and antisocial behavior demand a more complex and specialized intervention, which cannot be achieved with the usual medico-pedagogical methods but by a long process of reeducation, correction, and social isolation (*sotsial'naia izoliatsiia*)."[89]

Striking a similarly uncompromising tone, Poznyshev's statement of the time-honored etiological combination of heredity and milieu was swiftly succeeded by his rather more trenchant declaration that "crime serves to externalize psychology." Indeed, when he insisted that "there are those who commit crimes largely for endogenous reasons—because of their psychological constitution," the intellectual force of his argument suggested that this constituency was a good deal more expansive than that of criminals impelled chiefly by circumstance. Poznyshev identified moral degeneracy as one of the most frequent causes of crime: "Through the complete or partial atrophy of the moral faculties, degeneration prepares an individual psychologically for crime."[90] Osipov made much the same point, arguing that one should not conclude that all hooligans were simply the unfortunate victims of their corrupting environments. Employing categories familiar from degeneration theory, he asserted the need for "coercive healing" of some hooligans: "The hooligan is created by the conditions of the surrounding environment, by those circumstances that evolved unfavorably. Yet among the hooligans are also clearly pathological types, morally defective, unbalanced, degenerate individuals with various manifestations of diseased deviations from the norm [*s razlichnymi proiavleniiami boleznennykh uklonenii ot normy*]."[91]

---

88 See the same arguments in Hellbeck, *Revolution on My Mind*, 34.

89 Pavel I. Liublinskii, *Bor'ba s prestupnost'iu v detskom i iunosheskom vozroste (sotsial'no-pravovye ocherki)* (Moscow: Narkomiust, 1923), 255. For similar statements in textbooks on psychology, see Raymond Bauer, *The New Man in Soviet Psychology* (Cambridge, MA: Harvard University Press, 1952), 147–49.

90 Poznyshev, *Uchebnik ugolovnogo prava*, 169, 189, 199.

91 Osipov, "K voprosu o khuliganstve," 88.

This insistence on the importance of the biopsychological constitution of the individual as a primary causal factor in the etiology of crime served additionally to blur the distinction between actual and potential perpetrators. In 1929, Ivan Nikolaevich Vvedenskii (1875–1960) declared that "the criminal act itself is irrelevant—what matters are attitudes and tendencies that pose a threat to the health of society."[92] The criminologist Boris Samoilovich Utevskii (1887–1970) came in 1927 to the view that "there is no basis on which to distinguish between punishment for a crime that has just been committed by a dangerous criminal and preventive detention."[93] This conflation of the actual and potential criminal was central to the development of the legal concept of "social danger." The psychiatrist Mark Zakharovich Kaplinskii observed that "in order to decide the question of social danger and take measures of social defense of a medical character, we must on every occasion take an individual, detailed approach to each case, considering not merely the manifestations of social danger but also the potential urges and capacities fixed within the individual."[94] The writings of criminologists of this period support Peter Holquist's observation that Bolshevik judges were less concerned about guilt or innocence than about "whether one was redeemable (and hence subject to detention and correction) or incorrigible (and hence subject to elimination)."[95]

The concept of "social danger" and suggestions for a corresponding raft of legal policies known as "social defense" had been coming into vogue in Europe in the first decade of the twentieth century in both legal and psychiatric circles. These precepts began to be implemented in the first two legal codes of the new Soviet state. Dmitrii Aleksandrovich Amenitskii (1873–?) applauded the 1922 legal code for its recommendation of the incarceration of "mentally and morally defective" criminals in special institutions as a form of social defense.[96]

Like their prerevolutionary predecessors, many Soviet psychiatrists and criminologists hailed the replacement of the concept of criminal responsibility

---

92   Ivan N. Vvedenskii, "Prinuditel'noe lechenie dushevno-bol'nykh i psikhopatov," in *Dushevno-bol'nye pravonarushiteli i prinuditel'noe lechenie,* ed. P. V. Gannushkin (Moscow: NKVD, 1929), 13, 19.

93   Boris S. Utevskii, "Retsidiv i professional'naia prestupnost'," in *Problemy prestupnosti,* ed. E. Shirindt, F. Traskovich, and M. Gernet, vyp. 3 (Moscow: NKVD, 1927), 107.

94   Mark Z. Kaplinskii, "K voprosu o prinuditel'nom lechenii," in *Dushevno-bol'nye pravonarushiteli i prinuditel'noe lechenie,* P. V. Gannushkin (Moscow: NKVD, 1929), 61.

95   Holquist, "State Violence as Technique," 42.

96   Dmitrii A. Amenitskii, "K voprosu o prinuditel'nom lechenii i o sotsial'no-opasnykh dushevno-bol'nykh i psikhopatakh," in *Dushevno-bol'nye pravonarushiteli,* ed. Gannushkin, 24. The rise of social defense in European "positivist" penal codes of the 1920s was especially marked in Italy under the influence of Enrico Ferri. See Daniel Pick, *Faces of Degeneration: A European Disorder, c. 1848–c. 1918* (Cambridge: Cambridge University Press, 1989), 145–52. Ferri's proposed codex was much discussed by criminologists in the Soviet Union. See, for example, Lents, "Zadachi i plan," 112. On the German case, see Wetzell, *Inventing the Criminal,* 125–78.

with that of social danger as a progressive development in the interests of both the criminal and wider society. Udal'tsov declared that "we have to welcome in every way the concept of social danger, which has been able to replace the concept of criminal responsibility. People who manifest anti-social reactions and are therefore enemies of society should be isolated with the aim of coercively healing or reeducating them."[97] Osipov boasted,

> Our legal system has assimilated this biosocial perspective [*biosotsial'naia tochka zreniia*], the logical consequence of which is a root and branch change in the approach to the question of *punishment* for crime. The concept of punishment, as with retribution for the violation of social and personal interests, has been replaced by the assertion of measures of *social defense* from harmful and dangerous antisocial elements.[98]

Accordingly, criminology and psychiatry came to regard violations of the law as the manifestation of biosocial illnesses to be treated by the coercive power of the state. Indeed, arguments in favor of social defense could, on some accounts, supersede the claims of the legal process. Kaplinskii declared that "treatment" could not be subordinated to the law: "If a person is sick, if he or she is in need of treatment, if a person's behavior, determined by their illness, brings them into conflict with those around them, brings them into conflict with the law, then treatment must begin even before the start of the legal process."[99]

The biomedical discourse of treatment remained extremely elastic. Lents observed that the term "socially dangerous requires special explanation because it enjoys such a wide field of applicability, embracing rabid dogs, enraged bulls, a carrier of TB or some other contagious infection—these are all socially dangerous elements." Seeking to define the principle that inhered in this revealing set of examples, Lents argued that if "analysis of an accused reveals that his social reactions boil down to permanent conflicts with, and frequent violations of, the existing legal order, then we can consider him socially dangerous." Lents noted the similarities between his own and the German psychiatrist Gustav Aschaffenburg's (1866–1944) definition of "socially dangerous": "'those individuals whose psychological characteristics lead us to expect with a great probability that they cannot be at large without coming into conflict with the law.'"[100]

Amenitskii was more alive to the pernicious potential of the term's indeterminacy, claiming that it needed to be treated "with great care." In what

97   Udal'tsov, "Pravonarusheniia v voiskakh," 132.
98   Vladimir P. Osipov, "K voprosu o khuliganstve," in *Khuliganstvo i prestuplenie*, ed. Orshanskii et al., 85.
99   Kaplinskii, "K voprosu o prinuditel'nom lechenii," 58.
100   Lents, "Zadachi i plan," 112–13. On Aschaffenburg's career, thought, and influence, see Wetzell, *Inventing the Criminal*, 62–68.

surely stood as an acutely prophetic commentary on the state's policies of gathering and retaining discriminatory information about individuals or groups in Soviet society, Amenitskii noted that "it was enough to attach the label 'socially dangerous' to a particular offender, whether he had only committed one crime or was a recidivist, or even for reasons of a previous judgment, for his presence outside the walls of a hospital or a prison to be deemed completely intolerable. . . . Declaring a particular subject to be socially dangerous on the basis of an old judgment, without taking account of the possibility of his having changed and having regenerated over the lengthy preceding period, is for many a more severe punishment than a long period of incarceration in prison."[101] Amenitskii perceived that the limitless nature of social defense might merge fatefully with a definitional vagueness leading to "all manner of possible errors . . . an arbitrary and excessively subjective interpretation of the concept by individuals in the localities."[102] Such cautionary voices were, however, few and far between.

Coercive Rehabilitation: The Civilizing Process

As had been the case before the revolution, so in the 1920s practitioners of the human sciences manifested both optimism and pessimism as they confronted a recalcitrant society. For the Bolsheviks, too, this was a decade in which anxiety about their inheritance from the old regime stood side by side with a bold confidence in the state's ability to transform that society. Illiteracy, high rates of infant mortality, poverty, and ignorance would all be swept aside by the power of science and reason.[103] It is precisely in this context that the advocacy of "coercion" and "coercive healing" is to be understood.

Most clinicians hailed the sanction of the unlimited use of force as something not primarily repressive but therapeutic—a productive and useful engine of both individual and societal transformation.[104] Osipov gave an example of this precept in practice: "When psychiatric expertise establishes that a hooligan has a diseased condition, he should be subject to coercive treatment [*prinuditel'noe lechenie*] best of all, in the framework of curative-labor colonies [*lechebno-trudovye kolonii*]."[105] Coercion was understood, therefore, to wield reconstitutive powers; and the more intense its visitation, the greater the rehabilitative benefits.

101 Amenitskii, "K voprosu o prinuditel'nom lechenii," 31.
102 Ibid., 40.
103 Lewis H. Siegelbaum, *Soviet State and Society between the Revolutions, 1918–1929* (Cambridge: Cambridge University Press, 1992), chap. 4.
104 See the similar arguments made by Holquist, "State Violence as Technique."
105 Osipov, "K voprosu o khuliganstve," 88.

Chalisov saw the entire repressive apparatus of the state as an inalienable constituent feature of the broader concern with forging a new citizenry, what some scholars have termed, following Nobert Elias, "the Stalinist civilizing process."[106] "Measures of social defense" elaborated precisely "the forms of external restraint" that the prerevolutionary era had failed to instill in the population. Chalisov argued that "in those cases in which, as a consequence of biological peculiarities, the internal restraints have developed badly, then we have to turn to the establishment of external ones, which the state does with real success." Addressing the particular issue of swindlers, he endorsed "an intensification of the repression. . . . General coercion acts as a considerable restraint on them."[107]

Shirvindt also saw the penal system as a workshop in which to forge a new citizen. He explained that "social defense" served not merely the "general prevention [of crime], but also the adaptation of the criminal to communal living conditions."[108] Osipov saw the function of social defense in analogous terms: "The struggle with crime should be and is carried out along two lines—the strategy of social defense and the correction of the criminal in the sense of inoculating [*privivka*] him with new social habits, solid foundations that will turn him if not into a useful then a harmless member of society."[109] He called for the "organization of curative labor colonies, in which individuals would be able to acquire useful skills [*navyki*]."[110] In 1920, Bukharin demonstrated the political currency of these ideas, declaring that outright "enemies" were to be subjected to the "concentrated force" of the dictatorship and stripped of their property and ways of thinking as part of their "psychological reeducation," making them capable of "socially useful work" within the state.[111]

By the late 1920s, many Soviet criminologists and psychiatrists had begun to universalize the principle of social defense, coming to see biosocial hygiene as the essence of societal progress. In a volume edited and with a foreword by then-People's Commissar of Internal Affairs Vladimir Nikolaevich Tolmachev (1886–1937), Segalov argued that the pressures of modern,

106 Vadim Volkov, "The Concept of *Kul'turnost'*: Notes on the Stalinist Civilising Process," in *Stalinism: New Directions*, ed. Sheila Fitzpatrick (London: Routledge, 2000), 210–30; David L. Hoffmann, *Stalinist Values: The Cultural Norms of Soviet Modernity, 1917–1941* (Ithaca: Cornell University Press, 2002).
107 Chalisov, "Opyt bio-sotsial'nogo obsledovaniia," 74. Echoes of Bogdan Kistiakovskii's 1909 lament of Russia's low level of legal culture are not difficult to discern. See introduction, 17–18.
108 Shirvindt, "O problemakh prestupnosti," 10.
109 Osipov, "K voprosu o khuliganstve," 88.
110 Vladimir P. Osipov, "Predislovie," in Lents, *Kriminal'nye psikhopaty*, 7.
111 Nikolai Bukharin, *Ekonomika perekhodnogo perioda: Obshchaia teoriia transformatsionnogo protsessa* (Moscow, 1920), 140–46, cited in Yanni Kotsonis, "'No Place to Go': Taxation and State Transformation in Late Imperial and Early Soviet Russia," *Journal of Modern History* 76, no. 3 (September 2004): 571.

urban, industrial existence meant the state had to discharge certain prophylactic functions that had earlier been a natural constituent feature of
less-developed societies:

> It would be appropriate here to turn our attention to a certain natural pro-
> phylaxis by which during the precapitalist era unbalanced and psychopathic-
> unfortunate elements were swept out of the general life of citizens . . . the
> particular prophylactic expediency [*profilakticheskaia tselesoobraznost'*] for
> the healing of the contemporaries of that age of medieval institutions [was] in
> the form of a huge army of brothels and monasteries. All the unbalanced, mis-
> chievous, unfortunate, and criminally minded humanity had the opportunity
> to leave the world and pass behind the walls of either monasteries or dens of
> iniquity, or move to the fringes of the state.[112]

Segalov noted ruefully that the capitalist era, with its system of conscription
and a unitary tax, had deprived these unfortunates of the opportunity of
"stealing away from life's labors and taxes . . . the more developed a state
is, the more effort each individual has to make to keep in step with his co-
citizens, at an ever increasing pace. . . . Those left without any particular
solicitous supervision, the unbalanced, traumatized, psychopathic personalities, represent an ever greater social danger."[113]
Segalov continued by noting that the new demands of production, compounded by the dire shortage of housing in the Soviet Union, left the authorities with no option but to isolate those disruptive and corrupting elements of
the population whose conduct and ideas might prove harmful to the socialist project: "Securing the life and work of the healthy by means of isolating
the sick [*vydelenie bol'nykh*], by means of filtering out those who have not
adapted to particular labor processes, particular living conditions, a prophylactic renovation [*profilakticheskoe ozdorovlenie*] of the population—is
the essential task."[114] Segalov's call for the reestablishment of a neofeudal

112   Timofei Segalov, "Prestupnoe khuliganstvo", 73–74. On Tolmachev's career and
fate, see Lynne Viola, "A Tale of Two Men: Bergavinov, Tolmachev and the Bergavinov Commission," *Europe-Asia Studies* 52, no. 8 (December 2000): 1449–66.
113   Segalov, "Prestupnoe khuliganstvo." For a recent article stressing the expansion of
taxation as a hallmark of Russian modernity, see Kotsonis, "'No Place to Go,'" 531–77. For
an excellent examination of the Bolshevik's concern with the surveillance of the Soviet population in the context of other European states, see Peter Holquist, "'Information Is the Alpha
and Omega of Our Work': Bolshevik Surveillance in Its Pan-European Context," *Journal of
Modern History* 69, no. 3 (September 1997): 415–50.
114   Segalov, "Prestupnoe khuliganstvo," 73–74. The Bolsheviks' apparent preference
for prophylactic over therapeutic measures is borne out by Susan Gross Solomon's comparison
of the differing approaches in 1928 of a joint German-Soviet scientific expedition to the Buriat,
where syphilis was rife. The German scientists were concerned first and foremost with develop-
ing a cure for the disease, but the Soviet team sought to isolate the infected and to identify the
mechanisms for transmission. See Solomon, "The Soviet-German Syphilis Expedition to Buriat
Mongolia, 1928: Scientific Research on National Minorities," *Slavic Review* 52, no. 2 (Summer 1993): 204–32.

system of social marginalization and exclusion lent, of course, a theoretical sanction to the burgeoning Soviet gulag.[115] In the eyes of Segalov and his colleagues, the elaboration of a system of curative labor colonies, administered by the state, was a way of usurping the natural course of societal evolution, of accelerating and directing society toward rational and harmonious ends. The greater the degree of uniformity and stability to which the state aspired, the more intense and sustained the mechanisms of coercion it endorsed.

The consolidation of a biomedical discourse of individual deviance, which served to highlight the "social danger" represented by certain constituencies within society, was an important part of the intellectual climate that legitimated the leadership's assault on enemies real and imagined during the violent years of the Great Breakthrough. Paradoxically, just at the moment when the regime appeared to be moving decisively against all social constituencies whose real and imagined adaptive failures to the new regime imperiled the Bolsheviks' mission, the very disciplines that had so emphatically sanctioned the assault were themselves extinguished. When the dispute over Soviet criminology erupted in 1929, the legal establishment led a drive for Marxist conformity, which resulted in rapid and complete destruction of serious research on criminality.[116] The closure of the research institutes that had generated the steady stream of literature emphasizing the threats of biopsychological deviance did not, however, signal the disappearance of a public role for biomedical discourse.[117]

Perhaps the most explicit endorsement of the institution of the gulag in the public culture of the 1930s lay in the special commemorative volume, edited by Maksim Gor'kii, celebrating the completion of the White Sea

115   Jeffrey Brooks has noted that "the enemies denounced in the 1930s differed from earlier opponents because they had no place in society. Previous enemies could not be fully excluded because there was no cleansed social space from which to expel them." Yet Segalov's proposals indicate that Soviet jurists and penologists were at least already confronting this dilemma in the late 1920s. Jeffrey Brooks, *Thank You, Comrade Stalin! Soviet Public Culture from Revolution to Cold War* (Princeton: Princeton University Press, 1999), 134.

116   See Shelly, "Soviet Criminology: Its Birth and Demise, 1917–1936," 624. See also idem, "The 1929 Dispute on Soviet Criminology," *Soviet Union* 6, no. 2 (1979): 175–85. More generally on the impact of the Cultural Revolution on Soviet science, see David Joravsky, *Soviet Marxism and Natural Science* (London: Routledge, 1961); Loren R. Graham, *The Soviet Academy of Sciences and the Communist Party, 1927–1992* (Princeton: Princeton University Press, 1967); Michael David-Fox, *Revolution of the Mind: Higher Learning among the Bolsheviks, 1918–1929* (Ithaca: Cornell University Press, 1997).

117   Of course, the study of the continuing influence of biopsychological explanations of crime into the 1930s and beyond, although not the subject of this study, might prove an interesting field of further inquiry. Their sublimation into the regime's flirtation with racial politics might be one possibility worth exploring. See the discussion of race by Eric Weitz, Francine Hirsch, Amir Weiner, and Alaina Lemon in *Slavic Review* 61, no. 1 (Spring 2002): 1–65; Terry Martin, "The Origins of Soviet Ethnic Cleansing," *Journal of Modern History* 70, no. 4 (December 1998): 813–61; Weiner, "Nature and Nurture in a Socialist Utopia: Delineating the Soviet Socio-Ethnic Body in the Age of Socialism," *American Historical Review* 104, no. 4 (October 1999): 1114–55.

Canal in 1934. Gor'kii, clearly drawing on the discourse of coercive adaptation elaborated by the human sciences over the previous decade, introduced the work with bold claims of the therapeutic benefits of forced labor. He hailed "the process of returning to health the socially-ill and 'dangerous,'" noting that some of those cured of the diseases of the past even "polemicized with Lombroso." One former kulak observed gratefully: "'I always think what nonsense thick-skulled bourgeois scholars like Lombroso talk, claiming that criminality is an inheredited condition [*prestupnost' est' vrozhdennost'*] against which it is impossible to struggle.'"[118]

Holquist has insisted on a sharp distinction between sociological and biological paradigms as the key to understanding what distinguished Bolshevik from Nazi repression. Whereas the National Socialist regime used a biological-racial standard to categorise individuals and ethnic communities, the Soviet regime keyed individual and group experiences to its universal class matrix.[119] Yet the persistent conflation of biological and psychological categories throughout the 1920s and into the 1930s suggests that any analytical attempt to draw hard and fast lines between sociological and biological "paradigms" is deeply problematic. Gor'kii's language betrayed the tendency, consolidated over the previous half century, to read social experience through a biological lens. Although they could, and did, repudiate the existence of Lombroso's born criminal, early Soviet criminologists in effect saw class consciousness and class instincts as something that could be (excepting the beneficent and timely intervention of the state) transmitted from parents to offspring. Of course, the Bolsheviks did remain convinced (officially at least) that the environment would triumph over heredity—but with the important caveat that it needed time and space to do so.[120]

That certain deviants, criminals, and even oppositionists were corrupted to the extent that their pathologies lay beyond the rehabilitative powers of the state did not amount to an endorsement of the finality of biological determinism. Rather, skeptical medical voices cautioned that the defective biopsychological heredity of these individuals or groups had been reinforced by a pathological environment to such an extent that its ill effects could no

118   M. Gor'kii, L. Averbakh, and S. Firin, eds., *Belomorsko-Baltiiskii Kanal imeni Stalina. Istoriia stroitel'stva 1931–1934 gg.* (Moscow: OGIZ, 1934; repr. 1998), 12, 19, 595, 593. On the creation of the canal and the myths surrounding it, see Cynthia A. Ruder, *Making History for Stalin: The Story of the Belomor Canal* (Gainesville: University Press of Florida, 1998).
119   Holquist, "State Violence as Technique," 44–45. For similar arguments, see also Amir Weiner, "When Memory Counts: War, Genocide, and Postwar Soviet Jewry," in *Landscaping the Human Garden*, ed. Amir Weiner, 167–88.
120   Indeed, Hirsch has shown that the Soviet retreat from biological models of identity had more to do with a desire to distance Soviet ethnography and anthropology from the hierarchical race science of the Nazis than with a fundamental rejection of biologism per se. Francine Hirsch, *Empire of Nations: Ethnographic Knowledge and the Making of the Soviet Union* (Ithaca: Cornell University Press, 2005), chap. 6.

longer be reversed within an individual's lifetime or within the time the state believed it had at its disposal given the threat of war and counterrevolution. It is in this context that the general (though not total) Russian rejection of biological determinism could coexist with a latent biologization of the social.

This paradox provides some historical context for Amir Weiner's observation of an increasing emphasis on the role of hereditary factors, often understood in terms of ethnicity, in determining individual and group behavior toward the end of the 1930s and certainly after World War II. Although the Bolsheviks ventured down the path of a racial differentiation of human beings only in the aftermath of the war, the potential for that radicalization had long lain dormant within their theoretical understanding of deviance, their avowals of a purely Marxist approach to the social notwithstanding.[121] Official repudiation of biological determinism coexisted with an acceptance of neo-Lamarckian acquired characteristics, which might help to explain the simultaneous resurgence of biological/racial models in relation to Soviet Jewry and the rise to prominence of Lysenko's Michurinist biology after World War II.[122]

Scientific Modernity and Stalinist Repression

By the eve of the Bolshevik regime's frontal assault on the vestiges of the old order—the campaigns against kulaks and the petty traders of the NEP era in the collectivization and industrialization drives, and against priests, bourgeois specialists, and other "former people" in the Cultural Revolution—Soviet practitioners of the human sciences had elaborated a vision of modernity defined in a language of social excision and coercive rehabilitation. Indeed, they came to conceive the entire revolutionary project in terms

121   For a comparative discussion of human heredity in the interwar period, see Mark B. Adams, Garland E. Allen, and Sheila Faith Weiss, "Human Heredity and Politics: a Comparative Institutional Study of the Eugenics Record Office at Cold Spring Harbor (United States), the Kaiser Wilhelm Institute for Anthropology, Human Heredity, and Eugenics (Germany), and the Maxim Gorky Medical Genetics Institute (USSR)," *Osiris* 20 (2005): 232–62.

122   Weiner, "When Memory Counts"; idem, *Making Sense of War: The Second World War and the Fate of the Bolshevik Revolution* (Princeton: Princeton University Press, 2001). Indeed, Nikolaus Wachsmann's study of state prisoners in the Third Reich has demonstrated that in their biopsychological analysis of Germans, rather than racially "different" constituencies, the practitioners of the human sciences in Nazi Germany employed categories virtually indistinguishable from their Soviet counterparts in the 1920s. "'Annihilation through Labour': The Killing of State Prisoners in the Third Reich," *Journal of Modern History* 71, no. 3 (September 1999): 624–59. On Lysenko, see David Joravsky, *The Lysenko Affair* (Cambridge, MA: Harvard University Press, 1970); Kirill O. Rossianov, "Editing Nature: Joseph Stalin and the 'New' Soviet Biology," *Isis* 83, no. 4 (December 1993): 728–45; Boris Gasparov, "Development or Rebuilding: Views of Academician T. D. Lysenko in the Context of the Late Avant-Garde," in *Laboratory of Dreams: The Russian Avant-Garde and Cultural Experiment*, ed. John E. Bowlt and Olga Matich (Stanford: Stanford University Press, 1996), 133–50.

of social renovation, moral and social purification, and forced adaptation to the new socialist order.

Such a vision did not, however, in and of itself, preordain the massive eruption of state repression during the Great Breakthrough. Zygmunt Bauman and Detlev Peukert have both argued that the horrors of Nazism and Stalinism were the logical outcome of the very project of modernity. Bauman has argued that "the most extreme and well documented cases of global 'social engineering' in modern history (those presided over by Hitler and Stalin), all their attendant atrocities notwithstanding, were neither outbursts of barbarism not yet fully extinguished by the new rational order of civilization, nor the price paid for utopias alien to the spirit of modernity." On the contrary, they were "legitimate offspring of the modern spirit, of that urge to assist and speed up the progress of mankind toward perfection that was throughout the most prominent hallmark of the modern age—of that optimistic view, that scientific and industrial progress in principle removed all restrictions on the possible application of planning, education and social reform in everyday life."[123] Yet Stalinist repression is neither reducible to, nor explicable primarily in terms of, modern social knowledge. The intellectual antecedents of repression are rather to be found in the meshing of the human sciences with the revolutionary discourse of Soviet Marxism.

Both before and after 1917, modernizing elites struggled to articulate a vision of a harmonious and stable society, in part by identifying the forces impeding its emergence. These forces, it was argued, were embodied in the person of the deviant. For the intellectual, manufacture of a healthy, beautiful, and conflict-free society of the future was enormously indebted to the anxious investigation of disorder in the present. Accordingly, the project of investigating, categorizing, and ultimately transforming the deviant is to be understood as a central feature of ongoing attempts to renovate the social order. The biomedical sciences claimed to offer an empirical explanation for the links between economics and subjectivity that seemed to flesh out the sustained effects on individuals and classes of exposure to certain economic milieu (in the sense both of material and ideological conditions).

Manichean and born of violent hostility toward certain social constituencies, Soviet Marxism proved a form of cognitive software eminently

---

123   See Zygmunt Bauman, *Modernity and Ambivalence* (Cambridge: Polity Press, 1991), 29. Peukert has similarly argued that . . . [the scientific and academic disciplines and the social-welfare institutions and professions] swung between the dual poles of their claim to comprehensive validity and control on the one hand and the depressing fact of their limited efficacy on the other. . . . It was . . . possible . . . and this was the more likely eventuality, given the astonishing breakthroughs made by the human and social sciences around the turn of the century—that the frustrating and recalcitrant features of social and human reality would have been seen as obstacles that had to be surmounted or abolished by yet more rapid advance." Detlev J. K. Peukert, "The Genesis of the 'Final Solution' from the Spirit of Science," in *Reevaluating the Third Reich*, ed. Thomas Childers and Jane Caplan (New York: Holmes and Meier, 1993), 238.

compatible with these biomedical constructions of the social. It endorsed and celebrated class struggle as an engine of social change, yet it was less cogent in its explanation of the threat posed by the "dying classes" once Bolshevik victory in the Civil War had been secured and the active forces of counterrevolution crushed. The disciplines of criminology, psychiatry, and their related fields lent coherence and specificity to the Bolsheviks' fears about the residual effects of capitalism on the mentality and morality of its citizens after 1917. They explained, for example, why a former capitalist might represent a threat, even if no longer engaged in "capitalist" activity.

Biomedical constructions of deviance were thus carriers of anxiety; they provided the Bolsheviks with a ready-made framework in which to explore and articulate their fears about their own biopsychological inheritance. They mediated between theories of societal transformation on the one hand and individual and group transformation on the other. By elaborating the nature of threats and strategies for their neutralization, the assumptions, categories, and arguments of the human sciences furbished the new regime's own transformative project with immediacy, tangibility, and urgency. In this arena, the meshing of the biomedical sciences with Marxism was both productive and enabling—productive in the sense that it generated compelling narratives about the nature of the threats posed both by the remnants of the old order and capitalists; enabling in the sense that it articulated and sanctioned the excisionary means to combat them. Definitions of the deviant became radicalized under the impact of the millenarian language of class struggle within Soviet Marxism to produce the Bolsheviks' intractable and violent insistence on acceptable individual conduct and class heredity. Within the human sciences in the 1920s, excision and coercive rehabilitation came to be one of the principal measures of progress toward the harmonious socialist society of the future.[124]

In the absence, however, of a dictatorship characterized by both a millenarian Marxist agenda of radical social transformation and a readiness (undoubtedly strengthened by the long years of conflict between 1914 and 1921) to deploy unprecedented levels of violence, the coercive strategies conceived and elaborated by contemporary intellectuals might never have been

---

124   My arguments here build on a number of thoughtful attempts to elucidate the relationship between "modernity," Soviet Marxism, and repression. See Weiner, "Nature and Nurture"; David L. Hoffmann, "European Modernity and Soviet Socialism," in *Russian Modernity*, ed. Hoffmann and Kotsonis, 245–60; Stephen Kotkin, "Modern Times: The Soviet Union and the Interwar Conjuncture," *Kritika* 2, no. 1 (Winter 2001): 111–64; Peter Holquist, "New Terrains and New Chronologies: The Interwar Period through the Lens of Population Politics," *Kritika* 4, no. 1 (Winter 2003): 163–76; idem, "State Violence as Technique." For criticisms of the very use of the term "modernity," see Matthew Lenoe, *Closer to the Masses: Stalinist Culture, Social Revolution, and Soviet Newspapers* (Cambridge, MA: Harvard University Press, 2004), 3–5, 248–54. For an overview of these debates, see Daniel Beer, "Origins, Modernity, and Resistance in the Historiography of Stalinism," *Journal of Contemporary History* 40, no. 2 (April 2005): 363–79.

put into practice on the scale witnessed at the end of the 1920s.[125] Biomedical theories of deviance were not a primary cause of state repression; they were, however, one of its conditions of possibility.[126] Their particular vision of "social renovation" made the repressive practices of Stalinism theoretically possible, made them imaginable. What made the practices real was the creation of a dictatorship that acknowledged no limits on either its own ambitions or on its entitlement to use violence in their realization.[127] Yet in their emphatic insistence on the need for societal renovation, the human sciences offered a powerful theoretical legitimation for state repression.[128]

Long before the Bolsheviks came to power with their dreams for remaking the world, liberal practitioners of the human sciences had endeavored to enlighten and improve their populations, to direct their development toward the formation of a cohesive and stable law-bound society governed by order and rationality. In so doing, they bequeathed a legacy infused with a potential for both expansion and radicalization. The Bolshevik discourse of violent class struggle and radical social transformation proved the catalyst.

125   On the radicalizing impact of the First World War on imperial, provisional and Bolshevik governments, see Peter Holquist, *Making War, Forging Revolution: Russia's Continuum of Crisis, 1914–1921* (Cambridge, MA: Harvard University Press, 2002).

126   Geoff Eley has made similar arguments about the importance of eugenic thinking for Nazi racial policy in "Introduction 1: Is There a History of the *Kaiserreich?*" in *Society, Culture, and the State in Germany, 1870–1930,* ed. Geoff Eley (Ann Arbor: University of Michigan Press, 1996), 28.

127   Yet even in this context, the identification and stigmatization of "the socially dangerous" could only be implemented at all because of the structures and dominance of what Dickinson, describing the Nazi state, has termed a "*Maßnahmenstaat*'—a political system that operated by administrative fiat rather than by the law." I have deliberately echoed his conclusion that "the development of the science of human heredity and the ambition of total social 'renovation' . . . made Nazi policies theoretically possible, made them imaginable. What made them real was the creation of a totalitarian dictatorship. To put it in a few words: no dictatorship, no catastrophe." "Biopolitics, Fascism, Democracy," 17–18.

128   Moreover, both David Shearer and Paul Hagenloh have pointed to the genealogy of state terror in the 1930s stretching from the campaigns against *sotsanomalki* (social misfits), kulaks, and *nepmen* in the midst of the collectivization and industrialization drives to the Great Terror. Hagenloh has noted that "policing practices against 'harmful elements' . . . are a much stronger bridge between the period of collectivization, dekulakization, and forced industrialization, on the one hand, and the Terror, on the other, than are trends related to political repression." Examining the "vocabularies, procedures and classifications of targets that were employed in 1937–8 against marginal strata," he argues that they owed much to the understanding of social deviants in the late 1920s and early 1930s. Paul M. Hagenloh, "'Socially Harmful Elements' and the Great Terror," in *Stalinism: New Directions,* ed. Sheila Fitzpatrick (London: Routledge, 2000), 287–88. David Shearer, "Elements Near and Alien: Passportization, Policing, and Identity in the Stalinist State, 1932–1952," *Journal of Modern History* 76, no. 4 (December 2004): 835–81; idem, "Social Disorder, Mass Repression and the NKVD during the 1930s," in *Stalin's Terror: High Politics and Mass Repression in the Soviet Union,* ed. Barry McLoughlin and Kevin McDermott (London: Palgrave, 2003), 85–117.

Conclusion

In 1929, Ivan Vvedenskii argued that psychiatry was the branch of medicine in which coercion was "the rule rather than the exception." He explained that

the principle of coercion is deployed specifically and systematically in psychiatry. . . . The premise for the deployment of psychiatric coercion is the thought that mental illness distorts the individual's capacity to understand his situation and his interests, rights, and obligations, disrupts his reciprocal relations with the surrounding environment, and in so doing deprives him of the right autonomously to decide his own actions and to bear the responsibility for them.[1]

Vvedenskii's statement offers a distilled expression of the axis of intellectual continuity that runs throughout the revolutionary era in Russia. Confronting a still overwhelmingly peasant society at the turn of the twentieth century, Russian liberal practitioners of the human sciences struggled to articulate the conditions necessary for the modernization of the country, the civic, material and spiritual emancipation of its population, and the creation of a functioning *Rechtsstaat*. In so doing, they invalidated the claims of contemporaries to individual autonomy and sovereignty and asserted that Russia's salvation only lay in a scientifically structured understanding of normality that was theirs to define.

Propelled by the moderns' hybrid of boundless optimism and bottomless despair, the human sciences grappled with the forces of vice, disorder, and subversion. Practitioners of the disciplines of psychiatry, criminology, and

---

1   Ivan N. Vvedenskii, "Prinuditel'noe lechenie dushevno-bol'nykh i psikhopatov," in *Dushevno-bol'nye pravonarushiteli i prinuditel'noe lechenie*, ed. P. V. Gannushkin (Moscow: NKVD, 1929), 8.

psychology throughout the revolutionary period (both liberal "fathers" in the *fin-de-siècle* and their more radical "sons" working under the Bolsheviks) applied a biopsychological model of deviance to an ever-expanding range of moral, social, and political conduct deemed antithetical to the well-being of society and its future prospects. Soviet totalitarianism distinguished itself from liberal forms of government through the limitless application of Vvedenskii's principle of coercion to all social and political constituencies understood to have failed in their adaptation to the new order. Yet the Bolsheviks' own conception of societal renovation (and the nature of the forces impeding it), was heavily indebted to visions of reform and progress articulated by liberal elites in the *fin-de-siècle*.

It was precisely in their enthusiasm for order, improvement, and the creation of a law-bound society (in which Kistiakovskii's internal restraints would do away with the need for external ones) that Russia's liberal elites in the scientific, medical, and legal professions could not but endorse, albeit with deep reservations, a tutelary program of coercive modernization. A priori, they claimed a privileged understanding of the needs and interests of the population on whose behalf they sought reform. Alarmed by the backwardness of the Russian people and the violence and disorder they perceived to be expanding throughout the empire in tandem with modernization, liberals within the human sciences came to argue for a series of draconian measures intended temporarily to withhold the democratic rights of the Russian people and to sanction the coercive treatment of the socially dangerous. Yet once reconfigured within the millenarian framework of Soviet Marxism, such arguments came to sanction not the temporary but rather the indefinite subjugation of the population to a disciplinary program of societal and individual transformation.

Such a view leads us to a reconceptualization of the fate of liberal modernity in the Russian Revolution.[2] Laura Engelstein has articulated what is probably a majority opinion among historians of the period:

> Whether one believes that Russian liberalism ought to have triumphed, had any reasonable chance of succeeding, or was inevitably doomed, the liberal project has an unavoidable pathos in the social and political environment of late

---

2   Much has been written in the last decade or so exploring continuities across the 1917 divide. The nature and duration of the continuity depends very much on the thematic focus of the analysis. Oleg Kharkhordin has, for example, claimed to undercover deep continuities in practices of self-formation that stretch back to the sixteenth century in his comparison of the monastery statutes of Saint Joseph Volotskii (1503) and the disciplinary techniques employed in the Soviet educationalist Anton Makarenko's labor colony of the 1930s. Oleg Kharkhordin, *The Collective and the Individual in Russia: A Study of Practices* (Berkeley: University of California Press, 1999), 54, 117–22. Bernice Glatzer Rosenthal has meanwhile argued that Stalinism's violent transformative agenda was deeply indebted to Nietzsche's influence on Russian intellectuals in the late imperial period. *New Myth, New World: From Nietzsche to Stalinism* (University Park: University of Pennsylvania Press, 2002).

imperial Russia. . . . The ultimate drama of . . . [the Russian liberals'] situation rests perhaps in the nation's failure to enter the difficult and flawed terrain of postabsolutist public life, its failure to create a polity in which citizens might have struggled with the imperfections of the civic condition in terms supplied by the arsenal of liberal thought.[3]

I have argued, by contrast, that as the Russian Empire disintegrated and became reconstituted under the Soviet regime, its citizens did continue to struggle "with the imperfections of the civic condition in terms supplied by the arsenal of liberal thought."[4] To be sure, the terms in which that condition was understood were modified in the wake of 1917, but their configuration remained eminently recognizable. The most basic continuity between late imperial Russian liberalism and early Soviet radicalism lies in the assumption that human material could and should be remolded. Peter Fritzsche has remarked that "renovation and experimentation are distinctive modernist practices but because they presume both the extreme malleability and impermanence of the material world and are also often undertaken in conditions of apprehension they can serve dangerously adventurous ends."[5] It was paradoxically in their quest to define and forge a renovated society that liberal practitioners of the human sciences in the late imperial period themselves elaborated a discourse of social and individual transformation within which the Bolsheviks' own anxieties and aspirations could subsequently be explored, concretized, and legitimated.

Rather than viewing the late imperial period as a liberal experiment that failed, opening up the path to the Bolshevik dictatorship, I have argued that the period leading up to the revolution is more instructively understood in terms of a laboratory of modernity that bequeathed an ambiguous legacy to its successor regime. The Bolsheviks' ideology of class struggle and social transformation did not enslave or subjugate the human sciences to its own oppressive ends; rather, it meshed with them, generating radical theories of change and sanctions for repression. Russian liberalism in the late imperial period did not "fail"; rather, it contained—precisely in its modernist

3   Laura Engelstein, *The Keys to Happiness: Sex and the Search for Modernity in Fin-de-Siècle Russia* (Ithaca: Cornell University Press, 1992), 8.

4   There have been some challenges to an alleged rupture in policymaking across 1917. In an examination of the state's mounting regulation of the economy between February and October 1917, William G. Rosenberg has argued that the subsequent role of the Bolshevik state in Soviet society represented essentially a radical extension, rather than a revolutionary break, with the past. "Social Mediation and State Construction(s) in Revolutionary Russia," *Social History* 19, no. 2 (May 1994): 169–88. Peter Holquist has demonstrated that many of the draconian and interventionist policies associated with War Communism had in fact been pioneered by the late imperial and provisional governments. Peter Holquist, *Making War, Forging Revolution: Russia's Continuum of Crisis, 1914–1921* (Cambridge, MA: Harvard University Press, 2002).

5   Peter Fritzsche, "Did Weimar Fail?" *Journal of Modern History* 68, no. 3 (September 1996): 649.

preoccupations with science, crisis, and solutions—a dangerous potential that could be radicalized and implemented in unforeseen ways.

Unforeseen and yet not entirely unforeseeable. Radicalization was, so to speak, hard-wired into the Bolshevik mainframe. Holquist has noted that "Bolshevism was distinct not so much because it was ideological, or even utopian, but on account of its specifically Manichean and adversarial nature."[6] This latter ideological component was a crucial escalatory ingredient in the intellectual history of state repression under the Bolsheviks. The revolution in 1917 brought about a substantial reconfiguration of the discriminatory apparatus of the human sciences and generated increasingly threatening visions of disorder and radical proposals for its elimination. The late imperial practitioners of the human sciences certainly had elaborated theories of social categorization and strategies for the normalization of society; but although their theories had undoubtedly contained a utopian impulse, they had remained loyal to the idea of reform as a gradual way of managing social problems. Indeed, the critique of the status quo firmly embedded in most biomedical theories of deviance meant that all coercive attempts to rehabilitate socially marginal or dangerous elements were advocated in a mood of paternal indulgence.

Clinicians and scientists continued in the postrevolutionary period to forge a discursive axis around which threats and solutions could be identified and acted upon. Under the Bolsheviks, the ambiguous legacy of these liberal elites became, however, infused with the concrete and discrete facts of the Marxist imagination so that there emerged, notionally at least, far more explicit borders around civil society and political community than had ever existed before 1917.[7] In the 1920s, the human sciences offered a particular articulation of Marxism's division of society into classes in conflict with each other, furnishing the abstract language of collectivities with a concrete, tangible quality that reverberated with urgency and the necessity of a decisive confrontation with social and political disorder. Moreover, whereas as the liberals' sense of social responsibility for the iniquities of the late imperial social order had impeded them from reacting with unadulterated hostility to the deviants they confronted, the Bolsheviks had no such qualms. Their Manichean worldview, predicated on the Marxist division of society into classes, gave no quarter in their struggle to cleanse Soviet society of the pathologies of the old order. The Bolsheviks' transformative program came increasingly to be understood in terms of a coercive rehabilitation of

---

6   Peter Holquist, "Violent Russia, Deadly Marxism? Russia in the Epoch of Violence, 1905–21," *Kritika* 4, no. 3 (Summer 2003): 652.

7   Halberstam has noted that "the concrete and comprehensive ideologies of totalitarian movements appear less ephemeral, less ideal, and more 'real' than the abstract political principles of liberalism that emphasise the pragmatics of the political process and the indeterminacy of human nature." Michael Halberstam, "Totalitarianism as a Problem for the Modern Conception of Politics," *Political Theory* 26, no. 4 (August 1998): 472.

those amenable to treatment and the isolation (and even elimination) of those who were not.

Although by 1934, the Soviet regime ridiculed "thick-skulled bourgeois scholars like Lombroso," ironically these liberal practitioners of the human sciences had made an important intellectual contribution to the Bolsheviks' own program of social transformation and to the articulation of strategies for combating the disorder this program engendered.[8] Russian liberalism proved a spectacular *political* failure in the revolution. Yet it also proved to be the unwitting architect of significant features of the project that triumphed over it.

8   M. Gor'kii, L. Averbakh, and S. Firin, eds., *Belomorsko-Baltiiskii Kanal imeni Stalina. Istoriia stroitel'stva 1931–1934 gg.* (Moscow: OGIZ, 1934; repr. 1998), 593.

Bibliography of Primary Sources

Alekseev, A. "Alkogolizm i nasledstvennost'." *Priroda*, no. 3 (1914): 351–70.

Alekseev, P. S. "Kriminogennoe svoistvo alkogolia," *Vrachebnaia gazeta*, no. 36 (1906): 958–62; no. 37 (1906): 982–85.

Alelekov, A. N. "Iz oblasti psikhiatrii." *Russkaia mysl'* (August 1893): part 2: 102–28.

Amenitskii, D. A. "K voprosu o prinuditel'nom lechenii i o sotsial'no-opasnykh dushevno-bol'nykh i psikhopatakh." In *Dushevno-bol'nye pravonarushiteli i prinuditel'noe lechenie*, edited by P. V. Gannushkin, 23–40. Moscow: NKVD, 1929.

Anuchin, D. N. "Izuchenie psikhofizicheskikh tipov." *Vestnik Evropy* (May 1890): 331–43.

Aronovich, G. D., and Z. A. Bannikova. "Biogeneticheskii analiz (kachestvennyi i kolichestvennyi) fizicheskikh degenerativnikh priznakov u defektivnykh i zdorovykh detei." *Pedologicheskii zhurnal*, no. 3 (1923): 17–27.

Arsen'ev, K. K. "Novyi istorik sovremennoi Frantsii." *Vestnik Evropy*, no. 1 (1891): 313–42; no. 2 (1891): 784–814; no. 4 (1892): 913–51.

Astvatsaturov, M. I. "Biologicheskie osnovy klassifikatsii fizicheskikh degenerativnykh priznakov." *Nauchnaia meditsina*, no. 10 (1922): 40–49.

Avdeev, V. B., ed. *Russkaia rassovaia teoriia do 1917 goda.* Moscow: Feri-V, 2002.

Bakhtiiarov, A. A. *Briukho Peterburga: Ocherki stolichnoi zhizni.* 1887. St. Petersburg: Fert, 1994.

Baudrillart, H. J. L. *Histoire de luxe privé et public depuis l'antiquité jusqu'à nos jours,* 4 vols. Paris: Hachette, 1878–80.

Bazhenov, N. N. *Oblast' i predely vnusheniia.* Moscow: I. N. Kushnerev, 1891.

———. *Psikhiatricheskie besedy na literaturnye i obshchestvennye temy.* Moscow: A. I. Mamontov, 1903.

———. *Psikhologiia i politika.* Moscow: I. D. Sytin, 1906.

Bekhterev, V. M. "Lichnost' i usloviia ee razvitiia i zdorov'ia." In *Trudy Vtorogo s''ezda otechestvennykh psikhiatrov, proiskhodivshego v g. Kieve c 4-go po 11-e sentiabria 1905 goda,* 28–52. Kiev: S. V. Kul'zhenko, 1907.

———. *Lichnost' i usloviia ee razvitiia i zdoroviia.* St. Petersburg: K. L. Rikker, 1905.

——. *Ob''ektivno-psikhologicheskii metod v primenenii k izucheniiu prestupnosti.* St. Petersburg: V. Anderson and G. Loitsiaskii, 1912.

——. "O prichinakh samoubiistva i o vozmozhnoi bor'be s nim." In *Trudy Pervogo s''ezda russkogo soiuza psikhiatrov i nevropatologov,* 84–117. Moscow: Tipografiia Shtaba Moskovskogo Voennogo Okruga, 1914.

——. *Vnushenie i ego rol' v obshchestvennoi zhizni.* St. Petersburg: K. L. Rikker, 1898.

——. *Vnushenie i ego rol' v obshchestvennoi zhizni.* Third edition. St. Petersburg: K. L. Rikker, 1908.

——. "Voprosy nervno-psikhicheskogo zdorov'ia v naselenii Rossii." In *Trudy Tret'ego s''ezda otechestvennykh psikhiatrov,* 43–66. St. Petersburg: Tipografiia pervoi Sankt-Peterburgskoi trudovoi arteli, 1911.

——. "Voprosy vyrozhdeniia i bor'ba s nim." *Obozrenie psikhiatrii, nevrologii i eksperimental'noi psikhologii,* no. 9 (1908): 518–21.

Belen'kii, G. S., and E. V. Eremeeva. "O sotsial'no-bytovykh motivakh samoubiistva zhenshchin." *Leningradskii meditsinskii zhurnal,* no. 4 (1928): 3–15.

Beliakov, S. A. "Antropologicheskoe issledovanie ubiits." *Arkhiv psikhiatrii, neirologii i sudebnoi psikhopatologii* 4, no. 1 (1884): 19–48; no. 2 (1884): 12–52.

Belilovskii, K. A. *K voprosu ob antropologicheskom tipe prestupnika.* St. Petersburg: Ia. I. Liberman, 1895.

Berg, L. S. "Brachnost', rozhdaemost' i smertnost' v Leningrade za poslednie gody." *Priroda,* nos. 7–12 (1924): 101–8.

Bernshtein, A. N. "Psikhicheskie zabolevaniia zimoi 1905–1906 g. v Moskve." *Sovremennaia psikhiatriia* (March 1907): 49–67.

Blokhin, N. *Alkogol' i potomstvo potrebliaiushchikh ego.* Tver: Mir, 1913.

Borodin, D. N. *P'ianstvo sredi detei.* St. Petersburg: Vilenchik, 1910.

Bourneville, D. M. *De la contracture hysterique permanente.* Paris: Delahaye, 1872.

Brailovskii, V. V. "O biologicheskikh korniakh prestupnosti." In *Sbornik po psikhonevrologii,* 545–48. Rostov-on-Don: Severnyi Kavkaz, 1928.

——. *Opyt bio-sotsial'nogo issledovaniia ubiits (po materialam mest zakliucheniia Severnogo Kavkaza).* Rostov-on-Don: Donskaia Pravda, 1929.

——. "O vegatativnoi nervnoi sisteme ubiits." *Voprosy izucheniia prestupnosti na Severnom Kavkaze,* no. 2 (1927): 83–103.

Brokgauz, F. and Efron, I. *Entsiklopedicheskii slovar',* 43 vols. St. Petersburg: F. A. Brokgauz and Efron, 1890–1907.

Brukhanskii, N. P. "K vorposu o psikhicheskoi zarazitel'nosti." *Obozrenie psikhiatrii, nevrologii i refleksologii* 24, nos. 4–5 (1926): 279–90.

——. *Ocherki po sotsial'noi psikhopatologii.* Moscow: M. and S. Sabashnikovy, 1928.

——. "Vvedenie v kriminal'nuiu psikhopatologiiu." In *Sudebno-meditsinskaia ekspertiza. Sbornik 1.,* edited by Ia. L. Leibovich, 39–97. Moscow: Narkomzdrav, 1925.

Bugaiskii, Ia. P. *Khuliganstvo kak sotsial'no-patologicheskoe iavlenie.* Moscow: Molodaia Gvardiia, 1927.

——. "K klinike i psikhopatologii khuliganstva v sviazi s voprosom o determinirovannosti povedeniia dushevno-bol'nykh." *Obozrenie psikhiatrii, nevrologii i refleksologii,* no. 1 (1927): 57–68.

Bunak, V. V. "Antropologicheskoe izuchenie prestupnika, ego sovremennoe polozhenie i zadachi." *Arkhiv kriminologii i sudebnoi meditsiny* 1, no. 3 (1927): 535–69.

———. "Novye dannye k voprosu o voine kak biologicheskom faktore." *Russkii evgenicheskii zhurnal* 2, nos. 1–2/3 (1922): 223–32.

Chalisov, M. A. "Opyt bio-sotsial'nogo obsledovaniia rastratchikov v Rostove n-D." *Voprosy izucheniia prestupnosti na Severnom Kavkaze*, no. 2 (1927): 45–75.

Chekhov, A. P. *Polnoe sobranie sochinenii i pisem.* 30 vols. Moscow: Nauka, 1974–84.

Chizh, V. F. *Prestupnyi chelovek pered vrachebnym sudom.* Kazan: Tipografiia Imperatorskogo Universiteta, 1894.

———. *Uchebnik psikhiatrii.* St. Petersburg-Kiev: Sotrudnik, 1910.

Danilovich, L. *Espinas i Tard ob obshchestve.* Moscow: I. N. Kushnerev, 1902.

Davidov, P. N. "K voprosu o vyrozhdenii russkogo naroda ot p'ianstva." *Trudovaia pomoshch'*, no. 1 (1906): 83–101.

Déjérine, J. J. *L'hérédité dans les maladies du système nerveux.* Paris: Asselin and Houzeau, 1886.

Dement'ev, E. M. *Fabrika: chto ona daet naseleniiu i chto ona u nego beret.* Moscow: I. N. Kushnerev, 1893.

Despine, P. *De la contagion morale. Faits démontrants son existence.* Marseilles: E. Camoin, 1870.

D-ov, I. [Dobrovol'skii, I. I.]. "Psikhologiia 'prestupnoi' tolpy." *Russkaia mysl'* (December 1894): part 2: 130–58.

———. "Tsezar' Lombrozo kak uchenyi i myslitel'." *Russkaia mysl'* (July 1895): part 2: 1–23; (August 1895): part 2: 1–28; (October 1895): part 2: 20–42.

Dokhman, A. M. *Nasledstvennost' v nervnykh bolezniakh.* Kazan: Tipografiia gubernskogo pravleniia, 1887.

"Dokladnaia zapiska Vitte Nikolaiu II," *Istorik-marksist* 2–3, nos. 42–43 (1935): 131–38.

Dril', D. A. "Antropologicheskaia shkola i ee kritiki." *Iuridicheskii vestnik* 6, no. 4 (December 1890): 579–99.

———. "Chto govorilos' na mezhdunarodnom ugolovno-antropologicheskom kongresse v Briussele." *Russkaia mysl'* (February 1893): part 2: 88–104; (March 1893): part 2: 60–87.

———. "Iavleniia vyrozhdeniia i usloviia obshchestvennoi sredy v sviazi s voprosami vospitaniia." *Vestnik psikhologii, kriminal'noi antropologii i gipnotizma*, no. 10 (1906): 265–94.

———. *Maloletnie prestupniki. Etiud po voprosu o chelovecheskoi prestupnosti, ee faktorakh i sredstvakh bor'by s nei.* Moscow: A. I. Mamontov, 1884.

———. *Prestupnost' i prestupniki (ugolovno-psikhologicheskie etiudy).* St. Petersburg: Ia. Kantorovich, 1895.

———. "Prestupnyi chelovek." *Iuridicheskii vestnik*, no. 11 (1882): 401–22; no. 12 (1882): 483–550.

———. *Psikhofizicheskie tipy v ikh sootnoshenii s prestupnost'iu.* Moscow: A. I. Mamontov, 1890.

———. "Tiuremnyi mir." *Russkaia mysl'* (February 1891): part 2: 63–81.

———. *Uchenie o prestupnosti i merakh bor'by s neiu.* St. Petersburg: Shipovnik, 1912.

———. "V chem zhe sostoiat uvlecheniia antropologicheskoi shkoly ugolovnogo prava?" *Russkaia mysl'* (June 1890): part 2: 132–46.

———. "Zadachi vospitaniia i rol' nasledstvennosti." *Vestnik psikhologii, kriminal'noi antropologii i gipnotizma*, no. 10 (1906): 1–26.

Droznes, M. Ia. "Vazhneishiie zadachi sovremennoi prakticheskoi psikhiatrii." In *Trudy Vtorogo s"ezda otechestvennykh psikhiatrov proiskhodivshego v g. Kieve c 4-go po 11-e sentiabria 1905 goda*, 202–13. Kiev: S. V. Kul'zhenko, 1907.

——. *Zadachi meditsiny v bor'be s sovremennoi nervoznost'iu.* Odessa: Aktsionnoe Iuzhno-Russkoe obshchestvo pechatnogo dela, 1907.

Dugdale, R. *The Jukes: A Study in Crime, Pauperism, Disease, and Heredity.* New York: Putnam, 1877.

Dumas, G. "Contagion mentale: épidémies mentales, folies collectives, folies grégaires," *Revue Philosophique* 71 (January–June 1911): 225–44.

Edel'shtein, A. O. "Khuliganstvo kak bio-sotsial'naia problema i ego sotsial'nopsikhiatricheskie izucheniia." *Vestnik sovremennoi meditsiny,* no. 12 (1926): 19–23.

——. "Opyt izucheniia sovremennogo khuliganstva." In *Khuliganstvo i ponozhovshchina,* 28–80. Moscow, Moszdravotdel, 1927.

Esipov, V. V. *"Revoliutsiia" v Rossii. Populiarnye ocherki.* Warsaw: Tipografiia Varshavskogo Uchebnogo Okruga, 1907.

Espinas, A.-V. *Des sociétés animales: Étude de psychologie comparée.* Paris: G. Baillière, 1877.

——. *Sotsial'naia zhizn' zhivotnykh.* Translated by F. Pavlenkov. St. Petersburg: M. A. Khan, 1882.

Esquirol, J.-É. *Des maladies mentales considerées sous le rapport médical, hygienique et médico-légal.* Paris: G. Ballière, 1838.

Feinberg, Ts. M., E. K. Krasnushkin, and G. M. Segal. *Prestupnik i prestupnost'. Sbornik I.* Moscow: Moszdravotdel, 1920.

——. *Prestupnik i prestupnost'. Sbornik II.* Moscow: Moszdravotdel, 1927.

Féré, C. *Dégénérescence et criminalité.* Paris: F. Alcan, 1888.

Ferri, E. *Criminal Sociology.* New York: D. Appleton, 1897.

——. *Prestuplenie i prestupniki v nauke i v zhizni.* Odessa: N. Leinenberg, 1890.

——. *Ugolovnaia sotsiologiia.* Foreword by E. Ferri and D. Dril'. Translated from the 4th Italian edition. St. Petersburg: Prosveshchenie, 1910.

Florinskii, V. M. *Usovershenstvovanie i vyrozhdenie chelovecheskogo roda.* St. Petersburg: Riumin, 1866.

Gall, F. J., and J. C. Spurzheim. *Observations sur la phrénologie, ou la connaissance de l'homme moral et intellectuel, fondée sur les fonctions du système nerveux.* Paris, 1810.

Gal'ton, F. [Galton, F]. *Nasledstvennost' talanta, ee zakony i posledstviia.* St. Petersburg: Znanie, 1875.

Genik, E. A. "Tret'ia epidemiia isterii v Moskovskoi gubernii." *Sovremennaia psikhiatriia* (August 1912): 588–604.

——. "Vtoraia epidemiia istericheskikh sudorog v Podol'skom uezde, Moskovskoi gubernii." *Nevrologicheskii vestnik* 6, no. 4 (1898): 146–59.

Ger'e, V. "Ippolit Ten i ego znachenie v istoricheskoi nauke." *Vestnik Evropy,* no. 1 (1890): 5–65; no. 2 (1890): 463–500.

German, I. S. "O psikhicheskom rasstroistve depressivnogo kharaktera, razvivshemsia u bol'nykh na pochve perezhivaemykh politicheskikh sobytii." *Zhurnal nevropatologii i psikhiatrii,* no. 3 (1906): 313–23.

Gershenzon, M. O. "Tvorcheskoe samosoznanie." In *Vekhi. Intelligentsiia v Rossii: Sbornik statei, 1909–1910,* 2nd ed., 70–96. Moscow: V. M. Sablin, 1909.

Gertsen, A. I. *Sobranie sochinenii.* 30 vols. Moscow: Akademiia Nauk SSSR, 1954–65.

Golosov, A. "Pamiati Dmitriia Andreevicha Drila." *Vestnik psikhologii, kriminal'noi antropologii i gipnotizma,* no. 4 (1911): 80–94.

Golovin, N. N. *Issledovanie boia.* St. Petersburg: Ekonomicheskaia tipografiia, 1907.

Gorbunov, A. V. "Vliianie mirovoi voiny na dvizhenie naseleniia Evropy." *Russkii evgenicheskii zhurnal* 1 (1922): 40–64.

Gor'kii, M. "Razrushenie lichnosti." *Ocherki filosofii kollektivizma*. St. Petersburg: Znanie, 1909: 353–403.

——. *Polnoe sobranie sochinenii*, 25 vols. (Moscow: Akademiia Nauk SSSR, 1968–76).

Gor'kii, M., L. Averbakh, and S. Firin, eds. *Belomorsko-Baltiiskii Kanal imeni Stalina. Istoriia stroitel'stva 1931–1934 gg.* Moscow: OGIZ, 1934; repr. 1998.

Granovskii, L. B. *Obshchestvennoe zdravookhranenie i kapitalizm (Tuberkulez, alkogolizm, venerizm i nervnost' i usloviia bor'by s nimi).* Moscow: Obshchestvo russkikh vrachei v pamiat' N. I. Pirogova, 1907.

Iakobii, P. I. "Religiozno-psikhicheskie epidemii." *Vestnik Evropy*, no. 10 (1903): 732–58; no. 11 (1903): 117–66.

Iakovenko, V. Ia. "Epidemiia istericheskikh sudorog v Podol'skom uezde, Moskovskoi gub." *Vestnik obshchestvennoi gigieny, sudebnoi i prakticheskoi meditsiny* 15, no. 3 (March 1895): 93–109.

——. "Nasledstvennost' u dushevno-bol'nykh." *Zhurnal nevropatologii i psikhiatrii* 4, nos. 1–2 (1904): 1–50.

——. "Psikhicheskaia epidemiia na religioznoi pochve v Anan'evskom i Tiraspol'skom uezdakh Khersonskoi gub." *Sovremennaia psikhiatriia* (March 1911): 191–98; (April 1911): 229–45.

——. "Zdorovye i boleznennye proiavleniia v psikhike sovremennogo russkogo obshchestva." *Zhurnal obshchestva russkikh vrachei v pamiat' N. I. Pirogova* 13, no. 4 (May 1907): 269–87.

Iaroshevskii, S. O. "Materialy k voprosu o massovykh nervnopsikhicheskikh zabolevaniiakh." *Obozrenie psikhiatrii, nevrologii i eksperimental'noi psikhologii* 11, no. 1 (1906): 1–9.

Iaroslavskii, E. M. *Vozhd' rabochikh i krest'ian.* Leningrad: Gosizdatel'stvo, 1924.

——. "Preduprezhdat' simptomy bolezni," *Pravda*, December 8, 1925.

Iudin, T. I. "O kharaktere nasledstvennykh vzaimootnoshenii pri dushevnykh bolezniakh." In *Trudy Pervogo s''ezda russkogo soiuza psikhiatrov i nevropatologov*, 854–63. Moscow: Tipografiia Shtaba Moskovskogo Voennogo Okruga, 1914.

Jacoby, P. [Iakobii, P.], *Études sur la selection chez les hommes.* Paris: G. Baillière, 1881.

Juquelier, P., and A. Vigoroux. *La contagion mentale.* Paris: Doin, 1905.

K proverke, peresmotru i ochistke partii. Irbit: RKI, 1921.

Kablits, I. [Iuzov, I.]. *Osnovy narodnichestva.* St. Petersburg: A. M. Kotomin, 1882.

Kandinskii, V. Kh. *Obshcheponiatnye psikhologicheskie etiudy.* Moscow: A. Lang, 1881.

Kanel', V. Ia. *Alkogolizm i bor'ba s nim.* Moscow: I. D. Sytin, 1914.

Kapterev, P. F. "O podrazhatel'nosti v psikhologicheskom i pedagogicheskom otnosheniiakh." *Obrazovanie*, nos. 7–8 (1893): 1–41.

Kaplinskii, M. Z. "K voprosu o prinuditel'nom lechenii." In *Dushevno-bol'nye pravonarushiteli i prinuditel'noe lechenie*, edited by P. V. Gannushkin, 55–61. Moscow: NKVD, 1929.

Kistiakovskii, B. A. "V zashchitu prava (Intelligentsiia i pravosoznanie)." In *Vekhi: Sbornik statei o russkoi intelligentsii*, 2nd ed, 125–55. Moscow: V. M. Sablin, 1909.

Koenker, D. P., and R. D. Bachman, eds. *Revelations from the Russian Archives.* Washington, DC: Library of Congress, 1997.

Korganov, N. N. "K voprosu o znachenii biologicheskogo faktora v razvitii antisotsial'nykh detei." *Voprosy izucheniia prestupnosti na Severnom Kavkaze,* no. 1 (1926): 55–62.

Kovalevskii, M. M. "N. K. Mikhailovskii kak sotsiolog." *Vestnik Evropy,* no. 4 (1913): 192–212.

———. "Ocherk istorii razvitiia sotsiologii v kontse XIX i v nachale XX veka." In *Istoriia nashego vremeni,* edited by M. M. Kovalevskii and K. A. Timiriazev, no. 27 (no date): 20–42.

Kovalevskii, P. I. *Dushevnye bolezni: Kurs psikhiatrii dlia vrachei i iuristov,* 5th ed. St. Petersburg: "Vestnik dushevnykh boleznei," 1905.

———. *Obshchaia psikhopatologiia.* Kharkov: Kaplan and Biriukov, 1886.

———. *Sudebnaia psikhiatriia.* Warsaw: "Arkhiv psikhiatrii, neirologii i sudebnoi psikhopatologii," 1896.

———. *Vyrozhdenie i vozrozhdenie. Genii i sumasshestvie. Sotsial'no-biologicheskie ocherki.* St. Petersburg: M. I. Akinfiev and I. V. Leont'ev, 1899.

———. *Vyrozhdenie i vozrozhdenie. Prestupnik i bor'ba s prestupnost'iu (Sotsial'no-psikhologicheskie eskizy),* 2nd ed. St. Petersburg: M. I. Akynfiev and I. V. Leont'ev, 1903.

Kozlov, A. A. *Tard i ego teoriia obshchestva.* Kiev: Tipografiia Imperatorskogo Universiteta Sviatogo Vladimira, 1887.

Krainskii, N. V. *Porcha, klikushi i besnovatye.* St. Petersburg: M. I. Akynfiev and I. V. Leont'ev, 1900.

Krasnushkin, E. K. "Chto takoe prestupnik." In *Prestupnik i prestupnost'. Sbornik I,* 6–33. Moscow: Moszdravotdel, 1926.

———. "K psikhologii khuliganstva." In *Khuliganstvo i ponozhovshchina,* edited by E. K. Kranushkin, G. M. Segal, and Ts. M. Feinberg, 150–7. Moscow: Moszdravotdel, 1927.

———. *Sudebno-psikhiatricheskie ocherki.* Moscow: M. & S. Sabashnikovy, 1925.

Krasnosel'skii, A. I. *Mirovozzrenie gumanista nashego vremeni: Osnovy ucheniia N. K. Mikhailovskogo.* St. Petersburg: B. M. Vol'f, 1900.

Krestovskii, V. V. *Peterburgskie trushchoby: Kniga o sytykh i golodnykh.* 2 vols. Leningrad: Khudozhestvennaia literatura, 1990.

Krieken, A. T. von, *Über die sogennante organische Staatstheorie.* Leipzig: Duncker and Humblot, 1873.

Kriukov, A. I. "O degeneratsii cherepa." *Arkhiv kriminologii i sudebnoi meditsiny* 1, nos. 2–3 (1927): 705–14.

———. "O degeneratsii cherepa u samoubiits." *Sudebno-meditsinskaia ekspertiza,* no. 1 (1925): 18–24.

Kropotkin, P. *Mutual Aid as a Factor of Evolution.* New York: McClure, Philips and co., 1902.

Lavrov, P. L. *Istoricheskie pis'ma.* St. Petersburg: A. Kotomin, 1870.

Lebedev, N. N. "Bor'ba s prestupnost'iu v Amerike. Operativnyi sposob uluchsheniia roda chelovecheskogo." *Vestnik obshchestvennoi gigieny, sudebnoi i prakticheskoi meditsiny* (January 1911): 1–11.

Le Bon, G. *Psychologie des foules.* Paris: F. Alcan, 1896.

LeBon, G. [Gustave Le Bon]. *Psikhologiia narodov i mass.* Translated by A. Fridman and E. Pimenova. St. Petersburg: F. Pavlenkov, 1896.

LeGrain, P. M., and V. Magnan. *Les dégénérés: État mental et syndromes épisodiques.* Paris: Rueff, 1895.

Legrand du Saulle, H. *Le délire des persécutions.* Paris: H. Plon, 1871.

——. *La folie héréditaire*. Paris: Adrien Delaye, 1873.

Lenin, V. I. *Bor'ba s naslediem kapitalisticheskoi kul'tury*. Moscow: Gosizdatel'stvo, 1926.

——. *Polnoe sobranie sochinenii*, 5th ed. 55 vols. Moscow: Gosizdatel'stvo politicheskoi literatury, 1958–62.

Lents, A. K. *Kriminal'nye psikhopaty (sotsiopaty)*. Foreword by V. P. Osipov. Leningrad: Rabochii sud, 1927.

——. "Zadachi i plan sovremennoi kriminal'no-psikhiatricheskoi ekspertizy." In *Sudebno-meditsinskaia ekspertiza. Trudy II Vserossiiskogo s''ezda sudebno-meditsinskikh ekspertov, Moskva, 25 fevralia—3 marta 1926*, edited by Ia. L. Leibovich, 108–17. Ul'ianovsk: Ul'ianovskii Kombinat PPP, 1926.

Lesevich, V. V. "Ekskursii v oblast' psikhiatrii." *Russkaia mysl'* (February 1887): part 2: 1–34; (March 1887): part 2: 49–82.

Lewes, G. H. *The Study of Psychology; Its Object, Scope, and Method*. London: Truber and Co., 1879.

Liadov, M. N. *Voprosy byta*. Moscow: Kommunisticheskii universitet im. Sverdlova, 1925.

Likhachev, A. "Novye raboty v oblasti ugolovnoi statistiki i antropologii. Teoriia Ferri." *Grazhdanskoe i ugolovnoe pravo*, no. 3 (1883): 1–24.

Lisianskaia, E. A. "Prinuditel'noe lechenie kak mera sotsial'noi zashchity." In *Dushevno-bol'nye pravonarushiteli i prinuditel'noe lechenie*, edited by P. V. Gannushkin, 41–54. Moscow: NKVD, 1929.

List, F. von [Franz von Liszt]. *Nakazanie i ego tseli*. St. Petersburg: I. Iurovskii, 1895.

——. *Prestuplenie kak sotsial'no-patologicheskoe iavlenie*. St. Petersburg: A. V. Orlov, 1903.

——. *Uchebnik ugolovnogo prava. Obshchaia chast'*. Translated from the 12th German edition by R. El'iashchevich. Moscow: A. I. Mamontov, 1903.

Liublinskii, P. I. *Bor'ba s prestupnost'iu v detskom i iunosheskom vozraste (sotsial'no-pravovye ocherki)*. Moscow: Narkomiust, 1923.

——. "Novaia mera bor'by s vyrozhdeniem i prestupnost'iu." *Russkaia mysl'* (March 1912): part 2: 31–56.

Lobach, Ia. M. "O mekhanizme prestupnoi agressivnosti." In *Sbornik po psikhonevrologii*, 549–56. Rostov-on-Don: Severnyi Kavkaz, 1928.

Lobas, N. S. *Ubiitsy (nekotorye cherty psikhofiziki prestupnikov)*. Moscow: I. D. Sytin, 1913.

Lombroso, C. *L'uomo delinquente studiato in rapporta alla anthropologia, alla medicina legale ed alle discipline carcerarie*. Milan, 1876.

Lombrozo, Ch. [Lombroso, C.]. *Prestuplenie*. Translated by G. I. Gordon. St. Petersburg: N. K. Martynov, 1900.

Lucas, P. *De l'imitation contagieuse ou de la propagation sympathique des névroses et des monomanies*. Paris, 1833.

Manassein, V. A. *O znachenii psikhicheskikh vliianii*. St. Petersburg: L. F. Pantaleev, 1877.

Merzheevskii, I. P. "Ob usloviiakh, blagopriiatstvuiushchikh razvitiiu dushevnykh i nervnykh boleznei v Rossii i o merakh, napravlennykh k ikh umen'sheniiu." In *Trudy Pervogo s''ezda otechestvennykh psikhiatrov, proiskhodivshego v Moskve s 5 po 11 ianvariia 1887 g.*, 15–38. St. Petersburg: M. M. Stasiulevich, 1887.

Michels, R. *Zur Soziologie des Parteiwesens in der modernen Demokratie: Untersuchungen über die oligarchischen Tendenzen des Gruppenlebens*. Leipzig: W. Klinkhardt, 1911.

Mikhailovskii, N. K. *Sochineniia.* 6 vols. St. Petersburg: Russkoe Bogatstvo, 1896–97.

Mikhnevich, V. O. *Iazvy Peterburga. Opyt istoriko-statisticheskogo issledovaniia nravstvennosti stolichnogo naseleniia.* St. Petersburg: Limbus Press, 2003. First published 1886 by F. Sushchinskii.

Mintslov, R. "Osobennosti klassa prestupnikov." *Iuridicheskii vestnik,* no. 10 (1881): 216–46; no. 11 (1881): 355–418; no. 12 (1881): 577–606.

Moreau de Tours, J.-J. *La psychologie morbide dans ses rapports avec la philosophie de l'histoire.* Paris: V. Masson, 1859.

Morel, B. A. *Traité des dégénérescences physiques, intellectuelles, et morales de l'espèce humaine.* Paris: G. Baillière, 1857.

Mumortsev, A. N. "O sovremennom pessimizme i samoubiistvakh." *Sovremennaia psikhiatriia* (November 1914): 861–81.

Nabokov, V. D. *Ob "opasnom sostoianii" prestupnika kak kriterii mer sotsial'noi zashchity.* St. Petersburg: Obshchestvennaia pol'za, 1910.

——. "Poslednee slovo kriminalistiki," *Pravo* no. 13 (1908): 805–07.

Nordau, M. *Vyrozhdenie.* Translated under editor R. I. Sementkovskii. St. Petersburg: P. P. Soikin, 1894.

Novombergskii, N. I. *Po puti k vyrozhdeniiu. Sotsial'no-gigienicheskie ocherki.* St. Petersburg: A. M. Lassman, 1913.

O rabote Moskovskoi KK RKP po 15 Aprel' 1924. Moscow: RKKI, 1924.

Obninskii, P. N. "*Contagion morale* i kholernye besporiadki." *Zhurnal grazhdanskogo i ugolovnogo prava,* no. 1 (January 1893): 1–14.

——. "Illiuzii pozitivizma," *Zhurnal grazhdanskogo i ugolovnogo prava* (March 1890): 1–11.

Obolenskii, L. E. "Noveishaia psevdo-nauka." *Russkaia mysl'* (November 1893): part 2: 122–42.

Orshanskii, I. G. *Atavizm i vyrozhdenie.* Moscow: I. N. Kushnerev, 1910.

——. *Nashi prestupniki i uchenie Lombrozo.* St. Petersburg: E. Arnol'd, 1891.

——. *Rol' nasledstvennosti v peredache boleznei.* St. Petersburg, 1897.

Orshanskii, L. G. "Khuligan. Psikhologicheskii ocherk." In *Khuliganstvo i prestuplenie. Sbornik statei,* edited by L. G. Orshanskii, A. A. Zhizhilenko, and I. Ia. Derzibashev, 55–82. Leningrad and Moscow: Rabochii sud, 1927.

——. *Kriminal'naia antropologiia i sudebnaia meditsina.* St. Petersburg: G. Pozharov, 1903.

Osipov, V. P. "K voprosu o khuliganstve." In *Khuliganstvo i prestuplenie. Sbornik statei,* edited by L. G. Orshanskii, A. A. Zhizhilenko, and I. Ia. Derzibashev, 83–90. Moscow: Rabochii sud, 1927.

——. "O kontrrevoliutsionnom komplekse u dushevno-bol'nykh." *Obozrenie psikhiatrii, nevrologii i refleksologii,* no. 2 (1926): 85–95.

——. "O politicheskikh ili revoliutsionnykh psikhozakh." *Nevrologicheskii vestnik* 17 (1910): 437–92.

——. *O politicheskikh ili revoliutsionnykh psikhozakh.* Kazan: Tipografiia Imperialisticheskogo Universiteta, 1910.

——. "Otvet doktoru Rozenbliumu." *Obozrenie psikhiatrii, nevrologii i refleksologii,* no. 3 (1926): 211–13.

——. "Predislovie," in A. K. Lents, *Kriminal'nye psikhopaty (sotsiopaty).* Leningrad: Rabochii sud, 1927: 1–9.

Pinel, P. *Traité medico-philosophique sur l'aliénation mentale, ou la manie.* Paris: Caille et Ravier, 1801.

Pinel', F. [Pinel, P.]. *Vrachebno-filosofskoe nachertanie dushevnykh boleznei*. Moscow: I. Roshetnikov, 1829.

Pisarev, D. *Sochineniia*. 4 vols. Moscow: Khudozhestvennaia literatura, 1955–56.

Plekhanov, G. V. *Sochineniia*. 24 vols. Moscow: Gosizdatel'stvo, 1924–27.

Pobedonostsev, K. P. "Bolezni nashego vremeni." In idem, *Moskovskii sbornik*, 92–139. Moscow: Sinodal'naia tipografiia, 1896.

Podvysotskii, V. V. *Osnovy obshchei patologii*, 2 vols. St. Petersburg: K. L. Rikker, 1894–96.

Popov, V. A. *Psikhologiia tolpy*. Moscow: S. P. Iakovlev, 1905.

Portugalov, Iu. V. "Nauchnye problemy kriminologii." *Vestnik psikhologii, kriminal'noi antropologii i pedologii*, no. 7 (1904): 456–78.

Poznyshev, S. V. "K psikhologii sovremennogo banditizma." *Zhurnal psikhologii, nevrologii i psikhiatrii* 3 (1923): 56–71.

———. *Uchebnik ugolovnogo prava: Ocherk osnovnykh nachal obshchei i osobennoi chasti nauki ugolovnogo prava. 1. Obshchaia chast'*. Moscow: Narkomiust, 1923.

Preobrazhenskii, S. A. "Khirurgicheskaia profilaktika vyrozhdeniia." *Sovremennaia psikhiatriia* 6, no. 2 (1912): 110–16.

Przheval'skii, V. V. *Prof. Frants List i ego vozzreniia na prestuplenie i nakazanie*. St. Petersburg: M. M. Stasiulevich, 1895.

Radishchev, A. N. *Puteshestvie iz Peterburga v Moskvu*. St. Petersburg: Tipografiia Radishcheva, 1790.

Rakovskii, K. G. *Etiologiia prestupnosti i vyrozhdaemosti*. Moscow: Gosizdatel'stvo, 1927.

Rambosson, J. *Phénomènes nerveux, intellectuels et moraux, leur transmission par contagion*. Paris: Firmin-Didot, 1883.

Reich, E. D. *Die Entartung des Menschen. Ihre Ursachen und Verhütung*. Erlangen: F. Enke, 1868.

Reikh [Reich], E. D. *Prichiny vyrozhdeniia cheloveka, nepolnota i nepravil'nost' ego telesnogo i dushevnogo razvitiia v nastoiashchee vremia*. Edited by O. Mil'chevskii. Moscow: A. I. Mamontov, 1870.

Reitts, G. V. "Patologicheskaia prestupnost' i umen'shennaia vmeniaemost'." *Sovremennaia psikhiatriia* (June 1912): 427–62; (July 1912): 511–30.

Rezanov, A. S. *Armiia i tolpa: Opyt voennoi psikhologii*. Warsaw: Varshavskaia esteticheskaia tipografiia, 1910.

Ribo, T. *Bolezni voli*, trans. from the French under ed. Dr. B. V. Tomashevskii. St. Petersburg: S. S. Riabchenko, 1884.

Ribot, T. *Les maladies de la volonté*. Paris: G. Ballière, 1883.

———. *L'hérédité psychologique*. Paris: G. Ballière, 1873.

Rozenbakh, P. Ia. "Nasledstvennost' boleznei i vyrozhdenie." *Entsiklopediia semeinogo vospitaniia i obucheniia*, no. 9 (1899): 31–50.

———. "O prichinakh sovremennoi nervnosti i samoubiistv." *Novoe slovo*, no. 11 (1909): 41–47.

———. "Vnushenie." In *Entsiklopedicheskii slovar'*, 43 vols., edited by F. Brokgauz and I. Efron, 11:689–91. St. Petersburg: F. Brokgauz and I. Efron, 1890–1907.

Rozenblium, I. "Po povodu kontrrevoliutsionnogo kompleksa u dushevno-bol'nykh." *Obozrenie psikhiatrii, nevrologii i refleksologii*, no. 3 (1926): 209–11.

Rybakov, F. E. "Alkogolizm i nasledstvennost'." *Trudy Vtorogo s"ezda otechestvennykh psikhiatrov, proiskhodivshego v g. Kieve c 4-go po 11-e sentiabria 1905 goda*. Kiev: S. V. Kul'zhenko, 1907: 651–664.

———. "Dushevnye rasstroistva v sviazi s tekushchimi politicheskimi sobytiiami." *Russkii vrach*, no. 51 (1905): 1593–95.
———. *Gipnotizm i psikhicheskaia zaraza*. Moscow: V. Rikhter, 1905.
———. "Nasledstvennost' i alkogolizm." *Zhurnal nevropatologii i psikhiatrii*, no. 1 (1910): 338–48.
Sazhin, I. V. *Alkogol' i nasledstvennost'*. St. Petersburg: Ia. Trei, 1910.
———. *Alkogolizm i nervnaia sistema*. St. Petersburg: P. P. Soikin, 1907.
———. *Nasledstvennost' i spirtnye napitki. Rol' i znachenie spirtnykh napitkov v oblasti dukhovnogo i fizicheskogo vyrozhdeniia*. St. Petersburg: P. P. Soikin, 1908.
———. *Vliianie alkogolia na razvivaiushchiisia organizm*. St. Petersburg, Tipografiia Shtaba otdela korpusa zhandarmov, 1902.
Shcheglov, A. L. "D. A. Dril' kak kriminalist-antropolog." *Obozrenie psikhiatrii, nevrologii i eksperimental'noi psikhologii* (January 1911): 1–16.
———. "Prestupnik kak predmet izucheniia vrachebnoi nauki." *Vestnik psikhologii, kriminal'noi antropologii i pedologii*, no. 1 (1913): 1–21.
Shcherbak, A. E. *Prestupnyi chelovek po Lombrozo (Vrozhdennyi prestupnik—nravstvenno-pomeshannyi epileptik)*. St. Petersburg: P. I. Shmidt, 1889.
Segalov, T. E. "Mery sotsial'noi zashchity meditsinskogo kharaktera po UK 1926 g." In *Problemy prestupnosti*, no. 3, edited by E. Shirvindt, F. Traskovich, and M. Gernet, 173–88. Moscow: NKVD, 1927.
———. "Prestupnoe khuliganstvo i khuliganskie prestupleniia." In *Khuliganstvo i khuligany. Sbornik*, edited by V. N. Tolmachev, 63–74. Moscow: NKVD, 1929.
Semashko, N. A. "Khuliganstvo—ostatki 'starogo byta.'" In *Khuliganstvo i prestuplenie*, edited by N. A. Semashko, L. G. Orshanskii, A. A. Zhizhilenko, and I. Ia. Derzibashev, 117–19. Leningrad-Moscow: Narkomzdrav, 1927.
———. "Sotsial'naia gigiena, ee sushchnost', metod i znachenie." *Sotsial'naia gigiena*, no. 1 (1922): 5–11.
Sementkovskii, R. I. "Nazad ili vpered?" Foreword to Russian edition of Maks Nordau, *Vyrozhdenie*, translated under editor P. I. Sementkovskii, ii–xxvii. St. Petersburg: P. P. Soikin, 1894.
Sheinis, L. I. "Prestupnost', ee evoliutsiia i sotsial'noe znachenie." *Vestnik znaniia*, no. 9 (1905): 57–68.
Shirvindt, E. G. "O problemakh prestupnosti." *Problemy prestupnosti*, no. 1 (1926): 3–13.
Sholomovich, A. S. "K voprosu o dushevnykh zabolevaniiakh, voznikaiushchikh na pochve politicheskikh sobytii." *Russkii vrach*, no. 20 (1907): 715–20.
———. *Nasledstvennost' i fizicheskoe vyrozhdenie*. Kazan: Tipo-litografiia Imperatorskogo Universiteta, 1915.
Shumkov, G. E. *Psikhika boitsov vo vremia srazheniia*, St. Petersburg: B. I. 1909.
———. "Rasskazy i nabliudeniia iz nastoiashchei russko-iaponskoi voiny (Voenno-psikhologicheskie etiudy)." *Voprosy nervno-psikhicheskoi meditsiny*, no. 1 (January–March 1905): 1–60.
Sigele, S. [Sighele, S.]. *Prestupnaia tolpa: Opyt kollektivnoi psikhologii*. St. Petersburg: F. Pavlenkov, 1893.
Sighele, S. *La foule criminelle, essai de psychologie collective*. Translated by Paul Vigny. Paris: F. Alcan, 1892.
———. *La psychologie des sectes*. Paris: V. Giard and E. Brière, 1898.
Sikorskii, I. A. "Biologicheskie voprosy v psikhologii i psikhiatrii." *Voprosy nervno-psikhicheskoi meditsiny*, no. 1 (1904): 79–114.

——. *Ekspertiza po delu ob ubiistve Andriushi Iushchinskogo.* Kiev: A. S. Suvorin, 1913.

——. *Epidemicheskie vol'nye smerti i smertoubiistva v Ternovskie Khutora.* Kiev: I. N. Kushnerev, 1897.

——. *Psikhopaticheskaia epidemiia 1892-go goda v Kievskoi gubernii.* Kiev: Tipografiia Imperatorskogo Universiteta Sviatogo Vladimira, 1893.

——. "Zadachi nervno-psikhicheskoi gigieny i profilaktiki." In *Trudy Pervogo s"ezda otechestvennykh psikhiatrov, proiskhodivshego v Moskve s 5 po 11 ianvariia 1887 g.,* 1055–64. St. Petersburg: M. M. Stasiulevich, 1887.

Skliar', N. I. "Eshche o vliianii tekushchikh politicheskikh sobytii na dushevnye zabolevaniia." *Russkii vrach,* no. 15 (1906): 448–49.

Sluchevskii, V. K. "Tolpa i ee psikhologiia." *Knizhki nedeli,* no. 4 (1893): 5–38; no. 5 (1893): 5–23.

Sol'ts, A. A. *O partetikete.* Moscow: PKK, 1925.

Stancheva, E. [Rakovskii, E. K.], *"Neschastnen'kie": O prestupleniiakh i prestupnikakh. Ocherk po obshchestvennoi patologii i gigiene.* St. Petersburg: Sever, 1900.

Stelletskii, M. [*sic*—Ivan] I. "K voprosu o vyrozhdenii. (Teoriia degeneratsii)." *Zhurnal nevropatologii i psikhiatrii imeni S. S. Korsakova,* nos. 5–6 (1911): 802–25.

Sulima, K. P. "Epidemiia ikoty (Singultus) v selenii Ketrosy, Iamol'skogo uezda, Podol'skoi gubernii." *Vestnik obshchestvennoi gigieny, sudebnoi i prakticheskoi meditsiny* 4 (October–December 1889): 36–40.

Sviatlovskii, V. V. *Priadil'noe proizvodstvo v sanitarnom otnoshenii.* Moscow: Russkaia Tipografiia, 1891.

——. *Sukonnoe i sherstomoinoe proizvodstvo v sanitarnom otnoshenii.* Chernigov: Zemskii vrach, 1890.

Taine, H. *Les origins de la France contemporaine.* 6 vols. Paris: Hachette, 1876–94.

Tard, G. [Tarde, G.]. *Lichnost' i tolpa. Ocherki sotsial'noi psikhologii.* Translated by E. A. Predtechenskii. St. Petersburg: A. Bol'shakov and D. Golof, 1903.

——. *Obshchestvennoe mnenie i tolpa.* Translated by P. S. Kogan Moscow: A. I. Mamontov, 1892.

——. "Prestupleniia tolpy." *Nevrologicheskii vestnik* 1, no. 1 (1892): 4–17.

——. *Prestupleniia tolpy.* Translated by I. F. Iordanskii. Kazan: N. Ia. Bashmakov, 1892.

——. *Zakony podrazhaniia.* St. Petersburg: F. Pavlenkov, 1892.

Tarde, G. "Études criminelles et pénales." *Revue philosophique* 32 (July–December 1891): 483–547.

——. "Foules et sectes au point de vue criminel." *Revue des deux mondes* 120 (November 1893): 349–87.

——. *Les lois de l'imitation.* Paris: F. Alcan, 1890.

——. *Philosophie pénale.* 2nd ed. Paris: A. Storck, 1891.

——. "Qu'est-ce qu'une société?" *Revue philosophique* 18 (July–December 1884): 489–510.

Tarnovskaia, P. N. "O nekotorykh antropologicheskikh izmereniiakh i fizicheskikh priznakakh vyrozhdeniia u privychnykh prostitutok." In *Trudy Pervogo s"ezda otechestvennykh psikhiatrov, proiskhodivshego v Moskve s 5 po 11 ianvaria 1887 g.* 884–93. St. Petersburg: M. M. Stasiulevich, 1887.

Tarnovskaia, P. N. *Vorovki. Antropologicheskoe issledovanie.* St. Petersburg: T-vo khudozhestvennoi pechati, 1902.

Tarnovskii, E. N. "Religioznye prestupleniia v Rossii." *Vestnik prava*, no. 4 (1899): 1–27.

Teleshov, N. D. *Zapiski pisatelia. Vospominaniia.* Moscow: Khudozhestvennaia literatura, 1943.

Ten, I. [Taine, H.]. *Proiskhozhdenie obshchestvennogo stroia sovremennoi Frantsii*, vol. 1. St. Petersburg: I. I. Bilibin, 1880.

——. *Proiskhozhdenie obshchestvennogo stroia sovermennoi Frantsii*, 5 vols. Translated by A. V. Svyrov. St. Petersburg: M. V. Pirozhkov, 1907.

Tereshkovich, A. M. "Nasledstvennost' u prestupnikov." *Russkii evgenicheskii zhurnal* 4, no. 2 (1926): 76–84.

——. "Vliianie voiny i revoliutsii na psikhicheskuiu zabolevaemost'." *Moskovskii meditsinskii zhurnal*, no. 4 (1924): 67–74.

Thompson, B. "The Hereditary Nature of Crime." *Journal of Mental Science* 17, no. 75 (October 1870): 321–50.

Tokarskii, A. A. *Gipnotizm i vnushenie.* St. Petersburg: M. F. Zilberberg, 1887.

——. *Psikhicheskie epidemii.* Moscow: I. N. Kushnerev, 1893.

Tolmachev, V. N., ed. *Khuliganstvo i khuligany. Sbornik,* Moscow: NKVD, 1929.

Tolstoi, L. N. *Polnoe sobranie sochinenii.* 91 vols. Moscow: Khudozhestvennaia literatura, 1929–64.

Tolstoy, L. *War and Peace.* Translated by Louise Maude and Aylmer Maude. London: Wordsworth Classics, 1993.

Towne, E. T. *Die Auffassung der Gesellschaft als Organismus, ihre Entwicklung und ihre Modifikation.* Halle: C. A. Kammerer, 1903.

Trotskii, L. D. *Literatura i revoliutsia.* Moscow: Krasnaia Nov', 1923.

Trudy Pervogo s"ezda russkogo soiuza psikhiatrov i nevropatologov. Moscow: Tipografiia Shtaba Moskovskogo Voennogo Okruga, 1914.

Trudy II s"ezda sudebno-meditsinskikh ekspertov. Moskva, 25 fevralia–3 marta 1926 g. Edited by Ia. Leibovich. Ul'ianovsk: Ul'ianovskii kombinat PPP, 1926.

Trudy Tret'ego s"ezda otechestvennykh psikhiatrov. St. Petersburg: Tipografiia pervoi Sankt-Peterburgskoi trudovoi arteli, 1911.

Tsetlin, S. L. "Degenerativnaia psikhopatiia." *Sovremennaia psikhiatriia*, no. 1 (1913): 36–49.

Tutyshkin, P. P. *Rol' otritsatel'nogo otbora v protsesse semeinogo vyrozhdeniia (Darvinizm v patologii).* Kharkov: M. Zilberberg, 1902.

——. "Zadachi tekushchego momenta russkoi obshchestvennoi psikhiatrii." In *Trudy Tret'ego s"ezda otechestvennykh psikhiatrov,* 735–44. St. Petersburg: Tipografiia pervoi Sankt-Peterburgskoi trudovoi arteli, 1911.

——. "Zhiznennye voprosy sudebno-psikhiatricheskoi ekspertizy, vydvigaemye kazuistikoi pri sovremennykh russkikh usloviiakh." In *Trudy Pervogo s"ezda russkogo soiuza psikhiatrov i nevropatologov,* 404–13. Moscow: Tipografiia Shtaba Moskovskogo Voennogo Okruga, 1914.

Udal'tsov, G. N. "Pravonarusheniia v voiskakh s tochki zreniia patologicheskoi fiziologii." *Obozrenie psikhiatrii, nevrologii i refleksologii,* no. 2 (1927): 119–32.

Ukhach-Ugorovich, N. A. *Psikhologiia tolpy i armii.* Kiev: S. V. Kul'zhenko, 1911.

Ukshe, S. A. "Vyrozhdenie, ego rol' v prestupnosti i mery bor'by s nim." *Vestnik obshchestvennoi gigieny, sudebnoi i prakticheskoi meditsiny* (June 1915): 798–816.

Utevskii, B. S. "Retsidiv i professional'naia prestupnost'." In *Problemy prestupnosti.* Edited by E. Shirindt, F. Traskovich, and M. Gernet. no. 3, 91–109. Moscow: NKVD, 1927.

Vershinin, A. P. *Gnilye ustoi.* Viatka: P. D. Kharitonov, 1907.

———. *Vyrozhdenie (Itogi zhizni).* Moscow: S. F. Razsokhin, 1915.

Viazemskii, T. I. *Vyrozhdenie i alkogolizm.* Moscow: Tipografiia Shtaba Moskovskogo Voennogo Okruga, 1913.

Vidorchuk, N. A. "Politicheskie psikhozy i politicheskie samoubiistva." *Obrazovanie,* no. 12 (1907): part 2: 51–64.

Viktorov, L. L.[*sic*—P. P.] *Uchenie o lichnosti i nastroeniiakh.* St. Petersburg: Knizhnoe delo, 1904.

Vladimirov, L. E. "Psikhicheskie osobennosti prestupnikov po noveishim issledovaniiam." *Iuridicheskii vestnik,* nos. 7–8 (1877): 105–41; nos. 9–10 (1877): 3–31.

Vorob'ev, V. V. "K voprosu ob osobennostiakh fizicheskogo stroeniia dushevnobol'nykh. O "degenerativnom ukhe." *Voprosy nervno-psikhicheskoi meditsiny* 4, no. 4 (1899): 506–26.

———. "K voprosu o tak nazyvaemom zatylochnom tipe stroeniia cherepa vyrozhdaiushchikhsia dushevnobol'nykh." *Zhurnal nevropatologii i psikhiatrii,* no. 2 (1901): 384–99.

Vorotynskii, B. I. "Biologicheskie i sotsial'nye faktory prestupnosti." *Zhurnal Ministerstva Iustitsii,* no. 7 (September 1901): 1–34.

———. "Psikho-fizicheskie osobennosti prestupnika-degenerata." *Uchenye zapiski Kazanskogo Universiteta,* no. 3 (1900): 87–106.

Vvedenskii, I. N. "Prinuditel'noe lechenie dushevno-bol'nykh i psikhopatov." In *Dushevno-bol'nye pravonarushiteli i prinuditel'noe lechenie,* edited by P. V. Gannushkin, 7–22. Moscow: NKVD, 1929.

Zakrevskii, I. P. "Ob ucheniiakh ugolovno-antropologicheskoi shkoly." *Zhurnal grazhdanskogo i ugolovnogo prava,* no. 1 (1893): 65–132.

———. *Ugolovnaia antropologiia na Zhenevskom Mezhdunarodnom Kongresse.* St. Petersburg: Tip. Pravitel'stvuiushchego Senata, 1897.

"Zarazitel'nost' umstvennykh zabluzhdenii." *Znanie* (November 1871): 91–117.

Zernov, D. N. *Kriticheskii ocherk anatomicheskikh osnovanii kriminal'noi teorii Lombrozo.* Moscow: Universitetskaia tipografiia, 1896.

Zhbankov, D. N. "Travmaticheskaia epidemiia v Rossii (Aprel'–mai 1905 g.)." *Prakticheskii vrach* 4, nos. 32–35 (1905): 633–37; 656–61; 681–86; 703–6.

———. "Travmaticheskaia epidemiia v Rossii (fevral' 1905 g.–iiun' 1907 g.)." *Prakticheskii vrach* 6, nos. 34–38 (1907): 609–15; 624–25; 644–45; 661–64; 680–83.

———. "Travmaticheskaia krovavaia epidemiia v Rossii." *Prakticheskii vrach* 5, nos. 32–35 (1906): 533–36; 552–55; 569–71; 584–88.

Zhilekhovskaia, V. P. "Vyrozhdenie." *Russkoe obozrenie* 43 (January 1897): 41–67; 43 (February 1897): 647–79; 44 (March 1897): 171–91; 44 (April 1897): 620–44; 45 (May 1897): 142–66; 45 (June 1897): 685–719; 46 (July 1897): 93–130.

Zhizhilenko, A. A. "Mery sotsial'noi zashchity v otnoshenii opasnykh prestupnikov." *Pravo,* no. 35 (1910): 2078–91; no. 36 (1910): 2136–43; no. 37 (1910): 2167–77.

Zhukovskii, M. N. "Morel' i sovremennoe uchenie o psikhicheskikh priznakakh degeneratsii." *Obozrenie psikhiatrii, nevrologii i eksperimental'noi psikhologii,* no. 10 (1908): 612–24; no. 11 (1908): 641–55.

———. *O vliianii obshchestvennykh sobytii na razvitie dushevnykh zabolevanii.* St. Petersburg: P. P. Soikin, 1907.

Newspapers

Peterburgskaia gazeta (1881)
Pravda (1925)
Russkie vedomosti (1893, 1902)
Novosti i birzhevaia gazeta (1893)
Sovetskaia Rossiia (1918)

Index